Experimental and Applied Analysis of Human Behavior

WITHDRAWN
FROM

D1628674

Experimental and Applied Analysis of Human Behavior

Edited by

Julian C. Leslie
University of Ulster, Northern Ireland

and

Derek Blackman
University of Wales, Cardiff

CONTEXT PRESS
Reno, Nevada

KEELE UNIVERSITY
LIBRARY

12 DEC 2001

B|29977

Library of Congress Cataloging-in-Publication Data

Experimental and applied analysis of human behavior / edited by Julian
C. Leslie and Derek Blackman.
    p. cm.
    Includes bibliographical references.
    ISBN 1-878978-37-3
1. Behaviorism (Psychology) I. Leslie, Julian C. II. Blackman, Derek E.

    BF199 .E887 1999
    150.19'43—dc21

                        99-052328

© 2000 Context Press
933 Gear Street, Reno, NV 89503-2729

All rights reserved.

No part of this book may be reproduced, stored in a retrieval system, or transmitted in
any form or by any means, electronic, mechanical, photocopying, microfilming,
recording, or otherwise, without written permission from the publisher.

Printed in the United States of America

Preface

The contributors to this book attended the Third European Meeting for the Experimental Analysis of Behaviour which was held in Dublin in July 1997. This was the first time for a number of years that this meeting had been held, as the two previous meetings in this series were held in Liege, Belgium, in 1983 and 1988 respectively. The Third European Meeting for the Experimental Analysis of Behaviour meeting was a great success, both in terms of its scientific content which is reflected, we feel, in the excellent contributions to this volume, and in the completely international and extremely friendly atmosphere at the meeting. The success of the meeting has led to the Fourth European Meeting for the Experimental Analysis of Behaviour meeting being planned for Amiens, France in July 2000.

Both the Dublin meeting and this subsequent volume would not have come about without help from many quarters. For planning the meeting we are indebted to the Behaviour Analysis in Ireland group, in particular Roisin McKee and Marion Staunton; the meeting was held in the delightful surroundings of Trinity College Dublin and for that we are indebted to the Psychology Department, and in particular Howard Smith and Pat Holahan; the book could not have been produced without the support of Steve Hayes, Tim Weil and Michael Clayton at Context Press, Geraldine Leader at the University of Ulster, and, most importantly, the authors.

Julian C. Leslie
Derek Blackman
April 2000

Table of Contents

Selectionism, Relational Learning and Radical Application

> Julian C. Leslie
> *University of Ulster*

Ten Points Every Behavior Analyst Needs to Remember About Reinforcement

> A. Charles Catania
> *University of Maryland Baltimore County*

Structure and Function in Selectionism: Implications for Complex Behavior

> José E. Burgos and John W. Donahoe
> *University of Guadalajara
> and University of Masssachusetts, Amherst*

Synthesizing Equivalence Classes and Natural Categories From Perceptual and Relational Classes

> Lanny Fields and Kenneth F. Reeve
> *Queens College and the Graduate School of the
> City University of New York*

Stimulus Control Topography Coherence and Stimulus Equivalence: Reconciling Test Outcomes with Theory

> W. J. McIlvane, R. W. Serna, W. V. Dube, and
> R. Stromer
> *E. K.Shriver Center and Northeastern University*

Chapter 1

Selectionism, Relational Learning and Radical Application

Julian C. Leslie
University of Ulster

The contributors to this book attended the Third European Meeting for the Experimental Analysis of Behaviour which was held in Dublin in July 1997. This proved to be an exciting time to hold and attend an international meeting in behaviour analysis. As the chapters of this volume show, behaviour analysis now has a well established conceptual framework, strongly grounded in the experimental work carried out over the last 50 years primarily with non-human animal participants, and it is progressing in at least two directions. In one direction, the framework is being extended, incrementally, to encompass more areas of human behaviour, while in another direction behaviour analysis is being applied in more ways to a greater range of human behavioural issues and problems.

The early chapters of this book deal with general and conceptual issues. Those chapters in the middle part of the book are concerned with the developments that have grown rapidly out of Murray Sidman's pioneering work on stimulus equivalence from the 1970's onwards into analyses of the concept of the stimulus, relational learning and the analyses of human verbal behaviour. The final group of chapters is concerned with new developments in applied behaviour analysis and other aspects of interpretation and application.

There is no doubt that the agenda of the behaviour analysis community has changed considerably, and that issues of primary current concern are reflected in the chapters of this volume. I offer here some summary comments on three major themes in that current agenda.

Selectionism

The idea that operant conditioning is a process whereby certain classes of behaviour are selected and thus become more frequent is of course fundamental to Skinner's (1938) position and thus cannot be described as "new". However, we need to be continually concerned both with its implications within behaviour analysis and with the widespread misunderstanding of this principle by psychologists not trained in behaviour analysis. To cite one incident, Roitblat (1982a) in reviewing theories of memory in nonhuman animals, asserted that behaviour analysis offers only an S-R theory of how behavioural change was retained from one occasion to another. In commentaries on his paper, a number of behaviour analysts roundly rejected this and re-stated their, selectionist, position that any explanation for the change in behaviour of an animal as a result of a conditioning history should involve reference to that history, rather than the postulation of hypothetical internal changes in the animal (for example, Branch, 1982; Catania, 1982; Epstein, 1982). In reply, Roitblat (1982b) simply stated that their proposed selectionist explanation did not make sense. Thus, it appeared that almost 50 years after the *Behavior of Organisms* provided an alternative to S-R mechanisms, some researchers in closely related fields of research had learned little about the mechanisms behavioural change proposed there. Nor is there any no reason to believe that matters have changed more recently. Perhaps we should not be surprised at this; although selection has been the preferred explanatory principle for natural selection amongst scientists for 100 years or more, most scientific and quasi-scientific explanations involve proximal causes and this type of explanation is completely dominant in many fields of psychology. However, in this volume Burgos and Donahoe, whose chapter is discussed a little later, address directly the issue as to how selectionist and structural accounts of memory can be reconciled.

Within behaviour analysis, it behooves us to be aware of the range and complexity of the effects of the selection mechanism of positive reinforcement. Catania's chapter, written somewhat ironically as a tutorial or revision class, ranges over diverse effects of reinforcement. Some of these are subtle, while others are frequently unknown or misunderstood. His review reminds us that, in interpreting the phenomena of the complex human social world, we must be as radical and relentless in identifying applications of the law of effect as evolutionary biologists are in their parallel task of speculating about the evolutionary function of both usual and unusual characteristics of species.

A recurrent theme of this volume is the interplay between experimental analysis and interpretation. While the experimental analysis of behaviour is always to be preferred, the contribution of interpretation of phenomena, *post hoc* or where experimental intervention is not possible, is increasingly widely appreciated. This reflects the recognition in behaviour analysis that, just as physicists cannot predict the exact trajectory of a piece of paper when a gust of wind blows it from the table -although they have long understood the basic principles involved- we should be able to offer an increasingly rich account of the human social world even when we are not directly able to control the crucial environmental variables.

The exercise in which Catania engages resembles to some extent and in microcosm that which Skinner (1953) carried out in *Science and Human Behavior*. Catania, however, can draw on a much richer literature in the experimental analysis of behaviour for his interpretations. He also addresses a range of issues that have recently arisen only recently with authors who wish to challenge what they believe to the "behaviourist" position. Although behaviour analysis develops steadily and does not abandon any of its established principles, challenges to its account of human behavioural phenomena come from the changing cultural context and thus those challenges vary and must be addressed afresh from time to time. Arguably, behaviour analysts should devote more of their time not preaching to the unconverted, but carefully presenting arguments to the sceptical.

A feature of Catania's chapter, and throughout the volume, is concern with functional accounts of behaviour (rather than structural or topographic ones) and awareness that the function of behaviour is not generally readily visible or instantly detected. We must realize that those not trained in behaviour analysis do not easily come to understand what functional analysis involves. Indeed, functional definitions and functional analyses tend to be surreptitiously replaced by structural ones, even within behaviour analysis. In their chapter, McIlvane, Serna, Dube, and Stromer point out that contemporary models of stimulus classes – a major concern of several chapters – often use unhelpful structural analogies.

The central importance of selection is also the starting point of Burgos and Donahoe's chapter, but they go further and remind us of the importance of articulating the relationships between structure and function: it is only by engaging with this issue that we may succeed in disarming those critics mentioned earlier who believe that explanations arising from behaviour analysis must, like those arising from other approaches to psychology, be essentially structural even to count as explanations. In Burgos and Donahoe's skilful analysis, there are three key aspects of behavioural development and change: variation, selection and retention. Considerations of structure arise, they believe, when we seek to establish the mechanisms of retention. These mechanisms cannot be the hypothetical constructs favoured by mentalists or cognitivists, however, because those constructs are inherently unobservable and thus cannot be the subject of legitimate scientific enquiry. Despite this and the fact that the experimental analyses of behaviour does not directly reveal retention mechanisms, we need not abandon our investigation of retention because we can investigate neural processes.

Burgos and Donahoe do not accord the status of "primary causes" to neural processes. Rather they state that there are genotypic neural structures that have been selected through interaction with the environment over generations, and phenotypic neural structures which "allow for the conservation of the products of selection by reinforcement in the individual environments of the past and the present." (p. 44). Thus, selection by the environment is inevitably responsible for all aspects of neural structure. In this argument we see the notions of selection of the evolutionary biologist and of the behaviour analyst brought together to form a coherent whole. The central part of Burgos and Donahoe's chapter is the presentation of a simulation experiment which is intended to capture the relationship between neural phenotypic structure and the behaviour generated by schedules of reinforcement. This is an exercise in interpretation because it involves postulating neural networks with properties that are plausible – given current knowledge of neural science – rather than directly observed. The simulation generates a range of phenomena that are seen in actual experiments with the same reinforcement schedules. However, changing the size of the hypothesised neural network alters the pattern of responding obtained. This suggests that a certain level of complexity is required to retain different environment-behaviour relationships, and that neural structure may consequently impose constraints on the environment-behaviour relationships that can be selected by consequences. The notion that biological constraints can constrain learning has been familiar since the 1970's (see, for example, Hinde & Stevenson-Hinde, 1973), and Burgos and Donahoe's formal modelling and interpretation takes us significantly further in organising an account of the nature of the interaction between environmental and biological factors. In so doing, it provides an account of the interdependence of behavioural function with neural structure.

Relational Learning

The most significant change in the research agenda of the experimental analysis of behaviour came as the implications of Sidman's (1986, 1990, 1994; Sidman & Tailby, 1982) pioneering work on stimulus equivalence were grasped. Some of the most exciting work in this area is reviewed in six chapters of this volume. As research on stimulus equivalence developed, researchers in behaviour analysis were often asked whether they were engaged in cognitive psychology. After all, one of the defining features of behaviour analysis up until around 1980 was that it seemed to have little to say about the issues that had preoccupied the cognitive movement since 1960, but now many of those same issues were being addressed in behaviour analysis research. Every contributor to the six chapters of this volume is at pains to demonstrate that their work constitutes behaviour analysis, not cognitive psychology, because the explanatory principles used are those of behaviour analysis. Indeed, the debate within this volume is partly about whether explanation of these "cognitive" phenomena can proceed without additions to the explanatory principles already used frequently to explain other behaviour, largely in nonhuman species, or whether there needs to be a limited increase in the explanatory principles used.

A unifying theme, and one that engenders excitement in all the contributors of these chapters (Fields & Reeve; McIlvane, Serna, Dube, & Stromer; Pilgrim & Galizio; Barnes, Healy, & Hayes; Horne & Lowe; Luciano), is that our knowledge of human relational learning, that is the ways in which relationships between stimuli come to control behaviour, is developing rapidly while the stringent standards of evidence that characterise the experimental analysis of behaviour are being maintained. The behaviour analysis community is deeply conservative in that it requires scientific phenomena to be replicable, directly and systematically, in individual experimental participants. In the modern era, many phenomena of relational learning have been demonstrated within experiments with verbally-competent human participants. However, this scientific conservatism has generated heated debate as to whether any of these can be seen in young, pre-verbal, children, in developmentally-delayed adults, or in any other species (the Californian sea lion is a possible candidate, see Schusterman & Kastak, 1993).

In their chapter, Fields and Reeve discuss the most basic type of relational learning, establishment and membership of stimulus classes. The fact that it is stimulus *classes* that enter into relationships with behaviour, and that *all* stimulus classes consist of a number of nonidentical members, is a fundamental tenet of behaviour analysis which went largely unexamined until Sidman and co-workers (see, for example, Sidman, 1990, for a review) pointed out that we continually use stimulus classes with physically disparate members (for example, the sight of a chair, the written word "chair", the spoken word /chair/, etc.) in a way that suggests that all members of the class are psychologically equivalent or identical.

There has been a tendency to treat "Sidman's" stimulus classes (those established through experiments or training and often consisting of previously meaningless items) as different in kind from the physically-defined perceptual or relational stimulus classes with which psychologists have long been familiar. Fields and Reeve meticulously describe the possible links between the two sets of concepts, and persuasively suggest that we are simply examining different aspects of a single phenomenon. They conclude that perceptual and relational classes are best established through presentation of many positive and negative exemplars, that the emergence of a class is inferred from a multiple exemplar generalisation test, that class formation must be confirmed by showing that the stimuli are discriminable from each other, that primary stimulus generalisation is important in relational as well as perceptual classes, and, of course, that class members must be functionally equivalent in controlling the same behaviour. Furthermore, they argue, reflexivity, symmetry, and transitivity are types of relational class. These, of course, are regarded as the defining characteristics of stimulus equivalence classes (Sidman & Tailby, 1982), and Fields and Reeve demonstrate that the emergence of equivalence classes is enhanced by the prior establishment of reflexivity, symmetry, and transitivity as relational stimulus classes. Finally, they suggest how the procedures that generate both perceptual classes and equivalence classes can account for real-life natural categories. Overall, they provide an account of how a small set of familiar behavioural processes may account for these apparently different types of stimulus classes.

The concept of the stimulus is further developed by McIlvane, Serna, Dube, and Stromer in their chapter. They use the concept of stimulus control topography to capture a subtle and often ignored aspect. We are familiar with the careful physical description of stimuli used within experiments. An example of this might be: three horizontal black lines, 10 cm long, 3mm wide, separated by 3 cm (centre to centre), presented on light grey background on a computer screen at eye level 50 cm in front of a seated experimental participant. McIlvane et al. argue convincingly that when scientists read such descriptions they make assumptions about the effective stimulus which may not be true, particularly for young children or people with developmental delay. If, for example, the "horizontal lines" stimulus is presented for a few seconds and then removed and followed by another which requires a selective response (as might be the case in a matching-to-sample procedure), we assume that "the stimulus" will have been the three 10-cm lines, visually presented. While this is very likely to the case with a verbally-competent adult who has seen the display several times, it may well not true for a child or adult with developmental delay who may look at different aspects on different occasions. In effect, what is presumed to be one stimulus may be several, each controlling a different response. Their research program is primarily concerned with the development of techniques to remove this generally unwanted source of variability. Importantly, they report that reflexivity (for example) can be taught using their techniques to a wide range of people with developmental delay, even though other researchers have failed to teach this in similar studies.

McIlvane et al.'s chapter is an excellent restatement of several key objectives of behaviour analysis. Our primary objective should be to gain control of a phenomenon in the laboratory and then extend this control to real-world contexts. Evidence of "failure" to obtain consistent effects within single-subject designs should lead us to redouble our efforts and show increased ingenuity in experimental procedures, until we can establish the conditions under which the phenomenon does and does not occur.

There are strong links between the material presented in Pilgrim and Galizio's chapter, and that in those by Fields and Reeve and by McIlvane et al. Pilgrim and Galizio's research program developed from findings which undercut some conventional wisdom about stimulus equivalence classes. Roughly speaking, it had been thought that conditional discrimination training (for example, training AB and AC relationships) resulted in the formation of equivalence classes (for example, A1B1C1 and A2B2C2) that then functioned as behavioural units. Demonstrations of reflexivity, symmetry and transitivity were then taken as evidence for that unity. However, Pilgrim and Galizio showed that subsequent training with reversal of the AC relation (reinforcing choice of C2 given A1, and of C1 given A2) led to those newly-trained relations being established and the symmetrical relations emerging (given C2, A1 was chosen; given C1, A2 was chosen), while the previously established transitivity relations were maintained (for example, given B1, C1 was chosen; given B2, C2 was chosen). Further studies reported in the present chapter have confirmed the independence of the various equivalence properties.

If these relations can be shown to be potentially independent, why do they occur together so often that it had previously been assumed that one could not occur without the other two? Pilgrim and Galizio suggest that the paradox may be resolved by using an account of operant units of increasing size from two- to five-term contingencies proposed by Sidman (1986). Reflexivity, symmetry, and transitivity can each be described as a four-term contingency, and this cluster of four-term units might be selected in a five-term contingency, thus producing the range of phenomena usually labelled as stimulus equivalence class formation. Here, as in many other places in this volume, we are offered proposals – and some data – indicating how apparent inconsistencies in published data may be resolved by looking more carefully at the procedures used and identifying basic, and familiar, behavioural processes.

At the beginning of their chapter, Barnes, Healy, and Hayes immediately set our their aim. This is to provide a functional account of language through an extension of the relational learning paradigms that they and others have developed. Their central thesis is that this requires a shift from the focus on stimulus classes, which has been the tradition in this area, to one on stimulus relationships which can subsume the account of stimulus classes. They review and extend Hayes's relational frame theory to show how it may account not on only for various types of stimulus relationships but also rule-governed behaviour. We noted earlier that an outcome of equivalence training is that stimuli in different modalities (such as the written word "chair", the spoken word /chair/, etc.) are treated as equivalent. Barnes et al. state that this is one of a number of types of derived relational responding (or relational learning) which parallel phenomena of natural language. In their words, "the equivalence effect constitutes an empirical analogue of the symbolic properties of natural language" (p. 151).

Relational frame theory seeks to explain equivalence and other derived relational responding using two concepts, the functional definition of operant response classes and the capacity of organisms to respond to relationships among events. Functional definition of response classes means that form or structure of response cannot define response class membership and that the same class can have infinitely many forms. The capacity to respond to relationships is familiar; for example, members of many species can learn to select the smaller of two stimuli, but in relational frame theory this notion is intended to arbitrary application. That is, to cases where the stimuli do not have the relational property specified, as in "x is smaller than y" where the symbols x and y are not different in size. Rather than the physical properties of the stimuli presented resulting in relational responding, cues such as the words "smaller than" have come to control the relational response.

According to Barnes et al., arbitrarily applicable relational responding comes about through a similar process of multiple exemplar training as that specified by Fields and Reeve for the development of stimulus classes. Additionally, they believe that natural language learning in children involves innumerable examples of the same relational cue being presented in different contexts, and this history gradually abstracts out specific cues for various types of arbitrarily applicable relational responding. In their view, equivalence is one of a number of types of derived relational responding, and all in turn are types of operant behaviour. They review some of their research on other types of derived relational responding (such as the same-different relation) and, given these demonstrations of various types of arbitrarily applicable relational responding within experiments, are critical of the view that all relational responding can be understood solely in terms of the concept of stimulus class. Interestingly, they also present data from research with a novel procedure (the "relational evaluation procedure") intended to allow rule-governed behaviour to be investigated in experiments that parallel those on stimulus equivalence.

Horne and Lowe's chapter addresses some of the same issues as that of Barnes et al. However, this chapter builds on a ground-breaking earlier publication (Horne & Lowe, 1996) where they explicitly deviated from the position broadly shared by the authors of the previous four chapters. They maintain that an additional process, the symbolic relationship of naming, is required to make progress in a functional analysis of human language. In the present chapter, they recapitulate their previous development of Skinner's (1957) account of verbal behaviour and go on to present novel data from studies with infants and young children. As Luciano notes in the present volume (see below), Skinner's account neglected the role of the listener while providing an account of the speaker in functional terms, but listening has a crucial role in Horne and Lowe's theory. In their view, speakers (including young children) can listen to their own speech and thus a circular naming relationship is established between an object (for example), and the corresponding verbal response. In the case where a child sees a chair, and says the word "chair", she will then hear the sound /chair/. Listening to the spoken name refers the child back to the named object, thus closing a loop which can continue indefinitely. Naming, they believe, can account for the generativity of language, which has attracted such attention from linguists, and for rule-governed behaviour. Generativity occurs because once the name relation has been established with one exemplar of a class of objects it will generalise to other physically similar stimuli, and also to other stimuli that are members of the same functional class. Rule-governed behaviour, they maintain, is also to be understood primarily in terms of naming because a common name for physically different objects provides a means of establishing new behaviour to all members of the class. For example, the instruction, "throw out the rubbish" can be applied to all the physically dissimilar items labelled as rubbish. The studies reported, with infants or young children, are consistent with their view that the name relation is a union of speaking and listening that involves tact, echoic and listener relations, and provide experimental analyses that go well beyond the correlations between ability to name and capacity to succeed in equivalence tasks that has been well established in previous publications.

While there are open disagreements between Barnes et al. and Horne and Lowe about some of the key element of the conceptual apparatus that is required to advance the behaviour analysis of relational learning and language, the uncommitted reader will see many similarities in the two accounts. Furthermore, both research groups share the methods and standards of evidence of the experimental analysis of behaviour, and thus there is a framework within which the conceptual issues may be resolved. Finally, and crucially, both research groups are implementing new experimental procedures to test out their ideas.

In the final chapter of this group of six, Luciano examines the practical implications of research on rule-governed behaviour. She concludes, as do other contributors to this volume, that earlier definitions of rule-governed behaviour were incomplete or unclear. Again, there is a tension between functional accounts and more frequently used structural or formal accounts. A functional account is concerned with the functions of antecedent verbal stimuli in the various contexts where behaviour passes various tests (such as those suggested by Hayes, 1986) for establishing that it is rule governed. Relevant experimental research procedures include say-do correspondence, and equivalence class formation. Applications include procedures to increase the probability of rule following including self-instructional training, and studies of the indirect effects of rules through transfer of function across equivalence classes. There are also areas of application where the objective is to break existing behaviour-behaviour relationships.

Looking across the chapters by Barnes et al., Horne and Lowe, and Luciano, we see that there is now a large and growing range of behavioural techniques available to investigate human language and rule-following behaviour. The data generated are orderly, in accord with traditions of the experimental analysis of behaviour, but unsurprisingly they are complex and lead to disagreements about satisfactory conceptualisation. The most important features of this developing landscape are that innovations in experimental procedures are continuing and enabling us to capture increasing amounts of the field generally termed cognition within an experimental analysis, while retaining the selectionist and functional framework of behaviour analysis.

Radical Application

Radical behaviourism is the philosophy underpinning the science known as the experimental analysis of behaviour, and applied behaviour analysis is the application of principles derived from that science to real-life human problems. "Radical" here means "thoroughgoing" and, while applied behaviour analysis has gone from strength to strength in the past 20 years, some commentators have argued recently that the scope of applied behaviour analysis has become too narrow, and thus "un radical". In particular, the range of principles derived from the experimental analysis of behaviour that have been routinely applied is a small fraction of the full range that has been established through laboratory research. However, this is changing and applications are becoming more radical, in the sense of becoming thoroughgoing. This development is well illustrated by the final seven chapters of this volume.

In his chapter, Wacker notes the lack of interaction of applied behaviour analysis with the experimental analysis of behaviour in recent times, and defines bridge studies as those that provide a link between basic and applied research. Such studies inform both domains by advancing knowledge of basic processes and having implications for applied problems. He stresses the importance of two-way interaction between the fields. Until application is attempted, we do not know the value of basic processes investigated in the laboratory, nor which aspects deserve further investigation. Indeed, it can be argued that basic research is literally worthless until application has been carefully attempted.

Bridge studies also have other more subtle but equally important features: they can alter the ways in which treatment is studied, and they can improve the ways in which behaviour change is assessed. Both these aspects are illustrated, Wacker argues, in the development of functional analysis for aberrant behaviour. Classic bridge studies supported the hypothesis that apparently-similar aberrant behaviours can be maintained by different reinforcers and different contingencies. This led to the abandonment of the earlier assumption that aberrant behaviour could be defined by its topography (eye gouging, head banging, etc.), and thus bridge studies have completely changed our view of this type of behaviour. This is a further example of the importance of functional definitions of response classes, stressed by Barnes et al., and has the crucial applied consequence that we can now match treatment to function of the aberrant behaviour. Although Wacker is able to point to several other important groups of recent bridge studies, they are still relatively rare. However, their great potential importance for progress in behaviour analysis means that editorial policies in both the experimental analysis of behaviour and applied behaviour analysis should be modified to favour them rather than only those studies that lie closer to the ends of the experimental-applied continuum.

The next two chapters are examples of good practice of the type recommended by Wacker. In the first of these, Fisher, DeLeon, and Kuhn take further the account of the functional analysis of aberrant behaviour. Following a review of aspects of the recent literature, they introduce the concept of precurrent contingencies (using a term provided by Skinner, 1953). A precurrent response is one that creates the opportunity for reinforcement of a subsequent response. Based on some published experimental studies, they hypothesise that precurrent contingencies develop between destructive behaviour and the probability of reinforcement for mands (categories of verbal behaviour that are reinforced by the listener's compliance; Skinner, 1957). For example, a child may demand food from a parent, and the parent may comply, or, on those occasions when this reinforcement does not occur the mand may be followed by destructive or self-injurious behaviour. Their research program has shown that this model is supported by the results of some functional analyses and has led to interventions that are effective in reducing destructive behaviour. This extension of functional analysis methodology to include relationships between behaviours (in this case, verbal behaviour and destructive behaviour) raises many possibilities of further application.

In their chapter, Taylor, O'Reilly and Lancioni re-examine a tenet of behaviour analysis that, like several others scrutinised in this volume, has been neglected until recently. Although summaries of the most basic tenets of behaviour analysis state that current behaviour is a function of the history of reinforcement in relevant situations, as well as the reinforcement contingencies prevailing at present (see, for example, Leslie, 1988), and experimental studies (in humans and other species) have established the systematic effect of extended exposure to one reinforcement schedule on behaviour subsequently maintained by a different schedule, applied studies have nonetheless generally examined only the current contingencies. This is beginning to change, and Taylor et al. are able to review a number of studies examining effects of behavioural history. Two of their own studies illustrate the applied importance of these effects. In one, a 7 year-old girl showed higher levels of aggression in analogue assessment when this followed a period in which the teacher attended to aggressive behaviour. In another study, differing effects of prior social conditions on levels of aggression in analogue assessment were shown for two individuals. As well as being important demonstrations that assessment outcomes depend on recent behavioural history, these findings confirm that our account of the environment must refer to previous as well as present features if we are to successfully account for behaviour. This undermines the prevailing – but incorrect – assumption that the environment can act only as a proximal cause of behaviour.

The next chapter, by Gewirtz and Peláez-Nogueras, makes a radical assault on other prevailing and incorrect assumptions. These are those that pervade developmental psychology and attribute much problem behaviour in infants and young children solely to maturational and other "prewired" biological factors. In a series of studies, Gewirtz and Peláez-Nogueras illustrate brilliantly that well-established operant principles can generate, and eliminate, a number of these behaviours including protests at departure of and separation from the parent, fear of the dark, and jealousy between twin siblings. All these experiments involved minor, but crucial, changes to the naturally occurring interactions between mothers and infants or young children, so that increases or decreases in a functionally-defined class of protest behaviours were differentially reinforced by just those maternal behaviours that occurred routinely. In a further study, they examined eye-contact in very young infants of depressed mothers. Such infants are typically found to be depressed in turn by the age of 3 months, in that they show gaze avoidance, low activity levels etc. Selective reinforcement of eye-contact with the experimenter was successful, suggesting that this could be used as a protective intervention with infants of depressed mothers. It appears that behaviour usually regarded as indicative of depression in infants, similarly to that taken to be indicative of separation, fear of the dark, or jealousy, is susceptible to change in accordance with operant reinforcement contingencies. Furthermore, as Gewirtz and Peláez-Nogueras conclude, the changes in everyday mother-infant interactions used to demonstrate operant control were so small, that there is every reason to believe that it was normal, and caring, parental practices that generated the problems in the first place.

Gewirtz and Peláez-Nogueras's work illustrates another theme in the history of the relationship between behaviour analysis and general psychology. Very often it has been assumed that a behavioural approach is ineffective with a particular problem in the absence (or even the presence, see Leslie, 1997, for examples) of well-designed studies. It appears that ideological, rather than empirical, reasons for rejecting a behavioural analysis have carried the day in such cases, and it is necessary for behaviour analysts not only to do the crucial experiments, as has been done here, but also to bring them to the attention of other psychologists. In fact this is hard to do directly, and may be best achieved by demonstrating the effectiveness of behavioural techniques to potential clients (in this example, parents of very young children with behaviour problems) in the first instance. This has been happening recently in many countries in the case of behavioural approaches for young children with autistic behaviour, where there is now high parent-led demand for programs based on methods devised by Lovaas (for example, 1987).

The final three chapters are concerned with broad aspects of interpretation and application of behaviour analysis. Hobbs, Cornwell, and Chiesa address the so-called "misrepresentation" of behaviour analysis in psychology texts, and promote a behaviour-analytic approach to this issue. They recommend the analysis of referencing of publications in behaviour analysis within those texts, in terms of quantity and accuracy, as a more objective measure than some of those previously used, but concur that behaviour analysis is not properly treated in introductory psychology texts. As well as suggesting some tactics for correcting or improving presentations of behaviour analysis to students, they go on to examine textbook writers' behaviour.

Textbooks are selected by instructors, and their choices will be of books that reflect their views of mainstream psychology; this has the unfortunate "side effect" that there is little pressure on current writers to include an adequate account of behaviour analysis. More generally, Hobbs et al. note some parallels between the contingencies under which textbook writers work and those affecting journalists and storytellers. As increasing numbers of more popular textbooks are sold, these contingencies become more salient. There are pressures to "tell a good story" which operate at several levels, all of which can be construed in terms of contingencies whereby the writer is selectively reinforced for including easy, familiar, and perhaps amusing material, rather than material which is soundly based on scientific findings. This cogent analysis not only provides an appropriate warning to textbook writers but, more importantly, illustrates how further complex human phenomena can be interpreted within a behaviour analysis framework..

The notion of interpretation is dealt with at the outset of Foxall's chapter, in introducing his Behavioural Perspectives Model and its application to consumer behaviour. Interpretation of consumer behaviour in his model involves three stages: operant classification, allocation to contingency categories, and identification of consumer situations. Operant classification is done in terms of the relative importance (high or low) of utilitarian reinforcement and of informational reinforcement for that consumer behaviour; this four-way classification is combined with open or closed behaviour settings to produce a set of eight contingency categories. Finally, these categories are applied to specific consumer situations. Foxall points to the particular problems of finding out about relevant behavioural history in consumer situations. Given these, he makes the important assumption that elements of the current behaviour setting are broadly the same the same as those that have shaped and maintained similar behaviour in the consumer in the past. While this is an assumption, it can be checked against verbal reports by the consumer.

Foxall's chapter is an extended exercise in interpretation in behaviour analysis, potentially dealing with a huge range of phenomena that have usually been regarded as well beyond the current reach of behaviour analysis. The exercise is radical in its scope- it is intended to cover all aspects of consumer behaviour rather than some narrowly defined aspects- and it is also important for another reason. Consumer behaviour is most often the point at which human behaviour makes contact with the world of commerce. Ever since John B. Watson worked in advertising the 1920's, commercial interests have enthusiastically used behavioural methods to influence the behaviour of consumers. It is more than time that the behaviour-analytic community began to conceptualise and investigate that behaviour scientifically.

In our final chapter, Richelle takes an approach to *Walden Two* (Skinner, 1948) which is radical in that he addresses how specific recommendations for social practice made within Skinner's novel might contribute to modern society in general, rather than being concerned only with whether communities similar to Skinner's fictional one might "work". A major theme is that many of the problems identified by Skinner fifty years ago in social democracies are even more severe today, and Skinner's suggested alternatives remain fresh and interesting. Richelle elegantly demonstrates that many popular "remedies" for social problems in Western democracies, such as early retirement to reduce unemployment or the use of unfettered free markets, generate as many problems as they solve and are much less original, or radical, than Skinner's proposals. Interestingly, we are here again dealing with interpretation of behavioural principles in the broadest sense, rather than with direct links to scientific findings. Richelle concludes that this is not a matter for concern, but that our aspiration should be to examine the efficacy of the practices recommended with those currently used.

Conclusion

The contributors to the Third European Meeting for the Experimental Analysis of Behaviour were asked to examine the current state of the interaction between the experimental analysis of behaviour and applied behaviour analysis. I have been able to find three unifying themes in the material they have presented, but there is of course a fourth. This is the way in which so many current and novel developments can be linked directly to the innovations of B.F. Skinner (1904-1990). Truly we owe him an enormous debt.

References

Branch, M. (1982). Misrepresenting behaviorism. *Behavioral and Brain Sciences, 5,* 372-373.

Catania, A.C. (1982). Anti-misrepresentationalism. *Behavioral and Brain Sciences, 5,* 374-375.

Epstein, R. (1982). Representation - a concept that fills no gaps. *Behavioral and Brain Sciences, 5,* 377-378.

Hayes, S. C. (1986). The case of the silent dog-verbal reports and the analysis of rules: A review of Ericsson and Simon's 'Protocol analysis: Verbal reports as data". *Journal of the Experimental Analysis of Behavior, 45,* 351-363.

Hinde, R.A., & Stevenson-Hinde, J. (Eds.) (1973). *Constraints on learning: limitations and predispositions.* London: Academic Press.

Horne, P.J., & Lowe, C.F. (1996). On the origins of naming and other symbolic behavior. *Journal of the Experimental Analysis of Behavior, 65,* 185-241.

Leslie, J.C. (1988). Behavioural analysis of professional competence. In R. Ellis (Ed.), *Professional competence and quality assurance in the caring professions* (pp. 179-198). London: Croom Helm.

Leslie, J. C. (1997). Applied psychology from the standpoint of behavioural analysis. In K. Dillenburger, M. F. O'Reilly, & M. Keenan (Eds.), *Advances in behaviour analysis* (pp. 103-112). Dublin: University College Dublin Press.

Lovaas, O. I. (1987). Behavioral treatment and normal educational and intellectual-functioning in young autistic-children. *Journal of Consulting and Clinical Psychology, 55,* 3-9.

Roitblat, H.L. (1982a). The meaning of representation in animal memory. *Behavioral and Brain Sciences, 5,* 353-372.

Roitblat, H.L. (1982b). Representations and cognition – response. *Behavioral and Brain Sciences, 5,* 394-401.

Schusterman, R., & Kastak, D. (1993). A California sea lion (Aalophus californianus) is capable of forming equivalence relations. *The Psychological Record, 43,* 823-840.

Sidman, M. (1986). Functional analysis of emergent verbal classes. In T. Thompson, & M. D. Zeiler (Eds.), *Analysis and integration of behavioral units* (pp. 213-245). Hillsdale, NJ: Erlbaum Associates.

Sidman, M. (1990). Equivalence relations: Where do they come? In D.E. Blackman & H. Lejeune (Eds.), *Behaviour analysis in theory and practice: Contributions and controversies* (pp. 93-114). Hillsdale, NJ: Erlbaum.

Sidman, M. (1994). *Equivalence relations and behavior: A research story.* Boston, MA: Authors Cooperative, Inc.

Sidman, M., & Tailby, W. (1982). Conditional discrimination vs. matching to sample: An expansion of the testing paradigm. *Journal of the Experimental Analysis of Behavior, 37,* 5-22.

Skinner, B.F. (1938). *The behavior of organisms.* New York: Appleton-Century-Crofts.

Skinner, B.F. (1948). *Walden Two.* New York: Macmillan.

Skinner, B.F. (1953). *Science and human behavior.* New York: Macmillan.

Skinner, B.F. (1957). *Verbal behavior.* New York: Appleton Century.

Chapter 2

Ten Points Every Behavior Analyst Needs to Remember About Reinforcement

Charles Catania
University of Maryland, Baltimore County

Operant behavior is behavior that is sensitive to its consequences. When operant behavior becomes more likely because of the consequences it has had, we speak of reinforcement. Some consequences produce increases in the likelihood of operant behavior, and others do not. Ubiquitous but not universal, reinforcement is not a matter of associations or stimulus-response connections. Rather, it is a variety of selection, in many ways analogous to the phylogenic selection of biological populations over evolutionary time. In ontogenic selection, or the selection of operant behavior, populations of responses are selected by their consequences. As in phylogenic selection, ontogenic selection is constrained by the range of variations available in the current population, and it can either occur naturally or be arranged artificially.

With regard to phylogenic selection, artificial selection was taken for granted, as in horticulture, even while arguments for natural selection continued to face serious challenges long after Darwin's insight. Similarly, most critics of behavior analysis allow that procedures for the selection of behavior are useful in some contexts, such as animal training, even as they deny the relevance of the ontogenic selection of behavior in natural environments. Shaping is artificial selection and is easily demonstrable, but natural ontogenic selection is harder to document The decades of debate over whether any reinforcement contingencies operate in language acquisition provide an example.

As suggested by Skinner (1971), some of the resistance to the concept of reinforcement can be attributed to verbal traditions in contemporary Western culture, including the languages of freedom and control. Perhaps that is one reason why research on how extrinsic reinforcers might undermine the potency of intrinsic reinforcers has led some of its proponents to argue that these presumed hidden costs should bar the use of reinforcement in schools, businesses and other institutions (Kohn, 1993), even though the claimed effects are only inconsistently demonstrable and are small and transient when they do occur.

But other sources of resistance can be found in misunderstandings of reinforcement and how it works. The relations among behavior and its consequences in reinforcement seem simple, but they have subtle properties, some of which become evident only in special contexts. When those properties are not taken into account, reinforcement can appear to be ineffective or to be accompanied by undesirable side-effects. It is therefore prudent to review the properties of reinforcement and to consider the circumstances in which they may mislead us as we deploy techniques of reinforcement and evaluate their effects. In the interests of preventing misconceptions and misunderstandings, it is probably even more important to remind ourselves of these properties whenever we present what we know about reinforcement to those outside of the field of behavior analysis. To those who argue that reinforcement should not be studied because it can be misused, the appropriate rejoinder is that detailed familiarity with its properties may be the best defense against its misuse.

In its concern for accountability, behavior analysis typically assesses current behavior before modifying it in an intervention. Let us be consistent with that concern by assessing our understanding of some properties of reinforcement in a brief quiz before we proceed further. Ten true-false questions follow that are correlated with ten points we need to remember about reinforcement. This is not meant to imply that these ten points are mutually exclusive or that they are the only points we need to remember; in fact, some items on the list are implicit in other items and the list is surely incomplete.

The reader may wish to answer these questions in writing, whether on these pages or on a separate paper, so that the answers will be easily available for later reference. An answer key will be offered in the context of successive discussions of the several questions, although many readers will not need it and perhaps some will even disagree with one or more of the keyed answers. In the latter case, readers may wish to give themselves partial credit or modify their scores in other ways as they see fit. There is no penalty for guessing and grades will presumably remain confidential.

A True-False Quiz on Reinforcement

1. Chain pulls produce food and lever pressing increases. This illustrates reinforcement.
2. The response classes produced by reinforcement are defined in terms of their forms or topographies.
3. Reinforcers work because they make the organism feel good or because the organism likes them.
4. A more probable response may be reinforced by an opportunity to engage in a less probable response.
5. Extinction depends on an active suppression of the previously reinforced responding.
6. If reinforcers have produced problem behavior, the best solution is simply to take the reinforcers away: to reduce a child's bad behavior, extinguish it.
7. Following a long string of errors, do not miss a chance to reinforce the next correct response.

8. Cases in which responses seem to be insensitive to their consequences demonstrate that some responses cannot be reinforced.
9. Extrinsic reinforcers applied to behavior maintained by intrinsic reinforcers undermine the potency of the intrinsic reinforcers.
10. The advantages of reinforcement make techniques of reinforcement more likely to spread through a culture than techniques of punishment.

Before proceeding, the reader may wish to review the items to be sure that no answers have been omitted.

Point 1: Specificity of Reinforcers

By definition, reinforcement always increases responding relative to what it would have been like without reinforcement. Also by definition, that increase must be specific to the response that produced the consequence. If response *A* produces food and only response *B* increases, we do not say that response *B* has been reinforced. Thus, *false* is the answer to Question 1: It is not correct to say that reinforcement has been demonstrated when chain pulls produce food and lever pressing increases. The specificity of reinforcement effects to the response that produces the reinforcer distinguishes reinforcement from other processes that produce increases in behavior. Question 1 is therefore a useful diagnostic tool when introducing students to the topic of reinforcement.

The vocabulary of reinforcement includes the terms reinforcer as stimulus and reinforce as a verb. For example, when a rat's lever presses produce food and lever pressing increases, we say that the food is a reinforcer and that the lever presses are reinforced with pellets. The response that increases must be the one that produces the consequences. For example, if a rat's lever press produces shock and only the rat's jumping increases, it would be inappropriate to speak of either pressing or jumping as reinforced.

It is because reinforcement operates on responses that we speak of reinforcing responses rather than organisms. We say that food reinforced a rat's lever press or that a pigeon's key peck was reinforced with water, but not that food reinforced the rat or that the pigeon was reinforced for pecking or that a child was reinforced. It is too easy to be ambiguous about contingencies when we fail to identify the response that was reinforced. If we have been told only that a child has been reinforced, we do not know much about actual contingencies. This grammatical restriction forces us to be explicit about which response has been reinforced but it does not prevent us from mentioning the organism whose behavior had consequences. The moral is that in our descriptions of reinforcement procedures we should be explicit about what behavior has been reinforced by what consequences.

Point 2: Topography and Function

Reinforcement creates response classes that are defined by their functions and not by their forms or topographies, so *false* is also the correct answer to Question 2. Common contingencies select the members of operant classes, and they do so even if the relations among members are arbitrary. A lever press is a lever press whether the rat presses with right paw, left paw, both paws, chin or rump (Skinner, 1935; consider also the arbitrariness of the sets of slides in the discriminated operant classes in Vaughan, 1988).

The distinction between function and topography is particularly crucial as it enters into diagnostic categories. The self-injurious behavior of two children may be similar in topography, but if the behavior of one child is reinforced socially by attention and the behavior of the other is reinforced by avoidance of compliance with simple requests, effective treatment programs designed for the two children will have to be radically different (Iwata, Pace, Kalsher, Cowdery, & Cataldo, 1990). The first child must be taught more effective ways of engaging the attention of others and must be brought into situations where attention is more readily available. Requests must be selected for the second child that are appropriate to the child's competence and the child's compliance with those requests must be reinforced (perhaps in the past such behavior has instead been punished).

What the behavior does is more important than what the behavior looks like. The moral is that we must define the response classes created by reinforcement in terms of their functions and not in terms of their forms or topographies.

Point 3: Assessing Reinforcers

Our verbal behavior is often correlated with our nonverbal behavior, so we should not be surprised that events that are effective as reinforcers are sometimes described in terms of positive feelings or strong preferences. Such descriptions are subject to the inconsistent practices of verbal communities, however, and we must therefore be wary of using them to predict whether particular events will serve as reinforcers. It is tempting to equate reinforcers with events that are colloquially called rewards. But contrary to Question 3, which is false, reinforcers do not work because they make the organism "feel good" or because the organism "likes" them. Our everyday language does not capture what is important about reinforcers. For example, in assessments of the reinforcers that might be effective in managing the behavior of people with profound handicaps, predictions based on staff opinion of what would work for each individual were inconsistent with the reinforcers identified by systematically assessing each individual's nonverbal preferences among those events (Green, Reid, White, Halford, Brittain, & Gardner, 1988; cf. Fisher, Piazza, Bowman, Hagopian, Owens, & Slevin, 1992).

We can sometimes make good guesses about what will be effective as a reinforcer because reinforcers often involve events of obvious biological significance. But reinforcers are not limited to such events. For example, sensory stimuli such as flashing lights can be powerful reinforcers of the behavior of autistic children (Ferrari & Harris, 1981). Restraint also seems an unlikely reinforcer, but in an analysis of self-injurious behavior, restraints that prevented children with severe developmental disabilities from poking or biting themselves were effective in reinforcing arbitrary responses such as putting marbles in a box (Favell, McGimsey, & Jones, 1978).

Whether particular events will be reinforcers can be a difficult judgment. In the final analysis, the primary criterion for reinforcement remains whether the consequences of behavior have raised the likelihood of that behavior. Reinforcers are defined by their behavioral effects and not by inconsistently correlated properties such as reports of feelings or preferences, so the moral is that when we try to identify which events will be effective as reinforcers we should assess, not guess.

Point 4: Relativity of Reinforcement

Reinforcement is relative, in the sense that it depends on relations between the reinforced response and the reinforcer. A less probable response may be reinforced by an opportunity to engage in a more probable response. The inverse relation, as in Question 4, does not hold. Again, *false* is the correct answer. For example, food is not always a reinforcer. When a parent only allows a child to go out and play with friends after the child has eaten, the opportunity to play may reinforce the eating.

Difficulties in estimating response probabilities at a given moment sometimes complicate analyses in terms of the relativity of reinforcement, but the reversibility of the reinforcement relation has been amply demonstrated experimentally (Premack, 1962). For example, levels of food and water deprivation can be selected so that drinking is reinforced by an opportunity to eat at one time and eating is reinforced by an opportunity to drink at another. In providing an *a priori* means for predicting whether an opportunity to engage in one response will reinforce some other response, the relativity of reinforcement also avoids the problems of circular definition that were inherent in some earlier definitions of reinforcement. We soon repeat ourselves if we begin by pointing to an increase in responding when asked how we know that a stimulus was a reinforcer and then explain that the response was reinforced when asked why the increase occurred.

The significance of reinforcers is based on the opportunities for behavior that they allow. For example, when time spent in isolation was used in an attempt to punish the tantrums of a 6-year-old autistic girl, her tantrums increased substantially instead of decreasing. This child often engaged in self-stimulation, such as waving her fingers over her eyes to create visual flicker, but that behavior was frequently interrupted by the staff. For her tantrums, time in the isolation room was a reinforcer rather than a punisher because the isolation room allowed her to engage in self-stimulation without interruption (Solnick, Rincover, & Peterson, 1977).

The relativity of reinforcement reminds us that we should not expect the effectiveness of reinforcers to be constant across different reinforced responses, different individuals, or even different time samples of the behavior of a single individual. The moral is that when a reinforcer is effective on some behavior in some context, we must not assume that it will be effective on other behavior or even on the same behavior in other contexts.

Point 5: Reinforcement and Extinction

The effects of reinforcers are not permanent. Extinction demonstrates that reinforcers have temporary effects. When reinforcement stops, the responding that it had maintained returns to its earlier lower levels. Thus, the decrease in responding during extinction is not a special process requiring a separate treatment. Rather, it is simply one of the properties of reinforcement. Earlier accounts of extinction treated it as a separate process that actively suppressed responding, but the phenomena that once seemed to support such accounts, including spontaneous recovery, disinhibition and rapid reacquisition after extinction, were eventually shown to be independently determined by different features of the transition from reinforcement to extinction (Catania, 1998, pp. 71-77). It is false to say, as in Question 5, that extinction depends on an active suppression of previously reinforced responding.

If the effects of reinforcement are temporary, then once we have created new behavior with reinforcers we cannot count on its maintenance after our intervention ends. Consider children learning to read. Only long after they have learned to name letters of the alphabet and to read whole words are they perhaps ready to read stories, so that reading can become "its own reward." Until that happens, teachers have no choice but to arrange artificial contingencies, using consequences such as praise or other extrinsic reinforcers to shape the components of reading. Responsible teaching adds extrinsic reinforcers only when there are no effective intrinsic consequences.

The effects of reinforcers are not permanent. The moral is that if we want to maintain behavior after we terminate artificial consequences, we should do so only if natural consequences are in place that will take over that maintenance.

Point 6: Side Effects

Reinforcement and extinction sometimes have side effects, effects that are independent of their defining properties. For example, aggressive responding is sometimes a side effect of extinction because extinction terminates reinforcer deliveries. If food is suddenly taken away from a food-deprived rat that has been eating, the rat becomes more active and perhaps urinates or defecates. If the food was produced by lever presses, the rat may bite the lever. If other organisms are in the chamber, the rat may attack them (Azrin, Hutchinson, & Hake, 1966). These effects and others, though observed in extinction, are not produced by the termination of the reinforcement contingency, because they also occur upon the termination of response-independent food deliveries. In either case, a rat that had been eating stops getting food. In extinction, the termination of a reinforcement contingency entails the termination of reinforcer deliveries, and the effects of the latter are necessarily superimposed on the decreases in previously reinforced responding.

If reinforcers have produced problem behavior, taking them away may produce undesired side effects. That is why extinction is not the method of choice for getting rid of behavior that has been created by reinforcement. For Question 6, as for its predecessors, "false" is the correct answer. Suppose a developmentally disabled boy engages in severe self-injurious behavior such as head-banging or eye-poking and we discover that his behavior is in large part maintained by staff attention as a reinforcer. Because of the harm he might do to himself if we ignore the self-injurious behavior, extinction is not well-advised. Giving him attention independently of the self-injurious behavior is one possibility, though that might reduce the behavior only slowly. Another is to use attention to reinforce alternative responses, and especially ones incompatible with the self-injurious behavior. The self-injurious behavior will decrease as the alternative responses increase.

In general, the solution is not to take the reinforcers away. The better way to reduce a child's misbehavior is to reinforce good behavior. Reinforcers that create problem behavior are important and, unless they are intrinsically harmful, taking them away will probably produce more problems than making good use of them by making them contingent on other behavior that is more manageable and more productive. Presumably that is why the experimental literature from applied settings provides relatively few examples of the use of extinction alone to get rid of problem behavior. The more typical practice in an applied setting is instead to use reinforcers already known to be potent, by virtue of the behavior they have created, to shape other behavior.

Sometimes we inadvertently teach the less effective alternative, especially when we present just a few basic facts about learning, as in the introductory psychology course. Based on a superficial account of reinforcement and extinction, a common misconception about what parents should do to get rid of a child's problem behavior is that they should not reinforce it. Instead, they should ignore it. Left unanswered are the inevitable subsequent questions, such as how the parents should handle things when other problematic behavior emerges that is maintained by the same reinforcer. We should not teach parents to ignore the behavior of their children; we should teach them how to use reinforcers more productively. The side effects of extinction typically make it an inappropriate method for getting rid of behavior that has been created by reinforcement. The moral is that rather than taking the reinforcers away we should make good use of them to strengthen alternative behavior.

Point 7: Delay of Reinforcement

The effects of a reinforcer depend on other responses that preceded it besides the one, usually most recent, that produced it. Thus, when one response is followed by a different reinforced response, the reinforcer may strengthen both. That means that the reinforcement of a single correct response after a long string of errors will strengthen the errors along with the correct response. It is therefore false to say, as in Question 7, that one should not miss a chance to reinforce the next correct response in such circumstances.

The effects of delayed reinforcers on responses preceding the ones that produced them are not restricted to a single operant class. For example, a pigeon's pecks on one key may be maintained because they are followed by reinforced pecks on a second key (Catania, 1971). In a task that involves correct responses and errors over trials, correct responses and errors can also constitute two separate operant classes. If we reinforce every correct response and repeat any trial with an error until the pigeon gets it right, this correction procedure guarantees that any sequence of errors will be followed by a reinforced correct response. Correct responses will probably dominate eventually, because the reinforcer most closely follows them. But errors may diminish only slowly and may even continue at a modest level though they never actually produce the reinforcer, because they are reliably followed after a delay by a reinforced correct response. Thus, always reinforcing a single correct response after a sequence of errors will probably maintain errors. An extended technical discussion of how to reduce the strengthening of errors while maintaining correction contingencies would take us too far afield, but all methods would involve increasing the separation between errors and subsequent reinforcers. One way is to extend the time to the next trial after every error; another is to draw from a set of error-prone problems after each error trial rather than repeating the same problem, so that errors for any given problem are further removed, on the average, from the eventual reinforced correct response.

Teachers must be alert for situations in which they may be strengthening incorrect responses along with correct ones that they reinforce. A reinforcer that follows a sequence of correct responses will probably do a lot more good than a reinforcer that follows a single correct response after several errors. Thus, teachers must judge whether correct responses are so infrequent that they should be reinforced even though preceded by errors or so frequent that the reinforcer can wait until the student has made several correct responses in a row.

Many practical applications of reinforcement may include other behavior that precedes the behavior that we target for reinforcement. When such behavior shares in the effect of the reinforcer, we may mistakenly conclude that the reinforcer is not doing its job very well. But if the reinforced behavior includes response classes that we did not intend to reinforce, it may simply be doing very well a job other than the one we wanted it to do. When one response is followed by a different reinforced response, the reinforcer may strengthen both, so the moral is that we should keep behavior that we do not want to reinforce from getting consistently close to reinforcers produced by other responses.

Point 8: Higher-Order Classes

Sometimes, when a response class appears insensitive to its consequences, it is part of a larger class other members of which continue to have the consequences it once shared with them. In such cases, the contingencies operating on the higher-order class may override those arranged for the original class. For example, once generalized imitation has been established, a child may continue to imitate some instance even though that particular imitation is never reinforced. That imitation may seem insensitive to contingencies, but it will be maintained by the contingencies that operate on the higher-order class as long as the higher-order class maintains its integrity. We would ordinarily expect subclasses for which reinforcement has been discontinued to be differentiated from the higher-order class, but that might not happen if the integrity of the higher-order class depends on its membership in other interlocking higher-order classes that continue to include the subclass (e.g., for generalized imitation, games such as *Simon Says* that occur in other contexts).

In any case, to demonstrate that responses are insensitive to their consequences is not to demonstrate that they cannot be reinforced, so Question 8 is another item for which "false" is the correct answer (this is not to say that all responses are reinforceable, but rather that unreinforceable responses are unreinforceable for different reasons). Let us now consider an institutionalized boy whose self-injurious behavior is reinforced by attention. Suppose we try to extinguish his self-injurious behavior by ignoring it. We might have trouble from the start because we cannot tolerate the damage he may do to himself. We persevere nevertheless and discover that his self-injurious behavior does not decrease. One possibility is that we have not adequately identified the relevant response class. If the function of this behavior is to produce attention, it is probably part of a much larger class of behavior that includes shouting obscenities, acting up, hitting or otherwise abusing the caregivers in the treatment center, and any number of other responses that might get attention (cf. Lalli, Mace, Wohn, & Livesey, 1995). This tells us how important attention is to this child; once again, we must consider a treatment program that uses attention to reinforce more effective and appropriate behavior. But the example should also remind us that we cannot define response classes by what they look like.

As in our discussion of Question 3, the criterion for defining response classes is function, but this case is distinguished from earlier examples by the embedding of one response class within another. The self-injurious behavior here was embedded in the larger class of attention-getting behavior. When a response class seems insensitive to its consequences, as when the self injurious behavior seemed not to extinguish, we must entertain the possibility that we have improperly specified the class and that it is part of a larger class the other members of which continue to have consequences it once shared with them. The hierarchical structure of some classes of behavior may sometimes make it appear that reinforcement is not working but it may be working on a response class larger than the one in which we have been interested. Contingencies operating on a higher-order class may override those arranged for one or more of its subclasses and thereby make reinforcement appear to be ineffective. The moral is that when reinforcement seems not to be working we should consider whether the response class in which we are interested is part of another larger class.

Point 9: Interactions with Verbal Behavior

Reinforcement may be obscured when human verbal and nonverbal behavior interact. For example, instruction-following is more than the following of particular instructions; it is a higher-order class of behavior held together by common contingencies (Catania, Matthews, & Shimoff, 1990; Estes, 1971). Following orders in the military is a product of extensive and powerful social contingencies, often based on aversive consequences, but in actual combat the long-term contingencies that maintain instruction-following in general as a higher-order class may be pitted against the immediate consequences of following a particular order. These points are therefore to some extent corollaries of the arguments considered in the context of Question 8.

Verbal behavior is involved in the distinction between intrinsic and extrinsic reinforcers, so it turns out not to be true, as stated in Question 9, that extrinsic reinforcers applied to behavior maintained by intrinsic reinforcers undermine the potency of the intrinsic reinforcers. An intrinsic reward or reinforcer is one that has a natural relation to the responses that produce it whereas an extrinsic one has an arbitrary relation to those responses. For example, music is an intrinsic consequence of playing an instrument but the music teacher's praise is an extrinsic one. Events presumed to function as reinforcers because their function has been instructed have been called extrinsic reinforcers (as when a child is told that it is important to earn good grades) but labeling them so does not guarantee their effectiveness.   In one experiment (Lepper, Greene, & Nisbett, 1973), one group of children received gold stars for artwork. After the gold stars were discontinued, children in this group engaged in less artwork than did those in a second group who never received gold stars. The gold stars, extrinsic reinforcers, were said to have undermined the intrinsic reinforcers, the natural consequences of drawing. The children had been told to earn the gold stars, however, and the experiment did not test their effectiveness as reinforcers. There were no data to show that children finger painted more when they got gold stars (cf. the discussion of Question 3).

Although extrinsic reinforcers are said to undermine the potency of intrinsic reinforcers, the claimed effects are only inconsistently demonstrable and are small and transient when they do occur (Cameron & Pierce, 1994). The evidence also suggests that problems are more likely to arise with extrinsic reward that is not contingent on performance than with contingent reward (Eisenberger & Cameron, 1996). In any case, if there is an effect its transience and small size is hardly consistent with the argument that extrinsic reinforcement may ruin the lives of children.

In the literature of the "hidden costs of reward", reinforcers have sometimes also been equated with bribes (Kohn, 1993), but it is unlikely that arrangements properly described as bribes involve the direct effects of reinforcers. Given that a bribe specifies behavior and its consequences ("If you put away your toys you can watch television"), bribes instead function as a stimuli that set the occasion for particular contingencies. The child who is frequently bribed will learn to discriminate between conditions in which bribes are in effect and those in which they are not, so the parent who often uses bribes will no doubt eventually find that the child complies only when a bribe is offered. The child will not learn to initiate appropriate behavior if the initiation rests with the one who offers the bribe. Over the long run, compliance with bribes will probably become a higher-order class that will interfere with the effects of more constructive contingencies. If reinforcement works here at all, it is in strengthening compliance with bribes, which is hardly the best way to make use of reinforcers.

Nonverbal effects of reinforcers must be distinguished from the social contingencies that maintain the verbal governance of behavior. The moral is that when situations involve verbal behavior there is a good chance that verbal governance will override more direct effects of reinforcement.

Point 10: Cultural Selection

We have considered phylogenic selection, as in the evolution of species, and ontogenic selection, as in the shaping of operant behavior within an individual lifetime. A third level of selection is cultural selection, which involves the selection of behavior as it is passed on from one individual to another (Skinner, 1981). Selection at any one of these levels need not be consistent with selection at the other two. For example, it may not matter how valuable one way of doing things is relative to some other way, if one is easy to pass on from one individual to another while the other can be passed on only with difficulty. The one that is easier to pass on may spread quickly and come to dominate in a culture relative to the other one even if the latter would be more beneficial in the long term.

A case in point is the application of techniques of reinforcement relative to the application of techniques of punishment. Unfortunately, the advantages of reinforcement do not make techniques of reinforcement more likely to spread through a culture than techniques of punishment. By now a trend should be apparent: None of the statements in Questions 1 through 10 were true.

The problem is that delivering a punisher is more likely to produce immediate consequences than delivering a reinforcer. Whatever else happens over the long term, if a parent shouts at or strikes a child thought to be misbehaving, the parent is likely to see some immediate change in the child's behavior, such as the onset of crying. That change will usually include the termination of the behavior that was of concern to the parent but may have little to do with whether the child's behavior will reappear on later occasions, especially in the parent's absence. If stopping the child's behavior is part of what reinforces the punishment of that behavior by the parent, its immediacy is an important factor in its effectiveness.

With reinforcement, on the other hand, the effects of delivering a reinforcer may not show up until some time has elapsed. In the shaping of a response, if a current response is reinforced that is closer to the target response than any other the shaper had seen before, the likelihood of that response will increase. Even so, many other responses might go by before the shaper sees another one like it. Unlike the punishment case, in which the immediate effects typically include the stopping of the target behavior, any immediate effects of reinforcement, as in the eating of a food reinforcer, involve behavior that is unrelated to the target response. Thus, the time periods over which deliveries of reinforcers have consequences by changing the probabilities of subsequent responses probably play an important role in determining how long it takes to teach shaping to students. If that makes it easier to teach aversive techniques than to teach techniques of reinforcement, perhaps it is also why punitive measures are so commonly used to maintain civil order in so many cultures.

Even as reinforcement begins to be more widely appreciated in our culture, we must not be complacent about teaching what we know about it. Some people are really good at shaping though they have not had explicit instruction, but mostly the effective use of reinforcers has to be taught. Despite the advantages of reinforcement, it is easier to teach the use of aversive techniques than to teach the use of reinforcers, and we have already reviewed here the various ways in which effects of reinforcement can be misunderstood or can be obscured by other processes. The moral is that we must remember that the effective use of reinforcers has to be carefully taught.

Other Points

Much remains. We have not discussed reinforcement based on stimulus removal (negative reinforcement). We have not considered symmetries with consequences that reduce rather than increase the likelihood of responding (punishers), nor have we examined some practical differences between reinforcement and punishment that make the former preferable and that limit the applicability of the latter. We have not dealt with the role of reinforcement rather than informativeness in the maintenance of observing behavior and the ways in which it may lead us to attend to what we want to hear rather than what we need to know (Dinsmoor, 1983). We have had little to say here about the interactions between behavior that has been reinforced and behavior that comes from phylogenic sources, nor about the relations between reinforcement and learning. Reinforcement is itself a phylogenically evolved process. It does not make learning happen; instead, the consequences of responding are what is learned.

These are just a few of many possibilities, because ours remains a rich subject matter with many areas still to be explored. The current list could have been a baker's dozen instead of ten, but then the temptation would have been to expand it still further. Instead, let us close our list here and pause for a review. Here is a new set of true-false items.

Another True-False Quiz on Reinforcement

1. If chain pulls produce food and lever pressing increases, this does not illustrate reinforcement.
2. Response classes created by reinforcement are defined in terms of their functions.
3. Reinforcers do not work because they make the organism "feel good" or because the organism "likes" them.
4. A less probable response may be reinforced by an opportunity to engage in a more probable response.
5. Extinction demonstrates that reinforcers have temporary effects.
6. If attention has reinforced problem behavior, using attention to reinforce an alternative response incompatible with the problem behavior is better than removing the attention.
7. Whenever possible, prevent errors from being followed immediately by reinforced correct responses.
8. When a response class seems to be insensitive to its consequences, it may be part of a larger class other members of which still have the consequences it once shared with them.
9. The claimed effects of extrinsic reinforcers on behavior maintained by intrinsic reinforcers are only inconsistently demonstrable and are small and transient when they do occur.
10. Delivering a punisher is more likely to produce immediate consequences than delivering a reinforcer, so it is easier to learn techniques of aversive control than techniques of reinforcement

In the first quiz, all of the items were false, but in this second one they are all true. Now we can summarize the ten points we have discussed and the morals we have drawn from each, again with the caveat that this list is not intended to be exhaustive nor are its several items mutually exclusive.

1. By definition, reinforcement is specific to the response that produces the reinforcing consequences, so we should be explicit about what is reinforced by what.

2. We must define the response classes created by reinforcement in terms of their functions, not in terms of their forms or topographies.

3. Reinforcers are defined by their behavioral effects and not by inconsistently correlated properties such as reports of feelings or preferences, so when we try to identify which events will be effective as reinforcers, we should assess rather than guess.

4. Reinforcement is relative, so when a reinforcer is effective on some behavior in some context, we must not assume that it will be effective on other behavior or even on that behavior in other contexts.

5. The effects of reinforcers are not permanent, so if we want to maintain behavior after we terminate artificial consequences we should do so only if natural consequences are in place that will take over that maintenance.

6. The side effects of extinction often make it an inappropriate method for getting rid of behavior that has been created by reinforcement, so rather than taking the reinforcers away we should make good use of them to strengthen alternative behavior.

7. When one response is followed by a different reinforced response, the reinforcer may strengthen both, so we should keep behavior that we do not want to reinforce from getting consistently close to reinforcers produced by other responses.

8. When behavior is a member of a higher-order operant class, contingencies operating on the higher-order class may override those arranged for the original class and make reinforcement appear to be ineffective, so when reinforcement seems not to be working we should consider whether the response class we are interested in is part of another larger class.

9. Nonverbal effects of reinforcers must be distinguished from the social contingencies that maintain the verbal governance of behavior, so when situations involve verbal behavior there is a good chance that verbal governance will override more direct effects of reinforcement.

10. Despite the advantages of reinforcement, it is easier to teach the use of aversives than the use of reinforcers, so we must remember that the effective use of reinforcers has to be carefully taught.

Conclusion

Reinforcement is a variety of selection. The relations among behavior and its consequences in reinforcement seem simple, but they have subtle properties, some of which become evident only in special contexts. When those properties are not taken into account, reinforcement can appear to be ineffective or to be accompanied by undesirable side-effects. Such inherent properties of reinforcement may have affected its acceptance, because they allow its effects to be masked in various ways. For example, when one response is followed by a different reinforced response, the reinforcer may strengthen both; when behavior is a member of a higher-order operant class, contingencies operating on the higher-order class may override those arranged for the original class; and, perhaps as a corollary, when human verbal and nonverbal behavior interact reinforcement may be obscured, as when human nonverbal behavior changes in ways inconsistent with reinforcement contingencies because other contingencies have operated on relevant verbal behavior. Alone or in combination, these and other factors may give the appearance that reinforcement does not work. On examination, we might instead conclude that it works more ubiquitously and more profoundly than we had originally imagined.

References

Azrin, N. H., Hutchinson, R. R., & Hake, D. F. (1966). Extinction-induced aggression. *Journal of the Experimental Analysis of Behavior, 9*, 191-204.

Cameron, J., & Pierce, W. D. (1994). Reinforcement, reward, and intrinsic motivation: A meta-analysis. *Review of Educational Research, 64*, 363-423.

Catania, A. C. (1971). Reinforcement schedules: The role of responses preceding the one that produces the reinforcer. *Journal of the Experimental Analysis of Behavior, 15*, 271-287.

Catania, A. C. (1998). *Learning* (4th ed.). Upper Saddle River, NJ: Prentice-Hall.

Catania, A. C., Matthews, B. A., & Shimoff, E. H. (1990). Properties of rule-governed behaviour and their implications. In D. E. Blackman & H. Lejeune (Eds.), *Behaviour analysis in theory and practice* (pp. 215-230). Hillsdale, NJ: Erlbaum.

Dinsmoor, J. A. (1983). Observing and conditioned reinforcement. *Behavioral and Brain Sciences, 6*, 693-728.

Eisenberger, R., & Cameron, J. (1996). Detrimental effects of reward: Reality or myth? *American Psychologist, 51*, 1153-1166.

Estes, W. K. (1971). Reward in human learning: Theoretical issues and strategic choice points. In R. Glaser (Ed.) *The nature of reinforcement* (pp. 16-36). New York: Academic Press.

Favell, J. E., McGimsey, J. F., & Jones, M. L. (1978). The use of physical restraint in the treatment of self-injury and as positive reinforcement. *Journal of Applied Behavior Analysis, 11*, 225-241.

Ferrari, M. & Harris, S. L. (1981). The limits and motivating potential of sensory stimuli as reinforcers for autistic children. *Journal of Applied Behavior Analysis, 14*, 339-343.

Fisher, W., Piazza, C. C., Bowman, L. G., Hagopian, L. P., Owens, J. C., & Slevin, I. (1992). A comparison of two approaches for identifying reinforcers for persons with severe and profound disabilities. *Journal of Applied Behavior Analysis, 25*, 491-498.

Green, C. W., Reid, D. H., White, L. K., Halford, R. C., Brittain, D. P., & Gardner, S. M. (1988). Identifying reinforcers for persons with profound handicaps: Staff opinion versus systematic assessment of preferences. *Journal of Applied Behavior Analysis, 21,* 31-43.

Iwata, B. A., Pace, G. M., Kalsher, M. J., Cowdery, G. E., & Cataldo, M. F. (1990). Experimental analysis and extinction of self-injurious escape behavior. *Journal of Applied Behavior Analysis, 23,* 11-27.

Kohn, A. (1993). *Punished by rewards.* Boston: Houghton Mifflin.

Lalli, J. S., Mace, F. C., Wohn, T., & Livesey, K. (1995). Identification and modification of a response-class hierarchy. *Journal of Applied Behavior Analysis, 28,* 551-559.

Lepper, M. R., Greene, D., & Nisbett, R. E. (1973). Undermining children's intrinsic interest with extrinsic reward: A test of the "overjustification" hypothesis. *Journal of Personality and Social Psychology, 28,* 129-137.

Premack, D. (1962). Reversibility of the reinforcement relation. *Science, 136,* 255-257.

Skinner, B. F. (1935). The generic nature of the concepts of stimulus and response. *Journal of General Psychology, 12,* 40-65.

Skinner, B. F. (1971). *Beyond freedom and dignity.* New York: Alfred A. Knopf.

Skinner, B. F. (1981). Selection by consequences. *Science, 213,* 501-504.

Solnick, J. V., Rincover, A., & Peterson, C. R. (1977). Some determinants of the reinforcing and punishing effects of timeout. *Journal of Applied Behavior Analysis, 10,* 415-424.

Vaughan, W., Jr. (1988). Formation of equivalence sets in pigeons. *Journal of Experimental Psychology: Animal Behavior Processes, 14,* 36-42.

Chapter 3

Structure and Function in Selectionism: Implications for Complex Behavior

José E. Burgos and John W. Donahoe
Universidad Central de Venezuela, Universidad Católica Andrés Bello and University of Massachusetts, Amherst

A major task throughout the history of psychology has been to define the place of internal processes in a science of behavior. What kinds of processes occur inside organisms when they behave, and what kinds of structures implement such processes? And, how are those processes and structures related to overt behavior and the external environment? The answers to these questions depend upon the positions one holds on the structure-function distinction. The main purpose of the present chapter is to discuss certain conceptual, philosophical, and empirical aspects of a selectionist position. Specifically, we intend to show how this position allows for structural considerations that are consistent with the basic tenets of behavior analysis as a functional science.

The chapter is divided into three major sections. In the first section, we describe a selectionist formulation of the structure-function distinction in terms of the relationships between experimental analysis, interpretation, neuroscience, and behavior analysis. We contrast this formulation to methodological behaviorism and cognitivism. In the second section, we describe a neural-network simulation based on that formulation. In the third section, we explore the implications of this simulation experiment and the underlying selectionist formulation for scientific interpretations of complex behavior.

Structure and Function in Selectionism

According to selectionism, complexity emerges from an interplay between simpler processes of variation, selection, and retention that occur repeatedly over ontogenetic and phylogenetic time (Donahoe & Palmer, 1994). Variation refers to differences observed between and within organisms. Selection encompasses mechanisms through which certain variations are favored over others by the environment. Retention includes mechanisms through which selected variations are preserved over time.

Experimental Analysis, Interpretation, Behavior Analysis, and Neuroscience

An epistemological thesis of selectionism is that basic processes of variation, selection, and retention can be discovered only through experimental analysis.

Experimental analysis allows for the discovery of basic processes through the definition and implementation of procedures. Procedures represent rules for manipulating independent variables, recording dependent variables, and controlling extraneous variables.

Procedures are implemented through experiments. The possibility of implementing procedures depends on their complexity, which increases with the number of variables. The more complex the procedure, the less possible it will be to implement it through an experiment. Also, the larger the number of variables, the more difficult it will be to analyze their functional relations quantitatively in order to derive general principles. Experimental analysis thus inevitably involves simplification. Precisely the point of experimental analysis is to simplify, so that it becomes feasible to determine how a certain few variables (chosen on the basis of empirical and/or theoretical considerations) are functionally related to one another, while ignoring many other variables.

Experimental analysis thus represents a suitable strategy for deriving general principles only when it is used to study relatively simple phenomena. Complex phenomena, in contrast, are not amenable to a direct experimental analysis. Any attempt to directly analyze complex phenomena experimentally would eliminate the very defining property of complexity. Hence, the impossibility of performing an experimental analysis of complex phenomena is not only practical but logical. Nonetheless, complex phenomena can be *interpreted* scientifically. In this sense, interpretation constitutes as much an aspect of science as experimental analysis.

According to selectionism, our interpretations of complex phenomena qualify as scientific only if they appeal to principles that have been derived from an experimental analysis of simpler phenomena. More specifically, complex behavior (e.g., verbal behavior) can be scientifically interpreted in terms of principles of behavioral variation and selection derived from an experimental analysis of simpler kinds of behavior (e.g., barpressing or keypecking). Here, variation refers to behavioral differences between and within organisms, whereas selection refers to the mechanisms that affect variation.

Principles of behavioral variation and selection can be derived through an experimental analysis of relatively simple behavior. This analysis, however, does not allow for a derivation of retention principles, because these usually refer to internal entities and processes, which take place at a level of observation different from the behavioral one. This nonbehavioral character of retention principles leaves us with three options. First, we can argue that principles of behavioral variation and selection are sufficient, and that retention principles are unnecessary for a complete interpretation of complex behavior. Second, we can formulate retention principles by making inferences about what happens inside organisms when they behave, without performing an experimental analysis of internal processes. Third, we can derive retention principles from an experimental analysis of such processes.

The first option forces us to remain silent about what happens inside organisms when they behave, whereas the second option leads to cognitivism. Silence about what happens inside organisms withdraws a crucial aspect of behavioral complexity, thus leading to seriously incomplete interpretations. And cognitivism violates the thesis according to which retention principles must be derived through a direct experimental analysis.

For selectionism, the choice is clear. If we want to talk about what happens inside organisms *and* avoid cognitivism, we must appeal to the principles derived from an experimental analysis of nervous systems, as performed by the neurosciences. Only then will our interpretations of complex behavior be more nearly complete and scientific.

As Skinner (1974) put it:

We shall eventually know much about the kinds of physiological processes, chemical or electrical, which take place when a person behaves. The physiologist of the future will tell us all that can be known about what is happening inside the behaving organism. His account will be an important advance over a behavioral analysis, because the latter is necessarily 'historical' —that is to say, it is confined to functional relations showing temporal gaps. Something is done today which affects the behavior of an organism tomorrow. No matter how clearly that fact can be established, a step is missing, and we must wait for the physiologist to supply it. He will be able to show how an organism is changed when exposed to contingencies of reinforcement and why the changed organism then behaves in a different way, possibly at a much later date. What he discovers cannot invalidate the laws of a science of behavior, but it will make the picture of human action more nearly complete (p. 215).

Selectionism thus appeals to the neurosciences because only they can provide us with experimentally derived principles that describe how selected environment-behavior relations are retained over time. Such principles refer to the kinds of processes that occur inside organisms when environment-behavior relations are selected, as well as the kinds of structures that implement such processes at the molecular, cellular, and anatomical levels. In this manner, the neurosciences allow us to introduce a second kind of variation, in addition to behavioral variation, namely, differences in retention processes and structures.

According to selectionism, the appeal to the neurosciences is considered necessary to deal with that aspect of complex behavior that relates to retention principles. However, neuroscientific principles by themselves are insufficient and, hence, cannot replace behavior-analytic ones. Just as behavior-analytic methods do not allow for an experimental analysis of nervous systems (and, hence, for a derivation of retention principles), neuroscientific methods do not allow for an experimental analysis of behavior (and, hence, for a derivation of principles of behavioral variation and selection).

Neuroscience, then, cannot put behavior analysis out of business, for even if we could derive specific principles of behavioral variation and selection solely from an experimental analysis of nervous systems, such principles would have to be empirically verified through an experimental analysis of behavior. Similarly, behavior analysis cannot put neuroscience out of business, for even if we could derive specific retention principles solely from an experimental analysis of overt environ-ment-behavior relations, such principles would have to be verified through an experimental analysis of nervous systems.

Selectionism and Methodological Behaviorism

By viewing retention principles as referring to internal processes and structures that are susceptible to an experimental analysis through the methods of the neurosciences, selectionism admits such processes and structures as scientifically legitimate. Selectionism thus separates itself from methodological behaviorism (Donahoe & Palmer, 1994). Based on the covert, publicly unobservable nature of internal processes and structures, methodological behaviorism rejects them as legitimate subject matters for scientific study (e.g., Skinner, 1974). Such a rejection arises from the assumption that direct, public observability is a condition for scientific legitimacy. Selectionism accepts this assumption, but qualifies it by clarifying that public observability is relative to our experimental methods. What is publicly unobservable with one method may become publicly observable with another. The covert nature of internal processes and structures certainly hinders an experimental analysis *at the level of overt behavior*. However, internal processes and structures are amenable to an experimental analysis at the neural level, which makes their study scientifically legitimate from an experimentalist perspective.

Just like the experimental analysis of behavior, the experimental analysis of nervous systems involves a great deal of simplification, which allows for the discovery of basic neural processes. Thanks to this simplification, what is publicly unobservable through behavior-analytic methods becomes publicly observable through neuroscientific methods. Public unobservability, then, is not an inherent property of retention processes and structures, but only a limitation of a certain kind of experimental methodology (viz., behavior analysis). What is internal in behavior analysis becomes external in neuroscience. Of course, in natural settings and everyday life, neural processes and structures are publicly unobservable, whereas overt environment-behavior relations are publicly observable. But, again, this separation arises from the fact that in such settings we are restricted to a certain kind of observation conditions. The internal-external and private-public distinctions thus seem to be more epistemological than ontological in that they refer to different ways of approaching reality, rather than different realities.

Although derivation from a direct experimental analysis represents a necessary condition for a principle to be scientifically legitimate, experimental analysis is not the only scientifically legitimate endeavor. Interpretation can also be considered as a legitimate (and, in some cases, inevitable) aspect of scientific activity. Scientific interpretation allows us to deal with complex neural processes and structures that are not amenable to a direct experimental analysis. That is to say, complex nervous systems can be interpreted in terms of neural principles just as complex behaviors can be interpreted in terms of behavior-analytic principles.

But interpretation also allows us to talk scientifically about what happens inside organisms when only relations between their overt behavior and environment have been experimentally analyzed. Neuroscientific principles, thus, may complement behavior-analytic ones. Neuroscience and behavior analysis do not have to interact directly at a methodological or theoretical level. In this sense, selectionism recognizes a kind of sovereignty in each discipline. Such a sovereignty, however, does not preclude the possibility of a collaborative relationship. A direct relationship involves the combination of methods and techniques from behavior analysis and neuroscience, to experimentally analyze the neural bases of learning. This kind of relationship is currently in progress, under names such as *biobehavioral science* or *behavioral neuroscience*. Less direct interactions involve combining principles that have been derived from independent experimental analyses of behavior and nervous systems. Such a combination represents a theoretical, logical endeavor, and can be applied to interpret simple as well as complex behavior.

Selectionism and Cognitivism

By accepting internal processes and structures as scientifically legitimate subject matters, selectionism could be misrepresented as a form of cognitivism. However, at least three differences can be identified, of which we have already mentioned two. First, selectionism rejects the cognitivistic strategy of inferring internal retention principles solely from an experimental analysis of environment-behavior relations (Palmer & Donahoe, 1993). Second, selectionism identifies retention principles with neurobiological processes and structures. A third difference relates to the causal status of the internal. A major tenet of cognitivism is that the internal represents a primary cause of overt behavior. In contrast, selectionism holds that the internal represents an effect of the external environment as much as does overt behavior. This view can be justified on empirical as well as logical grounds.

Empirically, the evidence from biobehavioral science (a hybrid discipline that combines behavior analysis with neuroscience) suggests that changes in neural processes, like changes in overt behavior, are effects of changes in an external environment. For example, the environmental manipulations involved in conditioned suppression have been shown to cause not only a characteristic overt-behavior pattern (referred to as "emotional"), but also certain states in specific regions of the organism's brain, particularly in the amygdala (e.g., Davis, 1992; LeDoux, 1992). This kind of evidence casts doubt upon the assumption that internal processes represent primary causes of overt behavior.

Logically, viewing internal processes as primary causes of overt behavior represents to the selectionist an artifact of prematurely ending our search for explanations. The example of the internal state of hunger and the overt behavior of eating (Skinner, 1974, p. 13) is to the point. In the presence of a person eating frantically, the question "Why is Person *A* eating so frantically?" will prompt the typical mentalist to answer "Because *A* is very hungry". The strategy of selectionism is to continue asking "But why is *A* so hungry?". The appropriate answer would be "Because *A* has not had food since yesterday". Thus, eating frantically (an overt behavior), as well as the covert state of hunger, can be explained in terms of a condition of the external environment (viz., the absence of food). For each question that leads to the postulation of internal states as causes, the selectionist can ask another one that leads to external causes. These causes account for the overt behavior we wanted to explain in the first place, as well as the internal states themselves, in which case the latter become effects.

The Origins of Structure: Evolution by Natural Selection

Selectionism appeals to the external environment not only to explain internal processes and overt behavior, but also to explain the kinds of structures that implement such processes. External environmental factors can explain present neural structures in two ways. First, neural structures result from developmental processes, which are partially determined by the individual's environment through epigenetic factors. Second, although development is also genetically determined, genotypes are structures that retain (in an encrypted form) the products of selection by the ancestral environment. Which genotypes are retained from generation to generation (and, hence, which nervous systems are developed) are ultimately determined by an ancestral selective environment. In this sense, present genotypes and present neural structures can ultimately be seen as effects of an external environment (ancestral as well as present).

Selectionism thus appeals to principles from evolutionary and molecular biology to explain present neural phenotypic structures that result from developmental processes, as well as the genotypic structures that determine such processes. This kind of explanation appeals to events in the ancestral environment as the ultimate causes of internal structures. Genotypic retention structures allow for the conservation of the products of natural selection by ancestral environments. Phenotypic neural structures allow for the conservation of the products of selection by reinforcement in the individual environments of the past and the present.

Description and Explanation

We thus arrive at a selectionist formulation of the structure-function distinction. Structures represent *retention media*, which can be of two types, namely, genotypes and neural phenotypes. Genotypes retain the outcome of evolution by natural selection in ancestral environments across phylogenetic time. Neural phenotypes (the structure of individual nervous systems) retain the outcome of selection of environment-behavior relations by reinforcement in the individual environment across ontogenetic time. Function refers to the kinds of processes permitted or implemented by retention media. Such processes can also be of two types, namely development and learning. During development, phenotypic structures are generated from genotypic ones through an interplay between genetic and epigenetic factors. Learning refers to changes in an individual's overt behavior and nervous system as a function of changes in the individual's environment.

In the above formulation, structure and function are so intimately related that one cannot be explained without the other, a codependence that is also emphasized in evolutionary theory (Sober, 1984). However, an explanatory codependence does not entail a descriptive one. Although structure and function cannot be explained without each other, they can be described independently. Here a distinction between description and explanation is crucial. It is precisely descriptive independence which gives the neurosciences and behavior analysis their sovereignty.

For example, a neuroanatomist can describe in detail how different regions in a nervous system are connected to each other without making any description of the function of such regions. It is also possible to describe genetic structure in molecular biology without describing development. Of course, the search for such structures is usually motivated by functional considerations. A description of how certain brain regions are connected is typically motivated by the idea that such regions must mediate certain changes in overt behavior. Structural descriptions thus become meaningful only in relation to certain functional considerations. But, operationally speaking, it is in principle possible to describe neural structure without describing behavioral function.

An independent description of structure is possible only through direct experimental analysis of nervous systems. If structure is inferred solely from function, as it is done in mentalism, then the former cannot be described without the latter. That is to say, inferring an underlying structure becomes possible only when functional considerations are taken as premises. In this way, a description of function becomes indispensable for mentalism in order to infer underlying retention structures. The difficulty with this strategy is that, in most cases, a given functional description entails multiple underlying structures, the empirical reality of which cannot be unequivocally established solely on the basis of such a description.

Behavior analysts, on the other hand, can (and typically do) describe changes in environment-behavior relations (a functional aspect of nervous systems), without describing the structure of nervous systems. This possibility suggests that function can be described independently of structure, although certain functional considerations may become meaningful only in relation to certain structural considerations. Such an independent description of function is possible only through an experimental analysis of environment-behavior relations.

The possibility of describing structure and function independently, however, does not entail the possibility of explaining them independently. To ask what is the structure or the function of a nervous system is very different from asking why such a structure and function are the way they are. In this regard, biological explanations of structure typically appeal to function, and vice versa. Thus, one may contend that current nervous systems possess a certain kind of structure because similar structures were suitable media for retaining certain kinds of environment-behavior relations throughout phylogenetic time (precisely, those kinds that increased individual reproductive success). Conversely, a nervous system allows for the retention of certain kinds of environment-behavior relations because it possesses a particular structure.

This is not to propose that neural structure explains overt behavior. To explain overt behavior by appealing to neural structure is like explaining the presence and organization of folders inside a filing cabinet by appealing to the cabinet's size and material. The structural features of the cabinet certainly impose general restrictions upon the number and size of folders that can be filed. But the presence of particular folders organized in a particular way inside the cabinet is due to the behavior of the person or persons using the cabinet, not to the cabinet's structural features. And even such features can be explained by appealing to the behavior of the persons who built the cabinet. In both cases, the explanatory factors are external to the cabinet's structural features.

By analogy, the structure of a nervous system imposes general restrictions on the number and kinds of environment-behavior relations that can be retained. But particular environment-behavior relations are selected under particular reinforcement conditions in the individual environment. An organism, hence, does not behave in a certain way because its nervous system possesses a particular structure, but because it has been exposed to certain environmental conditions. And even that structure can be explained in terms of natural selection by ancestral environments. In this sense, " ... the function of structure determines the fate of structure" (Donahoe, 1997, p. 1). Selectionism thus maintains the explanation of behavior at the level of the external environment.

From the perspective of selectionism, different kinds of scientific interpretation are possible (Donahoe & Palmer, 1994). In one kind, namely formal interpretation, principles derived through experimental analysis are expressed through mathematical models that are used for computer simulations. In the following section, we describe a simulation of the relationship between neural phenotypic structure and performance after selection by reinforcement, as an example of a formal interpretation of the structure-function distinction from a selectionist perspective. The motivation for the simulation was twofold. First, we intended to show how selectionist neural networks are capable of simulating a simple kind of structure-function interaction. Second, we intended to show how this approach allows for structural considerations that are consistent with a functional science. In the simulation, structure refers to the architecture of an artificial neural network, whereas function refers to environment-behavior relations selected through reinforcement.

A Simulation Experiment

The aim of this simulation was to study the relationship between the size of an artificial neural network (a structural variable) and its performance under certain operant-conditioning procedures (a functional variable). The networks consisted of neuron-like processing elements that functioned according to a neurocomputational model described elsewhere (Donahoe, Burgos, & Palmer, 1993). The model arose as a neural interpretation of a unified reinforcement principle that postulates a single reinforcement mechanism to account for behavior change under Pavlovian and operant procedures (Donahoe, Crowley, Millard, & Stickney, 1982). The model, thus, is based on general principles obtained through experimental analyses of nervous systems at the cellular and neuroanatomical levels.

Two handcrafted artificial neural networks were used (see Figure 1). Each network consisted of a set of elements organized into one input layer, two or more hidden layers, and one output layer. Elements represented abstract neurons, whereas connections represented abstract synapses. Elements were connected in a feedforward manner. That is, for any pair of connected elements, information flowed from the left (presynaptic) to the right (postsynaptic) element. Input-element activations were assigned according to a training protocol (see below). Activations of hidden and output elements were computed following an equation known as an *activation rule*. According to this rule, the activation of a given element was determined by the activation of its presynaptic elements and by the strengths or weights of the corresponding connections. Connection weights changed over time according to a *learning rule*, an equation that included a modulating reinforcing signal whose magnitude depended upon the activation of the *ca1* and *vta* elements over time (see below).

All activations and connection weights were represented as real numbers between 0 and 1, and time was conceptualized as a discrete variable measured in time-steps (*ts*). For details on the activation and learning rules and parameters, see Donahoe, Burgos, and Palmer (1993, pp. 39-40). All activation and learning parameters were the same as in our previous simulation research (Donahoe, Burgos, & Palmer, 1993; Donahoe, Palmer, & Burgos, 1997). Hence, the present experiment did not involve *ad hoc* parameter manipulation.

The input layer consisted of four input elements, of which only two were activated in the present experiment, namely S1 and S^R. Activations of S1 represented the occurrence of sensory stimuli (e.g., a light)[1]. Activations of S^R represented the occurrence of the kinds of stimuli typically used as primary (or, unconditional) reinforcers, such as food and water. Unlike S1, S^R was directly connected through a nonplastic strong connection to two kinds of elements, namely *vta* and CR/UR (see below). These connections constituted a pathway by which S^R unconditionally activated the CR/UR element, which simulated the occurrence of an unconditional response to a reinforcer. Although the presence, characteristics, and role of this response are not typically assessed in operant-conditioning procedures, such responses occur and play a crucial role in operant conditioning. The role of reinforcer-elicited responses and environmental stimulation in operant conditioning are incorporated within a single reinforcement mechanism that underlies behavioral change with both Pavlovian and operant procedures (Donahoe, Crowley, Millard, & Stickney, 1982; Donahoe, Palmer, & Burgos, 1997).

Hidden elements were organized into two kinds of layers, namely *sensory association* (*sa*) and *motor association* (*ma*). These elements differed mainly in two respects. First, *sa* elements activated *ca1* elements, whereas *ma* elements activated *vta* elements (which can also be activated by S^R). Activations of the *ca1* and *vta* elements provided the source of the reinforcing discrepancy signals that modulated changes in connection weights. Second, *sa* elements were closer to and, hence, more directly activated by the input elements, whereas *ma* elements were closer to and, hence, activated more directly the output elements.

The output layer consisted of two kinds of elements, namely R and CR/UR. Activations of the latter were produced by either activation of the S^R input element or the activation of the *ma* hidden elements that were activated by the S1 element through the *sa* elements. The R output element simulated the occurrence of

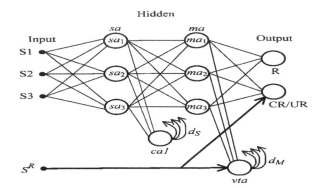

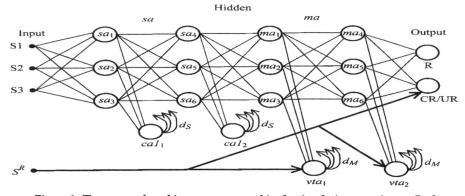

Figure 1. Two network architectures were used in the simulation experiment. Both networks consisted of three sensory input elements (labeled as S1, S2, and S3), one reinforcer input element (labeled as S^R), and two output elements (labeled as R and CR/ UR). The two networks differed only in the number of hidden layers. The smaller network (top) had two hidden layers, one sensory association (sa) and one motor association (ma). The larger network (bottom) had four hidden layers (two sa and two ma). Each hidden layer in both networks consisted of three elements, each of which was connected to one discrepancy element (ca1 for sa layers and vta for ma layers). Activations of discrepancy elements provided the signals that modulated changes in connection weights. Activations of S1, S2, and S3 represented the occurrence of sensory stimuli that could serve as environmental cues. In the present experiment, only S1 was activated, according to a predetermined training protocol (see text). Activations of the S^R input element represented the occurrence of a consequent stimulus (e.g., food). This element was activated at the end of an interval only if the activation of the R output element was larger than zero. Activation and learning parameters of all hidden and output elements were the same in both networks. Parameters were the same as those used in previous simulations (Donahoe, Burgos, & Palmer, 1993), except for the mean and standard deviation of the Gaussian distribution that determined the activation thresholds. In the present simulations, those parameters were 0.2 and 0.15, respectively. For details on equations and parameters, see Donahoe, Burgos, and Palmer (1993, pp. 39-40).

responses that are not unconditionally caused by any input element. This element thus could increase its activation only after operant conditioning (mediated by an increase in the strengths of the connections) has taken place. For the purpose of the present experiment, only activations of the R element are presented.

As Figure 1 shows, the networks differed only in the number of hidden layers. The smaller network (top portion) consisted of two hidden layers, whereas the larger network (bottom portion) consisted of four. Other structural traits (viz., number of input and output elements, number of elements per hidden layer, number of presynaptic connections per element, the number of *ca1* and *vta* elements per hidden layer, and activation and learning parameters) were identical in both networks.

The networks studied here can be seen as representing neural circuits that participate in different response systems, either in the same kind of organism or across different kinds of organisms. A specific application of this interpretation to the kinds of response systems studied in operant conditioning is still not feasible, for the relevant evidence is not yet available. At present, we assume only that the more complex the response of interest, the larger the underlying neural circuit. For example, responding under an intermittent schedule would seem to be more complex than responding under a *crf* schedule, to the extent that the former includes more interim responses than the latter. Hence, the circuit underlying the former would be expected to be larger than (and, to some extent, subsume) the circuit underlying the latter.

Procedure

Two reinforcement contingencies were used to train instances of the networks depicted in Figure 1. These contingencies simulated fixed-interval (FI) schedules in that reinforcement occurred only if a response occurred at the end of a sequence consisting of a fixed number of *ts*. In the short-interval schedule, an FI period consisted of a sequence of 3 *ts* during which the S1 input element was maximally activated. In the long-interval schedule, an FI period consisted of a sequence of 9 *ts* during which the S1 input element was also maximally activated. In each schedule, reinforcement could occur only at the last *ts* of an FI period. A reinforcement operation was simulated by maximally activating S^R at that *ts* only if the activation of the operant-response (R) output element was above zero. This element had a low level of spontaneous activation that simulated a larger-than-zero operant level at every *ts*, so reinforcement occurred from the very outset of training.

One instance of the smaller network was trained with the FI-3 schedule, and another instance was exposed to the FI-9 schedule. The same was done with the larger network. Training consisted of 300 FI periods for each of the four conditions of two network sizes and two FI schedules. The intertrial interval (the time between successive periods) was not explicitly simulated. Instead, we assumed that it was long enough for all activations to decay to low levels. As in other simulations, the initial connection weights (i.e., the weights before training, representing the state of a naive network) were set to a value of 0.01.

Results

Figure 2 shows the effects of training with FI-3 for one instance of the smaller network (top graph) and one instance of the larger network (bottom graph). The graphs represent cumulative records of responding across the last 450 *t*s of training (i.e., 150 FI periods for FI-3 and 50 FI periods for FI-9). Here, a response was defined as an R activation of 0.5 or more. The top records show relatively stable responding with a moderate overall response rate. Most FI periods are separated by relatively short breaks (i.e., intervals during which the R activation was below 0.5^2). Most of the breaks lasted 1 *t*s (e.g., the break separating the first two periods of the left record) and a few lasted 2 *t*s. In some cases, interspersed sequences of two (e.g., the first of the last ten periods of the middle record) and three periods (e.g., the first two periods of the right record) without a break can be observed. Also, the middle record shows a suggestion of two higher-order effects, one constituted by the first ten or eleven periods, and another constituted by the next six or seven periods.

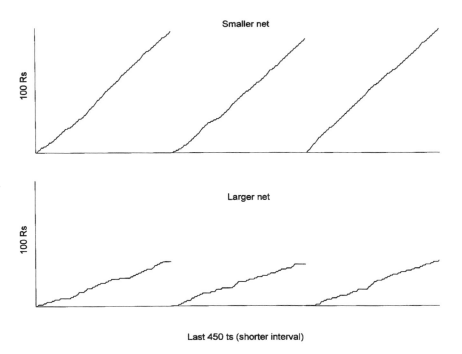

Figure 2. Cumulative records for the smaller (top) and larger (bottom) networks during the last 150 fixed-interval periods for the FI-3 schedule (a total of 450 ts). The vertical axis of both records represents a total of 100 responses. A response was defined as an activation of the R output element of 0.5 or more. Both networks showed break-and-run patterns, with most of the breaks occurring immediately after reinforcement. The overall response rate in the smaller network was substantially higher than the overall rate in the larger network.

In contrast, the bottom records show a less stable responding with a substantially lower overall response rate. A larger number of periods were separated by longer breaks. Only a few breaks lasted 1 *ts*, and most of the breaks lasted 2 *ts* (e.g., the break separating the first two periods of the left record) and 3 *ts* (e.g., the breaks separating the second and third, and third and fourth periods of the left record). A few breaks lasted 4 *ts* (e.g., the last two periods of the middle record). The presence of a larger number of long breaks produced higher-order deviations from stability. For example, the entire middle section of the left record and the first half of the middle record suggest negatively accelerated functions. Smaller "bumps" or "knees" (Ferster & Skinner, 1957, p. 164) occasionally appear throughout the three records.

Figure 3 shows cumulative records for an instance of each network under FI-9. The top records show that responding in the smaller network was even less stable than responding in the larger network under FI-3, with an even lower overall rate. Most of the breaks were substantially longer, some of them lasting up to 50 *ts*. A few runs can be seen interspersed throughout these records. There were only two pairs

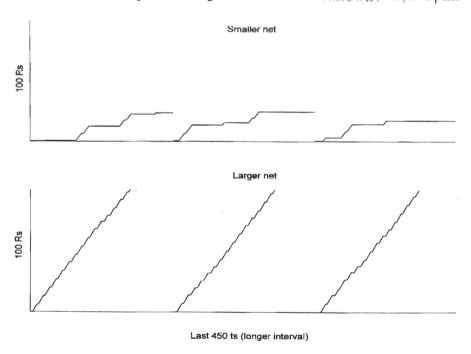

Figure 3. Cumulative records for the smaller (top) and larger (bottom) network under the last 50 fixed-interval periods for the FI-9 schedule (a total of 450 ts). The vertical axis of both records represents a total of 100 responses. A response was defined as an activation of the R output element of 0.5 or more. Both networks showed break-and-run patterns, with most of the breaks occurring immediately after reinforcement. The overall response rate in the smaller network was substantially lower than the overall rate in the larger network.

of periods consisting in runs that were separated by a break of 1 *t*s, one at the beginning of the second record and one at the beginning of the third record. Shorter runs can be seen towards the end of the first record, and the middle of the second and third records. Also, three pairs of runs are separated by a break of 2 *t*s, two in the first record and one roughly at the middle of the second record.

In contrast, the bottom records show that responding under FI-9 was far more stable in the larger network, with a higher overall response rate (the highest observed in these simulations). These records strongly resemble the kind of performance observed in real animals under relatively short fixed-interval and fixed-ratio schedules. Most of the periods were separated by breaks of 1, 2 or 3 *t*s. No conspicuous "knees" or higher-order effects were observed.

Discussion

In the above simulation, our primary goal was to show that selectionist neural networks are capable of simulating relatively simple structure-function codependences. We have shown how responding in these networks depended not only upon the reinforcement schedule, but also upon their structural features. Responding was substantially different when instances of the same kind of network were exposed to different schedules, and when instances of different kinds of networks were exposed to the same schedule. Our intention was not to simulate FI performance in any detail, nor to simulate particular interactions between reinforcement schedules and neural structures. Whether or not such interdependences specifically exist in real animals under the same kinds of reinforcement schedules represents an empirical question that awaits an answer from biobehavioral science.

The differences observed between the top records of each figure are consistent with the fact that responding becomes less stable and overall rate decreases as reinforcement becomes more intermittent or less frequent. Ferster and Skinner (1957) showed many examples of this phenomenon (e.g., compare Figure 149 on p. 157 to Figure 154 on p. 160). In operant conditioning, this phenomenon is typically explained in terms of extinction. That is, as reinforcement intermittence increases, the number of nonreinforced responses also increases, which produces a decrease in overall responding rate.

The bottom records of each figure, however, show the opposite tendency (i.e., more stability and higher overall rate under more reinforcement intermittence). This kind of result is also observed in operant conditioning, when a moderate value of an intermittent schedule produces higher overall rates than continuous reinforcement (crf). For example, Skinner (1938) showed that the overall barpressing rate under continuous reinforcement (e.g., see Figure 4, p. 68) is lower than the rate under an FI-2 min schedule (e.g., see Figure 30, p. 121). If reinforcement intermittence is further increased, then stability and overall rate decrease again.

This pattern of moderate to high to low overall rate under increasing degrees of reinforcement delay resembles the interstimulus-interval (ISI) function, a phenomenon observed in Pavlovian conditioning. The ISI function is an inverted U-shaped relation between the ISI and CR percentage, whose peak coincides with a set of intermediate ISI values. These values thus are considered as optimal. It is known that this function has roughly the same form across Pavlovian preparations such as nictitating-membrane response (NMR) in rabbits, autoshaping in pigeons, and conditioned emotional response (CER) in rats. It is also known that the absolute value of the peak of the ISI function varies widely from one preparation to another.

At this point, the best way to understand variations in optimal ISIs across Pavlovian-conditioning preparations is by combining functional with structural considerations, where the latter refer to the structure of the neural circuits underlying the response systems under observation. For example, the circuitry that serves as a retention medium for selected environment-behavior relations in NMR (e.g., Moore, Berthier, & Blazis, 1990) is very different from the circuitry involved in CER (e.g., LeDoux, 1992), and each preparation requires different optimal ISIs. In fact, the optimal ISI for NMR is far shorter (between 0.25 and 0.4 s) than the optimal ISI for CER (about 20 s). The present simulations suggest that such a variation in optimal ISIs may depend upon the size and architecture of the underlying neural circuits. Although there is no hard experimental evidence in this regard, it seems reasonable to believe that, neuroanatomically speaking, the NMR circuit is considerably smaller than the CER one.

According to the unified reinforcement principle, Pavlovian and operant conditioning involve similar kinds of environmental controlling events (Donahoe & Palmer, 1994). On this basis, we would expect phenomena like ISI functions and optimal-ISI variations to also occur in operant conditioning. Hence, we would also expect the above considerations about the role of neural structure to apply to operant conditioning. Under this view, the ISI in an operant procedure would be the interval between the onset of an antecedent stimulus and the onset of a consequent stimulus. Free-operant arrangements do not allow for precise measures of the ISI, because antecedent stimulation is not under experimental control. This problem does not arise in stimulus-control procedures, although a precise control of the onset of consequent stimuli may still be difficult. In any case, more experimental evidence is needed to determine what kinds of differences exist in optimal temporal parameters across response systems (within and between species) under different schedules.

Finally, how can we explain the relationship observed between responding under different reinforcement schedules and network size? At the present moment, we do not have a definite answer to this question. Preliminary simulations have shown that the manner in which hidden elements are organized throughout hidden layers, and the manner activations and connection weights are updated in a simulation represent important variables in this regard. If the number of hidden elements is increased while keeping the number of hidden layers constant (i.e., if the number of elements per hidden layer is increased), then the above effect disappears. Also, the effect is observed only when a particular procedure is used to update element activations.

To summarize, the size of a network imposed constraints on the kinds of environment-behavior relations it can retain. Extrapolating to real organisms, this signifies that the size of the neural circuit underlying the response system under observation imposes constraints upon the kinds of environment-behavior relations that such a circuit can retain.

Implications for Complex Behavior

The main implication of the present chapter is that structure imposes constraints on the kinds of environment-behavior relations that can be selected by consequences. Knowledge about internal structure thus becomes necessary, not only to understand differences in internal processes and overt environment-behavior relations but to interpret complex behavior in general. In the case of artificial neural networks, such knowledge arises directly from the network architecture. In the case of real organisms, knowledge about internal structures arises from an experimental analysis of the anatomy of nervous systems at the cellular and anatomical levels.

If internal structures are identified with neural structures, then the above implication leads to the idea that learning is constrained by biological structures. Selectionism is certainly consistent with this idea. However, selectionism is also consistent with the search for general laws of learning. The simulation described in the preceding section illustrates this point by showing that behavioral differences between individuals may arise from structural differences, even though the same reinforcement or learning mechanism is at work. Behavioral differences between networks were observed despite the fact that the very same neurocomputational model and parameters were used. This outcome suggests that the existence of individual differences between and within species, and the search for general laws of learning may not be as mutually exclusive as it once was thought, an idea that was anticipated by Hull (1945).

We find this possibility liberating for behavior analysis, in that individual and species differences should not represent a reason for fundamental concern. The presence of such differences does not necessarily indicate the existence of different learning laws. Also, interpreting complex behavior in terms of principles derived from an experimental analysis of nonhuman behavior remains a scientifically defensible endeavor. Selectionism, however, keeps our interpretations open to the possibility that individual and species differences, when observed under comparable environmental conditions, may arise from differences in neural structures.

Selectionism thus advises us to combine functional with structural considerations in order to achieve more complete interpretations of complex behavior. Each kind of consideration is insufficient by itself. Structural considerations become necessary when we are concerned with what happens inside organisms when they behave, especially to account for the mechanisms and structures that allow for the retention of the products of selection by consequences. Such an account cannot be achieved through a functional analysis alone, although, again, this kind of analysis is also indispensable. Any complementing structural considerations, however, must arise from principles generated through an experimental analysis of nervous systems at the molecular, cellular, and neuroanatomical levels of organization. Experimental analyses performed in biobehavioral science, of course, will also be most useful in this respect. However, complex behavior inevitably requires interpretation.

By considering neural structure as an integral part of our interpretations of complex behavior, selectionism could be seen as endorsing a kind of biological determinism. Whether or not this characterization is correct depends on what we mean by "determined". This issue has important ethical implications, for a lot of unnecessary suffering (human as well as nonhuman) has been produced in the name of misrepresentations of biological determinism. We want to make sure that selectionism is not identified with such misrepresentations.

If "determined" refers to an event that is caused, then selectionism may or may not represent a form of biological determinism, depending upon what kind of effect we are considering. As we have mentioned throughout this paper, selectionism does not view neural structures as causes of overt behavior, at least not in the efficient, Newtonian sense of the term. The ultimate efficient causes of overt behavior are to be found in the external environment. Hence, if the effect of interest involves changes in overt behavior, then selectionism is not biological determinism. If the effect is a nervous system, then selectionism can be seen as a form of biological determinism, insofar as nervous systems can be seen as products of natural selection by ancestral environments.

If "determined" refers to a system that can be described completely and unequivocally, then selectionism may or may not represent a form of biological determinism, depending on the kind of system under consideration. Systems like the networks used here are determined in this sense insofar as their structure and performance under certain conditions can be described completely and unequivocally. As network size increases, however, the possibility of a complete, unequivocal description decreases and, to this extent, the degree of determination also decreases. Most real nervous systems are far too large to be considered as determined in this sense. Even relatively "simple" nervous systems can be quite complex and, in this sense, undetermined. And if our concern is the human nervous system, which is the most complex structure ever produced by natural selection, then this sense of "determined" is untenable.

If "determined" signifies "destined", then selectionism most certainly does not represent a form of biological determinism. There is no scientifically justifiable sense in which a biological structure can be seen as imposing a destiny on an organism. Claims about destiny are predictions, insofar as they refer to the future. Science, of course, also involves making predictions. However, predictions about destiny possess a feature that is absent from scientific predictions, namely, necessity or inevitability. No serious scientist would consider that a given prediction is necessarily or inevitably true. Otherwise, there would be no reason to wait for the empirical evidence. Scientific predictions thus are *contingent*, in that they may or may not be true. Whether or not they are true ultimately depends on the empirical evidence. In contrast, predictions about destiny tend to be *tautological*, that is, they are considered as being inevitably true, which renders empirical evidence unnecessary. Such predictions do not belong in the realm of empirical science.

Finally, we want to emphasize that selectionism advises us to explain the structural differences themselves, before postulating them as ultimate explanations of performance differences. As mentioned before, selectionism explains structural differences in real organisms in terms of natural selection by ancestral environments. This kind of explanation does not apply to the present study, because the networks were handcrafted. The present structural differences can be explained only in terms of the behavior of the person who designed and built the networks. However, it is possible to generate structural differences between artificial neural networks through a simulated process of evolution. One of us (Burgos, 1997) has performed this kind of experiment using a *genetic algorithm* (a model of evolution by natural selection) to simulate the phylogeny of Pavlovian conditioning in artificial neural networks, obtaining similar structure-function codependences.

References

Burgos, J. E. (1997). Evolving artificial neural networks in Pavlovian environments. In J. W. Donahoe and V. P. Dorsel (Eds.), *Neural-network models of cognition: Biobehavioral foundations* (pp. 58-79). Holland: Elsevier.

Davis, M. (1992). The role of the amygdala in fear and anxiety. *Annual Review of Neuroscience, 15*, 353-375.

Donahoe, J. W. (1997). The necessity of neural networks. In J. W. Donahoe & V. P. Dorsel (Eds.), *Neural-network models of cognition: Biobehavioral foundations* (pp. 1-19). Amsterdam. Netherlands: Elsevier Science Press.

Donahoe, J. W., Burgos, J. E., & Palmer, D. C. (1993). A selectionist approach to reinforcement. *Journal of the Experimental Analysis of Behavior, 60*, 17-40.

Donahoe, J. W., Crowley, M. A., Millard, W. J., & Stickney, K. A. (1982). A unified principle of reinforcement: Some implications for matching. In M. L. Commons, R. J. Herrnstein, & H. Rachlin (Eds.), *Quantitative analyses of behavior: Vol. 2. Matching and maximizing accounts* (pp. 493-521). Cambridge, MA: Ballinger.

Donahoe, J. W., & Palmer, D. C. (1994). *Learning and complex behavior.* Boston: Allyn and Bacon.

Donahoe, J. W., Palmer, D. C., & Burgos, J. E. (1997). The S-R issue: Its status in behavior analysis and in Donahoe and Palmer's Learning and complex behavior. *Journal of the Experimental Analysis of Behavior, 67*, 193-211.

Ferster, C. B., & Skinner, B. F. (1957). *Schedules of reinforcement.* Englewood Cliffs, NJ: Prentice-Hall.

Moore, J. W., Berthier, N. E., & Blazis, D. E. J. (1990). Classical eye-blink conditioning: Brain systems and implementation of a computational model. In M. Gabriel and J. W. Moore (Eds.), *Learning and computational neuroscience: Foundations of adaptive networks* (pp. 359-387). Cambridge, MA: MIT Press.

Palmer, D. C. & Donahoe, J. W. (1993). Selectionism and essentialism in behaviorism and cognitive science. *American Psychologist, 47*, 1344-1358.

Skinner, B. F. (1938). *The behavior of organisms.* New York: Appleton-Century-Crofts.

Skinner, B. F. (1974). *About behaviorism.* New York: Alfred A. Knopf.

Sober, W. (1984). *The nature of selection: Evolutionary theory in philosophical focus.* Chicago, IL: The University of Chicago Press.

Notes

We thank V. P. Dorsel for useful comments. Correspondence concerning this paper can be addressed to José E. Burgos at Apartado 48276, Los Chaguaramos, Caracas 1041-A, Venezuela, South America. E-mail: *jburgos@ucab.edu.ve*

[1]For our neural networks to show conditioning, they must have at least one input element that is activated for at least one *ts*. This requirement is consistent with the idea (entailed by the unified reinforcement principle) that *all* operant-conditioning arrangements involve some antecedent stimulation that acquires a discriminative control over responding. In the case of free-operant arrangements, such a stimulation is assumed to arise from contextual stimuli (e.g., the sight of a lever). This assumption remains hypothetical for free-operant arrangements, because of the lack of experimental control of antecedent stimulation. The role of antecedent stimulation in operant conditioning is more readily assessed through discrimination arrangements, where antecedent stimulation is under experimental control. Input-element activations in our networks can be interpreted as representing discrete periods of contextual stimulation

[2]These activations were also reinforced, as long as they were larger than zero. The present simulation thus involved the definition of two responses, namely, an unlearned, spontaneous, low-level response used as a reinforcement criterion and a learned response used as a conditioning criterion. The first kind predominated early in training, whereas the second were more frequent towards the end of training.

Chapter 4

Synthesizing Equivalence Classes and Natural Categories from Perceptual and Relational Classes

Lanny Fields and Kenneth F. Reeve
Queens College and
the Graduate School of the City University of New York

Concept formation is inferred when the same response is spontaneously occasioned by many stimuli in a set or by many of the relations among the stimuli in a set (Keller & Schoenfeld, 1950; Dinsmoor, 1995). Following Hull's (1920) pioneering study of concept formation, experimental psychologists have studied how a diverse range of stimulus sets have come to control behavior. These sets, which differ in terms of their physical attributes, have been variously called perceptual classes (Bourne, Dominowski, & Loftus, 1979; Cook, Wright, & Kendrick, 1990; Domjam, 1998; Fields, Adams, Buffington, Yang, & Verhave, 1996; Fields, Reeve, Adams, Brown, & Verhave, 1997; Lea & Ryan, 1984) relational classes (Cook, Katz, & Cavoto, 1997; Edwards, Jagiello, Zentall, & Hogan, 1982; Lea & Ryan, 1984; Neiworth & Wright, 1994; Smoke, 1932), equivalence classes (Sidman, 1990; Sidman & Tailby, 1982), and superordinate semantic categories (Rosch & Mervis, 1975).

To date, experiments and theories that have addressed the formation of perceptual or relational classes have not addressed the formation of equivalence classes, and vice versa. When equivalence class formation is considered in isolation, one theory proposes that the formation of equivalence classes is a behavioral primitive that cannot be accounted for by other more fundamental behavioral processes (Sidman, 1990, 1994). To date, however, that assertion has not yet been empirically evaluated (McIlvane, Serna, Dube, & Stromer, this volume). Another theory attributes equivalence class formation to the transfer of previously learned repertoires of reflexivity, symmetry, and transitivity to the new stimuli that are to become members of the new classes (Boelens, 1994; Hayes & Hayes, 1989). The argument to support the latter theory remains to be fully unpacked and empirically evaluated. In addition, the latter theory does not relate the development of the prerequisite repertoires to the development of other more fundamental perceptual and relational stimulus classes. Finally, neither theory attempts to account for the emergence of superordinate semantic categories (Rosch & Mervis, 1975) or natural kinds (Gelman, 1988a, 1988b; Gelman & Markman, 1986, 1987), or to link them to the factors that influence equivalence class formation. The goal of this chapter is to present a unified, developmentally plausible, and behavior analytically simple account of the establishment of all of the above-mentioned conceptual classes.

We will begin by characterizing the physical attributes of perceptual classes and describing the general methods that have been used for their establishment. Then, we will characterize the physical attributes of relational classes, and show how they too can be established by procedures that are similar to those used to establish perceptual classes. In that context, we will also argue that the establishment of "relational frames" (Hayes, 1991, 1994; Barnes, 1994; Steele & Hayes, 1991) are also a consequence of the same general set of behavioral procedures. Finally, we will argue that the emergence of equivalence classes and naturally occurring categories can be accounted for by the generalization of perceptual and relational repertoires to new stimulus sets. The analysis will disclose some new ways of interpreting the performances that are used to assess the emergence of stimulus classes. It will also identify some new variables that might influence the emergence of equivalence classes and naturally occurring categories.

Characterization of Perceptual Classes

A perceptual class consists of stimuli that can be arrayed along some physically or psychometrically defined dimension. The characteristics of the dimensions define different types of perceptual classes. Three types of such classes will be considered: dimensional, fuzzy, and polymorphous.

Dimensional classes. In its simplest form, a dimensional class includes stimuli that are arrayed along a single physical dimension (Fields, Reeve, Adams, Brown, & Verhave, 1997; Zentall, Jackson-Smith, & Jagielo, 1990) such as length, weight, temperature, time, intensity, or frequency. Stimuli over a given range become members of one class, while stimuli over a different range become members of another. Thus, a child learns the line lengths that are called long and short, and the temperatures that are called cold, luke warm, and hot.

Some dimensional classes that have been established in laboratory settings consist of sets of stimuli that were arrayed along the dimensions of click frequency (Migler & Millenson, 1969; Cross & Lane, 1962), tonal frequency (Njegoven, Ido, Mewhort, & Weisman, 1995; Risley, 1964), line length (Fields, Reeve, et al., 1997), fill percentage (Reeve, 1998), time (Wearden, 1995), and object rotation (Wasserman, Gagliardi, Cook, Kirkpatrick-Steger, Astley, & Biederman, 1996).

More complex dimensional classes consist of stimuli that can be arrayed along mathematically created dimensions that are derived by combining values that characterize different aspects of a stimulus. For example, the compactness of a two-dimensional figure can be arrayed along a dimension that is defined by the length of its perimeter divided by the square root of its area (Hrycenko & Harwood, 1980). Another such dimension is apparent coldness of the weather which can be arrayed along a dimension that is defined by some combination of temperature weighted by wind velocity, and is referred to as the wind-chill factor. Thus, different combinations of temperature and wind that produce the same weighted value are judged to be of equivalent apparent coldness.

Fuzzy classes. Another type of perceptual category is called a fuzzy class (Bhatt, Wasserman, Reynolds, & Knauss, 1988; Blough, 1990; Fields, Adams, Buffington, Yang, & Verhave, 1996; Herrnstein, 1990), also referred to as an ill-defined (Bourne et al., 1979; Homa & Little, 1985; Omohundro, 1981; Neisser, 1967), natural (Herrnstein, 1990; Lea & Ryan, 1984; Wasserman & DeVolder, 1993; Wittgenstein, 1968), basic level (Rosch, 1978; Rosch & Mervis, 1975; Rosch, Mervis, Gray, Johnson, & Boyes-Bream, 1976), or probabilistic (Medin & Smith, 1984) category. A fuzzy class consists of a set of stimuli that contain an unspecified number of defining features. No single feature, however, is necessary to define class membership. In many cases, those features are identified by asking people to describe them. Each exemplar of a fuzzy class contains some of the defining features. No single stimulus feature, however, is present in all exemplars. Thus, each stimulus in a fuzzy class can be viewed as containing some of many defining features (Herrnstein, 1990; Jitsumori, 1993; Lea & Ryan, 1990; Medin & Smith, 1984; Rosch & Mervis, 1975; Wasserman, Kiedinger, & Bhatt, 1988).

Examples of fuzzy classes that have been established in laboratory settings by nonhuman subjects include pictures of fish (Herrnstein & de Villiers, 1980), humans (Malott & Siddall, 1972; Seigel & Honig, 1970), trees (Herrnstein, Loveland, & Cable, 1976), impressionist paintings (Watanabe, Sakamoto, & Wakita, 1995), classical music (Porter & Neuringer, 1984), leaves (Cerella, 1979), building locations on a college campus (Honig & Stewart, 1988), manufactured objects (Lubow, 1974), cars, cats, and flowers (Wasserman, Keidinger, & Bhatt, 1988). The formation of other fuzzy classes by human subjects has been studied by Homa and Chambliss (1975), Homa, Cross, Cornell, Goldman, and Swartz (1973), Homa and Little (1985), Homa, Sterling, and Treple (1981), Omohundro (1981), and Rosch and Mervis (1975).

All of the stimuli in a fuzzy class bear some degree of perceived similarity. This has been correlated with a family resemblance index that can be computed for each stimulus, which is equal to the number of defining features in an exemplar once each feature is weighted by its prevalence among all of the stimuli in the class (Rosch & Mervis, 1975). Stimuli with equal family resemblance values would be judged to be very similar to each other or to be of equal similarity to another stimulus judged to be prototypical for the class.

Polymorphous classes. A dimensional or a fuzzy class is said to be open-ended (Herrnstein, 1990) because each contains an infinite number of exemplars. Other perceptual categories called polymorphous classes, however, contain a specified number of defining features, designated by the letter N. Each class member contains some combination of the N features. No single feature, however, is common to all class members. Thus, a polymorphous classes is defined as a subset of stimuli all of which contain at least M of the N features (Aydin & Pearce, 1994; Jitsumori, 1993, 1996; Lea & Ryan, 1990). Because the values of M and N are finite, a polymorphous class contains a finite number of exemplars. Depending on the values of M and N, however, the number of exemplars in a class can be either very small or very large. Two examples can be drawn from biomedical settings: the diagnosis of autism in the DSM IV (American Psychiatric Association, 1994) is based on the observation of at least 8 of 16 behaviors exhibited by the population of individuals with autism, and the diagnosis of Chronic Fatigue Syndrome is based on the presence of any combination of at least 8 of 11 symptoms.

Some polymorphous classes consist of stimuli that contain features that are positionally specified. For example, Jitsumori (1996) created polymorphous classes of pictures of contrived butterflies that varied in terms of wing size, location, and pattern. Class membership required the presence of some combination of these elements that exceeded a particular value. Classes of this sort have been established by infrahuman subjects (Aydin & Pearce, 1994; Jitsumori, 1993, 1996; Blough, 1990; Lea & Ryan, 1984, 1990). Polymorphous classes can also be constructed of stimulus features that are not positionally constrained (Jitsumori, 1993, 1994, 1996; Lea & Harrison, 1978).

Functional Properties of Stimuli in Perceptual Classes

All of the stimuli in a perceptual class occasion the same response even though the response has been trained to occur in the presence of a small subset of class members (Lea, 1984; Herrnstein, 1990; Goldiamond, 1962, 1966). In addition, that response must occur with a much lower probability in the presence of stimuli that are not members of the class. These two provisos were eloquently characterized by Keller and Schoenfeld (1950) when they described concept formation as "...generalization within classes and discrimination between classes" (p. 155). Finally, many exemplars in the class must also be discriminable from each other even though they all can occasion the same response. While this caveat was also noted by Keller and Schoenfeld, its importance has been emphasized by Wasserman et al. (1988) and Fields, Reeve, Adams, Brown, and Verhave (1997).

According to this definition, the existence of a stimulus class can be inferred only when class-consistent performances are evoked by novel stimuli that are drawn from the same set. The existence of a stimulus class cannot be inferred when the same response is occasioned by many different stimuli as a direct result of training because such performances might simply indicate the memorization of responding to isolated stimuli rather than control by a class of stimuli (Herrnstein, 1990; Vaughan & Green, 1983).

Measuring Stimulus Classes

To measure the emergence of a perceptual class, let us assume that a discrimination was trained between two stimuli that occupy disparate positions along some stimulus domain. This would be followed by a primary generalization test that involves the presentation of the training stimuli and intermediate stimuli under extinction conditions. Although not depicted, other test stimuli could also be presented beyond the S^Δ and S^D. The test stimuli might produce performances like those shown in Figure 1 in which the response trained to the S^D is occasioned with the same likelihood by many other test stimuli. This region of the generalization

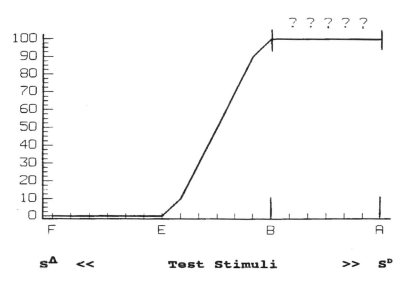

Figure 1. Likelihood of responding in the presence of test stimuli along some dimension.

gradient, bounded by the letters A and B, will be called a plateau. With further increases in disparity between the test stimuli and the S^D, likelihood of responding declines systematically and rapidly until the remaining test stimuli never occasion the response trained to the S^D. (See regions bounded by F and E.)

Clearly, the stimuli in the left portion of the gradient are not members of the same potential class as the S^D. In addition, the edges of the generalization gradient consist of stimuli that are discriminated from each other and from the S^D. They too are not functioning as members of the same potential class.

In contrast, the stimuli defined by the plateau may or may not be functioning as members of a perceptual class. On the one hand, these stimuli may occasion the same level of responding as the S^D because they are not behaviorally discriminable from each other or from the S^D. While physically different, since they are not discriminable, they would not be functioning as members of a perceptual class (Cook et al., 1990; Fields, Reeve, Adams, Brown, & Verhave, 1997; Wasserman, Kiedinger, & Bhatt, 1988). On the other hand, all of the stimuli on the plateau may be discriminable from each other and from the S^D even though they occasion the same response as the S^D. In that case, those stimuli would be functioning as members of a perceptual class (Cook et al., 1990; Fields, Reeve et al., 1997; Wasserman et al., 1988). This analysis raises two questions. What procedures ensure the emergence of generalization gradients with plateaus consisting of many discriminable stimuli? What procedures can be used to assess the discriminability of the stimuli in the plateau region of a generalization gradient?

Training and testing with single and multiple exemplars. Training that is conducted with only one S^Δ and one S^D frequently produces relatively narrow primary generalization gradients in which most stimuli occasion less responding than the S^D and also occasion differential responding among themselves (Hanson, 1959; Hearst, Koresko, & Poppen, 1964). In contrast, to conclude that a set of stimuli is functioning as a perceptual class, one must observe the occurrence of common responding occasioned by an S^D and some test stimuli. Therefore, single exemplar training is not a reliable method for establishing perceptual stimulus classes (Bhatt & Wright, 1992; Cook et al., 1990; Homa & Little, 1985; Malott & Siddall, 1972; Wright et al., 1988).

It is possible, however, that many test stimuli can occasion the same response as that trained to a single S^D (Cerella, 1979). Were that to occur, one possibility is that a stimulus class existed pre-experimentally. The effect of discrimination training would have been to link a new response to one member of the stimulus class. The generalization to the other stimuli would reflect transfer of responding to stimuli that were members of an already established class.

A much more reliable method for establishing dimensionally defined, fuzzy, or polymorphous classes involves discrimination training with many different positive and negative exemplars (Becker, 1971; Cook et al., 1990; Homa & Little, 1985; Lea & Ryan, 1990). The positive exemplars are all variations of each other and are more likely to share the defining characteristics of the class than the negative exemplars. The negative exemplars are also variations of each other and are less likely to share the defining characteristics of the positive exemplars. In addition, characteristics that are irrelevant to class definition are present with equal probability in the positive and negative exemplars (Becker, 1971; Bourne et al., 1979; Ferster, Culbertson, & Boren, 1975; Kelleher, 1958; Tiemann & Markle, 1990). After such multiple exemplar training, primary generalization gradients with relatively broad plateaus are observed (Bhatt & Wright, 1992; Cook et al., 1990; Homa & Little, 1985; Malott & Siddall, 1972; Wright et al., 1988). That is, many new stimuli occasion the same response as the S^Ds.

A number of studies have shown that the range of novel exemplars to which responding fully generalizes is a direct function of number of different training exemplars. This was found with animal subjects (Bhatt, Wasserman, Reynolds, & Knauss, 1988; Wright, et al., 1988) and human subjects (Becker, 1971; Homa, 1978; Homa, Cross, Goldman, & Schwartz, 1973; Homa & Vosburgh, 1976; Homa, Sterling & Treple, 1981; Posner & Keele, 1968).

Discriminability of stimuli. While generalization to new stimuli is necessary to document the emergence of a class, it is also necessary to show that those stimuli are discriminable from each other (Cook et al., 1990; Fields, Reeve, Adams, Brown, & Verhave, 1997; Lea, 1984; Wasserman et al., 1988). This is accomplished by use of one of three procedures: pseudo-concept discrimination training (Cook et al., 1990; Edwards & Honig, 1987; Herrnstein & de Villiers, 1980; Honig & Stewart, 1988; Wasserman, Kiedinger, & Bhatt, 1988), subcategory discrimination training (Wasserman, Kiedinger, & Bhatt, 1988), or discriminability training (Fields, Reeve, Adams, Brown, & Verhave, 1997). Because the inferences that can be drawn from these procedure are similar, only one will be considered to illustrate the process.

Let us assume that during class formation training, some variants of stimulus A were used as S^Ds and some variants of stimulus B were used as S^Δs. During testing, other variants of the A stimuli occasioned the same response as the S^Ds and other variants of the B stimuli did not occasion that response. When pseudo-concept discrimination training is to used to assess the discriminability of the stimuli in the classes, the A and B stimuli along with their variants would be randomly assigned as S^Δs and S^Ds for subjects in a control group. Under these conditions, a subject might respond differentially to the stimuli in accordance with the prevailing reinforcement contingencies. These performances would demonstrate that all of the A stimuli were discriminable from each other and likewise for the B stimuli. Thus, the stimuli that defined the plateau of the previously obtained gradient would be members of a perceptual class. Alternatively, the subject might respond with the same likelihood to all of the A and B stimuli regardless of the reinforcement contingencies. This failure to discriminate among the stimuli would indicate that they were not functioning as members of a perceptual class.

On nomenclature. Dimensional, fuzzy, and polymorphous classes have been subsumed under the hierarchical label of perceptual class, a term that was introduced by Bourne et al. (1979) and subsequently used by Lea and Ryan (1984). Classes of this type have recently been referred to as feature classes (McIlvane, Dube, Green, & Serna, 1993; Stromer & Mackay, 1997). The term feature class, however, is problematic since it can imply that all members of a class share some constant defining element or feature (Medin & Smith, 1984; Smith & Medin, 1981). The stimuli in a dimensional class, however, do not share a common feature. In addition, no single feature is present in all of the stimuli in a fuzzy or a polymorphous class. Therefore, the use of the term feature class does not appear to provide an optimal characterization of the stimuli in such classes. In contrast, all of the stimuli in a dimensional, fuzzy, or polymorphous class are perceptually similar to the other members of the same class. For this reason, the term perceptual would appear to better characterize the members of such classes. The only alternative that would appear to be a reasonable substitute for perceptual class would be similarity-based class (Wasserman & DeVolder, 1993).

Summary. The same procedures have been used to establish dimensional, fuzzy, and polymorphous classes. Training involves the presentation of a multiplicity of positive and negative exemplars. The emergence of the potential class is inferred from the outcome of a multiple exemplar generalization test. Class formation must be confirmed by showing that the stimuli in the potential class are discriminable from each other.

Relational Stimulus Classes

In addition to physical similarity, stimulus classes can also be defined by the formal or logical relation among the components of multi-element stimuli. These relations can be positional (as with representational art) and/or temporal (as with music). Such relational classes, like dimensional and fuzzy classes, are open-ended because they contain an infinite number of exemplars (Herrnstein, 1990).

Some relational classes are *element-specific*. In such a class, each member is defined by the presence of specific elements and a particular relation between those elements (Lea & Ryan, 1984). One example of an element specific relational class would be a "Circle in a Square." Positive exemplars can vary in terms of the size of the circle, the size of the square, and the location of the circle in a square. Negative exemplars include circles in a pentagon, a triangle in a square, or a circle alone. Smoke (1932) may have been the first to demonstrate the formation of an element specific relational class by use of multiple exemplar training and testing.

Other relational classes are element-independent. Stimuli in such classes are defined by the relation between the elements of a stimulus, apart from the stimulus elements themselves (Lea & Ryan, 1984). An example of one type of f element-independent class would be mirror image symmetry. Some positive exemplars are the block-printed upper case letters, A, T, and Y, as well as a top or front view of an automobile; in each case, folding the image of the stimulus along one axis produces a complete overlap or mirror image of features. Negative exemplars are the letters F, G, and Z, as well as a side or oblique view of an automobile. The formation of a mirror image symmetry class by pigeons through the use of multiple exemplar training and testing was demonstrated by Delius and Habers (1978).

Reflexivity. An example of another type of element-independent relational class would be reflexivity, also called generalized identity matching (Fields & Verhave, 1987; Schusterman & Kastak, 1993; Sidman, 1994; Sidman & Tailby, 1982). Members of such a class consist of two stimuli that are congruent spatially and temporally. These classes can be established with multiple exemplar training and testing conducted in the context of a conditional discrimination or matching-to-sample procedure (Cumming & Berryman, 1965). For example, consider four stimuli that are represented symbolically by the letters A, B, C, and D (see Figure 2). Training begins with the presentation of A as a sample with A and B as comparisons. Having learned to select the A comparison given the A sample, reflexivity tests are conducted with the presentation of novel stimulus sets. The first set involves the presentation of C as a sample with C and D as comparisons. Selection of the C comparison would demonstrate reflexivity. If reflexivity has not been demonstrated, the CC relation would be directly trained. These contingencies are repeated with novel stimulus sets until the subject selects comparisons that are identical to samples in a consecutive series of new tests, such as EE, GG, JJ, and LL. This general procedure was outlined first by Hull (1920) in his dissertation.

Similar procedures have been used to establish reflexivity repertoires in pigeons (Wright et al., 1988; Wasserman et al., 1988) and to document a reflexivity repertoire in very young children (Brown, Brown, & Poulson, 1995). Indeed, the procedure outlined above has been used routinely to establish relational classes of "same," "opposite," and "different," and to place each relational repertoire under the control of unique discriminative or contextual stimuli (Dymond & Barnes, 1995; Steele & Hayes, 1991). Steele and Hayes (1991) referred to this process as the establishment of relational frames. As with perceptual classes, confirmation of class formation

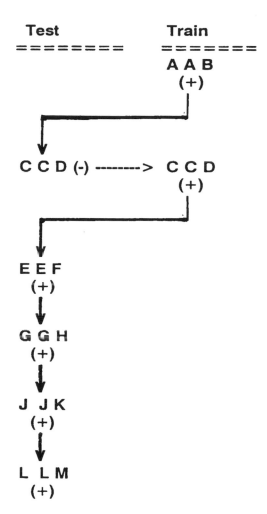

Test
========

Train
=======

A A B
(+)

C C D (-) --------> C C D
(+)

E E F
(+)

G G H
(+)

J J K
(+)

L L M
(+)

Figure 2. Sequence of conditional discrimination training and testing to establish a generalized identity matching or reflexivity repertoire. The first letter in each triad represents the sample stimulus. The second and third letters represent the positive and negative comparisons, respectively. The (+) indicates correct comparison selection while the (-) indicates an incorrect comparison selection.

would require tests of the discriminability of the potential class members. Such tests were conducted by Wasserman et al. (1988) but not by many others.

Other element-independent relational classes are "next to," "on top of," and "after." Positive exemplars of the "on top of" class would be an X above a Y, a bat above an airplane, or a shoe above a trivet. Negative exemplars would be the stimuli in each pair presented on the same horizontal plane, or the presentation of a single stimulus. Theoretically, these classes could also be established with multiple exemplar training and testing. These classes would be more complex than the previously mentioned relational classes because reinforcement would depend on the relation between elements in a stimulus as well as a response that was referenced to one of the elements in the stimulus.

Symmetry. An example of a more complex element-independent relational classes would be that of associative symmetry (see Figure 3) as opposed to geometrically defined mirror image symmetry (D'Amato, Salmon, Loukas, & Tomie, 1985). Associative symmetry will be referred to simply as symmetry.

Like reflexivity, multiple exemplar training and testing can be used to establish a relational class of symmetry. Training begins with the establishment of an arbitrary conditional discrimination such as AB. A is the sample and B is the comparison. Once a subject has learned to select B given A, symmetry is assessed by presenting B as a sample with A as a comparison under extinction conditions. Selection of A demonstrates

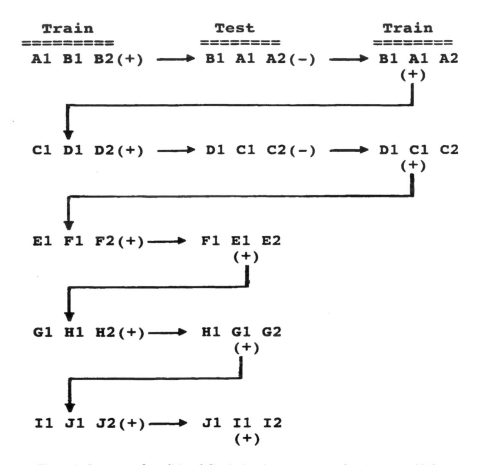

Figure 3. Sequence of conditional discrimination training and testing to establish a generalized symmetry repertoire. The first alpha-numeric symbol in each triad represents the sample stimulus. The second and third symbols represent the positive and negative comparisons, respectively. The (+) indicates correct comparison selection while the (-) indicates an incorrect comparison selection.

symmetry. If that does not occur, the symmetrical relation BA is trained directly. This contingencies are then repeated with novel stimulus sets, until a subject passes a consecutive series of symmetry tests such as FE, HG, and JI. The procedure was used to induce a stimulus class of symmetry in a sea lion by Schusterman and Kastak (1993).

Transitivity. A final example of an even more complex element-independent relational classes would be that of associative transitivity (D'Amato, Salmon, Loukas, & Tomie, 1985) as opposed to ordinal or inferential transitivity (Bryant & Trabasso, 1971; Gillan, 1981; Stevens, 1951; Stromer & Mackay, 1993). Associative transitivity will be referred to simply as transitivity.

Like symmetry, multiple exemplar training and testing can be used to establish a relational class of transitivity (see Figure 4). We begin by training at least two arbitrary conditional discriminations that share a common nodal stimulus. A node is a stimulus that is linked by training to at least two other stimuli (Fields, Verhave, & Fath, 1984). For example, if AB and BC are trained, the nodal stimulus, B, functions as a comparison for one relation and as a sample for the other. After training, the AC transitivity probe is presented under extinction conditions. The sample stimulus in the probe must have served the same function in training, and the comparison stimulus in the probe must have served the same function in training. Selection of C given A would demonstrate transitivity. If that does not occur, the AC relation is trained directly. These contingencies are then repeated with

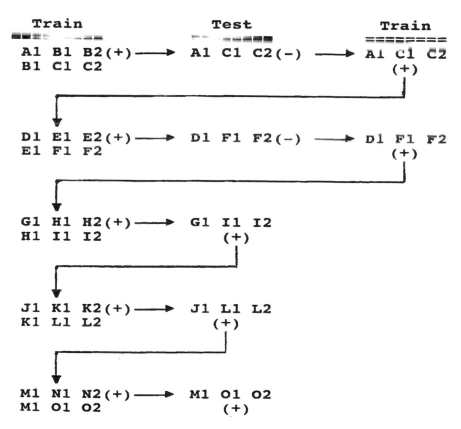

Figure 4. Sequence of conditional discrimination training and testing to establish a generalized transitivity repertoire. The first alpha-numeric symbol in each triad represents the sample stimulus. The second and third symbols represent the positive and negative comparisons, respectively. The (+) indicates correct comparison selection while the (-) indicates an incorrect comparison selection.

new stimulus sets until a subject passes a consecutive series of transitivity tests without the need of direct reinforcement, in this example, GI JL, and MO.

Interpretation of positive test performances. A number of inferences can be drawn from a succession of positive test outcomes with different stimulus sets. First, the existence of a generalizable relational repertoire becomes increasingly likely as a subject passes an increasing number of consecutively presented tests. Second, generalization occurs between the new test stimuli and those used in previous training and testing. Third, the relational repertoire transfers from the stimuli used in prior training and testing to the new stimuli used in a current test.

It is tempting to say that a series of positive test performances implies responding has come under the control of an abstract relation between stimuli, but has not come under the control of the particular stimuli. Indeed, that is a commonly accepted assumption (Wright, Cook, & Kendrick, 1989). If that premise is accepted, however, it is difficult to understand how the abstract relation transfers to novel stimuli and influences the performances occasioned by the new stimuli. Indeed, such an assumption requires the postulation of some executive agency to account for the transfer of the relational repertoire to new stimulus sets.

We would like to suggest an alternative view. During multiple exemplar training and testing, relational responding comes under the control of an increasingly wide range of particular stimuli. Each of these stimuli occasions generalization to other stimuli. These summed generalization gradients extend over an ever-increasing stimulus domain. Thus, the ever-increasing number of stimuli in that domain would occasion the relational response.

The apparent "abstractness" of a relation such as reflexivity, symmetry, or transitivity, then, may be more apparent than real. Test performances may simply reflect the operation of discrimination training with a multiplicity of exemplars, generalization testing with a multiplicity of novel exemplars, and primary generalization across stimulus sets.

Interpretations of negative test performances. A failed test might indicate that responding had not yet come under relational control. According to this outcome, correct responding on prior training trials probably reflected control by stimulus elements functioning as a compound (Sidman, 1994; Saunders & Green, 1992). Alternatively, a failed test might indicate that the relational repertoire had been established but a minimal amount of primary generalization occurred between the current test stimuli and those used for prior training and testing. Thus, an absence of generalization between stimuli would account for the lack of transfer of the relational repertoire. This interpretation, however, does not preclude generalization to other test stimuli that had not been used in the current tests. Failures of this sort may be similar to the cognitive phenomenon of domain-specific knowledge (VanLehn, 1989). Here, a repertoire used to solve problems in one domain is not used to solve problems in another stimulus domain even though the repertoire would be effective in the new domain.

When most tests are failed, it is likely that the relational repertoire has not yet been established. Therefore, a continuation of multiple exemplar training and multiple exemplar testing would be called for to establish the relational repertoire. When most tests are passed, it is more likely that the relational repertoire is present. Failure, then, is due to a lack of primary generalization between the new stimuli used in a current test and the other stimulus sets that evoked the relational responses. This outcome suggests that the transfer of the relational repertoires could be enhanced by some intervention that would increase generalization between stimuli, apart from the relational repertoire.

Application to the Emergence of Equivalence Classes

How can this information be used to account for equivalence class formation? The probes used to assess the emergence of equivalence classes are called reflexivity, symmetry, transitivity, and combined tests of symmetry and transitivity (Sidman & Tailby, 1982; Fields & Verhave, 1987). When used in this manner, the terms simply function as names of emergent relations tests. These terms, however, can also denote generalizable repertories that are controlled by different relational stimulus classes. Thus, it is possible that the prior existence of these relational repertoires are either necessary for or may enhance the emergence of new equivalence classes.

To illustrate the point, let us assume that separate relational repertoires of reflexivity, symmetry, and transitivity have been established with many different stimulus sets, designated by A-S. Thereafter, the conditional discriminations XY and YZ are established as the prerequisites for new XYZ equivalence classes. The emergence of these classes would be documented by the occurrence of class-consistent performances during reflexivity, symmetry, transitivity, and equivalence probes using the XYZ stimuli.

A positive outcome of these tests would indicate that a substantial amount of primary generalization occurred between the XYZ stimulus set and the A-S stimuli used in prior training and testing. A positive outcome could also indicate that the relational repertoires established in the presence of the stimulus sets A-S transferred to the new stimuli XYZ.

On the other hand, failure of the reflexivity, symmetry, or transitivity test conducted with the X, Y, and Z stimuli could not be attributed to the absence of relational repertoires because their existence had already been demonstrated with the A-S stimuli. Failure on these tests would probably result from poor generalization between the current stimuli used to establish the equivalence classes and those used to establish the relational repertoires. As mentioned earlier, that absence of generalization should be documentable apart from relational responding. This analysis also suggests that the relational repertoires would be either restricted to the stimuli used for prior training and testing or would generalize to a restricted range of new stimuli that did not include X, Y, and Z.

Finally, we have to consider the outcomes of the equivalence tests. Passing the equivalence test indicates that a substantial amount of generalization has occurred between the X, Y and Z stimuli and the A-S stimuli used in prior training and testing. It would also indicate that the relational repertoires of symmetry and transitivity that had been established in the presence of the stimulus sets A-S transferred to the new stimuli X-Z. Therefore, the positive test performances would indicate the conjoint function of symmetry and transitivity.

On the other hand, failure on an equivalence test cannot be attributed to the absence of the symmetry or transitivity repertoires because they had already been demonstrated. Failure could also not be attributed to an absence of generalization because symmetry alone and transitivity alone would have been demonstrated with the X-Z stimuli. Thus, failure of an equivalence test would have to result from an absence of the conjoint function of symmetry and transitivity.

Supporting data. A number of recent experiments provide partial support for the view that the emergence of equivalence classes can be enhanced by the prior establishment of prerequisite relational stimulus classes. Fields, Varelas, Rosen, Reeve, Belanich, and Hobbie (1997) showed that prior demonstrations of symmetry alone or transitivity alone with one set of stimuli enhanced the subsequent emergence of new equivalence classes formed with a different set of stimuli.

Pilgrim and Galizio (1990, 1995) and Pilgrim, Chambers, and Galizio (1995) showed that selective manipulation of a symmetrical relation influenced equivalence performances which require symmetry, but not transitivity-based performances. Dickins, Bentall, and Smith (1993) and Smith, Dickins, and Bentall (1996) showed that paired associate training that was in conflict with specific baseline conditional discriminations selectively disrupted symmetry, transitivity, or equivalence test performances.

Rosen, Fields, Reeve, Varelas, and Belanich (1996) described the effects of inducing a generalized transitivity repertoire on the emergence of new equivalence classes. College students attempted to learn 3-member equivalence classes consisting of nonsense syllables designated A, B, and C. After learning AB, they passed BA symmetry tests. After learning BC, they passed CB symmetry tests. A number of subjects then failed the AC transitivity tests. When that occurred, the experiment was stopped temporarily and a generalized transitivity repertoire was established using the multiple exemplar training and testing procedure described earlier.

As a result, subjects eventually passed eight consecutive transitivity tests, each conducted with distinctly different sets of visual stimuli. Thereafter, the original AC probes were reintroduced and subjects immediately passed them and went on to demonstrate the immediate emergence of 3-member classes. Thus, the induction of a transitivity repertoire that generalized across many stimulus sets enabled the emergence of equivalence classes constructed of other stimuli.

Buffington, Fields and Adams (1997) and Fields, Reeve et al. (1997) showed that emergence of new equivalence classes was substantially enhanced by the prior establishment of other equivalence classes. The establishment of the initial equivalence classes involved the demonstrations of symmetry and transitivity, alone and in combination. In addition, the stimuli used in the initial and the new equivalence classes were nonsense syllables. While primary generalization between the stimuli was not measured, it can be assumed that there was a great deal of generalization among all of the nonsense syllables. These are the theoretical conditions that should have, and indeed did, increase the likelihood of equivalence class formation.

Schusterman and Kastak's (1993) demonstration of equivalence class formation with a sea lion involved the use of multiple exemplar training and testing, and the demonstrations of symmetry alone and transitivity alone before assessments of equivalence. Symmetry eventually emerged after an extensive history of training and testing like that described earlier. In contrast, transitivity with novel exemplars was observed without direct training. Once both repertoires had been demonstrated, equivalence probes with novel stimulus sets immediately occasioned class-consistent performances. In addition to supporting the current analysis, the data also suggest that the establishment of equivalence classes with infrahuman subjects depends on the use of appropriate methodologies.

Implications for practice. The current analysis draws attention to the status of precursor relational repertoires when one does not observe the emergence of equivalence classes. Specifically, failure implies that some of the prerequisite relational repertoires may be absent or weak. Thus, they should be assessed directly with a range of stimuli other than those used for the equivalence class being formed. If absent or weak, they could be established or strengthened by multiple exemplar training and testing. If present in the context of other stimuli, the failure of equivalence class formation might be due to a lack of generalization between current stimuli and other stimuli that occasion the prerequisite repertoires. If so, increasing generalization between those stimuli should increase the likelihood of equivalence class formation. To date, however, these approaches have not been widely used to enhance the emergence of equivalence classes.

Comparison with current practice. It has become common to attribute a failure of equivalence class formation to stimulus control topographies that interfere with the emergence of equivalence (Sidman, Rauzin, Lazar, Cunningham, Tailby, & Carrigan, 1982; Sidman, 1992, 1994). This view is based on the assumption that equivalence relations are there to emerge but are blocked by other stimulus control topographies. This interpretation has led to the design of procedures that minimize the development of stimulus control topographies that could interfere with the emergence of equivalence. This in turn improves likelihood of class formation (McIlvane, Serna, Dube, & Stromer, this volume). These findings, however, do not confirm the theoretical assumption that equivalence is a behavioral primitive. In addition, these findings do not negate the assumption that the establishment of prerequisite repertoires is necessary for the emergence of equivalence classes, and the enhancement of equivalence class formation.

It would appear, then, that the establishment of equivalence classes can be enhanced by (a) strengthening the stimulus control repertoires that appear to be prerequisites for the emergence of equivalence classes, (b) increasing generalization between stimuli that occasion the prerequisite relational repertoires, (c) preventing the establishment of stimulus control topographies that interfere with class formation, and (d) suppressing the stimulus control topographies that can interfere with equivalence-based stimulus control topographies.

Application to the Emergence of Natural Categories

Let us now consider how the procedures used to account for the emergence of perceptual classes and equivalence classes can be used to account for the emergence of real life, complex naturally occurring categories, also called superordinate semantic categories (Rosch & Mervis, 1975), natural-kinds (Gelman, 1988a; 1988b, Gelman & Markman, 1986, 1987), or generalized equivalence classes (Fields, Adams, Buffington, Yang, & Verhave, 1996; Fields, Reeve, Adams, Brown, & Verhave, 1997). One example would be the class of furniture which consists of the words couch, lamp, and table. The class also contains pictures of the objects designated by each word, as well as the objects themselves. While the words do not resemble each other or the pictures they represent, all of the stimuli come to function interchangeably under some conditions. Finally, all of the stimuli in such a class will occasion the same response even though it is trained to occur in the presence of only a few

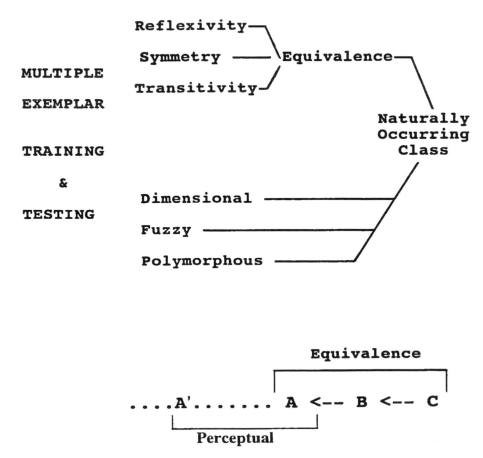

Figure 5. A nested hierarchy of stimulus classes that are prerequisites for other classes.

stimuli in the set. For example, under appropriate contextual conditions, all of the stimuli would be called furniture (Griffee, 1997).

Regardless of name, a naturally occurring class contains some stimuli that are perceptually similar and other stimuli that are perceptually disparate. The disparate stimuli can become members of an equivalence class through the generalization of already established relational repertoires of reflexivity, symmetry, and transitivity. As illustrated in Figure 5, those repertoires can be established through multiple exemplar training and testing. In addition, the stimuli that are similar to each other can become members of a perceptual class by use of the same multiple exemplar training and testing. Finally, for all of the perceptually similar and perceptually disparate stimuli to become members of a common class, one stimulus that is a member of the equivalence class must also be a member of the perceptual class (Adams, Fields, & Verhave, 1993; Fields, Reeve, et al., 1997). These processes have been empirically documented with generalization tests of emergent relations (Barnes & Keenan, 1993; Fields, Reeve, Adams, & Verhave, 1991; Lane, Clow, Innis, & Critchfield, in press; Lane, Innis, Clow, & Critchfield, in press; Mackay, Stromer, & Serna, 1997). In addition, other studies have shown that after an equivalence class has merged with a perceptual class, a response trained to one class member transfers to all members of the merged classes (Fields, Adams, Buffington, Yang, & Verhave, 1996; Mackay et al., 1997). This analysis, then, provides a behavior analytic account for the development of natural kinds, or superordinate semantic categories.

Summary. The combined effects of multiple exemplar training, multiple exemplar testing, primary stimulus generalization, and the transfer of response repertoires through generalization, have been used to account for the establishment of perceptual classes, relational classes, relational frames, equivalence classes, and complex naturally occurring categories. Essentially, repertoires controlled by simpler stimulus classes combine to synthesize more complex stimulus classes. The analysis, therefore, provides a unified, developmentally plausible, and behavior analytically simple account of the establishment of a wide range of stimulus classes. In addition, the account also suggests alternative ways of interpreting test performances, and suggests new variables that might enhance equivalence class formation.

References

Adams, B. J., Fields, L., & Verhave, T. (1993). Formation of generalized equivalence classes. *The Psychological Record, 43*, 553-566.

American Psychiatric Association. (1994). *Diagnostic and statistical manual of mental disorders* (4th Edition). Washington, D. C.

Aydin, A., & Pearce, J. M. (1994). Prototype effects in categorization by pigeons. *Journal of Experimental Psychology: Animal Behavior Processes, 20*, 264-277.

Barnes, D. (1994). Stimulus equivalence and relational frame theory. *The Psychological Record, 44*, 91-124.

Barnes, D., & Keenan, M. (1993). A transfer of functions through derived arbitrary and nonarbitrary stimulus relations. *Journal of the Experimental Analysis of Behavior, 59,* 61-82.

Barnes, D., & Roche, B. (1997). A behavior-analytic approach to behavioral reflexivity. *The Psychological Record, 47,* 543-572.

Becker, W. (1971). Teaching concepts and operations, or how to make kids smart. In W. Becker, (Ed.) *An empirical basis for change in education.* Science Research Associates.

Bhatt, R. S., Wasserman, E. A., Reynolds, W. F., Jr., & Knauss, K. S. (1988). Conceptual behavior in pigeons: Categorization of both familiar and novel examples from four classes of natural and artificial stimuli. *Journal of Experimental Psychology: Animal Behavior Processes. 3,* 219-234.

Bhatt, R. S., & Wright, A. A. (1992). Concept learning by monkeys with video picture images and a touch screen. *Journal of the Experimental Analysis of Behavior, 57,* 219-226.

Blough, D. S. (1990). Form similarity and categorization in pigeon visual research. In M. L. Commons, R. J. Herrnstein, S. Kosslyn, & D. Mumford (Eds.) *Models of behavior: Behavioral approaches to pattern recognition and concept formation.* Hillsdale, NJ: Erlbaum.

Boelens, H. (1994). A traditional account of equivalence. *The Psychological Record, 44,* 587-605.

Bourne, L. E., Dominowski, R. L., & Loftus, E. F. (1979). *Cognitive processes.* Englewood Cliffs, NJ: Prentice-Hall.

Brown, A. K., Brown, J. L., & Poulson, C. L. (1995). Generalization of children's identity matching-to-sample performances to novel stimuli. *The Psychological Record, 45,* 29-44.

Bryant, P. E., & Trabasso, T. (1971). Transitive infererences and memory in young children. *Nature, 232,* 456-458.

Buffington, D. M., Fields, L., & Adams, B. J. (1997). Enhancing the formation of equivalence classes by pretraining of other equivalence classes. *The Psychological Record, 47,* 1-20.

Cerella, J. (1979). Visual classes and natural categories in the pigeon. *Journal of Experimental Psychology: Human Perception and Performance, 5,* 68-77.

Cook, R. G., Katz, J. S., & Cavato, B. R. (1997). Pigeon same-different concept learning with multiple stimulus classes. *Journal of Experimental Psychology: Animal Behavior Processes. 23,* 417-433.

Cook, R. G., Wright, A. A., & Kendrick, D. F. (1990). Visual categorization by pigeons. In M. L. Commons, R. J. Herrnstein, S. Kosslyn, & D. Mumford (Eds.) *Models of behavior: Behavioral approaches to pattern recognition and concept formation.* Hillsdale, NJ: Erlbaum.

Cross, D. V., & Lane, H. L. (1962). On the discriminative control of concurrent responses: the relations among response frequency, latency, and topography in auditory generalization. *Journal of the Experimental Analysis of Behavior, 5,* 487-496.

Cumming, W. W., & Berryman, R. (1965). The complex discriminative operant: Studies of matching-to-sample and related problems. In D. I. Mostofsky (Ed.), *Stimulus generalization* (pp. 284-33). Stanford, CA: Stanford University Press.

D'Amato, M. R., Salmon, D. P., Loukas, E. & Tomie, A. (1985). Symmetry and transitivity of conditional relations in monkeys (cebus apella) and pigeons (columba livia). *Journal of the Experimental Analysis of Behavior, 44*, 35-48.

Delius, J. D., & Habers, G. (1978). Symmetry: can pigeons conceptualize it? *Behavioral Biology, 22*, 336-342.

Dickins, D. W., Bentall, R. P., & Smith, A. B. (1993). The role of individual stimulus names in the emergence of equivalence relations: The effects of interpolated paired-associates training of discordant associations between names. *The Psychological Record, 43*, 713-724.

Dinsmoor, J. A. (1995). Stimulus control: Part II. *The Behavior Analyst, 18*, 253-270.

Domjam, M. (1998). *The principles of learning and behavior*. Pacific Grove, CA: Brooks/Cole Publishing.

Dymond, S., & Barnes, D. (1995). A transformation of self-discrimination response functions in accordance with the arbitrarily applicable relations of sameness, more than, and less than. *Journal of the Experimental Analysis of Behavior, 64*, 163-184.

Edwards, C. A., & Honig, W. K. (1987) Memorization and "feature selection" in the acquisition of natural concepts in pigeons. *Learning and Motivation, 18*, 235-260.

Edwards, C. A., Jagielo, J. A., Zentall, T. R., & Hogan, D. E. (1982). Acquired equivalence and distinctiveness in matching to sample by pigeons: Mediation by reinforcer-specific expectancies. *Journal of Experimental Psychology: Animal Behavior Processes, 8*, 244-259.

Ferster, C .B., Culbertson, S., & Boren, M. C. P. (1975). *Behavior principles* (2nd Edition). Englewood Cliffs, NJ: Prentice Hall.

Fields, L., Adams, B. J., Buffington, D. M., Yang, W., & Verhave, T. (1996). Response transfer between stimuli in generalized equivalence classes: A model for the establishment of natural kind and fuzzy superordinate categories. *The Psychological Record, 46*, 655-684.

Fields, L., Reeve, K. F., Adams, B. J., Brown, J. L., & Verhave, T. (1997). Predicting the extension of equivalence classes from primary generalization gradients: The merger of equivalence classes and perceptual classes. Journal of the Experimental Analysis of Behavior, *68*, 67-92.

Fields, L., Reeve, K. F., Adams, B. J., & Verhave, T. (1991). The generalization of equivalence relations. A model for natural categories. *Journal of the Experimental Analysis of Behavior, 55*, 305-312.

Fields, L., Varelas, A., Rosen, D., Reeve, K. F., Belanich, J., & Hobbie, S. A., (May, 1997). *Effect of prior conditional discrimination training, symmetry, and transitivity probing on the emergence of new equivalence classes under the simultaneous protocol.* Paper presented at the Twenty-third Annual Convention of the Association for Behavior Analysis, Chicago, IL.

Fields, L., & Verhave, T. (1987). The structure of equivalence classes. *Journal of the Experimental Analysis of Behavior, 48,* 317-332.

Fields, L., Verhave, T., & Fath, S. (1984). Stimulus equivalence and transitive associations: A methodological analysis. *Journal of the Experimental Analysis of Behavior, 42,* 143-157.

Gelman, S. A. (1988a). Children's expectations concerning natural kind categories. *Human Development, 31,* 28-34.

Gelman, S. A. (1988b). The development of induction within natural kind and artificial categories. *Cognitive Psychology, 20,* 65-95.

Gelman, S. A., & Markman, E. M. (1986). Categories and induction in young children. *Cognition, 23,* 183-209.

Gelman, S. A., & Markman, E. M. (1987). Young children's inductions from natural kinds: The role of categories and appearances. *Child Development, 58,* 1532-1541.

Gillan, D. J. (1981). Reasoning in the chimpanzee II. Transitive inference. *Journal of Experimental Psychology: Animal Behavior Processes, 7,* 150-164.

Goldiamond, I. (1962). Perception. In A. J. Bachrach (Ed.). *Experimental foundations of clinical psychology* (pp.183-224). New York: Wiley.

Goldiamond, I., (1966). Perception, language, and conceptualization rules. In B. Klienmuntz (Ed.), *Problem solving* (pp. 183-224). New York: Wiley.

Griffee, K. (May 1997). *The roles of stimulus generalization and stimulus equivalence on hierarchical organization.* Paper presented at the Twenty-third Annual Convention of the Association for Behavior Analysis, Chicago, IL.

Hanson, H. M. (1959). Effects of discrimination training on stimulus generalization. *Journal of Experimental Psychology, 58,* 321-334.

Hayes, S.C. (1991). A relational control theory of stimulus equivalence. In L. J. Hayes, & P. N. Chase (Eds.) *Dialogues on verbal behavior* (pp. 19-40). Reno, NV: Context Press.

Hayes, S. C. (1994). Relational frame theory: A functional approach to verbal events. In S. C. Hayes, L. J. Hayes, M. Sato, & K. Ono (Eds.) *Behavioral analysis of language and cognition* (pp. 11-30). Reno, NV: Context Press.

Hayes, S. C., & Hayes, L. J. (1989). The verbal action of the listener as a basis for rule-governance. In S. C. Hayes (Ed.) *Rule-governed behavior: Cognition, contingencies, and instructional control.* New York: Plenum Press.

Hearst, E., Koresko, M., & Poppen, R. (1964). Stimulus generalization and response-reinforcer contingency. *Journal of the Experimental Analysis of Behavior, 7,* 369-380.

Herrnstein, R. J. (1990). Levels of stimulus control: A functional approach. *Cognition, 37,* 133-166.

Herrnstein, R. J. & de Villiers, P. A. (1980). Fish as a natural category for people and pigeons. In G. H. Bower (Ed.), *The psychology of learning and motivation: Vol. 14* (pp. 59-95). New York: Academic Press.

Herrnstein, R. J., Loveland, D. H., & Cable, C. (1976). Natural concepts in pigeons. *Journal of Experimental Psychology: Animal Behavior Processes, 4,* 285-301.

Homa, D. (1978). Abstraction of ill-defined form. *Journal of Experimental Psychology: Human Learning & Memory, 4,* 407-416.

Homa, D., & Chambliss, D. (1975). The relative contributions of common and distinctive information on the abstraction from ill-defined categories. *Journal of Experimental Psychology: Human Learning and Memory, 1,* 351-359.

Homa, D., Cross, J., Cornell, D., Goldman, D., & Schwartz, S. (1973). Prototype abstraction and classification of new instances as a function of number of instances defining the prototype. *Journal of Experimental Psychology, 101,* 116-122.

Homa, D., & Little, J. (1985). The abstraction and long-term retention of ill defined categories by children. *Bulletin of the Psychonomic Society, 23,* 325-328.

Homa, D., Sterling, S., & Treple, L. (1981). Limitations of exemplar-based generalization and the abstraction of categorical information. *Journal of Experimental Psychology: Human Learning & Memory, 7,* 418-439.

Homa, D., & Vosburgh, R. (1976). Category breadth and the abstraction of prototypical information. *Journal of Experimental Psychology: Human Learning & Memory, 3,* 322-330.

Honig, W. K., & Stewart, K. E. (1988). Pigeons can discriminate locations presented in pictures. *Journal of the Experimental Analysis of Behavior, 50,* 541-551.

Hrycenko, O., & Harwood, D. W. (1980). Judgements of shape similarity in the Barbary dove (Streptopelia risoria). *Animal Behaviour, 58,* 586-592.

Hull, C. L. (1920). Quantitative aspects of the evolution of concepts. *Psychological Monographs, 28, whole no. 123.*

Jitsumori, M. (1993). Category discrimination of artificial polymorphous stimuli based on feature learning. *Journal of Experimental Psychology: Animal Behavior Processes, 3,* 244-254.

Jitsumori, M. (1994). Discrimination of artificial polymorphous categories by Rhesus monkeys (Macaca mulatta). *Quarterly Journal of Experimental Psychology, 47,* 371-386.

Jitsumori, M. (1996). A prototype effect and categorization of polymorphous stimuli in pigeons. *Journal of Experimental Psychology: Animal Behavior Processes, 22,* 405-419.

Kelleher, R. (1958). Concept formation in the chimpanzee. *Science, 128,* 777-778.

Keller, F. S., & Schoenfeld, W. N. (1950). *The principles of psychology* New York: Appleton-Century-Crofts.

Lane, S. D., Clow, J., Innis, A., & Critchfield, T. S. (in press). Generalization of cross-modal equivalence classes: Operant processes as components in human category formation. *Journal of the Experimental Analysis of Behavior.*

Lane, S. D., Innis, A., Clow, J. S., & Critchfield, T. S. (in press). Preliminary evidence for cross-modal generalized equivalence classes. *Mexican Journal of Behavior Analysis.*

Lea, S. E. G. (1984). In what sense do pigeons learn concepts? In H. L. Roitblatt, T. G. Bever, & H. S. Terrace (Eds.) *Animal cognition* (pp. 263-276). Hillsdale, NJ: Erlbaum.

Lea. S. E. G., & Harrison, S. N. (1978). Discrimination of polymorphous stimulus sets in pigeons. *Quarterly Journal of Experimental Psychology, 30,* 521-537.

Lea, S. E. G., & Ryan, C. M. E. (1984). Feature analysis of pigeons' acquisition of concept discrimination. In H. L. Roitblatt, T. G. Bever, & H. S. Terrace (Eds.), *Animal cognition* (pp. 233-261). Hillsdale, NJ: Erlbaum.

Lea, S. E. G., & Ryan, C. M. E. (1990). Unnatural concepts and the theory of concept discrimination in birds. In M. L. Commons, R. J. Herrnstein, S. Kosslyn, & D. Mumford (Eds.), *Quantitative analyses of behavior: Behavioral approaches to pattern recognition and concept formation.* Hillsdale, NJ: Erlbaum.

Lubow, R. E. (1974). High-order concept formation in the pigeon. *Journal of the Experimental Analysis of Behavior, 21,* 475-483.

Mackay, H. A., Stromer, R., & Serna, R. W. (1997). Emergent behavior and intellectual functioning: Stimulus classes, generalization, and transfer. In S. Soraci & W. J. McIlvane (Eds.), *Perspectives on fundamental processes in intellectual functioning.* Norwood, NJ: Ablex.

Malott, R., & Siddall, J. W. (1972). Acquisition of the people concept in the pigeon. *Psychological Reports, 31,* 3-13.

McIlvane, W. J., Dube, W. V., Green, G., & Serna, R. W. (1993). Programming conceptual and communication skill development: A methodological stimulus-class analysis. In A. P. Kaiser & D. B. Gray (Eds.), *Enhancing children's communication: Research foundations of intervention.* Baltimore, MD: Paul H. Brookes.

Medin, D. L., & Smith, E. E. (1984). Concepts and concept formation. *Annual Review of Psychology, 35,* 113-138.

Migler B., & Millenson, J. R. (1969). Analysis of response rates during stimulus generalization. *Journal of the Experimental Analysis of Behavior, 12,* 81-87.

Neisser, U. (1967). *Cognitive psychology.* New York: Appleton-Century-Crofts.

Neiworth, J., & Wright, A. A. (1994). Monkeys (Macaca mulatta) learn category matching in a nonidentical same-different task. *Journal of Experimental Psychology: Animal Behavior Processes, 20,* 429-435.

Njegovan, M., Ito, S., Mewhort, D., & Weisman, R. (1995). Classification of frequencies into ranges by songbirds and humans, *Journal of Experimental Psychology: Animal Behavior Processes, 21,* 33-42.

Omohundro, J. (1981). Recognition vs. classification of ill-defined category exemplars. *Memory & Cognition, 9,* 324-331.

Pilgrim, C., Chambers, L., & Galizio, M. (1995). Reversal of baseline relations and stimulus equivalence: II. Children. *Journal of the Experimental Analysis of Behavior, 63,* 238-254.

Pilgrim, C., & Galizio, M. (1990). Relations between baseline contingencies and equivalence probe performances. *Journal of the Experimental Analysis of Behavior, 54,* 213-224.

Pilgrim, C., & Galizio, M. (1995). Reversal of baseline relations and stimulus equivalence: I. Adults. *Journal of the Experimental Analysis of Behavior, 63,* 225-238.

Porter, D., & Neuringer. A. (1984). Music discriminations by pigeons. *Journal of Experimental Psychology: Animal Behavior Processes, 10,* 138-148.

Posner, M. I., & Keele, S. W. (1968). On the genesis of abstract ideas. *Journal of Experimental Psychology, 77,* 353-363.

Reeve, K. F. (1998). *Effects of forced-choice generalization testing on the establishment of dimensionally based perceptual classes.* Unpublished doctoral dissertation, The Graduate School and University Center of the City University of New York.

Risley, T. (1964). Generalization gradients following two-response discrimination training. *Journal of the Experimental Analysis of Behavior, 7,* 199-204.

Rosch, E. H. (1978). Principles of categorization. In E. Rosch & B. B. Lloyds (Eds.), *Cognition and categorization.* Hillsdale, NJ: Erlbaum.

Rosch, E. H., & Mervis, C. B. (1975). Family resemblances: Studies in the internal structure of categories. *Cognitive Psychology, 7,* 573-605.

Rosch, E. H., Mervis, C. B., Gray, W. D., Johnson, D. M., & Boyes-Bream, P. (1976). Basic objects in natural categories. *Cognitive Psychology, 8,* 382-439.

Rosen, D., Fields, L., Reeve, K. F., Varelas, A., & Belanich, J. (May, 1996). *Remediation of transitivity failures using multiple exemplar training.* Paper presented at the Twenty-second Annual Convention of the Association for Behavior Analysis, San Francisco, CA.

Saunders, R. L. & Green, G. (1992). The nonequivalence of behavioral and mathematical equivalence. *Journal of the Experimental Analysis of Behavior, 57,* 227-241.

Schusterman, R., & Kastak, D. (1993). A California sea lion (Aalophus californianus) is capable of forming equivalence relations. *The Psychological Record, 43,* 823-840.

Seigel, R. K., & Honig, W. K. (1970). Pigeon concept formation: successive and simultaneous acquisition. *Journal of the Experimental Analysis of Behavior, 13,* 385-390.

Sidman, M. (1990). Equivalence relations: Where do they come from? In H. Lejuene & D. Blackman (Eds.), *Behavior analysis in theory and practice: Contributions and controversies* (pp. 93 - 114). Hillsdale, NJ: Erlbaum.

Sidman, M. (1992). Adventitious control by the location of comparison stimuli in conditional discriminations. *Journal of the Experimental Analysis of Behavior, 58,* 173-182.

Sidman, M. (1994). *Equivalence relations and behavior: A research story.* Boston, MA: Authors Cooperative, Inc.

Sidman, M., Rauzin, R., Lazar, R., Cunningham, S., Tailby, W., & Carrigan, P. (1982). A search for symmetry in the conditional discriminations of rhesus monkeys, baboons, and children. *Journal of the Experimental Analysis of Behavior, 37,* 23-44.

Sidman, M., & Tailby, W. (1982). Conditional discrimination vs matching to sample: an expansion of the testing paradigm. *Journal of the Experimental Analysis of Behavior, 37,* 5-22.

Smith, A. B., Dickins, D. W., & Bentall, R. P. (1996). The role of individual stimulus names in the emergence of equivalence relations II: The effects of interfering tasks prior to and after tests for emergent relations. *The Psychological Record*, 46, 109-130.

Smith E. E., & Medin, D. L. (1981). *Categories and concepts*. Cambridge MA: Harvard University Press.

Smoke, K. L. (1932). An objective study of concept formation. *Psychological Monographs, 42, whole no. 191.*

Steele, D., & Hayes, S. C. (1991) Stimulus equivalence and arbitrarily applicable relational responding. *Journal of the Experimental Analysis of Behavior, 56,* 519-561.

Stevens S. S. (1951). Mathematics, measurement, and psychophysics. In S. S. Stevens (Ed.), *Handbook of experimental psychology* (pp. 1-49). New York: John Wiley.

Stromer, R., & Mackay, H. M. (1993). Human sequential behavior: Relations among stimuli, class formation, and derived sequences. *The Psychological Record, 43,* 107-113.

Stromer, R., & Mackay, H. A. (1997). Naming and the formation of stimulus classes. In T. R. Zentall & P. M. Smeets (Eds.), *Stimulus class formation in humans and animals*. Amsterdam, NL: North-Holland.

Tiemann, P. W., & Markle, S. M. (1990). *Analysing instructional content: A guide to instruction and evaluation*. Champaign, Il: Stipes Publishing Co.

VanLehn, K. (1989). Problem solving and cognitive skill acquisition. In M. I. Posner (Ed.), *Foundations of cognitive science*. (pp. 527-580). Cambridge, MA: MIT Press.

Vaughan, W., Jr., & Green, S. L. (1983). Acquisition of absolute discriminations in pigeons. In M. L. Commons, R. J. Herrnstein, & A. R. Wagner (Eds.), *Quantitative analyses of behavior: Discrimination processes*. Cambridge, MA: Ballinger.

Wasserman, E. A., & DeVolder, C. L. (1993). Similarity and nonsimilarity-based conceptualization in children and pigeons. *The Psychological Record, 43,* 779-794.

Wasserman, E. A., Gagliardi, J. L., Cook, B. R., Kirkpatrick-Steger, K., Astley, S. L., & Biederman, I. (1996). The pigeon's recognition of drawings of depth-rotated stimuli. *Journal of Experimental Psychology: Animal Behavior Processes, 22,* 205-221.

Wasserman, E. A., Kiedinger, R. E., & Bhatt, R. S. (1988). Conceptual behavior in pigeons: Categorization of both familiar and novel examples from four classes of natural and artificial stimuli. *Journal of Experimental Psychology: Animal Behavior Processes, 3,* 235-246.

Watanabe, S., Sakamoto, J., & Wakita, M. (1995). Pigeons' discrimination of paintings by Monet and Picasso. *Journal of the Experimental Analysis of Behavior, 63,* 165-174.

Wearden, J. H. (1995). Categorical scaling of stimulus duration by humans. *Journal of Experimental Psychology: Animal Behavior Processes, 21,* 318-330.

Wittgenstein, L. (1968). *Philosophical investigations* (3rd Edition). Translated from the German by G. E. M. Anscombe. Oxford: Blackwell.

Wright, A. A., Cook, R. G.,& Kendrick, D. F. (1989). Relational and absolute stimulus learning by monkeys in a memory task. *Journal of the Experimental Analysis of Behavior, 52,* 237-248.

Wright, A. A., Cook, R. G., Rivera, J. J., Sands, S. F., & Delius, J. D. (1988). Concept learning by pigeons: Matching-to-sample with trial-unique video picture stimuli. *Animal Learning and Behavior, 16,* 436-444.

Zentall, T. R., Jackson-Smith, P., & Jagielo, J. A. (1990). Categorical color and shape coding by pigeons. In M. Commons, R. J. Herrnstein, S. M. Kosslyn, & D. B. Mumford (Eds.), *Quantitative analyses of behavior, vol. VIII: Behavioral approaches to pattern recognition and concept formation* (pp. 3-22). Hillsdale, NJ: Lawrence.

Notes

This research was conducted with support from Contract DASW01-96-K-0009 from the U.S. Army Research Institute. Address correspondence to. Lanny Fields, Department of Psychology, Queens College/CUNY, 65-30 Kissena Boulevard, Flushing, NY 11367.

Chapter 5

Stimulus Control Topography Coherence and Stimulus Equivalence: Reconciling Test Outcomes with Theory

W. J. McIlvane, R. W. Serna,
W. V. Dube and R. Stromer
E. K. Shriver Center and Northeastern University

In his recent book, Murray Sidman (1994) reemphasized a continuing theme of his thinking on stimulus equivalence. He wrote that "equivalence, while not derivable from more primitive behavioral functions, variables, or processes, is a direct outcome of reinforcement." (p. 362). Catania (1992) has come to a similar conclusion. When prominent theorists make strong assertions, they deserve careful consideration. That has not happened yet. Those who take seriously the possibility that equivalence is a basic process have written little on the topic. Those who have other opinions, however, have been articulate and even passionate in their critiques (e.g., Horne & Lowe, 1996).

Perhaps the most fundamental objection to the notion that equivalence is a basic process is that there are many examples in the equivalence literature in which research participants have failed to demonstrate equivalence relations. So the argument goes, if equivalence is a basic process, why the failures? Sidman has addressed this issue from time to time (e.g., Sidman, 1994), but no-one has given this fundamental issue the detailed consideration that it deserves. The main purpose of this chapter is to present one view of how one might reconcile failures on equivalence class tests with the notion that equivalence is a behavioral primitive. Our arguments are related to but not the same as those put forth by Sidman, in part because we emphasize somewhat different aspects of the basic problem and in part because we may have a slightly different interpretation of certain stimulus control processes. Nevertheless, the essential features of our position are compatible with the essential features of Sidman's position.

To articulate our position, we will first review our understanding of the status of basic behavior analytic processes in general, and discuss their relationship to the concept of the higher-level operant. Next, we will cover the essential features of a developing general theory of stimulus control that is emerging from many years of study in our laboratories and others. While the theory is only slowly taking shape (e.g., Dube & McIlvane, 1996), we feel that certain of its features have been developed sufficiently well for our present purposes. We will then summarize some relevant research that bears on the issue, and reinterpret certain findings in light of this developing theoretical position. We will conclude by offering an outline of a theoretically-inspired experimental program that might be undertaken to falsify our position.

Behavioral Processes and Higher-Level Operants

Behavior analysis is noteworthy among the behavioral sciences in that it specifies a very small number of fundamental processes. Ferster and Skinner (1957), for example, specified only four in their treatise on reinforcement schedules: reinforcement, discrimination, response differentiation, and conditioned reinforcement. Their elegant, parsimonious account of a rich set of complex behavioral phenomenon has stood as an inspiration for generations of behavior analysts who adhere closely to William of Occam's famous razor: When confronted with two otherwise competing explanations of a given phenomenon, choose the simplest. Indeed, Steven Hayes (1991) has proposed a "relational frame theory" that has the goal of accounting for stimulus equivalence and related behavioral phenomena without introducing new processes.

We agree with Hayes that behavior analysts should proceed cautiously when suggesting new processes, but if data compel that step and other theoretical alternatives are unsatisfactory, then so be it. Moreover, while we are sympathetic to many aspects of relational frame theory, we believe that it is best viewed as analogous to certain "molar" accounts of reinforcement processes (e.g., Baum, 1973). Such accounts may be contrasted with "molecular" accounts that are more in the spirit of Skinner's often expressed desire for "moment-by-moment" behavioral analyses. Our view is that both molar and molecular analyses have their place in behavior analysis, with the former seen as potentially instructive abstractions that may ultimately be reconciled with the latter.

With respect to relational frame theory specifically, Hayes has argued that equivalence and other derived relations are learned behavior. Analogies have been made, for example, to generalized imitation, which has been conceptualized as a higher-order operant response class established by reinforcement of many specific instances of imitative behavior (Baer, Peterson, & Sherman, 1967)[1]. Our main problem with the concept of the "higher level" operant is not that it is fundamentally wrong in principle but rather that it has not yet been sufficiently unpacked at the behavioral-process level. Without a detailed process-level developmental account in terms of specific ontogenic (and perhaps phylogenic) contingencies, the higher-level operant can have virtually the same status as the homunculus – the hidden entity invoked to "explain" unexplained phenomenon by investing within it the ability to produce the phenomenon. To be fair to Hayes, he has suggested behavioral histories that might plausibly be involved in establishing relational frames. What he has not done, however, is to (1) flesh out how those histories do the job in terms of the basic processes specified in behavior analysis, and (2) critique whether the specified processes are competent to account for the phenomena observed (see Dube, McIlvane, & Green [1992] for an initial step towards a process-level account of generalized identity matching to sample). When that has been attempted, Hayes may find the notion that equivalence is a basic process more congenial.

As will become apparent later on, we believe that the contingencies Hayes describes, or ones like them, are probably involved in bringing individuals to the point where they pass laboratory tests for stimulus equivalence. We part company in two areas. First, we believe that there may be other ways of interpreting findings that suggest that exposure to many exemplars may be needed to establish the potential for stimulus equivalence. Second, we question whether the concept of the "higher-level operant" constitutes an adequate explanation of behavioral emergence (see also Pilgrim & Galizio, this volume). For us, the higher-level operant raises more questions than it answers (e.g., How are a series of "lower-level" operants organized into a single "higher-level" operant?). It is merely an appetizer, where we think a seven-course dinner is called for. We are not yet in a position to serve that meal ourselves, but we may be able to add a course or two along the way.

Accounting for Variable Outcomes on Equivalence Class Tests

In his classic book *Tactics of Scientific Research*, Sidman (1960) suggested that accounting for behavioral variability was among the most important tasks for behavior science. We agree. To our present ends, we are challenged to address at least three critical questions. If stimulus equivalence is a basic behavioral process. (1) Why are equivalence test outcomes and/or tests for defining properties of equivalence relations often negative? (2) Why does altering baseline relations sometimes leave originally established classes unchanged? This question is important because if equivalence arises automatically out of reinforcement, it can be argued that changing a baseline via reinforcement should also change equivalence class membership. (3) Why have positive equivalence-test outcomes sometimes seemed to depend on prerequisite verbal behavior? This question is important because if equivalence classes depend upon verbal behavior in some central way, the suggestion that equivalence is a basic process would be clearly wrong.

To address these questions, we must first review the concept of the "stimulus control topography" and make some general points about our views of stimulus control. We would be hard pressed to characterize our views as "mainstream" in the sense that most behavior analysts would find our presentation familiar and comfortable. Nevertheless, we see no obvious violations of behavior analytic principles and certain clear advantages in thinking the way we do.

Stimulus Control Topography. As we define it, the concept and term "stimulus control topography" (SCT) refers to the discriminative stimuli's physical features, structure, and controlling properties. For example, if a research participant's behavior is controlled at one moment by some aspect of the form of a given stimulus and at another moment by its position in space, then these are two distinct topographies of stimulus control. As another example, in a matching-to-sample

(MTS) task, if the participant selects some stimuli directly and selects others only after rejecting incorrect alternatives, then different SCTs can be distinguished.

The SCT is directly analogous to response topography. Behavior analysts have no trouble differentiating touches with the left or the right hand as separate topographies. Although these topography differences are not differentiated by the recording apparatus which defines the operant class, they are obvious to visual inspection. In a 100-trial session, for example, behavior analysts would find it unremarkable that 80 responses were made with the right hand and 20 with the left. As a parallel in the analysis of stimulus control, is it such a leap to suggest that a participant's response is controlled by some defining feature on the right side of a visual stimulus on 80 trials and to a defining feature on the left on the other 20? If it is not a leap, then we think it appropriate to (1) term these different controlling relations different stimulus control topographies, and (2) suggest that different SCTs may occur with different frequencies in the same operant baseline.

The term "stimulus control topography" was first proposed by Barbara Ray (1969) to deal with certain problems of selective attending that had been ignored by mainstream behavior analysis. Her proposal was also ignored. A few years ago, McIlvane and Dube (1992) reintroduced and expanded the SCT concept to address the problems identified by Ray and other related problems. For some reason, this SCT proposal has not been ignored and has actually received a reasonably warm reception. Perhaps the proposal was timely. Prominent behavior analysts such as Mark Rilling (1992) have argued recently that behavior analysis cannot succeed unless it enriches its concepts of stimulus control. Indeed, this has been the position of Shriver Center researchers for decades (McIlvane & Dube, 1997; cf. Ray & Sidman, 1970).

Although the SCT term/concept is fully consistent with a functional analysis of behavior (see McIlvane, 1992), it has direct parallels in cognitive psychology and cognitive neuroscience. For example, SCT bears a formal resemblance to certain definitions of "representation" (e.g., the stimulus selected, the stimulus as encoded, etc.). It is not isomorphic with "representation," however, occupying a different place in behavior analytic theory. Behavior analysts define the "operant" as functional three-term unit involving (1) a class of antecedent stimuli that occasion behavior, (2) a class of responses that operate on the environment, and (3) a class of consequential stimuli that determine the frequency of behavior. As we have argued, it is perfectly meaningful to speak in terms of and experimentally analyze multiple SCTs and response topographies, each of which may occur at different frequencies within the behavioral stream. Such activities are often called "mircoanalyses," and represent efforts to expand and refine the traditional three-term analytical unit (see Thompson & Zeiler, 1986 for detailed discussion of issues pertinent to defining analytic units). By contrast, typical cognitive theories do not postulate multiple, separately analyzable representations of the same experimental environment.

We have been led to SCT analyses by research findings. For example, in work on discrimination learning of individuals with intellectual disabilities, one often encounters stable accuracy scores that are significantly above "chance" but substantially short of perfection (e.g., 83% correct on a two- or three-choice task). Continued training will often not produce improved accuracy. This general phenomenon was termed "a limitation on the law of effect" by House, Hanley, and Magid (1979), and, on its face, seems to present substantial theoretical challenges for behavior analytic researchers. When the problem is characterized in terms of multiple competing SCTs, however, one has not only a plausible explanation of stable intermediate accuracy (Dube & McIlvane, 1997) but also a potential solution path. The solution is to alter the teaching contingencies such that the desired SCTs are experimentally isolated and differentially selected by reinforcement (e.g., McIlvane, 1992; McIlvane, Kledaras, Stoddard, & Dube, 1990).

Stimulus control topography coherence theory. In brief overview, our suggestion is that unexplained behavioral variability can often be traced to a lack of coherence between (1) the SCTs that the experimenter/teacher intends to generate and (2) the SCTs actually generated by a given set of contingencies. We say "often" here because the stream of behavior has other sources of variability (e.g., endogenous factors) that also must be considered (cf. Thompson & Lubinski, 1986). Presuming that these latter sources of variability are effectively minimized, however, behavioral variability can be managed via procedures that establish or increase SCT coherence.

SCT coherence theory has its roots in an extensive series of early studies that demonstrated frequent lack of coherence between the stimulus control topographies that might be expected by the experimenter and those actually exhibited by research participants (e.g., Ray & Sidman, 1970; Sidman, 1969; Touchette, 1969; Stoddard & Sidman, 1971). It was found, for example, that stimuli such as line tilts, often used to test dimensional accounts of stimulus control (e.g., Thomas, 1969), were actually complex stimuli whose controlling properties could not be assumed in advance. Where experimenters tended to assume that line orientation was the controlling stimulus dimension, studies with individuals who were mentally retarded often revealed that the true controlling stimuli were different (e.g., a portion of the line appearing in spatial contiguity to a corner of the response key). More recently, we have reported findings that demonstrate, for example, lack of coherence between experimenter and participant topographies on tests of stimulus generalization (Stoddard & McIlvane, 1989) and during stimulus control shaping procedures (e.g., McIlvane & Cataldo, 1996; Serna, Wilkinson, & McIlvane, 1997).

As experimental tasks increase in complexity, problems in establishing SCT coherence become more pronounced. Relational (i.e., stimulus-stimulus) learning tasks are a case in point. Generalized "same"-"different" judgments, for example, were once thought to be beyond the capabilities of individuals with low mental ages (< 5 years) (e.g., House, Brown, & Scott, 1974; cf. Soraci & Carlin, 1992). Research by members of our group has since provided convincing evidence that past research had greatly underestimated the capabilities of developmentally-limited individuals in this regard. Our most recent paper (Serna, Dube, & McIlvane, 1997) has reported that procedures now available can teach generalized identity matching of abstract two-dimensional forms to virtually anyone who can master a basic form discrimination. Notably, our improved methods all seek to reduce the likelihood that task-irrelevant stimulus control (i.e., undesired SCTs) will inadvertently be established by the procedures.

Why is coherence so often lacking? We suggest that SCT coherence is difficult to achieve with developmentally limited individuals (i.e., young children and individuals with developmental disabilities) mainly because the experimenter and the research participant operate at different levels of behavioral development. It has often been reported, for example, that individuals with low mental ages respond to complex stimulus displays by attending to a restricted set of local stimulus elements or features (e.g., Burke, 1991; Stromer, McIlvane, Dube, & Mackay, 1993; Wilhelm & Lovaas, 1976; cf. Rudy, 1991). The experimenter, however, has a long history of broader attending; it would be unnatural for him/her to restrict attending to local stimulus elements. Moreover, it has also long been reported that low functioning individuals often attend to task-irrelevant stimuli (from the experimenter's viewpoint) despite protracted discrimination training (e.g., Zeaman & House, 1979). In one illustrative case from our own research, for example, we found that protracted failure to master a simple form discrimination was overcome merely by eliminating the then-standard response-key borders in our MTS software (see Dube, 1991 for a description of the relevant programs). From the experimenter's perspective, the borders were irrelevant, but they were clearly relevant for the research participant.

While atypical stimulus control development has long been observed in low-functioning individuals, our view is that the field has been slow to understand and come fully to terms with the phenomenon. Most frequently, atypical stimulus control has been thought of as a product of neurologically limited attentional resources, which may be overwhelmed by environmental complexity (e.g., Merrill, 1990). Our developing view, however, is that atypical control may have a more complex explanation. While attentional resources indeed may be limited in some sense, full understanding of the variables responsible for that limitation brings us outside the domain of "attention" *per se*. SCT coherence theory suggests that atypical attending has its roots in a complex interaction between attending and the consequences of attending.

While the importance of consequences has historically been appreciated by attention theorists such as Zeaman and House (1979), more recent work on attending de-emphasizes or ignores them (e.g., Posner, 1996). One reason may be that most of the recent work has been done with individuals who could understand syntactically complex verbal instructions. In the brief test protocols typically employed, instructional control may often suffice to establish and maintain performance. (Also, between-group experimental designs do not require that all participants understand and/or comply with the instructions.) Nevertheless, it can be demonstrated that consequences do matter in these procedures (e.g., by extending exposure to them [McIlvane, Dube, & Callahan, 1996]). Pertinent to SCT coherence theory, consequential variables must be more fully considered when working with developmentally limited participants; the consequences are an essential aspect of the teaching interaction (Sidman & Stoddard, 1966). Because one cannot assume that the participant attends to those aspects of the task defined as relevant by the experimenter, one must be especially attuned to how the schedule of reinforcement interacts with the participant's behavior. What follows is one simple example intended to make our arguments more concrete.

Suppose that the experimenter/teacher has decided to teach the elementary form discrimination shown in left portion of Figure 1. The task is to select the letter X and to reject the letter N (or alternately to select the odd stimulus in the display). From the experimenter's viewpoint, the schedule of consequences is as follows: (1) Selections of X are reinforced every time (FR1), (2) selections of N are never reinforced (EXT), and (3) selections of any given position, irrespective of form, are reinforced one-fourth of the time on average (VR4). In specifying these nominal schedule values, the experimenter is counting on the participant to detect the form differences and not to respond to the stimulus element that is common to both (\). He/she is also counting on the participant to detect the disparity between the FR1 schedule associated with X and the VR4 schedule associated with position stimuli, in order to discourage responding to the latter.

Suppose, however, that the participant responds not to X vs. N as integrated units, but rather to the constituent elements. What are the effective reinforcement contingencies? From an elemental perspective, one feature (/) defines the positive stimulus, one defines the negative (|), and one is common (\) (shaded for emphasis in Figure 1). If the participant can detect the line tilt differences, then the effective

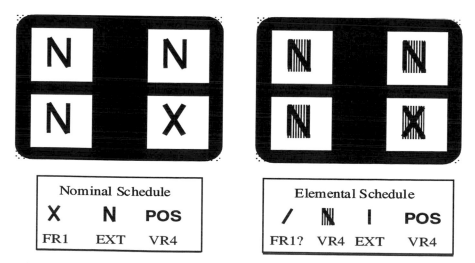

Figure 1. Two analyses of the effective reinforcement schedules in a simple simultaneous discrimination procedure. POS refers to positional stimuli.

element schedules are FR1, EXT, and VR4, respectively. But can one safely assume the prerequisite stimulus detection? Mirror image line tilt discriminations (/ vs. \) are notoriously difficult for participants with developmental limitations (Over & Over, 1967; Ray & Sidman, 1970). Even detection of the defining / vs. | stimulus difference must be suspect in this population. If the relevant differences are not detected, then the *de facto* schedule associated with *all* stimulus elements is effectively VR4 – the same as for responding to position stimuli. Even if the relevant stimulus differences are detectable, the participant must also detect the disparity between the FR1 and VR4 schedules – itself a signal detection problem (cf. Davison & Jenkins, 1985) that may challenge low-functioning individuals. Thus, from the experimenter's perspective, neither the letter nor the schedule detection task is challenging. But from the participant's perspective, *all* aspects of the task are potentially challenging. Perhaps it is not surprising that acquisition failures and variable, intermediate accuracy scores are commonplace in research with individuals with developmental limitations. Indeed, that is in part why fairly elaborate stimulus control shaping techniques have proven necessary to establish discriminative baselines in this population (e.g., Sidman & Stoddard, 1966; McIlvane, 1992).

SCT coherence theory and generalization. Also pertinent to an analysis of behavioral variability is the observation that behaviors established in one context may or may not be observed when the context is varied (cf. Kirby & Bickel, 1988). Here, SCT coherence theory makes virtually the same argument it makes in accounting for within-context variability (cf. Mackay, Stromer, & Serna, in press). In order for generalization to occur, (1) the stimuli that occasioned behavior in the original context (or members of the same equivalence class) must be present within the new context, (2) other stimuli in the new context must not occasion behaviors that compete with the behavior of interest to the experimenter, and (3) the *de facto* schedules of reinforcement in the new context must be sufficiently similar to the schedules that supported performance in the original context.

SCT Coherence Theory and Equivalence Classes

Returning to the matter most immediately at hand, what does coherence theory have to say about variability on tests for equivalence relations and/or their three defining properties (i.e., reflexivity, symmetry and transitivity)? By now, it should come as no surprise to find that coherence theory makes the same basic assertion as it does in accounting for behavioral variability: Outcomes on equivalence tests depend critically on coherence between the SCTs desired by the experimenter and those actually present in the participant's repertoire. To this basic point is added: (1) with SCT coherence established, outcomes on equivalence tests should always be positive, (2) provided that there is no procedural artifact and/or no behavioral history that sets up unresolvable competition between different SCTs established in the experiment and/or under similar circumstances in the participant's extraexperimental experience. This is an extremely strong, potentially falsifiable assertion. SCT coherence theory appears to be a good one in that regard. With the preceding information as background, we shall now turn to addressing the three challenges that were outlined earlier in the chapter.

(1) Why are Equivalence Test Outcomes Often Negative?

To this question, we answer "Why indeed?" In research at the Shriver laboratories, negative test outcomes are extremely rare. For example, we recently did a retrospective analysis of all of our readily available published and unpublished data with developmentally limited participants. To our surprise, we had no failures with 27 normally capable children aged 4 to 6 years. Even more surprising, our success rate with individuals with intellectual disabilities was nearly as great. With individuals having measured mental ages greater than 6 years, equivalence classes were obtained in 39 of 40 participants. With more severely impaired individuals, the success rate has exceeded 90%. Given our nearly routine success with developmentally limited individuals, we think it more than plausible that the occasional failure is due to artifact (i.e., inadequate care to assure coherence between experimenter-specified and participant SCTs and/or other uncontrolled historical variables).

In reporting these results, we hasten to add that other laboratories have not had the same findings. For example, the Kansas group has produced more negative outcomes (K. Saunders, personal communication), and together we have begun efforts to analyze these across-laboratory differences. At an early stage in this process, a few possibilities present themselves. For example, the Kansas group tends to make greater use of simple differential reinforcement techniques to establish the baselines needed for equivalence tests. The Shriver laboratories, by contrast, make much greater use of stimulus control shaping techniques in baseline training. Also, the Shriver group tends to make greater (but not exclusive) use of auditory-visual vs. all-visual stimulus control baselines. Green (1990) has reported that the former tend to encourage positive class outcomes.

These possibilities and other more subtle ones fit comfortably within a SCT coherence framework. For example, use of stimulus control shaping techniques may help to restrict the range of SCTs established by the contingencies, and thus encourage coherence. With respect to the all-visual testing, such procedures require the participant to differentiate among stimuli that inevitably share common physical features. Perhaps all-visual baselines may be more likely to encourage artifactual control by physical similarities. Auditory-visual procedures, by contrast, reduce the visual stimulus discrimination burden. While these and other possibilities require explicit experimental analysis, one thing is clear. It is incumbent upon proponents of coherence theory to explain such equivalence-test failures in terms of irrelevant and/or competing SCTs. If that cannot be done, then the theory falls.

Gradual emergence on equivalence tests. As one example of our efforts to account for variable outcomes on tests for stimulus equivalence, we will briefly summarize one recent account of the "gradual emergence" phenomenon (Dube & McIlvane, 1996). The observation is that equivalence-test scores often improve from low or intermediate levels to high levels as the tests are repeated, even if the tests are conducted under extinction conditions. Can an SCT formulation account for this observation? Early in training, we speculate, many different SCTs may occur across training trials, particularly if simple differential reinforcement (i.e., trial-and-error) methods are used. SCTs that are consistent with the reinforcement contingencies increase in frequency and those that are inconsistent decrease in frequency. As training progresses, SCTs of the former type are necessarily involved in many more reinforced trials, and thus may be expected to have greater behavioral momentum (Nevin, 1992). SCTs of the latter type, by contrast, are necessarily involved in fewer reinforced trials and less momentum.

Typical equivalence tests confront the participant with novel stimulus displays without prior adaptation. We speculate that novel displays may occasion a resurgence (Epstein, 1985) of previously low-frequency SCTs that compete temporarily with the high-frequency SCTs selected by the contingencies. Because the low-frequency SCTs have less momentum, the extinction schedule on the test has a relatively greater suppressive effect; their frequencies are rapidly reduced. The high-frequency SCTs, however, have substantial momentum, the extinction schedule has relatively less influence, and those SCTs occur more and more frequently. This account seems consistent with the gradual emergence phenomenon[2].

Negative outcomes in participants with relatively advanced behavioral repertoires. We are untroubled by the many reports of equivalence test failures in college students and others with extensive behavioral histories. We attribute these failures to two major variables. First, the practical realities of testing college students are such that they are often unwilling to participate beyond a few brief sessions. Facing this reality, experimenters have tried to develop complex baselines too rapidly in our opinion, and the participants have been overwhelmed by the learning burden of the procedures. (Indeed, Fields and colleagues [1997] have tried to tease out nodal distance effects by giving participants too much to learn in too short a time.) In the language of coherence theory, these procedures failed to control for the many irrelevant SCTs that the procedures might generate. Notably, introducing the emergence tests in a quasi-programmed manner improves test outcomes (Adams, Fields, & Verhave, 1993). The fact that programming encourages positive outcomes can be taken in two ways. Opponents of SCT coherence theory will ask why the programming is necessary, if equivalence is indeed a basic process. Proponents will ask why programming is ever *unnecessary*. In other words, they will question the meaning of negative test outcomes when the training procedures encourage artifacts such as potentially competing verbal strategies (Smith, Dickens, & Bentall, 1996) and uncontrolled sample-S- relations (Carrigan & Sidman, 1992).

The second reason that failures with college students do not trouble us is harder to characterize. Briefly stated, we suggest that the participants' extensive pre-experimental histories may interfere with test performance. Indeed, in post equivalence-test interviews, it is common for research participants to report use of elaborate strategies of the type that may be helpful in meeting their current educational contingencies. Indeed, college students must only very rarely experience circumstances in which they are presented with problem-solving situations that do not challenge preschool children and individuals with mental retardation.

Indeed, their experience is perhaps more often with problems that do not have immediately obvious solutions, for example, those presented on such tests as the Scholastic Aptitude Test, the Miller Analogies Test, and other tests required to gain admission to college. Consider the following analogy task: "camel" is to "truck" as "elephant" is to: (a) wagon, (b) car, (c) forklift, (d) jackhammer. Are the emergent behaviors targeted in equivalence experiments truly more demanding than those that are routinely required of and displayed by typical college students? Referring back to our successes with young children, is it plausible that educated adults would have trouble with problem-solving situations that preschooler resolve with relative ease? In layman's terms, is it not more plausible that these behaviorally sophisticated participants are merely reading too much into the task?

(2) Why Does Altering Baseline Relations Sometimes Leave Originally Established Equivalence Relations Unchanged?

The most important challenge to SCT coherence theory may come from findings in which it has been shown that certain equivalence test outcomes may not be affected even if one changes the contingencies that supposedly generated those test outcomes. In work with college students, for example, Pilgrim and Galizio (1990, and see this volume) have shown that reversing baseline relations and re-testing for newly derived relations does not have the effect that one might predict from a logical equivalence perspective. Pertinent aspects of their procedure and major findings are shown in Figure 2.

After the baseline reversal training, college students tended to show (1) reversed outcomes on symmetry tests and (2) unchanged outcomes on transitivity tests. How could this be if the test outcomes depended upon the equivalence relations established by baseline training? Can this apparent divergence be reconciled with the notion that equivalence arises directly from reinforcement? One possible reconciliation, admittedly somewhat speculative at this point, comes from early stimulus control topography analyses by Ray (1969) and Stoddard and Sidman (1971). Both studies showed that developing new stimulus control topographies that were incompatible with those established by prior training did not abolish the original topographies. Rather, the effect was to reduce the frequency of those topographies to zero or near-zero levels (see also Cohen, 1969). Stoddard and Sidman's study was particularly compelling. They showed that providing brief histories that reinstated key behavioral prerequisites immediately reinstated the original stimulus control topographies — the performances did not have to be reacquired.

Pilgrim and Galizio's procedures seem directly analogous to those used by Ray (1969) with rhesus monkeys and systematically replicated with human participants by Huguenin and Touchette (1980) and Huguenin (1987). In Ray's experiment, discriminations were separately established between two colors (e.g., red[S+], green[S-] and two line tilts (e.g., horizontal[S+], vertical[S-]). Then, the colors and forms were superimposed on each other and discriminative functions were arranged to create "conflict compounds." With reference to the example, the compound stimuli were (red+vertical[S+] and green+horizontal[S-]; in these compounds,

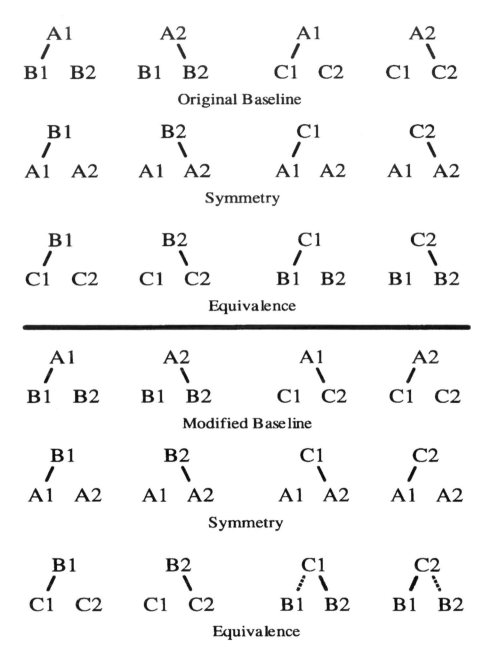

Figure 2. Diagram of procedures used by Pilgrim and Galizio (1990). Solid lines indicate relations that might be predicted from a logical equivalence analysis. Where participant behavior diverged from that predicted by such an analysis, the performance is indicated by dashed lines.

note that the line tilts had reversed discriminative functions from those originally established. When reliable discriminative control was established by the conflict compounds, probe trials evaluated control by the color and line-tilt elements. Had the conflict compound training reversed or abolished stimulus control by the tilts? Typically, it had not. The tilts exhibited the discriminative functions that had been established during the original training – not the reversed functions that would have been consistent with the conflict compounds. Thus, during the conflict-compound training, the frequency of the original tilt topographies was reduced to near zero, but that training had not altered the frequency of the established tilt topographies when the colors were not present.

Returning to Pilgrim and Galizio's experiment, reversing the baseline relations, we suggest, had the effect of reducing the frequency of the original SCTs to near zero levels. But doing that need not have abolished those stimulus control topographies. More importantly, from the SCT perspective, there is no reason to predict that the reversal training should have necessarily altered the transitive performances that depended upon the originally established topographies. To make that prediction, it would have been necessary to show that the prerequisite SCTs actually had been abolished. If re-reversing the contingencies led to an immediate (i.e., within a few trials) display of the original performances, for example, it would be difficult to argue that they had been abolished.

Yet to be explained, however, is why there was a reversal of the symmetry test outcomes. Here, one may point to the fact that symmetry tests merely reverse the sample and comparison positions of stimuli that were contiguously present during the reversal training. Conceivably, the contingency reversals may not have changed the original controlling stimuli but merely the stimuli that the participant touched. That is, participants selected C1 in the presence of A2 by *rejecting* C2. Support for this suggestion comes from the many studies of sample-S- controlling relations (e.g., McIlvane et al., 1987; Stromer & Osborne, 1982) (or "Type R control," Carrigan & Sidman, 1992). When the sample and comparison positions were reversed on symmetry test trials, Type R control was exhibited on those trials as well.

Equally plausible and perhaps more parsimonious, however, is to suggest that reversal training established new baseline sample-S+ topographies (i.e., A1:C2 and A2:C1). If so, the reversed symmetry test performance was merely consistent with those new topographies. And as Ray (1969) showed, creating new topographies need not abolish old ones. There is no requirement at the level of basic process that the transitivity test and symmetry test outcomes must conform to the simple logic of the procedures. To be clear, we do not suggest that Pilgrim and Galizio's (1990) participants were behaving illogically. Rather, we suggest that if logic is to be applied to analyze their performance, then that logic must be consistent with the full range of behavioral principles and processes that may have been operative in the experimental situation.

Should our SCT analysis of Pilgrim and Galizio's data prove to be essentially correct, equivalence researchers may have to learn to talk and write in new ways. There are many ways of talking about equivalence classes. For example, Sidman

(1994) has used the metaphor of a bag that contains the stimuli in a given class. In informal discussions with numerous colleagues, we have often heard hydraulic or electrical metaphors, with Pilgrim and Galizio's procedures seen as analogous to "rewiring" the connections between the class members. As tempting as these metaphors may be, we believe that all that suggest physical class structures should be used with extreme caution. Behavior analysis is committed to descriptive functionalism, not structuralism. It seems appropriate, therefore, to develop whatever metaphors are used with that in mind. Our own preference, however, is to try to dispense with metaphor and to speak whenever possible in the language of functional relations, behavioral frequencies, and so forth.

Zero-frequency operants and contextual control. The notion of zero-frequency SCTs and zero-frequency operants more generally, we suspect, will be unpalatable for behavior analysts accustomed to dealing with phenomena that are occurring – not those that are not occurring. In response, we suggest that SCTs are not occurring all the time, that fact is of major theoretical importance, and that behavior analysts deal with the phenomenon whenever they study conditional discrimination. What follows will develop this point.

Some years ago, Sidman (1986) discussed a possible extension of the traditional three-term unit of behavioral analysis, in part to address certain conceptual problems raised by the phenomenon of stimulus equivalence. Building upon the traditional three-term analysis of the discriminated operant, Sidman suggested that it might be necessary to add a fourth analytical term, the conditional stimulus, the function of which was to select or "activate" previously established three-term discriminated operants (see also Cumming and Berryman [1965] for a similar analysis of matching-to-sample procedures.). Sidman's language suggests, of course, that three-term behavioral units can have two states – active and inactive. Thus, Sidman's suggestion is very close to and perhaps isomorphic with our notion that operants may have a current frequency of zero under a given set of circumstances and other frequencies under other circumstances[3].

As Sidman pointed out in his 1986 chapter, however, conditional discrimination itself may be brought under conditional control. Consider the burgeoning research on so-called "contextual control" of class membership (or five-term contingencies in Sidman's analytical framework). A particularly illustrative example is the recent study by Perez-Gonzalez and Serna (1993), the essential procedures of which are illustrated in Figure 3.

In Phase Ia, Perez-Gonzalez and Serna established a conditional discrimination, AB. In Phase Ib, that conditional discrimination was put under contextual control, such that the original AB selections were reinforced in the presence of X1, but the opposite selections were reinforced in the presence of X2. Normally capable teenagers readily acquired this performance. In the Phase II test phase, participants demonstrated even more complex conditional stimulus control. In Phase IIa, a new conditional discrimination was established via unreinforced conditional selection (Stromer, 1986). (This widely-reported phenomenon occurs when participants with

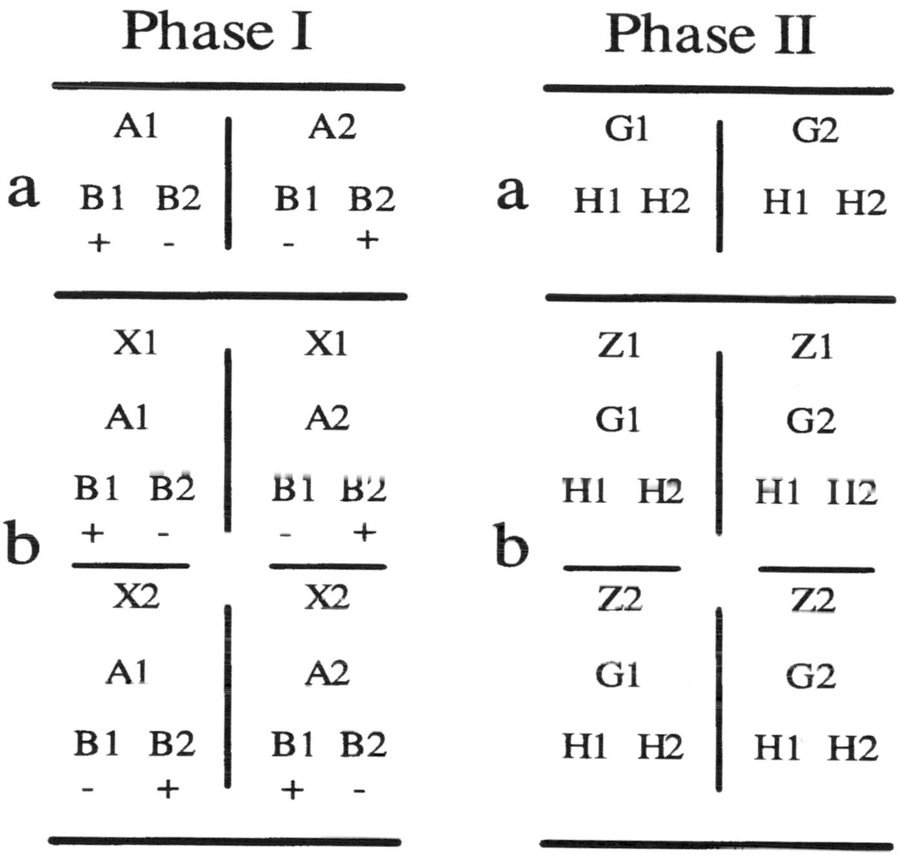

Phase I

	A1	A2
a	B1 B2	B1 B2
	+ -	- +

	X1	X1
	A1	A2
	B1 B2	B1 B2
b	+ -	- +
	X2	X2
	A1	A2
	B1 B2	B1 B2
	- +	+ -

Phase II

	G1	G2
a	H1 H2	H1 H2

	Z1	Z1
	G1	G2
	H1 H2	H1 H2
b	Z2	Z2
	G1	G2
	H1 H2	H1 H2

Figure 3. The procedures reported by Perez-Gonzalez and Serna (1993). Stimuli defined as positive and negative on each trial are indicated by + and -, respectively. Where performances were expected to emerge via unreinforced conditional selection, no discriminative functions are indicated.

extensive conditional discrimination histories are presented with new conditional problems without instructions or differential reinforcement. They nevertheless behave conditionally with respect to the new sample stimuli.) Unreinforced trials were presented until participants demonstrated stable conditional performance. The question posed in Phase IIb was whether the history provided in Phase I and Phase IIa was sufficient to establish unreinforced contextual performance. Would participants make selections consistent with their GH conditional discrimination in the presence of one novel contextual stimulus, but make the opposite selections in the presence of the other? The results were consistent with that possibility.

Three vs. higher-term behavioral units. Must behavior analysis specify further basic processes to account for unreinforced conditional selection and higher-order control of conditional discrimination? To answer provisionally, we do not yet feel compelled to postulate any processes beyond those already discussed. One certainly needs what we have termed "separability" to account for *all* emergent MTS performances (Stromer, McIlvane, & Serna, 1993). Taking a four-term contingency example, relations AB and AC cannot yield BC and CB unless the elements of the stimulus display are separable. Perez-Gonzalez and Serna's findings also point to the contextual stimulus as separable. How else could a novel fifth-term stimuli be substituted in an unreinforced conditional selection paradigm?

Given that MTS stimuli are manifestly separable, need one go further and imply different stimulus functions and/or a hierarchical relationship among the stimuli? This seems to be implied when stimuli are given different names, that is, the conditional stimulus of the four-term contingency and the contextual stimulus of the five-term contingency. Provisionally, we favor an analysis in which stimuli are joined in what we have termed a "separable compound" (Stromer, McIlvane, & Serna, 1993), analogous to a logical *and* function. The roles that stimuli play may be given different names by the experimenter, for convenience in specifying the *analytical unit*, but the relation among all stimuli in the compound is the same — equivalence arising from their participation in a three-term *behavioral unit* that includes a reinforcing stimulus. Viewing things in this way, we believe, helps keep our analysis of emergent performances more closely connected to established facts of behavior analysis. And, as we have argued, the notion that multiple stimuli can be combined and recombined in multiple SCTs is consistent with those facts.

SCTs and behavioral flexibility. One challenge for behavior analysis in general and equivalence research in particular is to provide a process-level account for the rich assortment of contextually-determined equivalence relations apparent in the behavioral repertoire of humans. For example, "saw" is equivalent to "hammer" if the context is "hand tools," but not if the context is "cutting tools." Perhaps even more important is the need to account for novel classifications, such as those involved in metaphor and analogy, which have no explicit reinforcement history. From the SCT perspective, it seems clear that one must explore possible parallels with the phenomena of resurgence (Epstein, 1985) and recombinative generalization (Goldstein, Angelo, & Mousetis, 1987) of previously established operants. In the latter paradigm, for example, components of previously established operants are spontaneously sequenced into orderly new performances that are consistent with current contingencies. If one adds contextually constrained equivalence relations to the mix, there is great potential for emergence of very complex stimulus relations[4]. Flexibility of this sort must be at the heart of any competent behavior analytic account of stimulus classification (or category formation [Rosch, 1975]). It is unsatisfying merely to claim that emergent classification has its roots in "the necessary behavioral prerequisites" without providing a plausible process-level account of how those prerequisites do the job.

Also essential to a competent SCT theory is a principled explanation of SCT competition (interference) and how competition is resolved. Recalling Ray's (1969) suggestion, the SCT notion is intended "to encourage testing of known behavioral principles that may readily apply to the phenomenon of selective attention" (p.

540). To us, it seems essential that competition resolution be related to basic reinforcement principles, such as current schedule, magnitude, history (e.g., behavioral momentum), and so on. We have already taken steps in this direction (McIlvane, Dube, & Serna, 1996), but much more is left to do.

We are left with the question of how one should refer to operants that have been in the behavioral repertoire, but are not currently occurring. Some years ago, we contributed a paper that asked "Do stimulus classes exist before they are tested?" (McIlvane & Dube, 1990). Our conclusion was that the question was not a good one, and it temporarily took the field in the wrong direction. In the present context, we find ourselves entering similar territory and perceive a similar risk. It is one thing to say that the frequency of a given SCT is zero (or of indeterminate status), and another to assert that SCTs exist independently of the behavioral analyses that document them.

Returning full circle to Pilgrim and Galizio's intriguing experiment, we suggest that it is meaningful talk about an SCT that one occurred frequently and is now not occurring — a zero-frequency SCT. Moreover, we suggest that SCTs that are not occurring in the current context may have some relationship to behavior that emerges when the context is varied. That is, zero-frequency topographies can and do serve as behavioral prerequisites for other performances (i.e., the preserved transitivity test outcomes). In fact, Pilgrim and Galizio's procedure and similar ones may provide an as yet unappreciated way to study how contingencies "break down" previously established equivalence relations (see Sidman, 1994, p. 522-524)[5]. As Sidman has frequently pointed out, there must be a way to constrain equivalence relations, or discrimination itself would be impossible. Perhaps, however, established equivalence relations are not so much "broken down" as they are reduced in frequency. Because they are not abolished but merely supplanted, they can reoccur under appropriate circumstances. What those circumstances may be — how the relevant SCTs, response classes, and reinforcement schedules interact — is only poorly appreciated at present. Much research will be necessary to give us a more complete picture.

(3) Why Have Positive Equivalence-Test Outcomes Seemed To Depend On Prerequisite Verbal Behavior?

There is perhaps no more controversial issue in contemporary behavior analysis than that of the role of the verbal repertoire in the formation of equivalence classes. Horne and Lowe (1996) have argued, for example, that equivalence classes depend upon a process termed "naming" that is said to emerge as one acquires speaking and listening skills. Horne and Lowe have supported their arguments with data that demonstrate negative equivalence class outcomes in young children that become positive outcomes when children are taught to name the stimuli. Hayes' group has also reported a very controversial study which reported (1) positive equivalence outcomes in young children who have demonstrable language and (2) negative outcomes in children who do not (Devany, Hayes, & Nelson, 1986). The difficulty in demonstrating equivalence classes in nonhumans also seemingly provides support for those who argue for an intimate relationship between language repertoires and equivalence classes.

Commenting on Horne and Lowe's article, McIlvane and Dube (1996) suggested that negative equivalence outcomes in nonhumans and nonverbal children are hard to interpret, as are facilitative effects of teaching naming (see also Stromer, 1996). In our view, experimental operations such as teaching participants to name the stimuli may be effective principally because they encourage coherence of participant- and experimenter-defined SCTs. For example, naming verifies the successive discriminations of stimuli that serve as samples (Saunders & Spradlin, 1990), a critical prerequisite for a successful test outcome. Notably, the Schusterman group's recent demonstration of equivalence in a sea lion (Schusterman & Kastak, 1993) was accomplished with a training regimen that featured a large number of different stimuli and stimulus relations. Providing multiple exemplars is a well-established technique for encouraging learners to attend to relevant aspects of the task being learned (e.g., Engelmann & Carnine, 1982; Repp, Karsh, & Lenz, 1990).

Another possibility is that teaching children to name the stimuli has other effects, perhaps increasing the frequency of sample-S+ SCTs in the baseline. Naming a stimulus may encourage the participant to look for that stimulus and engage other behavior with respect to it (e.g., if the name has an extra-experimental history, comparing this exemplar with others previously encountered). Even more subtle processes may be involved. For example, naming may encourage children to look at the stimuli as a whole rather than to their isolated (and potentially overlapping) features. Some support for this suggestion may be found in psycholinguistic studies of "operating principles" that are evident in early child word learning (Golinkoff, Mervis, & Hirsh-Pasek, 1994; cf. Wilkinson & McIlvane, 1997). These studies have shown that children are more likely to relate new words to items as a whole rather than to parts of items.

Buttressing our argument that stimulus naming may have a peripheral rather than a central role in equivalence class formation is the increasing number of demonstrations in our laboratories of equivalence classes in nonverbal, severely mentally retarded individuals (Wilkinson & McIlvane, unpublished data; Krendel-Ames & Green, unpublished data). None had appreciable skills as either speaker or listener, but all displayed reliable equivalence class outcomes. Deborah Carr (1997) has also demonstrated equivalence classes in a nonspeaking boy with autism. In addition, she reported the intriguing finding that equivalence outcomes may be related to whether or not the participant exhibits both sample-S+ and sample-S- relations after baseline training. Why such relations should matter is not clear, but it is possible that they merely verified that the participant discriminated each of the sample and comparison stimuli as separate rather than as part of a larger stimulus compound. When these case studies are reported more formally, we think they will present an insurmountable argument against the Horne and Lowe (1996) proposal.

Conclusion

To Horne and Lowe's credit, the pattern of data needed to falsify their naming hypothesis seems eminently clear — convincing evidence of stimulus equivalence in nonhuman animals and/or nonverbal humans. Should it be shown that equivalence is routinely demonstrable in either or both of these populations, we must nevertheless thank them for providing a testable hypothesis and for helping to frame questions that will further our understanding of nature. To show proper respect for that contribution, it seems incumbent upon those who offer alternative accounts to specify in advance the pattern of data that would be needed to falsify their accounts.

SCT coherence theory is testable. The procedures necessary to do it, however, are intricate, time-consuming, and expensive. Appropriate research participants would be nonhuman primates or minimally verbal humans. One must first develop a set of experimental stimuli all of which are discriminated both successively and simultaneously from one another, to show that any later failures of equivalence are not due to undesired SCT competition. This could be done via delayed matching-to-sample tests using the "blank comparison" procedure developed in our laboratories (e.g., McIlvane, Kledaras, Lowry, & Stoddard, 1992; Serna, Wilkinson, & McIlvane, in press). One must also adapt the participants to novel test displays, which might be done via prior experience with exclusion procedures (McIlvane et al, 1992). Then, effective stimulus control shaping techniques must be used to establish the necessary baseline performances with few or no errors, again to minimize undesired SCT competition. Highly stable and accurate baseline performances could be verified by overtraining, which would also build adequate momentum for subsequent tests. If equivalence tests are to be conducted without differential reinforcement, then the participants must be adapted to such trials. (An alternative would be to conduct the test with nondifferential reinforcement.) If, after such elaborate, competent preparation, the participants do not show reliable positive equivalence class outcomes, then SCT coherence theory as we have presented it here would not be supported. Indeed, if exposure to many problems in succession is always required (e.g., Schusterman & Kastak, 1993), then certain essential components of relational frame theory would become attractive.

If SCT coherence theory is ultimately supported, however, our field has another problem. As Sidman and others (e.g., Saunders & Green, 1992; Hayes, 1991) have often pointed out, equivalence relations are not the only stimulus-stimulus relations that can be specified. Relations such as "greater than," "father of," "next to," and so forth are not equivalence relations in the logical sense. Must these too be specified as behavioral primitives? Can the essence of such relations be captured by contextual control of equivalence relations? That is an intriguing possibility, which we will follow up as SCT coherence theory continues to develop.

References

Adams, B. J., Fields, L., and Verhave, T. (1993). Effects of test order on intersubject variability during equivalence class formation. *The Psychological Record, 43*, 133-152.

Baer, D. M., Peterson, R. F., & Sherman, J. A. (1967). The development of imitation by reinforcing behavioral similarity to a model. *Journal of the Experimental Analysis of Behavior, 10*, 405-416.

Baum, W. M. (1973). The correlation-based law of effect. *Journal of the Experimental Analysis of Behavior, 20*, 137-153.

Burke, J. C. (1991). Some developmental implications of a disturbance in responding to complex environmental stimuli. *American Journal on Mental Retardation, 96*, 37-52.

Carr, D. (1997). *Stimulus equivalence, naming and contextual control: Studies with language disabled, autistic adolescents.* Unpublished Ph.D. Dissertation, University of Wales, College of Cardiff.

Carrigan, P. F., & Sidman, M. (1992). Conditional discrimination and equivalence relations: A theoretical analysis of control by negative stimuli. *Journal of the Experimental Analysis of Behavior, 58*, 183-204.

Catania, A. C. (1992). *Learning* (3rd ed.). Englewood Cliffs, NJ: Prentice-Hall.

Cumming, W. W., & Berryman, R. (1965). The complex discriminated operant: Studies of matching-to-sample and related problems. In D. I. Mostofsky (Ed.), *Stimulus generalization* (pp. 284-330). Stanford, CA: Stanford University Press.

Cohen, L. R. (1969). Generalization during acquisition, extinction, and transfer of matching with an adjustable comparison. *Journal of the Experimental Analysis of Behavior, 12*, 463-474.

Devany, J. M., Hayes, S. C., & Nelson, R. O. (1986). Equivalence class formation in language-able and language-disabled children. *Journal of the Experimental Analysis of Behavior, 46*, 243-257.

Davison, M. & Jenkins, P. E. (1985). Stimulus discriminability, contingency discriminability, and schedule performance. *Animal Learning and Behavior, 13*, 77-84.

Donahoe, J. W. & Palmer, D. C. (1994). *Learning and complex behavior.* Boston, MA. Allyn & Bacon.

Dube, W. V. (1991). Computer software for stimulus control research with Macintosh computers. *Experimental Analysis of Human Behavior Bulletin, 9*, 28-30.

Dube, W. V., & McIlvane, W. J. (1996). Some implications of a stimulus control topography analysis for emergent stimulus classes. In T. R. Zentall & P. M. Smeets (Eds.), *Stimulus class formation in humans and animals* (pp. 197-218). North Holland: Elsevier.

Dube, W. V., & McIlvane, W. J. (1997). Reinforcer frequency and restricted stimulus control. *Journal of the Experimental Analysis of Behavior, 68*, 303-316.

Dube, W. V., McIlvane, W. J., & Green, G. (1992). An analysis of generalized identity matching-to-sample test procedures. *The Psychological Record, 42*, 17-28.

Engelmann, S., & Carnine, D. (1982). *Theory of instruction: Principles and applications.* New York: Irvington.

Epstein, R. (1985). Extinction-induced resurgence: Preliminary investigations and possible applications. *The Psychological Record, 35*, 143-153.

Ferster, C. B., & Skinner, B. F. (1957). *Schedules of reinforcement.* New York: Appleton-Century-Crofts.

Fields, L., Reeve, K. F., Rosen, D., Varelas, A., Adams, B. J., Belanich, J., & Hobbie, S. A. (1997). Using the simultaneous protocol to study equivalence class formation: The facilitating effects of nodal number and size of previously established equivalence classes. *Journal of the Experimental Analysis of Behavior, 67*, 367-389.

Goldstein, H., Angelo, D., & Mousetis, L. (1987). Acquisition and extension of syntactic repertoires by severely mentally retarded youth. *Research in Development mental Disabilities, 8*, 549-574.

Golinkoff, R. M., Mervis, C. B., & Hirsh-Pasek, K. (1994). Early object labels: The case for a developmental lexical principles framework. *Journal of Child Language, 21*, 125-155.

Green, G. (1990). Differences in development of visual and auditory-visual equivalence relations. *American Journal on Mental Retardation, 95*, 260-270.

Hayes, S. C. (1991). A relational control theory of stimulus equivalence. In L. J. Hayes & P. N. Chase (Eds.), *Dialogues on verbal behavior* (pp. 19-41). Reno, NV: Context Press.

Horne, P. J., and Lowe C. F. (1996). On the origins of naming and other symbolic behavior. *Journal of the Experimental Analysis of Behavior, 65*, 185-241.

House, B. J., Brown, A. L., & Scott, M. S. (1974). Children's discrimination learning based on identity or difference. In H. W. Reese (Ed.), *Advances in child development and behavior* (Vol. 9). New York: Academic Press.

House, B. J., Hanley, M. J., & Magid, D. F. (1979). A limitation on the law of effect. *American Journal of Mental Deficiency, 84*, 132-136.

Huguenin, N. H. (1987), Assessment of attention to complex cues in young children: manipulating prior reinforcement histories of stimulus components. *Journal of Experimental Child Psychology, 44*, 283-303.

Huguenin, N. H., & Touchette, P. E. (1980). Visual attention in retarded adults: Combining stimuli which control compatible behavior. *Journal of the Experimental Analysis of Behavior, 33*, 77-86.

Kirby, K. C., & Bickel, W. K. (1988). Toward an explicit analysis of generalization: A stimulus control interpretation. *The Behavior Analyst, 11*, 115-129.

Mackay, H. A., Stromer, R., & Serna, R. W. (in press). Emergent behavior and intellectual functioning: Stimulus classes, generalization, and transfer. In S. Soraci & W. J. McIlvane (Eds.), *Perspectives on fundamental processes in intellectual functioning: Vol. 1. A survey of research approaches.* Norwood, NJ: Ablex.

McIlvane, W. J. (1992). Stimulus control analysis and nonverbal instructional methods for people with intellectual disabilities. In N. W. Bray (Ed.), *International review of research in mental retardation* (Vol. 18, pp. 55-109). San Diego: Academic Press.

McIlvane, W. J., & Cataldo, M. F. (1996). On the clinical relevance of animal models for the study of human mental retardation. *Mental Retardation and Developmental Disabilities, 2,* 188-196.

McIlvane, W. J., & Dube, W. V. (1990). Do stimulus classes exist before they are tested? *The Analysis of Verbal Behavior, 8,* 13-17.

McIlvane, W. J., & Dube, W. V. (1992). Stimulus control shaping and stimulus control topographies. *The Behavior Analyst, 15,* 89-94.

McIlvane, W. J., & Dube, W. V. (1996). Naming as a facilitator of discrimination. *Journal of the Experimental Analysis of Behavior, 65,* 267-272.

McIlvane, W. J., & Dube, W. V. (1997). Units of analysis and the environmental control of behavior. *Journal of the Experimental Analysis of Behavior, 67,* 235-239.

McIlvane, W. J., Dube, W. V., & Callahan, T. D. (1996). Attention: A behavior analytic perspective. In G. R. Lyon & N. A. Krasnegor (Eds.), *Attention, memory, and executive function* (pp. 97-117). Baltimore, MD: Brookes.

McIlvane, W. J., Dube, W. V., & Serna, R. W. (1996). Analysis of behavioral selection by consequences and its potential contributions to understanding brain-behavior relations. In K. H. Pribram & J. S. King (Eds.), *Learning as self-organization* (pp. 75-100). Mahwah, NJ: Earlbaum.

McIlvane, W. J., Kledaras, J. B., Lowry, M. W., & Stoddard, L. T. (1992). Studies of exclusion in individuals with severe mental retardation. *Research in Developmental Disabilities, 13,* 509-532.

McIlvane, W. J., Kledaras, J. B., Munson, L. C., King, K. A., de Rose, J. C., & Stoddard, L. T. (1987). Controlling relations in conditional discrimination and matching by exclusion. *Journal of the Experimental Analysis of Behavior, 48,* 187-208.

McIlvane, W. J., Kledaras, J. B., Stoddard, L. T., & Dube, W. V. (1990). Delayed sample presentations in MTS: Some possible advantages for teaching individuals with developmental limitation. *Experimental Analysis of Human Behavior Bulletin, 8,* 31-33.

Merrill, E. C. (1990). Attentional resource allocation and mental retardation. In N. W. Bray (Ed.), *International review of research in mental retardation* (Vol. 16, pp. 51-88). New York: Academic Press.

Nevin, J. A. (1992). An integrative model for the study of behavioral momentum. *Journal of the Experimental Analysis of Behavior, 57,* 301-316.

Over, R., & Over, J. (1967). Detection and recognition of mirror-image obliques by young children. *Journal of Comparative and Physiological Psychology, 64,* 467-470.

Perez-Gonzalez. L. A., & Serna, R. W. (1993). Basic stimulus control functions in the five-term contingency. *Experimental Analysis of Human Behavior Bulletin, 11,* 50-53.

Pilgrim, C., Chambers, L., & Galizio, M. (1995). Reversal of baseline relations and stimulus equivalence: II. Children. *Journal of the Experimental Analysis of Behavior, 63,* 239-254.

Pilgrim, C., & Galizio, M. (1990). Relations between baseline contingencies and equivalence probe performances. *Journal of the Experimental Analysis of Behavior, 54,* 213-224.

Posner, M. I. (1996). Attention in cognitive neuroscience: An overview. In M. S. Gazzaniga (Ed.), *The cognitive neurosciences.* (pp. 615-624). Cambridge, MA: MIT Press.

Ray, B. A. (1969). Selective attention: The effects of combining stimuli which control incompatible behavior. *Journal of the Experimental Analysis of Behavior, 12,* 539-550.

Ray, B. A., & Sidman, M. (1970). Reinforcement schedules and stimulus control. In W. N. Schoenfeld (Ed.), *The theory of reinforcement schedules* (pp. 187-214). New York. Appleton Century Crofts

Repp, A. C., Karsh, K. G., & Lenz, M. W. (1990). Discrimination training for persons with developmental disabilities: A comparison of the task demonstration model and the standard prompting hierarchy. *Journal of Applied Behavior Analysis, 23,* 43-52.

Rilling, M. (1992). An ecological approach to stimulus control and tracking. In W.K. Honig & J.G. Fetterman (Eds.), *Cognitive aspects of stimulus control* (pp. 347-366). New York: Erlbaum.

Rosch, E. (1975). Cognitive representation of semantic categories. *Journal of Experimental Psychology: General, 104,* 192-233.

Rudy, J. W. (1991). Elemental and configural associations, the hippocampus and development. *Developmental Psychobiology, 24,* 221-236.

Saunders, K. J., & Spradlin, J. E. (1990). Conditional discrimination in mentally retarded adults: The development of generalized skills. *Journal of the Experimental Analysis of Behavior, 54,* 239-250.

Saunders, R. R. & Green, G. (1992). The nonequivalence of behavioral and mathematical equivalence. *Journal of the Experimental Analysis of Behavior, 57,* 227-241.

Schusterman, R. J., & Kastak, D. (1993). A California sea lion (Zalophus Californianus) is capable of forming equivalence relations. *The Psychological Record, 43.,* 823-839.

Serna, R. W., Dube, W. V., & McIlvane, W. J. (1997). Assessing same/different judgements in individuals with severe intellectual disabilities: A status report. *Research in Developmental Disabilities, 18,* 343-368.

Serna, R. W., Wilkinson, K. M., & McIlvane, W. J. (1997). A stimulus-class analysis of complex stimulus control shaping procedures. *Proceedings of the 30th Gatlinburg Conference on Research and Theory in Mental Retardation and Developmental Disabilities,* 117.

Serna, R. W., Wilkinson, K. M., & McIlvane, W. J. (in press). Blank-comparison assessment of stimulus-stimulus relations in individuals with mental retardation. *American Journal on Mental Retardation*.

Sidman, M. (1960). *Tactics of scientific research : Evaluating experimental data in psychology*. New York: Basic Books.

Sidman, M. (1969). Generalization gradients and stimulus control in delayed matching-to-sample. *Journal of the Experimental Analysis of Behavior, 33*, 285-289.

Sidman, M. (1986). Functional analysis of emergent verbal classes. In T. Thompson & M. D. Zeiler (Eds.), *Analysis and integration of behavioral units* (pp. 213-245). Hillsdale, NJ: Erlbaum.

Sidman, M. (1994). *Equivalence relations and behavior: A research story*. Boston: Authors Cooperative.

Sidman, M., & Stoddard, L. T. (1966). Programming perception and learning for retarded children. In N. R. Ellis (Ed.), *International Review of Research in Mental Retardation* (Vol. 2, pp. 151-208). New York: Academic Press.

Skinner, B. F. (1969). *Contingencies of reinforcement: A theoretical analysis*. New York: Appleton-Century-Crofts.

Smith, A. B., Dickins, D. W., & Bentall, R. P. (1996). The role of individual stimulus names in the emergence of equivalence relations II: The effects of interfering tasks prior to and after tests for emergent relations. *The Psychological Record, 46*, 109-130.

Soraci, S. A., & Carlin, M. T. (1992). Stimulus organization and relational learning. In N. W. Bray (Ed.), *International Review of Research in Mental Retardation* (Vol. 8, pp. 29-53). San Diego, CA: Academic Press.

Stoddard, L. T., & McIlvane, W. J. (1989). Generalization after intradimensional discrimination training in 2-year-old children. *Journal of Experimental Child Psychology, 47*, 324-334.

Stoddard, L. T., & Sidman, M. (1971). The removal and restoration of stimulus control. *Journal of the Experimental Analysis of Behavior, 16*, 143-154.

Stromer, R. (1986). Control by exclusion in arbitrary matching to sample. *Analysis and Intervention in Developmental Disabilities, 6*, 59-72.

Stromer, R. (1996). On the experimental analysis of naming and the formation of stimulus classes. *Journal of the Experimental Analysis of Behavior, 65*, 250-252.

Stromer, R., McIlvane, W. J., Dube, W. V., & Mackay, H. A. (1993). Assessing control by elements of complex stimuli in delayed matching to sample. *Journal of the Experimental Analysis of Behavior, 59*, 83-102.

Stromer, R., McIlvane, W. J., & Serna, R. W. (1993). Complex stimulus control and equivalence. *The Psychological Record, 43*, 585-598.

Stromer, R., & Osborne, J. G. (1982). Control of adolescents arbitrary matching-to-sample by positive and negative stimulus relations. *Journal of the Experimental Analysis of Behavior, 37*, 329-348.

Thomas, J. R. (1969). Maintenance of behavior by conditioned reinforcement in the signaled absence of primary reinforcement. In D. Hendry (Ed.), *Conditioned Reinforcement* (pp. 77-90). Homewood, Illinois: Dorsey Press.

Thompson, T. & Lubinski, D. (1986). Units of analysis and kinetic structures of behavioral repertoires. *Journal of the Experimental Analysis of Behavior, 46*, 219-242.

Thompson, T. & Zeiler, M. D. (Eds.) (1986*). Analysis and integration of behavioral units.* Hillsdale, NJ: Erlbaum.

Touchette, P. E. (1969). Tilted lines as complex stimuli. *Journal of the Experimental Analysis of Behavior, 12*, 211-214.

Wilhelm, H., & Lovaas, O. I. (1976). Stimulus overselectivity: A common feature in autism and mental retardation. *American Journal of Mental Deficiency, 81*, 26-31.

Wilkinson, K. M., & McIlvane, W. J. (1997). Contributions of stimulus control perspectives to psycholinguistic theories of vocabulary development and delay. In L. B. Adamson & M. A. Romski (Eds.), *Research on communication and language disorders: Contributions to theories of language development* (pp. 25-48). Baltimore, MD: Paul H. Brookes.

Zeaman, D., & House, B. J. (1979). A review of attention theory. In N. R. Ellis (Ed.), *Handbook of mental deficiency, psychological theory and research* (pp. 63-120). Hillsdale, NJ: Erlbaum.

Notes

The research reported here was supported by grants from the National Institutes of Child Health and Human Development (HD25995, HD23049, HD32506, & HD33802). We thank Krista Wilkinson and Gina Green for comments on an earlier version of this manuscript. This chapter is dedicated to Larry Stoddard, teacher, colleague, and friend. Although, like Skinner, he had little use for theory, his early stimulus control work was essential in its development. We hope that our proposal will stimulate empirical research by students of behavior analysis. That would make him happy.

Correspondence may be sent to the first author at the E. K. Shriver Center, Behavioral Sciences Division, 200 Trapelo Road, Waltham, MA 02254 USA.

[1]Notably, generalized imitation has been analyzed principally in terms of ontogenic contingencies. Surprisingly, however, we are not aware of anyone who has suggested that phylogenic contingencies (cf. Skinner, 1969) might play a role. Organisms having a genetic endowment that predisposes their offspring to rapid development of generalized imitation would have a clear advantage over reproductive competitors. Organisms with the genetic predisposition to "equivalence" would be similarly selected by phylogenic contingencies.

[2] Here, SCT coherence theory makes a clear prediction. Gradual emergence will be less likely if participants are adapted to novel test displays prior to equivalence tests. Also, gradual emergence will be more likely if (1) protracted baseline training (suggesting strong SCT competition) has been required to meet baseline accuracy criterion or (2) if baseline accuracy scores are fairly low (e.g., 85%-90% correct, suggesting ongoing SCT competition).

[3] Like the SCT analysis of Ray (1969), the frequency of SCTs among the discriminative stimuli changes from zero to one per trial on a moment-by-moment basis, depending upon which conditional stimulus is present.

[4] If those relations result from extraexperimental contingencies, tracing their specific histories may be impossible experimentally. Interpretation in terms of behavioral principles may be the best we can do (Donahoe & Palmer, 1994).

[5] Pilgrim and Galizio (1995) have shown that the procedures used in their earlier study have different outcomes with young children, disrupting previously established class membership. Notably, there have been almost no good demonstrations of tight contextual control of young children's stimulus classes. This may not be a coincidence.

Chapter 6

Stimulus Equivalence and Units of Analysis

Carol Pilgrim and Mark Galizio
University of North Carolina at Wilmington

The study of equivalence today is characterized by a number of different theoretical approaches. However, no single set of experiments has provided a critical test for deciding between these positions, a circumstance that suggests a closer look at the basic assumptions of the analytic approaches may be useful. Historically, when theoretical impasses have been reached, a reconsideration of basic units sometimes proved necessary before progress was made. This chapter begins with a brief recapitulation of several sets of data that raise questions about appropriate units in the analysis of stimulus equivalence (see Pilgrim & Galizio, 1996 for a more detailed analysis). These particular data sets are of interest because they challenge assumptions about equivalence patterns as a single, necessarily cohesive or integrated behavioral unit. In each of these cases, performances indicative of the defining properties of equivalence appear either to vary independently or to participate in somewhat different functional relations.

Evidence for Independence of Equivalence Properties

Baseline reversals. One type of finding that has posed difficulties comes from studies in which baseline conditional discriminations are modified following the emergence of equivalence performances. For example, Pilgrim and Galizio (1990) taught college students baseline AB and AC conditional discriminations that resulted in performances indicative of two three-member equivalence classes (i.e., A1B1C1 and A2B2C2). A reversal of the AC conditional discrimination was then arranged in which choosing comparison stimulus C2 was reinforced given A1 as a sample stimulus, and choosing C1 was reinforced given sample stimulus A2. One possibility was that this manipulation would produce patterns consistent with a reorganization of the classes, such that A1B1C2 and A2B2C1 would be treated as equivalent. Results showed, however, that while baseline and symmetry performances were immediately controlled by the reversed contingencies, the reflexivity and transitivity performances that were tested concurrently remained consistent with the original equivalence relations.

Equivalence classes are defined by complementary patterns of responding on all tests of equivalence properties, and baseline relations are commonly held to be the basis of such performances (Sidman & Tailby, 1982). Thus, both the inconsistencies between transitivity and baseline performances found by Pilgrim and Galizio and the contrast between transitivity and symmetry test performances were unexpected in light of the prevalent conceptualizations of stimulus equivalence.

In subsequent work, the stability of transitivity patterns obtained in our 1990 study, and the dissociation between symmetry and transitivity performances, were reproduced, and the experimental designs have helped determine that these effects could not be attributed to one particular training arrangement, to class size, to the ratio of changed to unchanged baseline relations that served as the context for testing, to practice on particular probe types prior to reversal, or not in any simple way at least, to Type-R stimulus control (Pilgrim & Galizio, 1995, 1996). Further findings, from both our laboratory and others, indicate that the determinants of performances on probe trials following baseline reversals will prove to be multiple and complex (Pilgrim, Chambers & Galizio, 1995; Pilgrim & Galizio, 1996; Spradlin, Saunders & Saunders, 1992). Even so, it has now been well established that baseline, reflexivity, symmetry, and transitivity/equivalence probe patterns can become inconsistent with each other under some conditions. Any complete account of stimulus equivalence and related phenomena must be reconciled with such findings.

Dube and McIlvane (1996) have offered one account in which reversal findings such as those described above are considered in terms of conflicting stimulus-control topographies (SCTs). They suggest that symmetry probes displaying the sample/comparison combinations for which contingencies were reversed may have set the occasion for the new SCT that was established during reversal training with those stimuli, while the transitivity/equivalence probes set the occasion for old SCTs that were established prior to reversal training. Thus, patterns of performance consistent with the new baseline relations would be seen on symmetry probes, while patterns consistent with the original baseline relations persisted on transitivity/equivalence probes. Such a possibility would maintain the functional integrity of the equivalence unit by positing two competing equivalence classes under contextual control. We agree that focus on sources of stimulus control will be critical to understanding data such as these. However, if the different equivalence properties are fully and functionally integrated, something beyond this basic SCT formulation seems needed to explain why different configurations of theoretically interchangeable stimuli should occasion topographies consistent with different equivalence classes in the particular steady-state patterns that were observed. For example, additional principles seem necessary to explain why transitivity probes should come to function as a context for old equivalence classes even while performances indicative of new equivalence classes are being demonstrated concurrently on relevant baseline- and symmetry-trial types. Entertaining the possibility that the three equivalence-defining stimulus-control relations may have the capacity to function as independent units under some conditions (such as baseline reversals) also seems entirely compatible with description in terms of differing stimulus-control topographies. At issue then is the nature of the unit of stimulus control.

Delayed emergence. There are also cases in which different probe-trial types give rise to reliable performance differences even under a constant set of baseline conditions. While the comparison selections on reflexivity, symmetry, and transitivity trial types typically co-vary in non-reversal conditions, thus providing the defining evidence of equivalence, there are indications that the different tests may reveal unique response characteristics.

One example is provided by the frequently reported finding that for many subjects in equivalence experiments, performances on probe trials do not become consistent with the predicted equivalence classes without repeated probe testing (e.g., Spradlin, Cotter, & Baxley, 1973). This delayed emergence of class-consistent responding is of particular interest here because the temporal order in which class-consistent patterns emerge for different probe-trial types is predictable, with symmetry patterns emerging before transitivity or equivalence patterns (e.g., Bush, Sidman, & de Rose, 1989; Dube Green, & Serna, 1993; Fields, Adams, Verhave, & Newman, 1990; Pilgrim & Galizio, 1995), and transitivity/equivalence relations involving a small number of nodal stimuli emerging prior to those involving a greater number (e.g., Dube, et al., 1993; Fields, et al., 1990) In addition, we have seen cases in which symmetry patterns have been demonstrated repeatedly with no evidence of transitivity even after hundreds of trials of exposure to those trial types (Pilgrim & Galizio, 1996). Collectively, these data might be interpreted as indicative of differential emergence of equivalence-defining properties. Again, Dube and McIlvane (1996) have provided a compelling account of the general phenomenon of delayed emergence in terms of a decreasing frequency of competing stimulus-control topographies over repeated testing. However, their proposal may need fuller development to explain the demonstrated regularities in order of emergence across trial types (e.g., are there *a priori* reasons to expect competing SCTs to be reliably more resistant to extinction or more numerous on transitivity trials than on symmetry trials, and if so, what accounts for immediate emergence in many subjects?).

Latency data. A second measure that reveals performance differences across probe-trial types is reaction time, or latency to make a comparison choice. Across a range of training, testing, and measurement procedures, latencies to respond on trained discriminations or symmetry trials have reliably proven to be shorter than the latencies shown on transitivity and equivalence trials (Bentall, Dickins, & Fox, 1993; Spencer & Chase, 1996; Wulfert & Hayes, 1988). Latencies on equivalence probes involving few nodes have been shorter than those on probes involving many nodes (Spencer & Chase, 1996), and across studies, mean latencies on symmetry test trials have been consistently longer than those for trained relations (although these were significant only in Spencer & Chase, 1996). Although differences in reaction time have never been considered as relevant to the identification of equivalence classes, there are still reasons to expect that such differences could be important. The relation between fluency, or response speed, and the long-term maintenance of behavior established in education settings has been noted by a number of theorists (Johnson & Layng, 1992). Thus, these reaction time data might be seen as indicating that the trial types typically used to define equivalence can give rise to performances that differ in functionally significant ways.

Reinforcer estimation. Another interesting example of differences in performances across probe-trial types comes from subjects' retrospective estimates of reinforcer frequency for each of the baseline and probe-trial types presented during a typical equivalence experiment (Pilgrim & Galizio, 1996). Despite the fact that reinforcers were never provided on any probe trial, subjects often indicated substantial reinforcer probability. For present purposes, the finding of greatest interest was that the different trial types generated clearly differentiated estimates for most subjects. The estimates given for baseline trial types were significantly higher than those given for symmetry trials, which in turn generated higher estimates than transitivity/equivalence trials. Reflexivity trials were discriminated reliably; that is, estimates were at or near zero for most subjects.

Summary of the problem. Performances on the different probe types that theoretically identify a single equivalence class can participate in different functional relations, and they sometimes vary independently. These facts seem challenging for most current views of equivalence. As we have noted elsewhere (Pilgrim & Galizio, 1996), it is understood that context must determine when functions will be shared among equivalence class members (e.g., Sidman, 1994; Hayes, 1991). However, delayed emergence, latency, and reinforcer estimation all occur within a single set of stimulus conditions, thus straining a contextual control interpretation. In these cases, the defining requirements for a given equivalence relation are satisfied, yet response functions vary with probe type.

Consideration of Equivalence in Terms of Analytic Units

A fundamental characteristic of any successful experimental analysis of behavior has been the identification of "the natural lines of fracture along which behavior and environment actually break" (Skinner, 1935, p. 40). One possible interpretation of the results reviewed above is that they point to such lines of fracture. This possibility has led us to wonder whether there might be some merit, even if only heuristic, to considering the nominal properties of equivalence as independent units in their own right. Recognizing this suggestion as somewhat of a departure from several current views of equivalence, it may be useful to remember that the mathematical definition of equivalence, which has proved so useful, does not specify the make-up of the behavioral unit(s) that include the required test outcomes. With Sidman (1994, 1997), we recognize the value and generality of the mathematical definition. As Sidman has emphasized, "to adopt the mathematical definition is to take the position that behavior is included among the many real-world specifics that the abstractions of mathematical set theory encompass" (1994; p. 553). In light of the cases described above for which set theory does not provide clear predictions, a behavioral definition that viewed equivalence not as a fundamental unit but rather as a correspondence among three independent stimulus-control relations might provide for even greater generality, while maintaining the precision and the rigor of the set-theory framework. By way of example, there is the mathematical set of symmetry operations (Hargittai & Hargittai, 1995), as well as of events related by equivalence. Thus, it may be possible to extend the range of behavioral specifics encompassed by mathematical sets.

Of course, all of this would beg another critical question. The fact is that in many, perhaps most, circumstances with human subjects, patterns indicative of reflexivity, symmetry, transitivity, and their combinations *do* vary together. Why might independent stimulus-control relations show such remarkable congruence in so many contexts? Consideration of the questions and issues just outlined provide additional reason to think that progress in understanding equivalence and other related phenomena will require more concentrated attention to appropriate units of analysis, the mechanisms that coordinate them, and the mechanisms that act to maintain their individual functional integrity.

The possibility and the importance of combining more basic units into increasingly larger functional entities has been considered by behavioral theorists for some time and for a variety of issues. Especially at a theoretical or interpretive level, coordination and integration within and between behavioral units has come to carry considerable conceptual weight in operant accounts of complex human performances, particularly those that take place over time in a seemingly cohesive fashion. The operating principle in these conceptual accounts is that orderly streams of human performances are constructed of fundamental functional components, combined in various patterns of complexity.

To illustrate by way of example, in their important 1986 chapter, Lubinski and Thompson outlined a hierarchy of levels of coordination among potentially independent fundamental response units. In their system, the generic term, "response class entity", was defined as a "class of behavioral components which co-vary as a function of a class of stimulus events that regulate their probability of occurrence" (p. 276). The levels of response class entities then, included first, fundamental response classes, these being elicited, emitted, or evoked responses identified in terms of proximal controlling variables. Next there are behavioral combinations, which are composites of two or more fundamental units (as when, for example, the sight of a flashing blue light atop a patrolman's car both elicits certain visceral conditioned responses and occasions pulling over to the highway shoulder). Response families or traits are defined as "clusters of fundamental units and behavioral combinations" (p. 276), while trait-clusters involve "two or more traits that co-vary" (p. 276). The point of emphasis here is that in order to make analytic headway, it is often necessary to conceptualize even highly integrated behavioral complexes in terms of their more fundamental components.

This sort of argument seems a compelling one, and one that would appear to be consistent with the views and strategies of behavior analysis. However, a matter of some concern is that many recent theoretical discussions of equivalence have become imprecise with respect to specifying the make-up of the analytic unit under consideration, and the manner in which the unit is organized. Consider a concept that has received increasing airtime as of late - the higher-order operant. The frequency of this and other similar terms (e.g., overarching relation) suggests that many behavior analysts find it natural and appropriate to apply the concept to the consideration of equivalence phenomena and other complex behavior (e.g., Catania, 1996; Hayes, 1991; 1996; Horne & Lowe, 1993). We agree that in thinking about equivalence performances, the notion of higher-order operant classes appears to hold some conceptual appeal. However, before the descriptive value of such a classification can be adequately considered, much less the explanatory value that is sometimes implied, we also believe that certain fundamental questions must be addressed.

What exactly is a higher-order operant class?

What are we really implying with respect to behavioral units when we classify a particular pattern of behavior as higher-order? Is the analytic unit really specified by the qualifier, "higher-order"? Although a complete review of the literature on higher-order operants lies beyond the scope of this chapter, our assessment is that not quite as much is known about such relations as current use of the term would suggest.

First, with respect to the specification of analytic units, we would point out that while "higher-order" carries important implications about certain features of a class (e.g., its breadth), the term itself connotes nothing precise about the nature of the behavior-environment relation at issue. Consider this definition from Catania's (1992) *Learning* text (notable in that it is the only definition of the term found among current introductory behavior-analysis textbooks), where the issue has perhaps received its fullest treatment at the generic level:

"Higher-order class of behavior: A class that includes within it other classes that can themselves function as operant classes. Control by the contingencies arranged for the higher-order class rather than for component classes defines these classes." (1992, p. 377).

A clear definition is a critical first step in the analysis of a problem of this sort, but consider whether a higher-order class defined in this way can carry either the descriptive precision or the explanatory load that is often asked of it. Note that nothing about the analytic unit is specified other than its operant basis, and while this is clearly an essential beginning, it is hardly a limiting case. Given this definition it is not clear how a higher-order operant would differ from any other operant class. Indeed, it might be argued that the distinction here between higher-order and basic operants is largely a matter of degree. Given that a range of topographies is always implied with an operant class, it is unclear what the designation of higher-order adds. Further, defining higher-order operants in terms of general relations (e.g., "the class is defined not by any particular stimuli or responses, but rather by relations that include those stimuli and responses as special cases"; Catania, 1992, p. 148) could also be seen as a matter of degree given the generic nature of stimuli and responses (Skinner, 1935). Still, it is probably this general, relational feature that is responsible for the greatest interest in higher-order operants in recent years, because it is here that we most clearly see opportunity for generativity; that is, novel instances of a behavioral relation prior to their explicit reinforcement.

Questions about the appropriate analysis of such operant classes become more apparent as one considers the kinds of performances that have been characterized as higher-order. Even a brief listing of such characterizations reveals considerable diversity with respect to the likely nature of the behavioral units involved. The list includes attention-getting, response novelty and variability, generalized imitation, instruction-following or rule-governed behavior, naming, tacting, manding, learning set, generalized identity or oddity matching, relational framing, and of course, stimulus equivalence, to name just a few. One question is whether current definitions capture the sorts of properties that are important for distinguishing all of these classes similarly as higher-order classes.

Catania (1992) notes that "common consequences are the glue that holds together higher-order classes of behavior" (p. 127). But in considering the examples listed above, the likely reinforcers seem as "generalized" as the class itself. Consider generalized imitation, for example. Imitating a model opening a cookie jar yields one reinforcer class, while imitating a model running in a video yields reinforcers of a very different kind. Imitating the dialect of a given geographic locale has consequences that are presumably social in nature, and imitating in some circumstances may help in avoiding contact with aversive stimuli. It seems to us that focus on common consequences is not sufficient to guide our understanding of higher-order classes. And if "common consequences" can include any form of reinforcement, what would be basis for distinct classes?

Complex Behavior and Analytic Units

Where some theorists have recommended a more exclusive focus on response rather than stimulus classes (Hayes, 1996; Hayes & Barnes, 1997), concerns like those outlined above suggest that restricted emphasis of response-consequence relations may prove insufficient to the task at hand. In contrast, issues of stimulus control seem to us to deserve even greater attention in the analysis of complex relational response patterns. How then might we return focus to basic behavioral units that emphasize stimulus-control dimensions? In his classic treatment, Sidman (1986) presents an elegant exposition of basic operant units as they increase systematically in size and complexity. In the progression from two- to five-term contingencies, a powerful case is made for the importance of delineating each element of the analytic unit and the relations between them. No mention of higher-order operants is made in this chapter, but the outline Sidman provided there may prove as useful for consideration of performances designated higher-order as it has been for their more basic counterparts. Consider the systematization added to the diverse array of earlier examples when considered in this framework.

Two-term units. The 2-term contingency might include examples such as attention-getting behavior, studying, or relaxing. Response novelty (e.g., Pryor, Haag, & O'Reilly, 1969) and response variability (e.g., Neuringer, 1986; Page & Neuringer, 1985) provide other interesting examples. In each of these cases the contingencies are not defined in terms of antecedent stimuli, but rather in terms of a class of responses with multiple subclasses and a class of reinforcers (Catania, 1996). Response novelty and variability are particularly interesting examples because, as Catania (1992) has pointed out, novelty or variability cannot be a property of an individual response. In these cases, a particular response instance can be defined as a member of the class only by virtue of its relation to previous responding; thus, a relation between separate instances of responding is critical to the definition of the class. Conversely, it might be argued that this dependence upon earlier responses necessarily reveals novelty as an example of a three-term contingency, which would simply bump the example to the next analytic unit. And consider that even with basic operant classes, each new instance of the class can be classified as a member only by virtue of its relation to previously reinforced responses or to previous (i.e., baseline) response distributions.

Three-term units. The 3-term contingency could include examples such as an echoic repertoire, tacting, generalized imitating, and instruction following (in simpler cases; for example, instructions can certainly be made more complex as can each of the other examples). These examples are, of course, distinguished from two-term units by the necessary inclusion of a discriminative stimulus in the contingency specification. They have been considered higher order because even novel instances of the antecedent stimulus class (for example, novel instructions or novel modeled actions) may occasion appropriately corresponding responses, this presumably due to a history of reinforcement for correspondences of a similar nature.

Another important point is that the 3-term contingency should allow for the selection of particular higher-order 2-term units from the subject's repertoire. Thus, the probability of studying versus relaxing might be influenced by announcing an exam. In so doing, a change in an entire cluster of responses - all those that make up and co-vary with studying - would be produced.

Four-term units. The 4-term contingency might add examples of generalized identity matching or generalized oddity. These cases are defined in terms of conditional relations between a sample stimulus, a comparison stimulus, a selection response, and a reinforcement opportunity. The classes are said to be generalized when novel stimuli are matched, or not, even prior to reinforcement for those particular matches. Each matching instance could stand as a 4-term conditional relation in its own right; the consistency of the general identity or oddity relation across multiple instances has been seen as constituting the higher order of the operant class.

Further, as was the case at the previous level, 4-term contingencies should allow for the selection of complex 3-term units from an individual's repertoire. By way of example, consider the adolescent's quandary with respect to parental cues: "Should I do what they say (i.e., instruction following), or what they do (i.e., generalized imitation)?" One might guess that the "appropriate" generalized 3-term unit will be determined by other environmental factors. And for the sake of the adolescent in question, one can also hope that in many situations, both 3-term classes will be appropriate. In this way it might be possible for a given environmental context to occasion multiple generalized classes, perhaps not unlike the clusters or response families described by Lubinski and Thompson (1986).

Now, in keeping with some of our earlier speculations about the independence of equivalence-defining components, we might consider here the possibility that separate classes of reflexivity, symmetry, and transitivity also fit into this category. Four-term relations continue to define the class (that is, sample stimulus, comparison stimulus, selection response, and reinforcement opportunity), as does the demonstration of novel instances of the relation prior to the delivery of reinforcement for those particular relations. And like the case of response novelty, symmetry or transitivity cannot be characteristics of an individual conditional relation. The class can only be defined in terms of prior response relations. (As before, if this necessitates the addition of a term, these classes should be moved along to the next analytic unit.)

Of course, if we grant the possibility that reflexivity, symmetry, and transitivity might indeed function as independent 4-term operants, the question remains regarding the frequent co-occurrence of these classes. Fortunately, there are additional levels of analytic units that may provide some assistance. At this point then, consider the possibility that particular clusters of 4-term units may be selected in a 5-term contingency. By this argument, the performance complex known as stimulus equivalence would suggest a context, or fifth term, effective in selecting the units of reflexivity, symmetry, and transitivity.

Given what we know about equivalence patterns, it seems likely that there are a number of such contexts. At the same time, different clusters of 4-term units may be occasioned in other contexts. Table 1 is taken from Sidman (1990), who presented these examples in support of his argument that equivalence is not a necessary logical outcome of conditional stimulus relations. In doing so, he also provided a very effective representation of the fact that the appropriate combination of properties will vary considerably depending on the particular case at hand. In many ways, this would appear to be consistent with the possibility that different combinations or clusters of component units (i.e., reflexivity, symmetry, and transitivity) might co-vary in any particular context.

At this point it seems important to issue a caveat, and make clear that the point of our argument here is not to champion the characterization of any particular example at any particular level of analytic unit. A number of questions could be asked of many, perhaps most, of the examples presented here. Our hope is that careful consideration of exactly these sorts of questions may better prepare us to identify sources of control and relevant relations in the attempt to analyze equivalence patterns and other complex performances.

So, at this point, what have we done? We have simply suggested a framework (and not an original one at that) that we think may prove useful in considering complex performances by focusing on analytic units. We clearly *have not* provided anything approximating an explanation for the selection of compounds that has been proposed at different analytic levels. Instead, we have emphasized that with this framework comes a great many questions, particularly with respect to the nature of

Table 1. Defining Properties of Equivalence in Various Relations
(after Sidman, 1990)

Relation	Reflexivity	Symmetry	Transitivity
Parallel To	+	+	+
Brother Of	X	X	+
Greater Than	X	X	+
Greater Than or Equal To	+	X	+
Lives Next To	X	+	X
Correlated With	+	X	X
Half Of	X	X	X

units involved. However, we also believe that empirical attention to these questions will comprise a profitable research agenda - even if the framework proves incomplete or incorrect regarding equivalence performances. Some of the more pressing issues to be addressed are as follows.

Basis for Creation of Higher-order Relations

One of the issues that we see as key to the understanding of equivalence performances was described well by Zeiler (1986) with respect to behavioral compounds more generally. In Thompson and Zeiler's *Analysis and Integration of Behavioral Units*, Zeiler wrote that, "if units are constituents of the whole, a complete picture requires not only unit specification, but also explication of the integration rules" (p. 2; 1986). For present purposes, the question is how functionally independent components might become organized or coordinated, how they might come to co-vary. Clearly this is not a new question (e.g., Lashley, 1951), but answers are still far from clear. With respect to the organization of complex performances, some of the most relevant suggestions regarding mechanisms for formation have included behavioral genetic endowment (e.g., Lubinski & Thompson, 1986), common contingencies (e.g., Catania, 1992; 1996), and the number of individual elements two response classes share (where the greater the number of shared elements, the more likely they will combine to form a larger cluster, even though some members may be nonoverlapping; Lubinski & Thompson, 1986)

While direct tests of the first possibility are tricky, the primary empirical approach relating the second and third suggestions to the creation of larger, or higher-order classes could be described as "exemplar training". When such training is said to be successful, correct responses to multiple examples of a given relation (e.g., different modeled behaviors to be imitated, or identity matching with various stimuli) are directly trained, with the result that correct responses to novel instances of the relation are also exhibited, prior to or in the absence of explicit reinforcement for those new instances. Thus, common contingencies are arranged across exemplars, and each potentially independent exemplar also has a relation in common with every other exemplar (e.g., corresponding modeled and imitative topographies, or identity in these two cases).

Fascinating as it is, and as useful as it has proved in behavioral applications, we have been able to find relatively little basic experimental analysis identifying the determinants of the effectiveness of exemplar training. The process underlying the extension to new examples has been described variously as generalization, as abstraction, and as emergence. More recently, Dube and McIlvane (1996) have suggested an interpretation of exemplar training in terms of its role in extinguishing stimulus-control topographies that could compete with the experimenter's target. This more molecular approach to understanding the mechanism behind abstraction bears considerable promise, and is deserving of empirical attention. Still, the range in effectiveness of exemplar training, particularly in basic studies with nonhuman subjects, implies that such procedures may not yet be fully understood. By way of example, consider the difficulty that has been encountered historically in generating generalized identity match-to-sample performances with non-human subjects (e.g., Carter & Werner, 1978; but also note exceptions like that of Schusterman & Kastak, 1993).

Additional concerns have been voiced regarding the mechanisms by which exemplar training might play a role in generating generalized arbitrary relations. As Sidman puts it, "A linguistically naive organism's abstraction of commonalities from a set of exemplars that share no physical feature requires more of an explanation than just a history of experience. Because the exemplars would possess no measurable feature in common, it is not at all evident that one might be able to generalize an arbitrary relation solely from exemplars. What aspect of several examples of symmetric event-name relations would permit a new example to be recognized or produced?" (p. 365, 1994). While at one level, the physical dimensions of stimulus location (i.e., for sample versus comparison) or temporal order of presentation seem just as sound a basis for generalizing symmetry as do the physical dimensions relevant to larger than, or brighter than, that Sidman and others appear comfortable with, the question of how subjects come to respond to novel arbitrary stimuli requires an answer that might again direct our attention to the issue of behavioral units. Given two completely physically dissimilar or arbitrary events, and even given that a conditional relation has been established between them, some other stimulus or context seems critical for determining the nature of the appropriate relation between the two. This emphasis on hierarchical stimulus control might be contrasted with an explanation that appeals exclusively to the operant of relating (Hayes, Gifford, & Wilson, 1996; Hayes & Barnes, 1997). Hayes argues that relational responding is a basic process based on observations of relational learning across different species (Reese, 1968), but not all relations have been observed in all species, and the sources of control by stimulus relations remain enigmatic even after years of research (Reese, 1968; Zentall & Smeets, 1996).

Implications for Flexibility of Higher-Order Relations

In addition to questions about the creation of larger classes of behavior, or integration rules, there are also important questions concerning the implications of higher-order organization for modification or flexibility of the class (disintegration rules?). There is a body of literature that seems interesting to consider in this context (e.g., that on stimulus control of instruction-following), but the determinants of when and how larger classes are partitioned are still unclear. Several theorists have made interesting suggestions along this line. Interestingly also, not all of the suggestions seem consistent.

For example, in his discussion of higher-order operants, Catania (1992) has emphasized that when contingencies for the class as a whole conflict with those for a particular component(s) of the class, the class contingencies may override the component contingencies. Thus, extinction procedures for some subset of a generalized class may have no effects on the probability of any member, as long as other class components continue to result in reinforcement. Further, the more overlapping or interlocking the components, the greater the stability of the class as a whole (Catania, 1996). In this way, component classes may be said to be "insensitive" to their individual consequences. Here then, the designation of the larger unit as a class implies that it will function in the same way as other, more fundamental classes. The probability of all members should be affected similarly given any particular manipulation.

In interesting contrast to these points, some theorists have argued that we need not expect larger functional units to be regulated by the same mechanisms that influence small or fundamental units. Lubinski and Thompson (1986) have pointed out examples such as behavioral contrast and symptom substitution to illustrate that a given contingency manipulation may affect components of a larger class in many different ways, decreasing some, increasing others, and leaving still others unchanged (see also Baer, 1982). Then add to this perspective the fact that we know very little about how, or when, differential contingencies separate components of larger units into distinct classes, although surely this occurs. Children learn fairly early which instructions to follow and which models to imitate, for example, and instruction following has been brought under stimulus control in the laboratory (e.g., Galizio, 1979). We wonder how once being part of a large class effects the integrity of individual components, and how removing components affects the integrity of the rest of the larger class. If interlocking or overlapping components are important, will "nonoverlapping" members show greater resistance to change than overlapping members? Is it easier to bring completely distinct classes under discriminative control than to do so with same-class members? Other things being equal, will punishment influence an isolated class more quickly than a larger class component? The laws describing the modification of complex operants and their components may be particularly relevant to an understanding of human perfor-mances. We have much work before us.

Summary

The emphasis of this paper has been that identification of appropriate analytic units may be critical to our increased understanding of complex, derived relational responding. We believe that a careful consideration of levels of stimulus control is called for. With respect to the different theoretical positions on equivalence, we remain agnostic. In our eyes, the data don't yet seem to compel adoption of any one particular position. Until they do, it should behoove us to consider the full range of possibilities that are consistent with the facts as we know them. A corollary of this stance is that given the unsure nature of the higher-order operant, we must be wary of accounts that grant such a unit an explanatory role. In short, we see so-called higher-order operants as an important target for exploration, rather than as an explanation. Following from the framework outlined here, it may be that even if the sorts of questions raised about higher-order operants can be answered, the concept will provide only a partial solution to understanding equivalence and other complex performances. Note that in the one possible scenario considered here, the equiva-lence complex is based on simultaneous contextual integration of three otherwise independent generalized relations. Perhaps it will come as no surprise if this sort of multiple determination proves to be one of the defining features of symbolic stimulus control (Skinner, 1957).

References

Baer, D. M. (1982). The imposition of structure on behavior and the demolition of behavioral structures. In D. J. Bernstein (Ed.), *Response structure and organization* (pp. 217-254). Lincoln, Nebraska: University of Nebraska Press.

Bentall, R. P., Dickins, D. W., & Fox, S. R. A. (1993). Naming and equivalence: Response latencies for emergent relations. *The Quarterly Journal of Experimental Psychology, 46B,* 187-214.

Bush, K. M., Sidman, M., & de Rose, T. (1989). Contextual control of emergent equivalence relations. *Journal of the Experimental Analysis of Behavior, 51,* 29-45.

Carter, D. E., & Werner, T. J. (1978). Complex learning and information processing by pigeons: A critical analysis. *Journal of the Experimental Analysis of Behavior, 29,* 565-601.

Catania, A. C. (1992). *Learning,* 3rd Edition. Englewood Cliffs, NJ: Prentice Hall, Inc.

Catania, A. C. (1996). On the origins of behavior structure. In T. R. Zentall, & P. M. Smeets (Eds.), *Stimulus class formation in humans and animals* (pp. 3-12). Amsterdam, The Netherlands: Elsevier Science B. V.

Dube, W. V., Green, G., & Serna, R. W. (1993). Auditory successive conditional discrimination and auditory stimulus equivalence classes. *Journal of the Experi-mental Analysis of Behavior, 59,* 103-114.

Dube, W. V., & McIlvane, W. J. (1996). Some implications of a stimulus control topography analysis for emergent behavior and stimulus classes. In T. R. Zentall, & P. M. Smeets (Eds.), *Stimulus class formation in humans and animals* (pp. 197-218). Amsterdam, The Netherlands: Elsevier Science B.V.

Fields, L., Adams, B. J., Verhave, T., & Newman, S. (1990). The effects of nodality on the formation of equivalence classes. *Journal of the Experimental Analysis of Behavior, 53,* 345-358.

Galizio, M. (1979). Contingency-shaped and rule-governed behavior: Instructional control of human loss avoidance. *Journal of the Experimental Analysis of Behavior, 31,* 53-70.

Hargittai, I., & Hargittai, M. (1995). *Symmetry through the eyes of a chemist,* 2nd Edition. New York, NY: Plenum Press.

Hayes, S. C. (1991). A relational control theory of stimulus equivalence. In L. J. Hayes & P. N. Chase (Eds.), *Dialogues on verbal behavior* (pp. 19-40). Reno, NV: Context Press.

Hayes, S. C., (1996). Developing a theory of derived stimulus relations. *Journal of the Experimental Analysis of Behavior, 65,* 309-311.

Hayes, S. C., & Barnes, D. (1997). Analyzing derived stimulus relations requires more than the concept of stimulus classes. *Journal of the Experimental Analysis of Behavior, 68,* 235-244.

Hayes, S. C., Gifford, E. V., & Wilson, K. G. (1996). Stimulus classes and stimulus relations: Arbitrarily applicable relational responding as an operant. In Zentall, T.R., & Smeets, P.M. (Eds.), *Stimulus class formation in humans and animals* (pp. 279-299). Amsterdam, The Netherlands: Elsevier Science B.V.

Horne, P. J., & Lowe, C. F. (1996). On the origins of naming and other symbolic behavior. *Journal of the Experimental Analysis of Behavior, 65,* 185-241.

Johnson, K. R., & Layng, T. V. J. (1992). Breaking the structuralist barrier: Literacy and numeracy with fluency. *American Psychologist, 47,* 1475-1490.

Lashley, K. S. (1951). The problem of serial order in behavior. In L. A. Jeffress (Ed.), *Cerebral mechanisms in behavior* (pp. 112-146). New York: Wiley.

Lubinski, D., & Thompson, T. (1986). Functional units of human behavior and their integration: A dispositional analysis. In T. Thompson, & M. D. Zeiler (Eds.), *Analysis and integration of behavioral units* (pp. 275-314). Hillsdale, NJ: Erlbaum Associates.

Neuringer, A. (1986). Can people behave randomly?: The role of feedback. *Journal of Experimental Psychology: General, 115,* 62-75.

Page, S., & Neuringer, A. (1985). Variability is an operant. *Journal of Experimental Psychology: Animal Behavior Processes, 11,* 429-452.

Pilgrim, C., Chambers, L., & Galizio, M. (1995). Reversal of baseline relations and stimulus equivalence: II. Children. *Journal of the Experimental Analysis of Behavior, 63,* 239-254.

Pilgrim, C., & Galizio, M. (1996). Stimulus equivalence: A class of correlations, or a correlation of classes? In T. R. Zentall, & P. M. Smeets (Eds.), *Stimulus class formation in humans and animals* (pp. 173-195). Amsterdam, The Netherlands: Elsevier Science B.V.

Pilgrim, C., & Galizio, M. (1995). Reversal of baseline relations and stimulus equivalence: I. Adults. *Journal of the Experimental Analysis of Behavior, 63*, 225-238.

Pilgrim, C., & Galizio, M. (1990). Relations between baseline contingencies and equivalence probe performances. *Journal of the Experimental Analysis of Behavior, 54*, 213-224.

Pryor, K. W., Haag, R., & O'Reilly, J. (1969). The creative porpoise: Training for novel behavior. *Journal of the Experimental Analysis of Behavior, 12*, 653-661.

Reese, H. W. (1968). *The perception of stimulus relations: Discrimination learning and transposition.* New York: Academic Press.

Schusterman, R. J., & Kastak, D. A. (1993). A California sea lion (Zalophus californianus) is capable of forming equivalence relations. *The Psychological Record, 43*, 823-839.

Sidman, M. (1986). Functional analysis of emergent verbal classes. In T. Thompson, & M. D. Zeiler (Eds.), *Analysis and integration of behavioral units* (pp. 213-245). Hillsdale, NJ: Erlbaum Associates.

Sidman, M. (1990). Equivalence relations: Where do they come? In D.E. Blackman & H. Lejeune (Eds.), *Behaviour analysis in theory and practice: Contributions and controversies* (pp. 93-114). Hillsdale, NJ: Erlbaum.

Sidman, M. (1994). *Equivalence relations and behavior: A research story.* Boston, MA: Authors Cooperative, Inc.

Sidman, M. (1997). Equivalence: A theoretical or a descriptive model? *Mexican Journal of Behavior Analysis, 23*, 125-145.

Sidman, M., & Tailby, W. (1982). Conditional discrimination vs. matching to sample: An expansion of the testing paradigm. *Journal of the Experimental Analysis of Behavior, 37*, 5-22.

Skinner, B. F. (1935). The generic nature of the concepts of stimulus and response. *Journal of General Psychology, 12*, 40-65.

Skinner, B. F. (1957). *Verbal behavior.* New York: Appleton-Century-Crofts.

Spencer, T., & Chase, P. (1996). Speed analysis of stimulus equivalence. *Journal of the Experimental Analysis of Behavior, 65*, 643-659.

Spradlin, J. E., Cotter, V. W., & Baxley, N. (1973). Establishing a conditional discrimination without direct training: A study of transfer with retarded adolescents. *American Journal of Mental Deficiency, 77*, 556-566.

Spradlin, J. E., Saunders, K. J., & Saunders, R. R. (1992). The stability of equivalence classes. In S.C. Hayes & L. J. Hayes (Eds.), *Understanding verbal relations* (pp. 29-42). Reno, NV: Context Press.

Wulfert, E., & Hayes, S. C. (1988). Transfer of a conditioned ordering response through conditional equivalence classes. *Journal of the Experimental Analysis of Behavior, 50*, 125-144.

Zeiler, M. D. (1986). Behavioral units: A historical introduction. In T. Thompson, & M. D. Zeiler (Eds.), *Analysis and integration of behavioral units* (pp. 1-12). Hillsdale, NJ: Erlbaum Associates.

Zentall, T. R., & Smeets, P. M. (Eds.). (1996). *Stimulus class formation in humans and animals.* Amsterdam, The Netherlands: Elsevier Science B.V.

Notes

Address correspondence to: Carol Pilgrim, Ph.D., Department of Psychology, UNC at Wilmington, Wilmington, NC 28403, USA, Telephone: 910-962-3288, Electronic mail: *pilgrimc@uncwil.edu*

Chapter 7

Putting the Naming Account to the Test: Preview of an Experimental Program.

Pauline J. Horne and C. Fergus Lowe
School of Psychology, University of Wales, Bangor

"It is the mother's language, internalized by the child, that allows it to move from sensation to 'sense', to ascend from a perceptual into a conceptual world." Sacks, (1989, p. 63, after Vygotsky, 1934/1987)

Mead (1934) and Vygotsky (1934/1987) both believed that language is learned or "internalized" by the child during social interaction between child and caregiver. Neither of them, however, explained exactly how. Skinner's explanation, presented in considerable detail in *Verbal Behavior* (1957), was based on the basic principles of reinforcement extrapolated from animal behavior. In his well-known review of that account, Chomsky (1959) objected that given that Skinner was not able to supply any empirical evidence as to the specific role of reinforcement in bringing about and maintaining verbal behavior, it was impossible to say whether reinforcement was a necessary condition for language learning or not. He thought Skinner offered no satisfactory explanation for the "generativity" of language and believed that until more were known about the specific character of verbal behavior a theoretical inquiry into its causation was premature. Though some behavior analysts have since challenged Chomsky's critique (Andresen, 1990; Czubaroff, 1988; Kany & Waller, 1995; Knapp, 1990; MacCorquodale, 1970; Richelle, 1993; Stemmer, 1990) and have defended Skinner's thesis, many psychologists still regard Chomsky's arguments as well-founded.

Chomsky's critique reflected his own interest in the highly developed verbal behavior that occurs in late childhood and adulthood. But language at this stage is very complex and many would argue that the pertinent reinforcers are all too often so subtle as to be essentially unidentifiable and so unmanipulable (and see Palmer, 1996; Vaughan & Michael, 1982). Furthermore, as Vygotsky (1987, pp. 58-75) has so cogently argued, observations of already fully-formed or "fossilized" behaviors may little avail understanding of the genesis of those behaviors. For these reasons, it is our view that the validity of Skinner's analysis needs to be considered within the context of a functional analysis of the development of verbal behavior from early infancy onwards. And systematic investigation of Skinner's account is certainly warranted, for although behavior analysts have had successes within applied linguistic domains, for example, in remedying language delay in humans with a variety of sensory impairments, (Lowenkron, 1988; Sundberg & Sundberg, 1990) no one has yet demonstrated experimentally the precise role of reinforcement in human language learning. Even among behavior analysts, Skinner's account has attracted criticism for its failure to provide a satisfactory definition either of "verbal behavior" itself or of "rule-governed behavior" - the key concepts that are central not just to behavior analytic theory but also to applied work with humans in clinical and other settings (see Hayes & Hayes, 1989; 1992; Sidman, 1990). Critics from this quarter view Skinner's failure to address the issue of generativity - how it is that new behavior "emerges" without reinforcement - as a fundamental deficiency in his account.

In the present paper, we consider why and how Skinner's theory needs to be modified in order to provide a convincing account of language acquisition. We also examine how language effects what Vygotsky argued is its supreme achievement - the transition that humans make from relating to particular objects in the world to a "generalized reflection of reality" in which, via naming, they come to categorize their environment, ever afterwards responding to those categorizations as much as to the world itself. We expand on elements of the account of verbal behavior that we have presented elsewhere (Horne & Lowe, 1996; 1997; Lowe & Horne, 1996) and we outline here for the first time a number of studies which, as part of an ongoing research program, employ novel experimental procedures to investigate how language is learned and comes to govern other behavior. The first study we describe is an investigation of the roles of listener and echoic relations in establishing the child's first name relations. The remaining studies investigate how training young children to name physically different stimuli generates unified categories or concepts and, consequently, a range of "emergent" behavior.

Skinner's Account

Skinner's theoretical analysis of the origins of verbal behavior was based upon the three-term contingency: discriminative stimulus, response, and reinforcer. Each of the verbal relations he described takes the form of a particular correspondence (which is arbitrary but conventional within a given verbal community) between either the discriminative stimulus and response (e.g., as in the *tact* and *echoic* relations), or the response and the reinforcer (as in the *mand* relation). A *tact* relation is said to obtain when, for example, a child says "apple" upon seeing an apple; the *echoic* relation when the child says, for example, "apple" upon hearing the spoken word /*apple*/; these basic relations are maintained by a variety of social and nonsocial reinforcers. Only in the case of the *mand* is there a tightly specified relation between the form of the response and the reinforcer that maintains it. Thus, for example, bread, and not some other item, such as water, must follow the mand response "bread" if the latter is to be reinforced. In all of these "verbal" relations, the response may occur in any modality (e.g., vocal or gestural), as accords with the conventions of the members of the relevant verbal community.

Entirely excluded from Skinner's (1957) taxonomy of basic verbal relations is the listener relation. Given that his definition of verbal behavior is "behavior reinforced through the mediation of other persons in accordance with the practices of the verbal community", this is surprising. When, as in this example of a typical listener relation, a child on hearing /look at the cat/ orients towards a cat, quite apart from any reinforcing effects of the sight of the cat itself, her listener response will usually be socially reinforced by other people voicing praise such as "yes, that's the cat!" According to Skinner, listener relations include both respondent and operant behavior. Thus an auditory stimulus (e.g., /apple/) can elicit Pavlovian responses such as salivation, seeing or hearing (Skinner, 1953, p. 266) and can also evoke operant responding such as visual orienting and reaching towards a particular stimulus or the performance of particular actions (e.g., running in response to /run!/). Just as is true of the relations he recognises as "verbal", however, the correspondence between the listener stimulus and the response it evokes is arbitrary and in accord with the conventions of the verbal community and, certainly, listener relations are maintained by reinforcers mediated by other persons. Nevertheless, as late as 1989, Skinner reaffirmed his view that the listener relation is not verbal "unless the listener is also to some extent speaking" (p. 90).

Another central feature of Skinner's taxonomy is that the basic verbal relations are functionally independent. Thus, teaching a child to say "cat" when she hears /cat/, as in an echoic relation, does not, according to his account, result in the emergence of the child saying "cat" when she next encounters a cat, as in a tact relation. Further, because these basic, functionally-independent, verbal relations are merely variations of the three-term contingency (discriminative stimulus, response and reinforcer), Skinner realised that, for his account to be internally consistent, he could no more attribute the properties of reference and representation to the tact relation than to any other operant relation; a child's saying "cat" upon seeing a cat is no different in status from a pigeon's pecking on a red response key. The response "cat" cannot be said to "mean", "refer to", or "represent" the cat any more than the peck can be said to "mean", "refer to", or "represent" the color red. At this basic level of Skinner's analysis there is, in other words, no functional relation that might be said to distinguish the behavior of humans from that of animals.

A New Theory of Verbal Behavior

In a recent theoretical paper (Horne & Lowe, 1996), we proposed that a "symbolic" relation, that is, a relation that does embody reference, representation and meaning, could however be developed from Skinner's framework if it were recognized that even during the early stages of verbal development, speakers can *listen to* their own speech, and so speak with understanding. We termed this relation *naming*. In our view, naming is essentially a circular relation between classes of objects and events and the verbal responses they occasion. Thus, when a child sees a chair and says "chair", the sound /chair/ is produced, listening to which returns (or refers) the child to seeing the particular chair and the class of "chairs" in general. This cycle of speaking a name that refers the speaker back to the named class of objects or events can continue indefinitely and it enables the speaker to "hold the object in consciousness" for just as long as the cycle continues. A name is thus far more than a mere audible response that dies on the air as it is uttered. We will argue that naming, including the "autoclitic" achievement of naming our naming (Horne & Lowe, 1997), confers the *generativity* that is characteristic of human language but that Chomsky and his successors failed to find in Skinner's *Verbal Behavior* (1957). As a generalizing and behavior-governing relation, we propose that naming, as we define it, also solves the conceptual riddle of what "rule-governed behavior" is, how it is learned, and how it establishes a distinctively human form of behavioral organization.

Listener Relations

In the normal course of human development, the child learns a repertoire of listener relations long before she learns to speak. Figure 1 (left) shows an example of a listener relation learned early in development: Upon hearing */where's shoe?/* , the child orients to a shoe. The ground work for the establishment of such a listener relation will have occurred earlier. The caregiver may have previously cued the child to look at the shoe by, for example, playfully putting it on and pulling it off the child's foot, and so on. Play sequences of this kind ensure that the child's attending to shoes is reinforced and that shoes become conditioned reinforcers. Next, in give-and-take games, the child may have learned to reach for the shoe when her caregiver shows it to her and praises her for doing so. These two steps will have established an initial relation between the reinforcers (i.e. shoes and social praise) and the behaviors destined to become listener responses. The caregiver may then place the shoe just out of reach and say, "where's the shoe?" in a voice that is likely to show the exaggerated prosody and high pitch universally characteristic of "parentese" (Fernald, 1992; Kuhl et al., 1997; Snow, 1977). If the child, upon hearing */where's shoe?/*, reaches for the shoe, she is praised and this early example of the listener relation is strengthened. If, on the other hand, the child fails to respond, the caregiver may point to the shoe, or prompt the child to reach for it. Such "scaffolding" (Bruner, 1977) or "shaping" behaviors on the caregiver's part will then be gradually faded out to the point at which the child can respond correctly to */where's shoe?/* on her own.

The listener relation depicted in Figure 1 may initially be context-bound, with listener responding tending to be directed only towards a particular object in response to a particular speaker in a particular setting. In the course, however, of repetitions of play sequences such as we describe above, in which a variety of caregivers present the discriminative stimulus for a particular listener behavior in an increasing variety of settings, control of irrelevant stimulus accompaniments to the listener stimulus will tend to diminish. At the same time, the generality of objects to which the child will respond when she hears */shoe/* will extend as caregivers reinforce the child's selecting any of a widening variety of shoes. The listener relation that results is depicted in Figure 1 (right): Upon hearing */shoe/* , the child scans her environment in order to orient to not just one, but possibly several shoes. According to Mead (1934), the child also, in response to the listener stimulus */shoe/*, may make preparatory, shoe-related responses irrespective of whether there are any shoes in her environment. She might also, in these same circumstances, engage in conditioned seeing of shoes (Skinner, 1953). That is, in the course of learning listener relations,

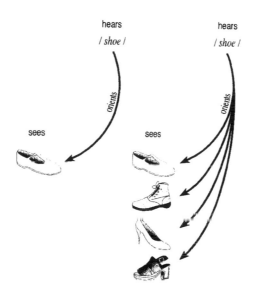

*Figure 1: In the above example of a listener relation, the child learns when she hears /
shoe?/ to orient not just to one particular shoe (left display) but to a class of objects which
her verbal community names "shoe" (right display). Though not shown here, this behavior
is reinforced by praise from caregivers.*

the child begins her progression from, in Vygotsky's terms, a "perceptual" to a
"conceptual" world. Increasingly, upon hearing a listener discriminative stimulus,
she orients to what is a culturally-specified set of diverse objects that will become ever
wider as she learns; because the verbal community deems that all the varied objects
within such a class share one or more common functions, the same listener stimulus
(e.g., /*shoe*/) is common to them all.

Study 1: A Longitudinal Investigation of Listener and Echoic Relations as Determinants of Naming

As far as we are aware, there are no published operant studies of human infants'
learning of listener relations. Our own research, conducted in collaboration with
Margaret Bell, set out to make good this deficit. In Study 1, 5 infants aged between
9.5 months and 16 months were taught three listener relations. The infants were
presented with three small and previously unfamiliar plastic objects and, as listener
stimuli, three unfamiliar auditory stimuli (e.g., /*pab*/, /*gek*/, /*dut*/); each listener
stimulus was assigned to correspond with one of the three objects. In Condition 1,
each object was presented accompanied by its corresponding listener stimulus (i.e.,
by the experimenter saying, for example, "pab, pab, it's a pab") on 27 separate

occasions. In Condition 2 all three objects were presented together in each trial and the experimenter asked the child, "where's pab?" (or alternatively, "where's gek?" or "where's dut?"). If, having heard the auditory stimulus /pab/, the child then touched or pointed to the object that the experimenter had designated as a pab, this behavior was reinforced by the experimenter saying, for example, "good girl", playing music and showing a toy. In trials where the auditory stimulus was either /gek/ or /dut/ the child's selection of the particular stimulus that had been designated either as a gek or a dut, respectively, was similarly reinforced. If the child selected the incorrect object the trial was terminated. Each auditory listener stimulus was presented with equal frequency and the spatial locations of each of the three experimental stimuli in relation to each other were systematically varied across trials. Training continued until the child reached a criterion of 8 out of 9 consecutively correct responses for each of the three listener relations.

In this and all subsequent conditions of the study, daily test trials for verbal production (i.e. the "tact" relation) were given before and after listener behavior training trials. For example, as she presented each object to the child, the experimenter would point at it and ask "what is it?" During the test trials there were no scheduled consequences for the infants' verbal productions. Listener behavior training was also maintained throughout all conditions of the study.

At the beginning of Condition 2 none of the children showed any evidence of having previously learned, in Condition 1, any of the experimentally required listener relations. Thereafter, under the reinforcement contingencies of Condition 2, it took several months of daily sessions for the infants to reach criterion on all 3 listener relations. The concurrent listener behavior repertoires of these infants in their home environments, as measured by the MacArthur Communicative Development Inventory (MCDI; see Fenson et al., 1993), increased from an average of 71 at the start of Condition 1 to 125 by the end of Condition 2.

This experiment was not designed to investigate the role of reinforcement in establishing listener relations; to do so would have required a multiple-baseline design in which each listener relation was successively reinforced. The study does, however, suggest that, for human infants, merely pairing an auditory stimulus with an object, at least over 27 trials, is not sufficient to establish listener behavior (cf. Stemmer, 1996, Whitehurst, 1996) and that, indeed, many reinforced trials may be required before listener relations are reliably established. This is clearly an issue that merits further experimental investigation.

We aimed in Condition 2 to determine whether infants, once having learned listener relations, would show emergence of the corresponding untrained speaker or tact relations. For example, after having learned, as in Condition 2, to select the correct object upon hearing /where's pab?/, would the infant, when presented with that same object but instead asked /what's this?/, then show emergent speaker behavior in the form of the vocalization "pab"? None of the 5 infants showed emergence of the tact relation simply as a result of listener training. This was true even though, by the end of Condition 2, the 5 infants had a verbal production repertoire of, on average, 20 "words" (ranging between 10 and 37 across children) as measured by the MCDI. These findings thus provide no support for the relational frame account of language acquisition which assumes that in such contexts speaker behaviors should "emerge" untrained, via a frame of coordination, from listener relations (Hayes, 1991; Hayes & Hayes, 1989, 1992; and see Horne & Lowe, 1996; 1997; Lowe & Horne, 1996). Our data do, however, provide strong support for Skinner's claim that speaking and listening, at least in the early development of verbal behavior in human infants, are functionally independent.

Echoic Relations

Although infants show an increasing range of vocal behavior in their first six months, it is only when they begin to "babble" (usually at around 7-10 months) that their vocalizations acoustically resemble adult speech. The particular syllabic responses constituting this repertoire are held to be universally the same and they are those that feature most frequently in the world's languages (Locke & Pearson, 1992). According to Lindblom and Engstrand (1989), these sounds result from the infant's tendency to alternately raise and lower the mandible while varying lip and tongue placement. When the mandible is raised the vocal tract is obstructed and consonant-like sounds are made; when it is lowered the vocal tract is opened and vowel sounds are produced. Babbling consists of three basic types: simple consonant-vowel syllables such as "ma" or "ba", reduplicated syllables such as "mama" or "bababa", and variegated syllable combinations such as "gaba" or "daba" (Locke, 1993).

Whatever the ambient language, most infants begin babbling at about the same age. However, there are a number of factors that are thought to have a negative influence on the onset, maintenance and development of the babble repertoire. First, there is evidence that the inability to hear others' speech may be a considerable obstacle to babbling. For example, in a study conducted by Oller and Eilers (1988) profoundly deaf infants showed very delayed and poorly differentiated babbling which deteriorated over time, and the one entirely deaf child in their study never babbled at all. Dennis (1941) showed that the onset of babbling in children who, though they had no hearing impairment, were exposed to very little speech throughout their infancy, was delayed for 4-6 months. And finally, along with the speech input of caregivers, the auditory self-stimulation attendant upon an infant's own vocalizing also appears to play an important role. For example, infants who have been tracheostomized prior to babbling show a delayed onset, and very slow development, of syllable production when, several months later, that obstacle to their babbling is removed (Kamen & Watson, 1991; Locke & Pearson, 1990).

It is clear, however, that whatever the variables necessary for establishing and maintaining the babble repertoire, the high frequency of many of the syllabic vocal responses within it, both singly and in combination, provides a vital pool of behaviors to which caregivers may selectively respond. There is now a large body of evidence that demonstrates that caregivers do indeed respond contingently to, and thus increase the frequency of, infants' syllabic babble utterances (Kaye, 1982; Papousek & Papousek, 1989; Pawlby, 1977; Uzgiris et al, 1989; Veneziano, 1988). These contingent responses usually consist of caregivers "echoing" their infant's

says   hears

"shoe"   / shoe /

Figure 2: In the echoic relation, the child learns to reproduce the verbal production of others. Here, when she hears /shoe/ she responds by saying "shoe" or some approximation to it. This behavior is reinforced by praise from caregivers.

vocalization, albeit in a slightly elaborated form. Given frequent exposure to "imitative" sequences of this kind, infants learn to produce vocal behavior that approximates that of their caregivers. This latter relation corresponds to Skinner's echoic relation, illustrated in Figure 2.

According to Locke (1993, p. 167), in such a sequence when the child utters a vocal response (e.g., "oo"), the caregiver often responds with a real-word vocal elaboration (e.g., "say, shoe ... shoe") of that utterance. That the caregiver's response serves as a reinforcer of the infant's utterance is supported by Veneziano's (1988) observation that in such episodes the infant usually emits the response ("oo") again. This provides the opportunity for massed training of that particular echoic relation (see also Moerk, 1977, 1983); when the caregiver's echoic stimulus /shoe/ is followed by the infant's vocal response "oo", the caregiver may often reinforce the echoic relation further by then saying, for example, "good girl!", before once more repeating the echoic stimulus.

The operant learning of echoic relations in 9- to 13- month-old human infants has been demonstrated in an experiment by Poulson, Kymissis, Reeve, Andreatos and Reeve (1991). In their study, 9 different sounds (chosen from the range of non-echoic vocal responses already in the infants' repertoires) were vocalized on separate occasions by parents in the presence of their respective infant. Following non-reinforced baseline trials, parental praise was given for the infants' echoic responses to 6 of the echoic stimuli; there were no scheduled consequences for echoic responses to the remaining 3. Echoic responding was established only in the conditions where there was contingent praise. However, once some echoic relations had been trained in this way via direct reinforcement, Poulson et al. report that echoic responding began to "emerge" to the echoic stimuli in the unreinforced trials also, thereby providing evidence for what they term "generalized echoic respond-ing".

Study 1: Condition 3. This consisted of a multiple baseline procedure similar to that employed by Poulson et al (1991). For the 5 infants, baseline trials consisted of the separate presentation of each of the three auditory stimuli (e.g. /pab/, /gek/, /dut/). In each trial the experimenter produced one of these stimuli (e.g., saying "say pab, pab") and the infant was given the opportunity to make the corresponding echoic response. In Baseline, there was no scheduled reinforcement for any of the infants' vocal productions. Then each of the three echoic responses was successively targeted for reinforcement. For example, if, following the experimenter saying "say pab", the child said "pab" or some approximation to it then this behavior was reinforced

There was little evidence of the children acquiring any of the three echoic behaviors over the many prompted-echoic baseline trials (ranging in number, across the 5 children, from 19 to 230 trials per echoic). Even when reinforcement was introduced, training of the echoic behavior to criterion levels took many sessions, conducted over several months. Across the five children training took an average of 208 trials for the first echoic relation to be established, 108 trials for the second echoic, and 55 trials for the third. The intensive training we found necessary to establish echoic relations in this study is consistent with the findings of Poulson et al., (1991) and accords with reports that in more naturalistic language learning contexts where children are given many thousands of exposures to potential echoic stimuli, their echoic repertoires develop slowly, even into the second year of life (Moerk, 1983, 1992) Our findings are also consistent with Skinner's account of the development of echoic relations and, together with those of Poulson et al (1991), they add weight to the argument that reinforcement is necessary for young children's learning of early echoic relations.

The name relation. In previous work (Horne & Lowe, 1996), we have argued that, when infants have learned a listener response relating a particular auditory stimulus to a particular object *and* an echoic response to that same auditory stimulus *in the presence of the object*, (given that the child orients to the object while she echoes), the conditions then exist for the corresponding "tact" relation to arise, and so complete the naming circle. These conditions are illustrated in Figure 3 (left) where, in the presence of one or more shoes, a caregiver says "shoe" to the child. The auditory stimulus /shoe/ serves simultaneously as a discriminative stimulus for both the child's echoic response "shoe" and for her listener response of orienting to the shoe (or shoes). In this way she may come to say "shoe" while she is looking at the shoe. We have proposed that, if they are frequently repeated, these are precisely the conditions under which the shoe itself may also come to serve as a discriminative stimulus for the saying of "shoe". And once the tact component is thus established, the functional circle of the name relation is made complete, as illustrated in Figure 3 (right).

Our naming account predicts, on the other hand, that if the echoic response is trained in the absence of the object to which its corresponding listener behavior relates, then naming may not be established. For unless it is present when the child is vocalizing, the object cannot have the opportunity to acquire discriminative control of that vocalizing, and there can be no naming relation without this tact component. This runs contrary to what might be predicted from the standpoint of equivalence theory. Saunders and Spradlin (1996), for example, have proposed that the tact relation should "emerge" untrained, via "equivalence", once the corresponding listener and echoic relations have been separately trained.

The findings of Study 1 support the naming but not the equivalence account. By the end of Condition 3, when listener and echoic relations had been established for all three auditory stimuli, none of the five infants had produced to criterion the

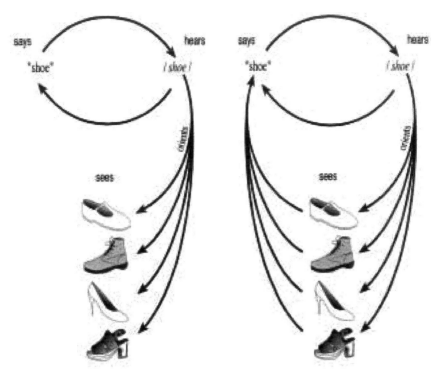

Figure 3: Having learned to echo the caregiver's spoken word "shoe", the child's own auditory stimulus /shoe/ comes to occasion her looking at not just one particular shoe but at any others that have been so named by the caregiver and for which she has already acquired listener behavior (left). These are the conditions under which a shoe itself may come to serve as a discriminative stimulus for the child's saying "shoe" (right). Naming may thus now be evoked either by the child's seeing a shoe, or her hearing /shoe/; it may be re-evoked either by her seeing a shoe again or via her echoic vocal response to her own auditory stimulus /shoe/. In this manner, objects in a class are bi-directionally related to each other through the speaker-listener relation they share.

correct tact response when presented with each of the corresponding objects in naming tests.

Study 1: Condition 4. All five children proceeded to Condition 4, in which echoing or otherwise producing the correct vocalization in the presence of the object was reinforced; within a multiple-baseline design each object was targeted in turn until the criterion for success on the naming test (i.e., 8 out of 9 consecutive correct responses, for each of the three stimuli) was met. All five children learned to name the objects under these conditions.

Using procedures similar to those in Study 1, we have conducted further studies of naming acquisition. Of the 14 infants thus far studied who reached criterion on listener and echoic training, 2 passed naming tests after they had, during subsequent listener behavior trials, "spontaneously" echoed the listener stimulus while also selecting the corresponding object; the remaining 12 required explicit training in producing the correct vocalization in the presence of the corresponding object before they succeeded on the naming tests.

The research we describe above is, we believe, rare in the language learning literature in providing so many single subject replications of infant learning of name relations that can only have been learned in the experimental setting. Our results indicate, as Skinner predicted, that reinforcement is necessary for the learning of both echoic and listener relations and that these relations are initially functionally independent. The findings also support our account of verbal behavior (Horne & Lowe, 1996; 1997; Lowe & Horne, 1996). Central to this is the hypothesis that when a child has learned both listener and echoic relations and both are evoked *in the presence of the relevant referent object*, the functional integration of those two relations may give rise to the learning of not only a tact relation but more importantly, of a name relation. This name relation - a functional union of speaking and listening that draws together tact, echoic, and listener, relations - is the basic unit of verbal behavior, upon which all of the complexities of human language are founded. It does not, however, feature in Skinner's account. Insofar as the Sidman "equivalence" and Hayes relational frame theories have anything to say about how infants learn to name the world of objects and events, which is in fact very little (e.g., Hayes & Hayes, 1992; Sidman, 1994, 1997; Wulfert & Hayes, 1988), then the empirical findings show both accounts to be almost entirely without foundation (see Horne & Lowe, 1996; 1997; Lowe & Horne, 1996).

Once the child has learned a number of name relations, naming becomes established as a higher-order class of behavior. From then on when she is taught object-speaker relations (e.g., when the caregiver looks at a horse and says "that's a horse" and the child then says "horse" herself) listener behavior (e.g., orienting to the horse) is also established, often without this behavior being directly trained or reinforced. Indeed, the generative properties of the child's existing listener repertoire may enable her, if subsequently so instructed, to "point to a horse", "go to a horse", "fetch a horse" and so on (Horne & Lowe, 1996, pp. 205-208; Lowe & Horne, p. 317-318)

Naming and Generativity

In conformity with the behavioral principle of stimulus generalization, once the name relation has been established with one exemplar of a class of objects it should extend to include other stimuli that physically resemble that exemplar. For example, in subsequent tests the name relations learned by infants in Study 1 generalized to objects that were of the same shape, but different in color, from those originally used in training. Name relations may also be extended by means other than stimulus generalization, however. If caregivers apply the same name to a range of exemplars, some physically similar, others not, and the child echoes this common name in the presence of the different exemplars, all of them, no matter how disparate their appearance, may come to be incorporated in the child's own common name relation. A name relation of this kind is a functional unit with extraordinary generative power. An example of this is depicted in Figure 4 which shows (left display) that when a child is taught to say "furniture" upon seeing such physically dissimilar items as toy chairs, chests of drawers, table-lamps and televisions, then appropriate listener behavior (e.g., orienting to any or all of these items in response to the auditory stimulus /furniture/) is also established at the same time. We (Horne & Lowe, 1996, p. 205) have proposed that because of the bi-directionality of the name relation, it may be sufficient for a child to be reinforced for putting just one of these items into a toy van following the instruction "put the furniture into the van" (Figure 4, right), for her afterwards to apply, without any direct training, that same "putting into the van" behavior to each of the remaining furniture items as well when she hears "put the furniture into the van."

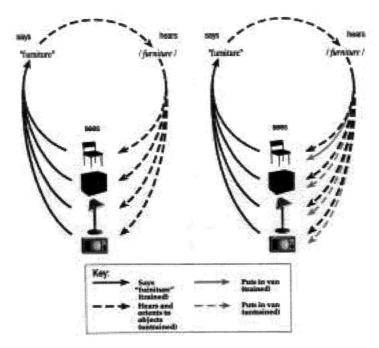

Figure 4: Schematic representation of ways in which naming brings about new behavior. A child is taught (left display) to emit the vocal response "furniture" (solid black lines) when she sees individual items of dolls' furniture (e.g., a chair, chest of drawers, lamp, television); listener behavior, such as orienting to each of these items, (broken black lines) is also generated by this training. Independently of this (right display) she is trained to load one of them (e.g., the chair) into a toy van (solid gray line); when she is subsequently instructed to "put the furniture in the van" she may show the untrained behavior (broken gray lines) of also putting the chest of drawers, lamp and television into the van.

Study 2: How Naming Generates New Behavior That Is Not Directly Trained

Whether naming might serve to bring about new behavior, as we proposed, was experimentally tested in Study 2, conducted in collaboration with Fay Harris and Carl Hughes. Four children aged between 2 years 9 months and 3 years 6 months participated. Each child was taught a common vocal response (either "zag" or "vek") for each of 2 sets of novel wooden objects (3 objects in each set) as illustrated in Figure 5 (the object sets varied across children).

In the common vocal response training sessions, each child was presented with successive pairs (each consisting of a zag and a vek) of all the zag and vek exemplars, the experimenter pointing to each object in each pair and saying, "this is a zag (or vek)... what is it?" Correct responding was reinforced by social praise. When the correct verbal response was produced by the child to each of the 6 stimuli, an entirely new behavior (e.g., hand waving) was trained in response to presentation of one of the zag stimuli, and another new behavior (e.g., hand clapping) in response to one of the veks. In test trials that followed, each of the remaining zag-vek pairs was presented in turn to each child. As each of the wooden objects was presented, the experimenter asked the child, "how does this go?" Every child responded to each of the two zag stimuli with the same response (e.g., hand-waving) as had been trained to the first zag stimulus, and to each of the vek stimuli with the same response (e.g., clapping) as had been trained to the first vek stimulus. Following the training of speaker behavior (i.e. saying "vek" or "zag"), each child was also tested for corresponding listener relations (e.g., by the experimenter asking "where is the zag?") and these were found to be in place. It is difficult, if not impossible, to account for the "emergence" of these new untrained behavioral relations in terms of traditional learning theories, but such generativity is readily explained within the naming account (Horne & Lowe, 1996).

Study 3: How Naming Generates Categorizing

As we have also previously argued (Horne & Lowe, 1996, p. 206), it follows directly from our account that if taught a common name for members of a class of physically different stimuli, a child may, when presented with a single exemplar of the class, select other class members without ever having been directly trained to do so previously. This prediction was put to the test in the next study which was conducted in collaboration with Fay Harris. Nine children ranging in age from 2 years 3 months to 4 years 3 months were each presented with three successive pairs of wooden stimuli similar to those used in Study 2. Again, as in Study 2, each child was taught to say "vek" when one of the pair of stimuli was indicated by the experimenter, and "zag" in the case of the other. In the category testing phase that followed, the experimenter presented all six stimuli in a random array, picked up one and said to the child "look at this... can you give me the others?" As is shown in Figure 6, our account predicts that under such conditions training a common vocal response, and hence common naming, for each of a range of items may be sufficient

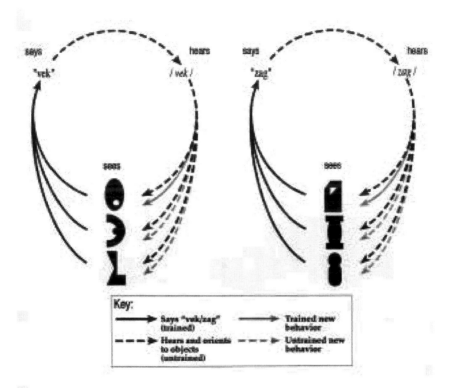

*Figure 5: Children were taught a different common vocal response (solid black lines),
either "vek" (left display) or "zag" (right display), for each of two sets of 3 physically
different objects, respectively. They were then taught a new behavior (e.g., hand-waving,
shown by a solid gray line, left display) in response to presentation of one of the vek objects,
and another behavior (e.g., hand clapping, shown by a solid gray line, right display) to one
of the zag stimuli. Several new behavior relations emerged including corresponding listener
behavior (broken black lines), hand waving (broken gray lines, left display) in response to
presentation of the remaining two vek stimuli, and hand clapping (broken gray lines, right
display) to the remaining two zag stimuli*

to establish stimulus classes or categories. In other words, when the child is presented
with one of the vek stimuli, she names it and this evokes her orientation to, and
selection of, all the remaining objects that she has named "vek". The same is true for
the zag stimuli. The findings of Study 3 bear out this prediction. Of the 9 children
given the categorization test (i.e., 18 unreinforced test trials), 3 sorted the stimuli
correctly on all trials, that is, in accordance with previously trained verbal responses;
selection of stimuli by most of the remaining children was unsystematic. However,
in their case, when the experimental procedure was changed so that the experimenter
asked "what's this?" (as she held up one of the objects), before she asked "where are
the others?", this prompted each of the remaining 6 children to make an overt

common vocal response and all then went on to sort the stimuli in terms of that common name.

Though little more than a simple "tact" was directly trained in Studies 2 and 3, listener behavior and, hence naming, "emerged". But this in turn gave rise to a range of new behaviors never directly trained so that, in Study 3, the children's seeing any one of the stimuli in a common-named class of stimuli gave rise to their selection of all the others in that class. Their behavior incorporates all the features of "emergent"

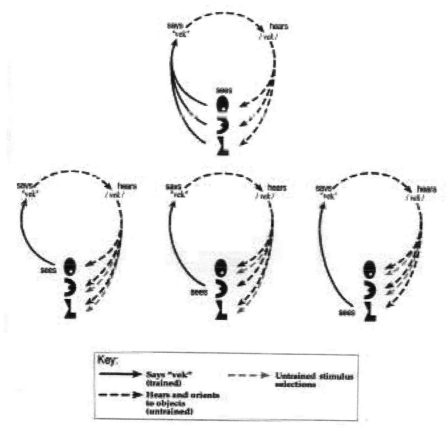

Figure 6: Children were taught a common vocal response (solid black lines), either "vek" or "zag", for each of two sets of 3 physically different stimuli, respectively. This gave rise to corresponding listener relations (shown for the vek stimuli in broken black lines, top display). When each of the six stimuli was presented on its own as a "sample" and the children were asked "can you give me the others?", they selected the other two stimuli (from the 5 remaining stimuli) that were members of the same name relation as the sample. According to the naming account, this occurs because, as the child is presented with each sample stimulus, she names it, either overtly or covertly, so that she reorients to and selects (broken gray lines, lower display) other members of that same name relation. This is shown for each of the three vek stimuli.

stimulus classes upon which researchers in behavior analysis have in recent years focused so much attention and which they have re-described in terms of theories of "stimulus equivalence" or "relational frames" (see Hayes & Hayes, 1992; Sidman, 1994). Unlike such theories, however, the naming account provides a functional analysis of these supposedly "emergent" behaviors, showing that they are a direct outcome of training particular kinds of verbal behavior. We know of no other way that categorization of physically different stimuli can be established.

Study 4: But Can Categorization Occur With Listener Behavior Alone?

We have, however, attempted to falsify the naming account by investigating whether the categorizing behavior we observed in Study 3 might not also occur if it were only common listener and not common speaker relations that were established between members of each stimulus class. Study 4, conducted in collaboration with Valerie Randle, was the same in most respects as Study 3 except that instead of the children being trained to make a vocal response to each member of the stimulus pairs, they were given common listener behavior training. This consisted of the experimenter prompting the child to make a selection by asking, for example, "where's the vek?". If the child chose the stimulus designated by the experimenter as a vek the behavior was reinforced; incorrect responses had no scheduled consequence. Having reached the criterion for correct responding on all three stimulus pairs, the children were then presented with categorization test trials as in Study 3. Of the 9 children (aged 1 year 7 months to 4 years 1 month) so far tested, none have succeeded in passing the category sorting test with only listener behavior training. However, after having subsequently received training in speaker relations - that is, after having been taught to respond to each object in a given set with its particular common vocal response - 6 of the children went on to pass the categorization tests. This strongly supports the view that naming is necessary for categorization of stimuli that physically differ.[2]

Naming And The Origins of Rule-Governed Behavior

The naming account has crucial implications for the distinction drawn by Skinner (1969, p. 147) between contingency-shaped and rule-governed behavior. Although "contingency-shaped" behavior is well understood as being behavior that is embraced by the three-term contingency (i.e., discriminative stimulus, response and reinforcer), Skinner's definition of "rule-governed" behavior as behavior that is under the control of "prior contingency-specifying stimuli" is more problematic. As a number of authors have observed (Hayes & Hayes, 1992; Sidman, 1990, 1992; Stemmer, 1992), Skinner did not make clear either what he meant by "specifying", or how the stimuli involved acquire their "specifying" function. The naming account, in our view, can make sense of his definition. Through naming, behavior and its consequences may indeed be specified; names are the basic components of rules, bi-directionally linking as they do speaker and listener behavior.

As we have already shown (see Studies 2 and 3), a common name for physically different objects can provide a powerful means of establishing entirely new behavior towards both the stimuli that are already encompassed within that name relation, and any future exemplars that come to be brought within the same relation. For within any name relation, the common auditory or listener stimulus evokes behavior that is applied to *all* of the common named stimuli. Take, for example, a young child who from her earliest days has a plastic bowl as one of her toys. Over a very long time she responds towards this unnamed stimulus much as a non-verbal mammal would, chewing it, hitting it on the ground, and so on. One day, however, her caregiver points to the bowl and says "boat", and because the child has previously been taught to name boats and been shown how they may, for example, float, sink, be used as vessels for toy passengers, her behavior towards the bowl may be instantly transformed. Transferring to the bowl all of the listener behaviors she has learned to apply to other "boats", instead of chewing the bowl she may now try to float it in the bath or fill it with toys. The power of a verbal stimulus to evoke an almost endless variety of behaviors that are only arbitrarily related to the form of the object to which they are applied may be appreciated when one considers that the caregiver might just as effectively have pointed to a bottle top, a piece of wood or a polystyrene block. Behavior that, like this, is under the control of name relations may be termed *verbally controlled behavior* (cf. Mead, 1934, p. 108).

With the increasing development of naming to include actions, properties of objects such as color, texture, shape, length and number, spatial and temporal relations between objects, and the "autoclitic" arrangements of these name responses, verbal control becomes increasingly complex and pervasive. As it does so the discrepancy between verbally controlled human behavior and the contingency-shaped behavior of animals widens inexorably. Thus, when a child says, "push boat", that naming governs her own behavior, and the behavior of others, of pushing the boat (see Horne & Lowe, 1996, pp. 211-212). And when she says " put people in the red ones here, and put animals in the green ones there" her own actions, and the actions of those whom she is instructing, are verbally governed in accordance with the operation of verbally-specified categories of objects. The prime distinction between such behavior and contingency-shaped behavior is founded, however, not on the fact that the former specifies contingencies but rather, that it specifies listener behavior. This is the critical feature of all verbal control. The accurate counter term to *contingency-shaped* should be, therefore, not *rule-governed* but *verbally governed*, or *verbally controlled* (and see Catania, 1998, pp. 264-270; p. 416). Only through naming, including naming of naming, and other autoclitic arrangements of naming, can verbal control reach the pinnacle of development where, through speech, it becomes possible, overtly or covertly, to instruct oneself to "see" any of a limitless variety of objects including the entirely hypothetical (talking swans?). It is this facility that lies at the heart of much of creative human thinking.

Conclusion

In this paper, we have tried to show what behavior analysis might contribute, both theoretically and empirically, to the study of how language is learned and how it transforms human behavior. We have built upon Skinner's account of verbal behavior but, drawing upon a range of other sources, we have developed his account in such a way as to deal with many of the criticisms that have been leveled at it, both from within and without, the field of behavior analysis.

The shortcomings of Skinner's approach have been, perhaps, at least partly responsible for the paucity of experimental research conducted on verbal behavior within behavior analysis in the 40 years since the publication of *Verbal Behavior* (1957). It has been a curious neglect, nevertheless, especially given that operant techniques have at the same time come to be widely used by others outside the tradition to investigate aspects of early language development in infancy (e.g., DeCasper & Fifer, 1980; Fernald, 1985; 1992; Kuhl et al., 1997). A central aim of the present chapter has been to show how experimental research on fundamental aspects of verbal behavior - what it is and how it comes about - might be conducted and, most importantly, how a range of fascinating "emergent" phenomena, driven by naming and categorization, might be fruitfully investigated. What we have described here, however, represents the mere beginnings of the extensive theoretical and empirical endeavor required for significant progress to be made in elucidating, from a behavioral perspective, the complexities of human thought and language. We have attempted elsewhere (Horne & Lowe, 1997) to extend the theoretical account beyond the relatively simple naming of objects and events to the naming of relations such as "same", "different", "more" and "less", and to the operation of names at higher levels of autoclitic complexity, including naming of names themselves. But a great deal remains to be done if we are to provide a comprehensive account of verbal behavior, and much of it, of necessity, is attendant upon further experimental investigations of the key phenomena. As we see it, behavior analysis has the opportunity to make a significant contribution to this enterprise which, if grasped, could bring about a renaissance within the field, returning it once again to the central focus of Skinner's radical behaviorism - verbal behavior and human consciousness.

References

Andresen, J. T. (1990). Skinner and Chomsky thirty years later. *Historiographia Linguistica, 17,* 145-166.

Bruner, J. S. (1977). Early social interaction and language acquisition. In H. R. Schaffer (Ed.), *Studies in mother-infant interaction* (pp. 271-289). New York: Academic Press.

Catania, A. C. (1998). *Learning* (4th edition). Englewood Cliffs, NJ: Prentice Hall.

Chomsky, N. (1959). Review of B.F. Skinner's Verbal Behavior. *Language, 35,* 26-58.

Czubaroff, J. (1988). Criticism and response in the Skinner controversies. *Journal of the Experimental Analysis of Behavior, 49,* 321-329.

DeCasper, A. J., & Fifer, W. P. (1980). Of human bonding: Newborns prefer their mothers' voices. *Science, 208,* 1174-1176.

Dennis, W. (1941). Infant development under conditions of restricted practice and of minimum social stimulation. *Genetic Psychology Monographs, 23,* 143-189.

Fenson, L., Dale, P. S., Reznick, J. S., Thal, D., Bates, E., Hartung, J. P., Pethick, S. & Reilly, J. S. (1993). *The Macarthur communicative development inventory: words and gestures.* San Diego, CA: Singular Publishing Group Inc.

Fernald, A. (1985). Four-month-old infants prefer to listen to motherese. *Infant Behavior and Development, 8,* 181-195.

Fernald, A. (1992). Human maternal vocalizations to infants as biologically relevant signals: An evolutionary perspective. In J. J. Barkow, L. Cosmides & J. Tooby (Eds.), The adapted mind: *Evolutionary psychology and the generation of culture* (pp. 391-428). Oxford: Oxford University Press.

Hayes, S. C. (1991). A relational control theory of stimulus equivalence. In L. J. Hayes & P. N. Chase (Eds.), *Dialogues on verbal behavior* (pp. 19-40). Reno, NV: Context Press.

Hayes, S. C., & Hayes, L. J. (1989). The verbal action of the listener as a basis of rule-governance. In S. C. Hayes (Ed.), *Rule governed behavior: Cognition, contingencies, and instructional control* (pp. 153-190). New York: Plenum Press.

Hayes, S. C., & Hayes, L. J. (1992). Verbal relations and the evolution of behavior analysis. *American Psychologist, 47,* 1383-1395.

Horne, P. J., & Lowe, C. F. (1996). On the origins of naming and other symbolic behavior. *Journal of the Experimental Analysis of Behavior, 65,* 185-241.

Horne, P. J., & Lowe, C. F. (1997). Toward a theory of verbal behavior. *Journal of the Experimental Analysis of Behavior, 68,* 271-296.

Kamen, R. S., & Watson, B. C. (1991). Effects of long term tracheostomy on spectral characteristics of vowel production. *Journal of Speech and Hearing Research, 34,* 1057-1065.

Kany, W., & Waller, M. (1995). Desiderata of a developmental theory of language acquisition: An alternative viewpoint to Chomsky nativist theory. *Zeitschrift für Entwicklungspsychologie und Padagogische Psychologie, 27,* 2-28.

Kaye, K. (1982). *The mental and social life of babies: How parents create persons.* Chicago: University of Chicago Press.

Knapp, T. J. (1990). Verbal behavior and the history of linguistics. *The Analysis of Verbal Behavior, 8,* 151-153.

Kuhl, P. K., Andruski, J.E., Chistovich, I. A., Chistovich, L. A., Kozhevnikova, E. V., Ryskina, V. L., Stolyarova, E. I., Sundberg, U., & Lacerda, F. (1997). Cross-language analysis of phonetic units in language addressed to infants. *Science, 277,* 684-686.

Lindblom, B., & Engstrand, O. (1989). In what sense is speech quantal? *Journal of Phonetics, 17,* 107-121.

Locke, J. L. (1993). *The child's path to spoken language.* London, England: Harvard University Press.

Locke, J. L. & Pearson, D. M. (1990). Linguistic significance of babbling: Evidence from a tracheostomized infant. *Journal of Child Language, 17,* 1-16.

Locke, J. L., & Pearson, D. M. (1992). Vocal learning and the emergence of phonological capacity: A neurobiological approach. In C. Ferguson, L. Menn, & C. Stoel-Gammon (Eds) , *Phonological development: Models, research, implications* (pp. 91-129). Timonium, MD: York Press.

Lowe, C. F., & Horne, P. J. (1996). Reflections on naming and other symbolic behavior. *Journal of the Experimental Analysis of Behavior, 65,* 315-340.

Lowenkron, B. (1988) Generalization of delayed identity matching in retarded children. *Journal of the Experimental Analysis of Behavior, 50,* 163-172.

MacCorquodale, K. (1970). On Chomsky's review of Skinner's Verbal Behavior. *Journal of the Experimental Analysis of Behavior, 13,* 83-99.

Mead, G. H. (1934). *Mind, self and society.* Chicago: University of Chicago Press.

Moerk, E. L. (1977). *Pragmatic and semantic aspects of early language acquisition.* Baltimore, MD: University Park Press.

Moerk, E. L. (1983). *The mother of Eve - as a first language teacher.* Norwood, NJ: Ablex.

Moerk, E. L. (1992). *A first language: Taught and learned.* Baltimore, MD: Paul H. Brookes.

Oller, D. K., & Eilers, R. E. (1988). The role of audition in infant babbling. *Child Development, 59,* 441-449.

Palmer, D. C. (1996). Achieving parity: The role of automatic reinforcement. *Journal of the Experimental Analysis of Behavior, 65,* 289-290.

Papousek, M., & Papousek, H. (1989). Forms and functions of vocal matching in interactions between mothers and their precanonical infants. *First Language, 9,* 137-158.

Pawlby, S. J. (1977). Imitative interaction. In H. R. Schaffer (Ed.), *Studies in mother-infant interaction* (pp. 203-224). London: Academic Press.

Poulson, C. L., Kymissis E., Reeve, K. F., Andreatos, M., & Reeve, L. (1991). Generalized vocal imitation in infants. *Journal of Experimental Child Psychology, 51,* 267-279.

Richelle, M. N. (1993). *B. F. Skinner: A reappraisal.* Hillsdale, NJ: Erlbaum

Sacks, O. (1989). Seeing voices. London, U.K.: Pan Books.

Saunders, K. J., & and Spradlin, J. E. (1996). Naming and equivalence relations. *Journal of the Experimental Analysis of Behavior, 65,* 304-308.

Sidman, M. (1990). Equivalence relations: Where do they come from? In D. E. Blackman & H. Lejeune (Eds.), *Behaviour analysis in theory and practice*: Contributions and controversies (pp. 93-114). Hillsdale, NJ: Erlbaum.

Sidman (1992). Equivalence relations: some basic considerations. In S.C. Hayes & L. J. Hayes (Eds.), *Understanding verbal relations* (pp. 15-27). Reno, NV; Context Press.

Sidman, M. (1994). *Equivalence relations and behavior: A research story.* Boston, MA: Authors Co-operative.

Sidman, M. (1997). Equivalence relations. *Journal of the Experimental Analysis of Behavior, 68,* 258-270.

Skinner, B. F. (1953). *Science and human behavior.* New York: Macmillan.

Skinner, B. F. (1957). *Verbal behavior.* New York: Appleton-Century-Crofts.

Skinner, B. F. (1969). *Contingencies of reinforcement: A theoretical analysis.* New York: Appleton-Century-Crofts.

Skinner, B. F. (1989). *Recent issues in the analysis of behavior.* Columbus, Ohio: Merrill Publishing Company.

Snow, C. E. (1977). The development of conversation between mothers and babies. *Journal of Child Language, 4,* 1-22.

Stemmer, N. (1990). Skinner's Verbal Behavior, Chomsky's review and mentalism. *Journal of the Experimental Analysis of Behavior, 54,* 307 - 315.

Stemmer, N. (1992). The behavior of the listener, generic extensions, and the communicative adequacy of verbal behavior. *The Analysis of Verbal Behavior, 10,* 69-80.

Stemmer, N. (1996). Listener behavior and ostensive learning. *Journal of the Experimental Analysis of Behavior, 65,* 247-249

Sundberg, C. T. & Sundberg, M. L. (1990) Comparing topography-based verbal behavior with stimulus selection-based verbal behavior. *The Analysis of Verbal Behavior, 8,* 31-41

Uzgiris, I. C., Benson, J. B., Kruper, J. C., & Vasek, M. E. (1989). Contextual influences on imitative interactions between mothers and infants. In J. Lockman & N. Hazen (Eds.) Action in a social context: *Perspectives on early development* (pp. 103-127). New York: Plenum Press.

Vaughan, M. E., & Michael, J. L. (1982). Automatic reinforcement: An important but ignored concept. *Behaviorism, 10,* 217-227.

Veneziano, E. (1988). Vocal-verbal interaction and the construction of early lexical knowledge. In M.D. Smith & J.L. Locke (Eds.) *The emergent lexicon: The child's development of a linguistic vocabulary* (pp. 109-147). San Diego: Academic Press.

Vygotsky, L. S. (1934/1987). Thinking and speech. In R. W. Rieber & A. S. Carlton (Eds.), *The collected works of L. S. Vygotsky,* (Vol 1, pp. 39-285). New York: Plenum. (Originally published in Russian, 1934).

Whitehurst, G. J. (1996). On the origins of misguided theories of naming and other symbolic behavior. *Journal of the Experimental Analysis of Behavior, 65,* 255-259.

Wulfert, E. & Hayes, S.C. (1988). Transfer of a conditional ordering response through conditional equivalence classes. *Journal of the Experimental Analysis of Behavior, 50,* 125-141.

Notes

The research reported here was supported by Ph.D. studentships awarded by the Economic and Social Research Council (to Margaret Bell and Valerie Randle), the Medical Research Council (to Carl Hughes), and the University of Wales, Bangor (to Fay Harris). We are grateful to Sue Peet and Gareth Horne for their assistance in producing the manuscript and are particularly indebted to Pat Lowe for her patient and skilful editorial contribution throughout. Correspondence should be addressed to either Pauline Horne or Fergus Lowe, School of Psychology, University of Wales, Bangor, Gwynedd, UK LL57 2DG.

[2] Taking Studies 1 to 4 together, it appears that training listener behavior in young infants may not immediately bring in corresponding speaker behavior. Instead the latter may, in its turn, have to be directly trained in order for naming to be established. Training young children's speaker behavior, on the other hand, does often establish corresponding listener behavior at the same time. For example, under normal circumstances, when an adult shows an object to a child and asks for its name (e.g., says, "it's a ball, what is it?") the child will not only respond "ball" as in a "tact" relation, but having heard /ball/ will show the typical listener behavior of looking again and otherwise attending to the object (and see Horne & Lowe, 1997, pp. 289-290).

Chapter 8

Relational Frame Theory and the Relational Evaluation Procedure: Approaching Human Language as Derived Relational Responding

**Dermot Barnes[1], Olive Healy[1]
and Steven C. Hayes[2]**
*[1]National University of Ireland, Cork,
and [2]University of Nevada, Reno*

Language is the Prize

Following Chomsky's lead, non-behavioral psychologists have tended to focus on structuralistic, and often mentalistic, analyses of language (e.g., Pinker, 1994). With the recent rise of social constructionism, structuralistic concerns have sometimes been supplemented and even replaced by more contextualistic perspectives, with a specific focus on communication (e.g., Owen, 1997). However, the vast majority of this contextualistic work has been of the descriptive or interpretive variety. Social constructionists have not been particularly active in conducting experimental analyses and thus their interpretations do not lead directly to an increased ability to influence language in a systematic or reliable fashion. Perhaps this is only to be expected in that one of the hallmarks of social constructionism is that each speech act is considered unique, and thus the idea that one could develop *general* methodologies for influencing language is totally inconsistent with this approach to psychological inquiry.

It is this context of structuralistic mentalism on the one hand, and the anti-experimental, non-interventional stance of social constructionism, on the other, that provides behavior analysis with a golden opportunity. It is our belief that the time is ripe for behavioral psychology to develop a truly effective analysis of human language. Such an achievement would surely be a great prize, not only for behavior analysis but for psychology in general.

This chapter will outline how we think this prize might be won. In particular, we will describe our ongoing efforts to subject language to a functional analysis. Although we believe that significant strides have been made in this regard, so much more work remains to be done. We hope to give a flavor of the work completed so far, and perhaps more importantly to impart some of the excitement that we feel for the research that must follow. We will do this in three major steps. First, the topic of derived stimulus relations, and the relational frame account of this phenomenon, will be examined. Second, some of our key reasons for favoring relational frame theory (RFT) over alternative accounts will be outlined. Third, recent methodological developments at the Cork and Reno laboratories will be described to illustrate how the focus on derived stimulus relations, provided by RFT, readily facilitates a functional analysis of rule governed behavior.

Derived Relational Responding and Relational Frame Theory

Derived Relational Responding

For over two decades now a growing number of behavioral researchers have been developing experimental procedures that generate derived relational responding. This form of responding is often studied using a "matching-to-sample" format to establish a number of related conditional discriminations among sets of stimuli. An example of this format might involve presenting one of three "sample" stimuli along with each of three "comparison" stimuli. The samples and comparisons may be nonsense syllables, abstract shapes, or any stimulus event, the only constraint being that the stimuli must not be related to each other along any consistent physical dimension (e.g., size, color). In accordance with tradition, we normally refer to the samples and comparisons using alphanumeric labels (subjects never see these labels). A typical procedure for studying derived relational responding might involve reinforcing the selection of comparisons B1, B2, and B3 in the presence of samples A1, A2, and A3, respectively, and reinforcing the selection of C1, C2, and C3 in the presence A1, A2, and A3, respectively. Once these conditional discriminations have been established, verbally-able humans will often reverse the explicitly reinforced conditional discriminations in the absence of any further training (i.e., they match A1, A2, and A3 to B1, B2, and B3, respectively, and match A1, A2, and A3 to C1, C2, and C3, respectively). When this occurs, responding in accordance with derived symmetrical stimulus relations has been shown. In addition, subjects also often respond in accordance with derived equivalence relations in the absence of any further training (e.g., they will match C1, C2, and C3 to B1, B2, and B3, respectively). When these types of matching performances emerge for a set of stimuli, the stimuli involved are said to participate in an equivalence class (Sidman, 1990, pp. 100-102; Sidman, 1992, pp. 18-19; see also Barnes, 1994; Fields, Adams, Verhave, & Newman, 1990). As an aside, there are many variations on the training and testing design described above. For instance, instead of training A-B and A-C relations, some studies have involved training A-B and B-C, and then testing for B-A and C-A symmetry relations, and C-A equivalence relations (see Sidman, 1990, p. 102).

Other patterns of derived relational responding have also been produced using stimulus equivalence procedures. For instance, when a simple discriminative function is established for one stimulus in an equivalence class, that function will often transfer to other stimuli in the class, without any further explicit reinforcement. This derived transfer of function effect in accordance with equivalence relations has been shown with discriminative (Barnes & Keenan, 1993; Barnes, Browne, Smeets, & Roche, 1995; de Rose, McIlvane, Dube, Galpin, & Stoddard, 1988; Gatch & Osborne, 1989; Kohlenberg, Hayes, & Hayes, 1991; Wulfert & Hayes, 1988), consequential (Hayes, Devany, Kohlenberg, Brownstein, & Shelby, 1987; Hayes, Kohlenberg, & Hayes, 1991), and respondent stimulus functions (Dougher, Auguston, Markham, Greenway, & Wulfert, 1994; Roche & Barnes, 1997). In Experiment 1 of the study reported by Roche and Barnes (1997), for example, a sexual arousal function was first established in a stimulus, C1, and then the following four stimulus relations were trained; A1-B1, A2-B2, B1-C1, B2-C2. Each subject was then tested for equivalence responding (C1-A1 and C2-A2), and subsequently for the derived transfer of sexual arousal functions from the C1 stimulus to A1. Two of four subjects showed a transfer of arousal functions (i.e., the increased arousal produced by C1 also emerged for A1).

Stimulus equivalence and derived transfer phenomena are not easily predicted using traditional behavioral concepts. In respondent or classical conditioning preparations, for instance, a conditioned stimulus (CS) predicts the onset of an unconditioned stimulus (UCS) and thus the CS acquires some of its functions. We do not, however, normally expect the UCS to acquire the functions of the CS via backward conditioning – in respondent conditioning the CS-UCS relation is *unidirectional*. In contrast, the relations between samples and comparisons in the equivalence procedure become *bi-directional* following training in one direction only (i.e., see sample → pick comparison, generates see comparison → pick sample).

Equivalence and derived transfer are interesting, to a large extent, because they appear to parallel certain types of natural language phenomena, including, for instance, naming behaviors. In the words of Hayes, Gifford, and Ruckstuhl (1996):

> If a child of sufficient verbal abilities is taught to point to a particular object given a particular written word, the child may point to the word given the object without specific training to do so. In an equivalence-type example, given training in the spoken word "candy" and actual candy, and between the written word CANDY and the spoken word "candy," a child will identify the written word CANDY as in an equivalence class with "candy," even though this performance has never actually been trained. In naming tasks, symmetry and transitivity between written words, spoken words, pictures, and objects are commonplace . . . (p. 285).

Research also indicates that the derivation of stimulus relations, such as equivalence, is related to verbal competence (Barnes, McCullagh, & Keenan, 1990; Devany, Hayes, & Nelson, 1986), and that equivalence procedures can be used effectively to establish basic reading skills (de Rose, de Souza, Rossito, & de Rose, 1992). To some behavior analysts, therefore, the equivalence effect constitutes an empirical analogue of the symbolic properties of natural language (e.g., Barnes, 1994, 1996; Barnes, Browne, Smeets, & Roche, 1995; Barnes & Holmes, 1991; Barnes & Hampson, 1993a, 1993b, in press; Barnes et al., 1990; Barnes, Lawlor, Smeets, & Roche, 1995; Barnes & Roche, 1996; Barnes, Smeets, & Leader, 1996; Biglan, 1995;

Chase & Danforth, 1991; Dymond & Barnes, 1994, 1995, 1996; Hayes, 1991; Hayes, et al., 1996; Hayes & Hayes, 1989; Lipkens, 1992; Lipkens, Hayes, & Hayes, 1993; Steele & Hayes, 1991; Watt, Keenan, Barnes, & Cairns, 1991).

Despite the fact that the study of stimulus equivalence has generated much excitement within behavior analysis, it is also the case that equivalence is simply a description of a set of procedures and a particular behavioral outcome; it does not constitute an explanation for the effect to which it refers. In contrast, RFT aims to provide an explanation for equivalence and other related effects, and also views these phenomena as having important implications for a behavior analytic approach to the study of human language (Barnes & Holmes, 1991; Barnes, 1994; Barnes & Roche, 1996; Hayes, 1991, Hayes & Hayes, 1989).

Relational Frame Theory

Relational frame theory attempts to explain equivalence, and derived relational responding more generally, by drawing upon two very common ideas in behavior analysis. The first of these is that a functional behavioral class cannot be defined in terms of the response forms of the members of that class. For example, a cat may press a lever with any of its paws, its nose or tail, or even by coughing on it if the lever is sensitive enough. Each of these response topographies may therefore become members of the same functional class. For the behavioral researcher, class membership is defined by the functional relations identified between responding and its antecedents and consequences, and hence the responses participating in any particular class may take on an infinite variety of forms.

The concept of a response class with an infinite range of topographies is a defining property of operant behavior. Nonetheless, topographical and functional classes of behavior-environment interactions quite often overlap, and thus the two may become confused. Lever pressing, for instance, may be defined by the effect of activity upon the lever, but almost all lever presses involve "pressing" movements. A sensitive lever may be activated by coughing, but for most purposes such instances can normally be ignored. Sometimes, however, the independence between topographical and functional classes is made very clear. The concept of generalized imitation (Baer, Peterson, & Sherman, 1967; Gewirtz & Stengle, 1968) provides one excellent example. After a generalized imitative repertoire is established, an almost infinite variety of response topographies may be substituted for the forms used in the earlier training. The behavior of imitating is generalized because it is not limited to any particular response topography. In a similar vein, some behavior analysts have argued that it is possible to reinforce "generalized attending" (McIlvane, Dube, Kledaras, Lennaco, & Stoddard, 1990; McIlvane, Dube, & Callahan, 1995), although *what* is being attended to will change.

Although these and other examples (see Neuringer, 1986; Pryor, Haag, & O'Reilly, 1969) constitute a simple extension of the three-term contingency as an analytic unit, specific qualifiers are often included when operant classes are not readily defined topographically. Such classes are referred to as "generalized," "higher order," or "overarching." These qualifiers are not used in this instance as technical terms, and they do not imply the existence of mediational processes leading to the formation of operants of this type. Instead, these qualifiers emphasize that a specific functional class cannot be defined by its response forms, a fact that is true in principle for all functional classes. Later, we will see how RFT draws heavily on this concept of a functionally defined, generalized operant class.

The second common behavioral idea used by RFT is concerned with the fact that organisms can respond to relations among events. The investigation of such responding has a long history in behavioral psychology, but most of the research has concentrated on responding that is controlled, in large part, by the formal properties of the related events. For example, mammals, birds, and even insects may be trained to select a stimulus as the dimmest of several options (see Reese, 1968, for a relevant review). The responding of complex organisms may thus be brought under the stimulus control of a particular property of a stimulus relationship along a formal stimulus dimension. Relational frame theory makes its contribution by suggesting that this form of relational responding may occur also in situations in which responding is brought under the contextual control of features of the situation that extend beyond the formal properties of the related events. Imagine a young girl, for instance, who is taught to respond to questions such as "Which bowl has more cereal?" or "Which bottle has more juice?" If a relational response can be brought under the control of situational features outside of the relative quantities, it may be *arbitrarily applied* to other events when the formal properties of those events do not occasion the relational response – for example, "p is more than q." Here, the relational response will be controlled by cues such as the words "more than" rather than by the relative sizes of the letters, p and q. At this point, of course, we might ask: How does a relational response come to be arbitrarily applied?

According to RFT, arbitrarily applicable relational responding is established, in large part, by an appropriate history of multiple exemplar training (see Barnes & Holmes, 1991; Barnes, 1994, 1996; Barnes & Roche, 1996; Hayes, 1991, 1994; Hayes & Hayes, 1989). Learning to name objects and events is perhaps one of the earliest and more important forms of arbitrarily applicable relational responding. For instance, a caregiver will often utter the name of an object in the presence of a young child and then reinforce any orienting response that occurs towards that object. We can describe this interaction as, hear name A → look at object B. Sometimes, the caregiver will also present an object to the child and then model and reinforce an appropriate "tact" (Skinner, 1957), and this interaction may be described as see object B → hear and say name A (see Barnes, 1994, for a detailed discussion). During the early stages of language training, each interaction may require explicit reinforcement for it to become established in the behavioral repertoire of the child, but after a number of name-object and object-name exemplars have been trained, the generalized, operant response class of "derived naming" is created. In other words, the multiple-exemplar training gradually *abstracts out* specific contextual cues as discriminative for the derived naming response. Suppose, for example, a child with this multiple exemplar naming history is told "This is your ball". Contextual cues, such as the word "is" and the naming context itself, will now be discriminative for symmetrical responding between the name and the object. In the absence of further training, therefore, the child will now point to the ball when asked "Where is your ball?" (name A → object B) and will say "ball" when presented with the ball and asked "What is this?" (object B → name A).

Relational frame theory argues that any stimuli may enter into arbitrarily applicable relational responding in the presence of the appropriate contextual cues, and moreover RFT views stimulus equivalence as an example of such relational responding. For instance, when the generalized operant of derived naming is established in the behavioral repertoire of a young girl, and she is then exposed to a matching-to-sample procedure, contextual cues provided by this procedure may be discriminative for equivalence responding. In fact, the matching-to-sample format itself is a likely contextual cue in this regard, because it is often used in preschool education exercises to teach picture-to-word equivalences (see Barnes, 1994, and Barnes & Roche, 1996, for detailed discussions). Relational frame theory therefore defines equivalence as a generalized operant response class insofar as it is created by a history of reinforcement with multiple exemplars, and once established, any stimulus event, regardless of form, may participate in an equivalence relation.

As indicated previously, RFT takes the position that stimulus equivalence and other related phenomena provide the beginnings of a functional analysis of human language. Consider the following example. Suppose that a young boy hears that he is going to the "Doctor" (Stimulus A), and subsequently experiences a painful injection. The boy may then learn at school that a "Surgeon" (Stimulus B) is a type of doctor. Later, on hearing that he is going to see a surgeon, the boy may show signs of distress despite having had no direct experience with surgeons. This transfer of function phenomenon is based on the psychological function of A and the derived relation between A and B. In effect, the boy need not experience any aversive consequences when attending a surgeon in order to show signs of anxiety (see Hayes & Hayes, 1989, 1992; Hayes & Wilson, 1994). This hypothetical example illustrates one of the core assumptions of the relational frame approach to verbal events; *a stimulus or response is rendered verbal by its participation in an equivalence or other type of derived relation* (examples of other types of derived relations will be outlined subsequently). Later in the current chapter we will show how this functional definition of verbal events provides an important foundation for the experimental and conceptual analysis of rule governed behavior.

Another core assumption for RFT is that if equivalence can be viewed as a form of generalized operant behavior, then so too should other relational activities, such as responding in accordance with the arbitrarily applicable relations of different, oppositeness, before/after, and so forth. In fact, a growing body of data provide empirical support for this assumption, thereby increasing dramatically the range of behavioral phenomena that might emerge from trained relational responding (e.g., Barnes & Hampson, 1993 a & b; Barnes & Keenan, 1993; Dymond & Barnes, 1994; Roche & Barnes, 1997; Steele & Hayes, 1991). Some relevant examples of these data will be considered subsequently, but first we need to outline the three defining properties of arbitrarily applicable relational responding (or relational framing). This needs to be done because relational framing phenomena often extend beyond the technical terms offered by equivalence researchers (e.g., symmetry, transitivity). The concept of symmetry, for instance, easily captures the bidirectional nature of relations involving equivalent stimuli (e.g., if A is the same as B then B is the same as A). However, if A and B participate in a frame of comparison, such that A is *less than* B, it does not follow that B is less than A (as required by "strict" symmetry) but rather that B is more than A. Given that the concept of symmetry does not easily capture such effects, a broader nomenclature is needed to describe the almost infinite variety of relations that may be derived between arbitrary stimuli.

Arbitrarily applicable relational responding, or relational framing, is said to involve the following properties.

1. *Mutual entailment:* If stimulus A is related to another stimulus B in a specific context, then a relation between B and A is entailed in that context. If the relation is one of equivalence (e.g., A is equivalent to B), then so too is the entailed relation (e.g., B is equivalent to A). As outlined above, however, trained and entailed relations may be dissimilar. For example, if A is *before* B, then an *after than* relation is entailed between B and A.

2. *Combinatorial entailment:* If stimulus A is in a relation to B, and B is in a relation to another stimulus C, then a relation is entailed between A and C and another between C and A. For example, if A is *bigger than* B, and B is *bigger than* C, then a *bigger than* relation is entailed between A and C, and a *smaller than* relation is entailed between C and A. Combinatorially entailed relations may differ in their specificity. For example, if B is *better than* A and C is *better than* A, the entailed relations between B and C and between C and B are unspecified (i.e., B and C may be the same, or one may be better/worse than the other).

3. *Transformation of stimulus functions:* If stimuli A and B participate in a relation, and stimulus A possesses a behavioral function, then in a relevant context the stimulus functions of B will be transformed in accordance with this relation. For example, if a subject is taught that stimulus A is *more than* stimulus B which elicits sexual arousal, then in some contexts stimulus A will elicit more sexual arousal than B. In other words, the functions of A and B differ in a manner consistent with the nature of the relation that obtains between them.

Parenthetically, it should be noted that when functions transform in accordance with equivalence relations, the term *transfer* is often used, instead of transformation (e.g., Barnes & Keenan, 1993). The reason for this is as follows. Imagine that stimuli A and B participate in an equivalence relation, and a sexually arousing function is established for B. In a suitable context, the previously neutral function of A may be transformed in accordance with this relation, in that A also acquires a sexually arousing function. One might also say, however, that the sexual function of B *transfers* to A (see Dymond & Barnes, 1995, 1996). Although using the term *transfer* is acceptable here, the term transformation is generic within RFT because functions do not necessarily transfer in accordance with non-equivalence relations. If, for example, A is the opposite of B, we would not expect a strong reinforcing function for B to transfer to A. Rather, the function of B would be transformed and would result in a greatly diminished reinforcing or even punishing function for A in contexts that produce a transformation of derived stimulus functions. To state this example in a less abstract way, suppose you are told that "dolor" is the opposite of "pleasure" (as indeed it is in Spanish). Although pleasure may be highly valued, "Do you want me to give you dolor?" will probably evoke avoidance, not approach. For this reason, relational frame theorists generally employ the term transformation.

Why Relational Frame Theory?

As we have seen, relational framing is characterized by patterns of responding involving mutual entailment, combinatorial entailment, and the transformation of stimulus functions, and furthermore RFT adopts the position that an event can only be considered verbal when it possesses these three properties. Relational frame theory therefore provides a relatively clear functional-analytic definition of verbal events. Furthermore, the empirical implications of RFT are already being explored in areas as diverse as emotional avoidance (Hayes, Stroshal, & Wilson, in press; Hayes & Wilson, 1993, 1994), emotional arousal (Dougher, Auguston, Markham, Greenway, & Wulfert, 1994; Roche & Barnes, 1997), social categorization (Watt, Keenan, Barnes, & Cairns, 1991), self-concept (Barnes, Lawlor, Smeets, & Roche, 1995) and analogical reasoning (Barnes, Hegarty, & Smeets, in press; Lipkens, 1992). It appears that the relational frame approach to the study of human language, in terms of derived stimulus relations, has stimulated a new enthusiasm for basic research in areas normally considered beyond the remit of behavioral psychology. We believe this to be a positive development for our discipline.

However, RFT is not the only approach that has been developed for the study of derived stimulus relations. Among several others, both Sidman (1994) and Horne and Lowe (1996) have argued for alternative perspectives. Furthermore, these researchers also see a clear connection between the modern work on derived stimulus relations and verbal phenomena. Why then do we favor RFT over these alternatives? Although we have many answers to this question (see Barnes & Roche, 1996; Hayes & Barnes, 1997; Hayes & Wilson, 1996), the most important one in the current context relates to the fact that the theoretical interpretations of both Sidman and Horne and Lowe share a central point; the centrality of stimulus class formation as an issue and a principle.

Stimulus classes are critically important to behavior analytic interpretations of many phenomena, so this focus on an important topic is good and worthwhile, but in this chapter we will argue that the concept of derived stimulus *relations* must also be accommodated. We suspect that this topic is essentially unavoidable in human psychology, and the attempt to interpret all phenomena in terms of classes rather than relations is hiding this need and distorting the class-based accounts that result.

The emphasis on class (to the exclusion of other issues) is partly conceptual but is also partly methodological. The matching-to-sample procedure has dominated over alternative procedures. This method has several characteristics that make class based analyses likely. The response is picking or pointing to a class member, and as such the only interesting issue is how the stimuli are partitioned into a class. However, a set of findings in the derived stimulus relations area, we believe, is beginning to reveal the limits of a class-based account. We will start by describing some of these findings – that we argue must be dealt with by any adequate theory of verbal relations – and then we will show why they undermine a class approach. Finally, we will outline some of our more recent work that clearly illustrates how important a focus on stimulus relations may be for the functional analysis of rule-governed behavior.

Multiple Stimulus Relations and the Transformation of Functions

Steele and Hayes (1991) were the first researchers to report an empirical demonstration of contextually controlled, matching-to-sample responding in accordance with multiple stimulus relations (i.e., same, different, and opposite). In a more recent study, Dymond and Barnes (1995) replicated and extended this earlier work. In the first part of their study, they demonstrated contextually controlled matching-to-sample responding in accordance with the stimulus relations of same, more-than, and less-than, but in the second and more critical part they also showed a *transformation* of self-discrimination functions in accordance with these three relations. These transformation data most clearly highlight the limits of class based analyses, and thus we will focus on this recent work.

In the Dymond and Barnes study, responding in accordance with sameness was trained using procedures similar to those developed by Steele and Hayes (1991) (e.g., subjects were trained to pick a short line comparison given a short line sample in the presence of the SAME contextual cue). Responding in accordance with more-than and less-than relations was established using comparisons that were either more than or less than the sample along some physical dimension. For example, subjects were trained to choose a two star comparison in the presence of a three star sample given the LESS-THAN cue, and were also trained to choose a six star comparison in the presence of the three star sample given the MORE-THAN cue. When the subjects had successfully completed the pretraining, they were then trained in six arbitrarily applicable relations using the three contextual cues. The four critical relations were; SAME/A1-B1, SAME/A1-C1, LESS-THAN/A1-B2, MORE-THAN/A1-C2. The subjects were then tested for seven derived relations, the following three relations being the most important; SAME/B1-C1, MORE-THAN/B1-C2, LESS-THAN/B1-B2 (see Figure 1).

To examine a transformation of self-discrimination functions in accordance with sameness, more-than, and less-than relations, three response functions were required. Subjects were trained, therefore, using three complex schedules of reinforcement to produce three response patterns; (i) no response, (ii) one response only, and (iii) two responses only. Dymond and Barnes predicted, that if the derived sameness, more-than, and less-than relations were established (i.e., B1 is the same as C1, B2 is less than B1, and C2 is more than B1), and choosing stimulus B1 after

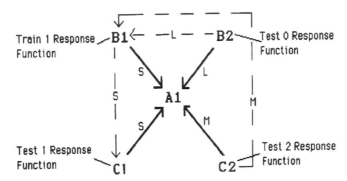

Figure 1. Schematic representations of the most important of the trained (solid lines) and tested (dashed lines) relations in the Dymond and Barnes (1995) study. Letters S, M, and L indicate the arbitrarily applicable relations of sameness, more-than, and less-than. The relational network from the Dymond and Barnes study also shows that a one-response function was trained using the B1 stimulus, and tests examined the transformation of the trained self-discrimination response function in accordance with the relations of sameness (C1, one response), more-than (C2, two responses), and less-than (B2, no response). (adapted from Dymond and Barnes, 1995; copyright the Society for the Experimental Analysis of Behavior, Inc., reprinted by permission).

making one response was reinforced, a subject, without further training, may then choose; (i) C1 following "one response" (i.e., C1 acquires the *same* function as B1), (ii) B2 following 'no response' (i.e., B2 acquires a response function that is *less-than* the B1 function), and (iii) C2 following "two responses" (i.e., C2 acquires a response function that is *more-than* the B1 function; see Figure 1, upper section). In fact, all four subjects demonstrated this predicted transformation of self-discrimination functions (see Dymond & Barnes, 1996 and Roche & Barnes, 1996, for related empirical research).

We believe that it is difficult to predict, or even describe, the test performances reported by Dymond and Barnes (1995) in terms of equivalence or stimulus classes. Consider the following. Because two different functions emerged for B2 and C2, and both of these functions differed from the trained B1 function, an equivalence or class-based account would require that we invoke three separate classes (i.e., one for each function), or alternatively we might invoke just one equivalence class in which the function transformation was controlled, to some extent, by the nodal distances between the stimuli participating in the class (see Fields, Adams, & Verhave, 1993). Neither of these class-based accounts seems plausible, however, because (a) simply invoking three different classes would not allow us to predict the specific transformation of functions observed in the study (i.e., even if B1, B2, and C2 were members of three distinct classes, establishing a one-response function for B1 leaves the untrained functions of B2 and C2 unspecified), and (b) B2 and C2 were both removed by one node (i.e., A1) from the B1 stimulus (see Figure 1, upper section), and thus nodal distance cannot differentiate between these stimuli. Furthermore, Dymond and Barnes examined two additional class-based accounts of their data, in terms of separable stimulus compounds and ordinal classes, and found these also to be inadequate (Dymond & Barnes, 1995, pp. 182-183). The question remains, therefore, is there some other way in which we might accommodate these types of findings in terms of stimulus classes?

To address this issue we will first consider Sidman's treatment of multiple stimulus relations, incorporating his most recent work published in 1994. Subsequently, we will examine the position offered by Horne and Lowe (1996, 1997) and Lowe and Horne (1996).

To our knowledge, the only place in which Sidman has directly addressed the issue of multiple stimulus relations is in the following sentence; "... the fact that a stimulus pair can be brought via contextual control into such differing relations as same, opposite, different, and so forth can be handled by any formulation of equivalence that recognizes the role of context" (1994, p. 561). At first blush, this simple statement may appear to accommodate the type of data reported by Steele and Hayes, and Dymond and Barnes. Upon closer inspection, however, we have found that if *any* relation between a stimulus pair is defined in terms of a contextually controlled equivalence class, we inevitably undermine the mathematical definition of equivalence in terms of reflexivity, symmetry, and transitivity (see Barnes & Roche, 1996). Consider, for example, a subject who is trained to choose B in the presence of A in "a more than" context. Presumably this subject should not then choose in the *same* context, A given B (i.e., A is in fact less than B) or A given A or B given B (a stimulus cannot be more than itself). In this particular example, therefore, we are left with neither symmetry nor reflexivity as defining properties of the subject's pattern of responding to the stimulus pair. In effect, if we define *any* stimulus pair that simply "go together", or partition into a set, as members of a contextually controlled equivalence class, we are thereby left with no *specific* pattern of behavior that can be isolated as an example of the formation of an equivalence class. What this means, is that in an effort to retain class as the core concept, and equivalence class as its main manifestation in derived stimulus relations, the distinction between equivalence and other classes has to be undermined. In short, we are left only with the word "equivalence."

A related issue is that although Sidman may prefer to define equivalence as a primitive or basic stimulus function, he agrees that the specific contextual control over it is learned (Sidman, 1994, see also Barnes, 1994, p. 94). So, even if we assume that multiple stimulus relations are just patterns of contextually controlled equivalence classes, we still have to account for those patterns in terms of the learning history that established them. For example, individuals would have to learn that if stimulus A is more than stimulus B, then B is less than A. But how would this be learned? First, it would seemingly have to be learned through the same type of history of multiple-exemplar training that RFT argues is necessary for establishing multiple stimulus relations. Second, this learning history would have to result in an operant that gave rise to stimulus relations, not classes. For instance, a "more-than" cue would have different functions in different parts of a stimulus network (e.g., "more-than"/ A → B is correct, but "more-than"/ B → A is incorrect). These functions are themselves difficult to interpret in class terms.

We have argued that equivalence cannot survive as a concept if the fundamental unit of analysis to cover all forms of relational responding is *stimulus class*. And indeed, evidence for this breakdown is all about us. Equivalence researchers are suggesting new forms of equivalence classes (e.g., ordinal/sequential; see Green, Stromer, & Mackay, 1993). Sidman has moved away from such key points as his 4-5 term contingency analysis (Sidman, 1994, pp. 378-379), and stimulus selection as the basis for equivalence class formation (Sidman, 1994, p. 399). And as we outlined above, Sidman's view of non-equivalence relations as contextually controlled equivalence classes (Sidman, 1994, p. 561) undermines his own set theory definition of equivalence in terms of reflexivity, symmetry, and transitivity. He is left with little else than the concept of partition, or class. It shows Sidman's intellectual honesty that he has been willing to take these radical steps, given all the work of his that he has to turn over to do so, but we argue that it also shows a fundamental error: the refusal to reconsider the foundational nature of stimulus class in this area has meant that the only way to save equivalence is to destroy it. Only "class" will remain standing, and that was a concept we had before equivalence arrived.

We can avoid destroying the functional utility of stimulus equivalence if the concept of stimulus relation is added to the concept of stimulus class. In this case equivalence is a type of relation, and of course other types of relation may be admitted. Learning would enter not just in the matter of contextual control over an inborn action, but into the nature of the operant activity itself. A more flexible version of the defining features of derived stimulus relations could be embraced and retained. And all of this is exactly what RFT does.

Naming and Stimulus Classes

In contrast to Sidman, Horne and Lowe (1996) present a much more elaborate view of stimulus equivalence, though it is one with considerably less empirical support. To their credit they do see stimulus class formation as the result of operant activity, but the end result is still simply a stimulus class. Allow us to explain. Horne and Lowe suggest that naming emerges, as a higher order behavioral relation, when listener and speaker behaviors combine (Lowe & Horne, 1996, p. 315). In their article, they describe in great detail how they imagine a young child's interaction with the verbal community establishes and maintains generalized or higher-order classes of listener and echoic behaviors. These behavioral repertoires then combine, according to Horne and Lowe, to produce the higher-order name relation. In their own words:

> . . when listener and echoic relations combine in the presence of particular objects or events, this creates the conditions for the emergence of a new response class of speaker behavior that is directly evoked by these objects

and events. Thus, objects now give rise to speaking and then to listening, that is, reorienting to the objects, which in turn reevokes speaker behavior and so on. This closes the circle and establishes a functional unity of these three generalized classes of behavior. At this point the higher order name relation is established. . . . the first instances of this new unit are explicitly reinforced by caregivers. What is now reinforced, of course, is the behavior class as a whole. With each reinforced repetition of the name relation, perhaps as new object class members are encountered (e.g., a new dog, a new chair), naming as a functional higher order class is further strengthened. Thereafter, explicit reinforcement by caregivers for new name relations become less important as the automatic reinforcing consequences of naming things become the more potent source of control (Lowe & Horne, 1996, pp. 317-318).

Having outlined how naming is established in the behavior of a young child, Horne and Lowe then attempt to use the concept of naming to explain the formation of stimulus classes. In particular, they suggest that the name relation helps to explain the formation of functional stimulus classes (pp. 204-206), and stimulus equivalence classes (e.g., p. 207). With regard to equivalence classes, Horne and Lowe (1996) suggest that naming may produce an equivalence class via common naming (pp. 215-218), via intraverbal naming (pp. 218-221), or via some other verbal behavior (pp. 221-222). The details of these explanations for the formation of equivalence classes are not important here. What matters, is that in focusing on naming explanations for the formation of stimulus classes, per se, Horne and Lowe have yet to provide an explanation for behavior that is not easily described in terms of stimulus classes alone.

In fact, Horne and Lowe were challenged on this very issue when they were asked to "explain the Steele and Hayes data using their approach" (Hayes, 1996, p. 311). In their initial response they simply replied that the subjects "will have used verbal behavior (i.e., names and rules) to solve the problems posed" (Lowe & Horne, 1996, p. 333). In effect, they indicated that the derivation of multiple stimulus relations requires rule-governance, a level of verbal ability that extends well beyond the name relation (Horne & Lowe, 1996, p. 212-213). In a more recent reply (Horne & Lowe, 1997), however, they appear to have backed off from this position, and have instead introduced some new concepts to account for multiple stimulus relations. They also offer a number of criticisms of RFT, and raise other issues, that need to be addressed if we are to show clearly why we believe RFT to be the best available conceptual framework for the functional analysis of human language.

Horne and Lowe (1997): Criticisms of RFT and other issues

1.   Horne and Lowe ask: What is the history that gives rise to a frame of coordination? And, how does the history work? As explained above, relational framing is considered to be a form of generalized operant activity that emerges from an appropriate history of multiple-exemplar

training. Specifying the exact details of the relevant histories is, for us, a largely empirical issue, not a theoretical one. The important answers will be found in the laboratory, and nowhere else. Horne and Lowe have been rather more willing to speculate about the details of history in the absence of data. This may be necessary given their elaborate model, but it carries a much larger burden to produce data quickly. Our specification of hypothetical histories has a humbler purpose since we wish only to argue that relational responding can be thought of an overarching operant class. So far as we know, multiple exemplars and the processes based on it (shaping, discrimination, and so on) are the basis of all operants.

2. Horne and Lowe suggest that we have attempted to disavow the concept of stimulus classes. We have not. We stated *very clearly* that the concept of stimulus class which has an important place in behavior analysis, needs to be added to, *not thrown over*. Apparently, Horne and Lowe do not agree that the concept of multiple stimulus relations should be *added* to the concept of stimulus class.

3. Horne and Lowe suggest that central to the relational frame account is the notion that it is the contextual stimulus *exclusively* that exerts control over the *relational response;* the latter is not occasioned by the formal properties (or physical characteristics) of the stimuli to be related. This is incorrect. In fact, for RFT the formal properties of events are often an important source of contextual control (see Barnes & Roche, 1997, pp. 199-200), and furthermore in a recent RFT study it has been shown that related events may also function simultaneously as contextual cues (Barnes, Hegarty, & Smeets, 1997). The early work on RFT was explicit in this regard. For example, Hayes (1991) said that framing events relationally was not due solely to the non-arbitrary characteristics of either the stimuli or the relation between them (p. 28). key word for our present purposes is the word 'solely.' If the formal properties of relata were not involved *at all* in relational frames it is hard to see how language could help humans interact with the physical world. This point has been made in a more extended section of a recent paper:

On the one hand, relational frames are arbitrarily applicable. On the other, they are rarely arbitrarily applied . . . As relational responding becomes freed from formal contextual control, it becomes more conventional and arbitrarily applicable . . . This is the essence of verbal behavior. But the utility of verbal behavior is hardly purely conventional. Verbal relations allow us to break up and to recombine the properties of the natural world, and thus to interact more effectively with the verbally analyzed world. Thus, a behavior that is arbitrarily applicable comes more and more under the control of subtle formal properties and components of these properties as contextual cues for relational responding. In other words, while verbal relations are arbitrarily applicable they are rarely arbitrarily applied outside of symbolic logic . . . [or it could also be argued, outside of the stimulus equivalence laboratory]. (Hayes, 1994, pp. 24-25).

It should also be noted that Horne and Lowe's misinterpretation of RFT invalidates their criticisms that are based on the assumption that the contextual cue for coordination must be *extrinsic* to the items to be coordinated.

4. Horne and Lowe suggest that early identity and oddity discriminations may serve as the basis for children's learning to name objects or events as "same" or "different", and their learning of those names is essentially no different from their learning to name "chair" or "red". This suggestion is entirely consistent with RFT. Horne and Lowe also outline how the ability to name a name may play an important role in some forms of relational responding. Consider the example they give. In an identity matching task the sample AA (that is, a sample containing two physically identical elements) may evoke the naming response "same" as will the comparison BB. However, if the subject can name the names evoked by the stimuli he or she may now respond to these two consecutive "same" responses with the *second-order naming* response "same". If reinforcement is then provided for choosing BB this would strengthen the naming of AA and BB "same" responses as "same" and help to establish the second-order name response as discriminative for selecting the correct comparison on future tasks. Horne and Lowe's (1997) description of naming a name is entirely consistent with RFT, but we would consider this behavioral effect to be an instance of multiple relational frames, or in other words a relational network. That is, A and A participate in one relation, B and B participate in a second, and AA and BB participate in a third, and each relation is defined by the function "same" (see, Barnes, et al., 1997, for a relevant empirical example). In other words, the *single* concept of relational frame can accommodate Horne and Lowe's description of naming a name. In contrast to RFT, however, notice how unwieldy the naming account of derived stimulus relations is becoming as Horne and Lowe bravely grapple with a relatively simple example of a relational network. The basic name relation itself is described as higher-order (although the exact nature of this relation remains undefined), and now Horne and Lowe have introduced the concept of a second-order name relation. In effect, we now have higher-order, second-order naming, and one is bound to wonder how many orders of naming will be needed to accommodate the rich

complexity of human behavior? Frankly, we suspect that this appeal to yet another level of naming shows that cracks are beginning to appear in Horne and Lowe's treatment of derived stimulus relations.

5. Horne and Lowe argue that the fact that young children learn to respond to "more" earlier than they do to "less" undermines an account of such behavior in terms of mutual entailment. But here again, Horne and Lowe misinterpret RFT. The term mutual entailment is not an explanation for derived relational responding, it is a term used to describe specific patterns of behavior. The explanation for those patterns is to be found in specifying the reinforcement contingencies that gave rise to them. If the contingencies operating in the verbal community normally establish "more" control before "less" control then that is a typical characteristic of the history that eventually gives rise to one example of mutual entailment. In fact, the flexibility and dynamic nature of derived relational responding, in general, is totally consistent with RFT (see Roche, Barnes, & Smeets, 1997; Wilson & Hayes, 1996). Furthermore, RFT would predict that suitable histories could be arranged to establish "less" control before "more" control, but this remains an empirical issue.

6. Horne and Lowe suggest that the failure of children, who have learned to name "more" and "less" appropriately, to show nonarbitrary transitive inferences, is inconsistent with RFT. More recent work than that cited by Horne and Lowe, however, has shown that the success or failure of children on transitive inference tasks appears to be determined in large part by specific features of the experimental procedure, rather than by some deficit on the part of the subjects (e.g., Holcomb, Stromer, & Mackay, 1996; Russell, McCormack, Robinson, & Lillis, 1996). These more recent findings are, of course, entirely consistent with the purely functional approach of RFT.

7. Horne and Lowe ask why relational frame researchers often use the Steele and Hayes pretraining procedure (outlined previously) rather than simply naming the contextual cues, "same", "different", "opposite", and so forth. This question has been asked and answered in a previous publication (Barnes & Roche, 1996). In short, pretraining establishes a similar history for each subject at the outset of the experiment, and thereby helps to control for the possibility that subjects may have learned to respond to words such as, "same", different, and so on, in slightly different ways. Furthermore, the pretraining procedure could easily be used with nonhuman subjects in a way that naming could not. Developing such procedures will obviously be important for making comparisons across species, an objective that Horne and Lowe would presumably applaud (see their treatment of Schusterman and Kastak's research).

8. Home and Lowe criticize relational frame researchers for testing derived stimulus relations until the subjects respond in accordance with the experimenter-defined relations. Although Steele and Hayes (1991) adopted this approach, more recent studies have not (e.g., Dymond & Barnes, 1995, 1996; Roche & Barnes, 1996). These latter experiments employed a stability criterion that required subjects to produce a stable, but not necessarily correct response pattern. The same sort of derived relational responses emerged as in the earlier research. On logical grounds it is not at all clear that this control is generally necessary, however, especially now that the results have been shown to be the same. Even a simple network of trained multiple stimulus relations results in hundreds of possible derived response patterns, but in a properly constructed network only one specific pattern is predicted by RFT. There is no evidence that mere recycling of training can produce such a specific result.

9. Home and Lowe argue that the large amounts of training and testing typically required to establish relational framing in the laboratory with verbally sophisticated adults is inconsistent with the RFT view that such performances are essentially verbal. Curiously enough, we have turned our attention to this very issue in recent times. However, we have adopted a behavior-analytic approach to the issue by assuming that the problem lies not in our subjects, but in the procedures we have been using to train and test for derived relations. The development of new procedures has been our response to this problem (see next section).

10. Home and Lowe criticize RFT for not offering an explanation for why there is a positive correlation between duration of reaction time and the "complexity" of the conditional stimulus relations tested in the probes (e.g., symmetry probes produce faster reaction times than probes for combined symmetry/transitivity). This "complexity effect" is totally consistent with the operant approach of RFT. Although the frame of coordination is defined in terms of mutual *and* combinatorial entailment, RFT takes the position that the generalized operant of mutual entailment will likely have been established before the generalized operant of combinatorial entailment (establishing an operant of mutual entailment may, however, facilitate combinatorial entailment [see Hayes & Wilson, 1996]). Moreover, subjects will almost certainly have far more experience of deriving symmetrical relations than equivalence relations in their day to day lives. Thus, in the laboratory it is no surprise that performance differences emerge across tasks of varying complexity. Indeed it has been shown that reaction times are longer when multiple stimulus relations are involved than when only one is involved, controlling for degree of nodality (Steele & Hayes, 1991). If Home and Lowe are correct, multiple stimulus relations are

based on the same action (naming), so this result seems surprising. If they are different operants, as RFT suggests, it is not surprising since it should normally take longer to do two different things than to do the same thing twice.

11. Horne and Lowe ask, if measures of response accuracy and latency do not covary on tests for derived stimulus relations, which is the "true" measure of these concepts? The question of which of these is the true measure makes little sense from a behavior-analytic perspective. The "true" measure is the one that helps the researcher or applied worker achieve his or her goals within a particular context. Thus the term "true measure" is an unworkable concept when it is presented in isolation, as it is by Horne and Lowe, rather than being firmly attached to more pragmatic or practical concerns, as would be demanded by a purely behavior-analytic perspective.

12. Horne and Lowe argue that the verbal reports of one of the subjects from Steele and Hayes (1991), who failed to pass the relational tests, supports the view that most of the performances observed in this study were controlled by subjects' verbal formulations and rules. We take the position that the experimental procedures normally obtained control over the subjects' verbal formulations *and* matching-to-sample re sponses, but occasionally this control was not forthcoming. This lack of control goes in both directions, a fact that Horne and Lowe seemingly cannot explain. It is not at all uncommon to have subjects who show complex patterns of derived stimulus relations but cannot verbalize why they are selecting one stimulus or the other (e.g., Smeets & Barnes, 1997, p. 75). This does not deny that verbal rules may control responding in the basic laboratory, particularly with adult subjects. Unlike Horne and Lowe's account, however, RFT provides an expla-nation of that very process (see next section). (Incidentally, Horne and Lowe [1996] suggested that naming is crucial for rule-governance, but they failed to specify exactly how the two phenomena are related. Clearly, much more will be needed to judge the adequacy of their naming account of rule-governance. In fleshing out the details, how ever, the lack of parsimony inherent in the concept of naming of naming [see point 4 above] will have to be addressed, and so too will the limitations recently identified for the concept of autoclitic behav-ior [see Cullinan, Barnes, & Lyddy, in press].)

Horne and Lowe conclude their criticism of RFT by suggesting that it consti-tutes "language-avoidance" research, and thus it will tell us little about complex human behavior. It seems to us, however, that Horne and Lowe have fixated on one (albeit important) property of human language, and this limited focus on naming will fail to provide the theoretical scope required for a truly useful functional analysis of human language. Given the limited data on naming, an empirical comparison between the functional utility of RFT and the naming account is simply not yet possible; we have no choice but to wait for the empirical research (both basic and applied) that *must* follow if the naming account is to be taken seriously. Furthermore, they argue that their existing data provide no support for RFT, and this is incorrect. Consider, for example, the research reported by Horne and Lowe that indicates that infants, once having learned listener relations, do not necessarily show the emergence of the corresponding untrained speaker or tact relations (i.e., once the children had learned to select a named object when asked "where's x?" they failed to utter the name of that object when asked "what's this?"). Horne and Lowe suggest that this finding is inconsistent with RFT because it assumes that speaker behaviors should "emerge" untrained, via the frame of coordination, from listener relations. This is a very surprising argument against RFT given that Hayes (1996), in his reply to Horne and Lowe's original article, outlined RFT research from his own laboratory (Lipkens, Hayes, & Hayes, 1993) that showed essentially the same effect as that reported by Horne and Lowe. In Hayes's (1996) words:

> We have shown that a 16-month-old infant can show symmetry in matching-to-sample procedures. . . The training was "see object" - "hear word". . . and the testing was "hear word" - "touch object." . . . At that early age, however, the child did *not* show symmetry when the training was "hear word" - "touch object" and the testing was "see object" - "say word." In our analysis we suggested that the child may have needed additional echoic training. But note that the child could clearly derive symmetrical stimulus relations (in the other task). This must mean that the lack of verbal echoic behavior merely limited the applicability of that repertoire to a specific overall performance. (pp. 310-311)

In our view, all of Horne and Lowe's criticisms of, and problems with, RFT are ill-founded. Furthermore, like Sidman they have refused to move beyond the concept of stimulus class, and in an attempt to deal with multiple stimulus relations they have introduced the unwieldy concept of higher-order, second-order naming. We cannot ourselves see how Horne and Lowe will account for responding in accordance with complex relational networks without the naming concept becoming cumbersome and unworkable. Conversely, however, RFT can explain all of the naming data quite readily, and without change it can also explain complex patterns of human behavior. It does so by allowing for the acquisition of a variety of relational operants, not just one (in the case of Horne and Lowe) or none (in the case of Sidman). The end result is not necessarily a stimulus class but is instead a stimulus relation. When stimulus relation is the core concept, stimulus classes can sometimes result (e.g., frames of coordination), but sometimes they do not.

To focus on this area more work needs to be done conceptually, but especially methodologically. Fortunately, new methods are being developed which will make it easier to focus on stimulus relations. In the following section we will describe one of these methods, and explain how it is shifting the focus away from stimulus classes

Flow Diagram of Trial Sequence

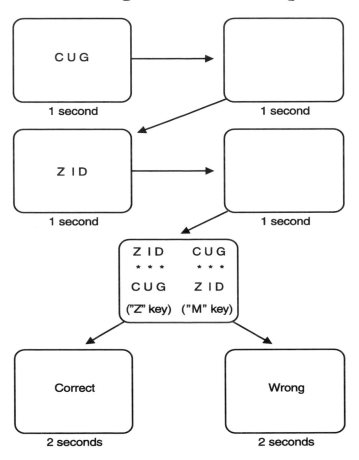

Figure 2. Schematic representation of a training trial used to establish responding in accordance with "Before" and "After" relations. Note that the three elements in the comparison stimuli were presented sequentially (i.e., the bottom elements were presented first, followed 0.2 s later by the middle elements, and then finally 0.2 s later by the top elements).

to stimulus relations, and is also providing the beginnings of a functional analysis of rule-governance.

The Relational Evaluation Procedure and the Analysis of Rule-Governance

The new methodology described here is called the Relational Evaluation Procedure (REP) because it was designed to allow subjects to report on, or evaluate, the stimulus relation or relations that are presented to them on a given task. This present example is focused on the derived stimulus relations of Before, After, Same and Different, but a similar approach can be used for virtually any relation. The core of the REP is this: establish a methodology in which subjects may confirm or deny the applicability of particular stimulus relations to sets of stimuli. In so doing, the focus shifts from stimulus partitioning and picking (with its class connotations) to relational specification and evaluation. And with this shift in emphasis, the door easily swings open to the functional analysis of rule-governed behavior.

Before/After Training

On each trial, a nonsense syllable (e.g., CUG) appears in the center of a computer screen for 1 s, disappears for 1 s, followed by a second syllable (e.g., ZID) for 1 s. The presentation of these two stimuli, one after the other, functions as a sample stimulus, and following a further 1-s delay two, three-element comparison stimuli appear on the screen, one in the lower left-hand corner, and the other in the lower right-hand corner. The three elements in the comparison stimuli are presented sequentially (i.e., the bottom elements are presented first, followed 0.2 s later by the middle elements, and then finally 0.2 s later by the top elements). Reading from bottom-to-top, both comparisons (which we will term here "statements") contain a nonsense syllable just displayed (e.g., CUG), an arbitrary relational contextual cue (e.g., XXX or VVV), and the other nonsense syllable just displayed (e.g., ZID) (for ease of communication, alphanumeric labels will be used in the following text). Subjects must select one of the two comparison statements, and are then given feedback (see Figure 2).

On one of the trials in which CUG (A1) was shown before ZID (B1) in the first part of the trial, choosing "A1 below XXX below B1" is correct while "B1 below XXX below A1" is not. Similarly, choosing "B1 below VVV below A1" is correct while "A1 below VVV below B1" is not. In this fashion, XXX is treated as functionally equivalent to "before", and VVV to "after". (For ease of communication, the words BEFORE and AFTER will be used subsequently.) Once the BEFORE and AFTER functions have been reinforced, they can then be tested using new stimuli (see Figure 3). What is critical for our present purposes is that, like statements in natural language, the correctness of the items cannot be distinguished on the basis of the two nonsense syllables, nor the relational contextual cue, but only on the relation of all of these to some prior event.

Evaluation of Statements

Once the meanings of the relational contextual cues are established, two statements can be presented and subjects can either affirm or deny that the statements agree with one another, rather than picking a statement from a set of comparison statements. For example, if B1 BEFORE A1 is presented, the statement A1 BEFORE B1 is incorrect, and the subject is reinforced for selecting one of two novel nonsense syllables (that is thus functionally equivalent to "No"; on other trials the "Yes" stimulus is selected). Once the "Yes" and "No" functions have been reinforced, they can then be tested using new stimuli (see Figure 4).

Before / After Training

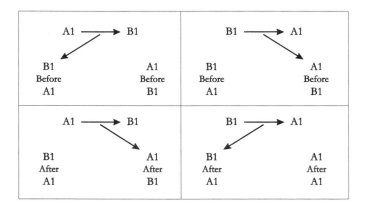

Before / After Test (No Feedback)

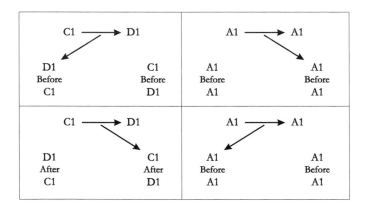

Figure 3. Schematic representation of the tasks used to train and test the contextual functions of BEFORE and AFTER. Arrows point to the "correct" comparisons.

Once such a procedure is established subjects can be trained and tested on entirely new sets of stimulus relations using the "Yes" and "No" stimuli. As in natural language, stimulus relations can even be trained without any explicit overt responding at all (e.g., A1 BEFORE B1/"Yes" might establish that A1 came first). Any relational stimulus can be similarly trained, provided only that pre-training exemplars can be provided (in fact, as outlined later, we have used this method to generate rule-following). Note also that this procedure does not require any instructions that would preclude its use with non-humans.

Four Training Tasks

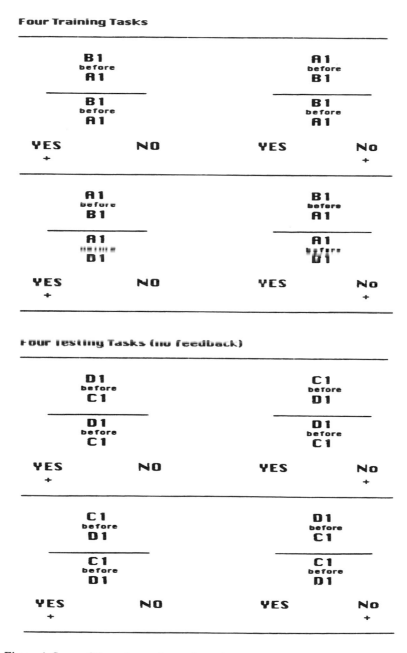

Figure 4. Some of the tasks used to train and test for the evaluation of two separate statements using arbitrary stimuli designed to function as "Yes" and "No". Correct responses are indicated by plus signs.

Our point in reviewing the REP is to show how much our current methods emphasize stimulus classes over stimulus relations, and to give an example of what methods focused on stimulus relations might look like. It is extremely difficult to think in terms of stimulus classes with REP performances. Consider, for example, the following test performance; C1 BEFORE D1 / D1 BEFORE C1 - pick "No". When the subject chooses the "No" nonsense syllable, should we define it as participating in an equivalence class with D1 BEFORE C1? If so, then its participation in this class must be under a complex form of contextual control because on other tasks D1 BEFORE C1 controls picking "Yes", and on yet other tasks D1 AFTER C1, and C1 AFTER D1 also control picking "No".

We are not suggesting here that a class-based account could not be constructed for these data, but we question the functional utility of doing so, particularly as we move towards rule-governance and more complex tasks with increasing multiple relations are used. In contrast to a class-based account, however, consider the relative ease with which REP data may be interpreted in terms of multiple stimulus relations. From this perspective, the subject is presented, on any given trial, with part of a relational network (e.g., one statement) which is to be compared to what is known about the network elsewhere (another statement). Thus, when a subject chooses "No" when presented with C1 BEFORE D1 / C1 AFTER D1, the response is controlled by the arbitrarily applicable relation C1 BEFORE D1, the arbitrarily applicable relation AFTER being applied to C1 and D1, and the relation of distinction that obtains between the two (i.e., the arbitrarily applied relation C1 BEFORE D1 is different than the arbitrarily specified C1 AFTER D1). This simple formulation in terms of a relational network may be applied with relative ease to any of the tasks outlined above, or to their more complex forms (see below). It is hard to think of REP performances in simple partitioning or class terms, because what distinguishes correct and incorrect responses is the applicability of stimulus relations, not mere stimulus partitions.

Modelling Rule-Governance

Perhaps the most significant contribution that the REP is likely to make is in the analysis of rule-governed behavior. As outlined earlier, the RFT definition of a verbal event requires that it involve, to some degree, a transformation of functions in accordance with mutual and combinatorial entailment. In the first publication outlining RFT, Hayes and Hayes (1989) used this definition of a verbal event to provide a functional-analytic definition of rule-following. In short, they suggested that following a rule involves, to some extent, a transformation of multiple functions in accordance with multiple stimulus relations. For example, the simple rule, "When it's cloudy, then bring an umbrella", establishes equivalence relations between the word "cloudy" and actual clouds, and between the word "umbrella" and actual umbrellas. Furthermore, a conditional relation is established between "cloudy" and "umbrella" and between actual clouds and umbrellas. As a result of hearing this rule, therefore, the function of clouds is changed such that their presence changes the function of umbrellas (i.e., when the listener sees clouds he or she will then seek out

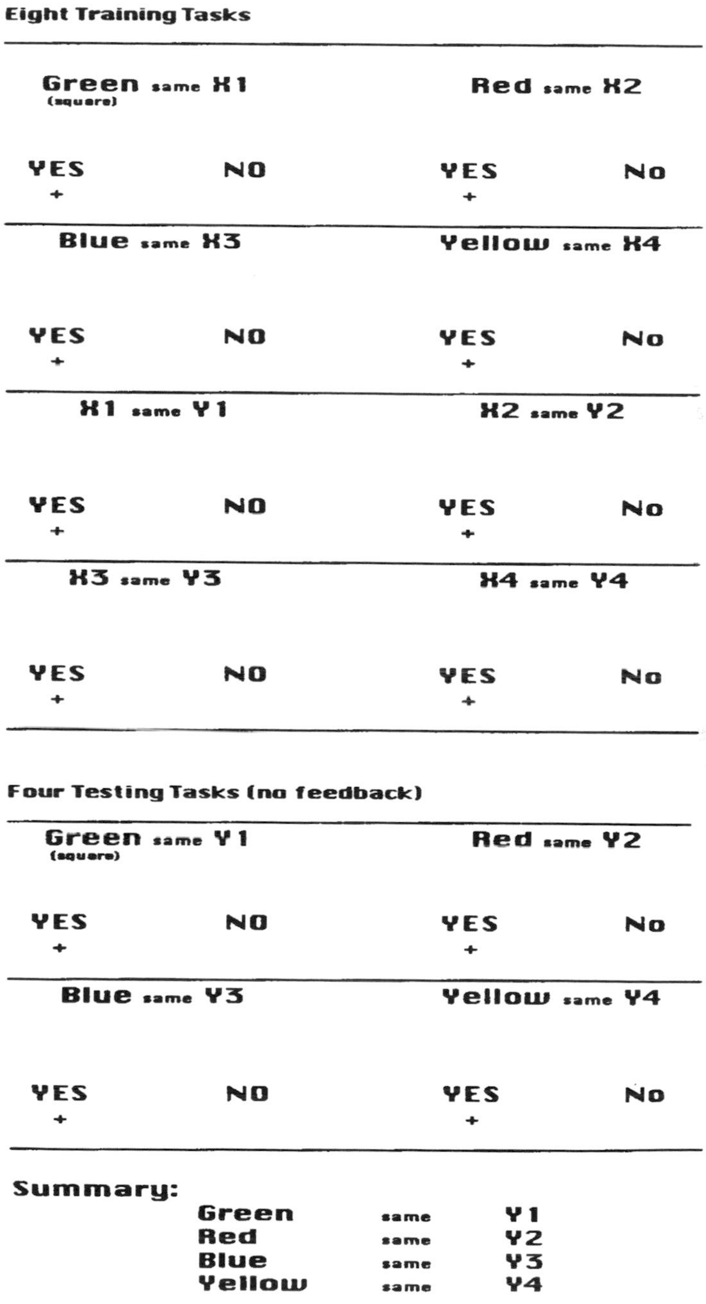

Eight Training Tasks

Green same **X1**
(square)

Red same **X2**

YES	NO	YES	No
+		+	

Blue same **X3**

Yellow same **X4**

YES	NO	YES	No
+		+	

X1 same **Y1**

X2 same **Y2**

YES	NO	YES	No
+		+	

X3 same **Y3**

X4 same **Y4**

YES	NO	YES	No
+		+	

Four Testing Tasks (no feedback)

Green same **Y1**
(square)

Red same **Y2**

YES	NO	YES	No
+		+	

Blue same **Y3**

Yellow same **Y4**

YES	NO	YES	No
+		+	

Summary:

Green	same	Y1
Red	same	Y2
Blue	same	Y3
Yellow	same	Y4

Figure 5. Some of the tasks used to train and test arbitrarily applicable sameness relations. Correct responses are indicated by plus signs.

an umbrella). In some of our most recent work we have attempted to model rule-following based on the RFT definition of verbal events. To do this we have used the REP to train and test for Before/After and Same/Different relations, and then used this history to generate novel sequence responses by presenting complex relational networks (i.e., rules) to our subjects. We will briefly describe the experimental sequence used in this research because it will provide a clear illustration of how RFT, combined with the REP, may be used to examine highly complex forms of human behavior.

Subjects were first trained in Before and After responding, as outlined in the previous sections. Afterwards, they were exposed to Same and Different training and testing. This involved three stages. In the first stage subjects were presented with tasks that were designed to establish the contextual functions of Same and Different in two arbitrary stimuli (|||| and +++). On one task, for example, V1 SAME V1 was presented and choosing the "Yes" stimulus was reinforced. On another task V1 SAME W1 was presented and choosing "No" was reinforced. In this way the stimulus |||| became the contextual cue for SAME. Similar tasks were used to establish the stimulus +++ as the Different contextual cue. For example, when V1 DIFFERENT V1 was presented choosing "No" was reinforced, and when V1 DIFFERENT W1 was presented choosing "Yes" was reinforced.

During the second stage, the contextual cues were used to train and test for the arbitrarily applicable relations of Same and Different. On one task, for example, subjects were trained to choose the "Yes" stimulus when presented with a red square, SAME, and the nonsense syllable X1, and on another task choosing "Yes" was reinforced given X1 SAME Y1. Afterwards, and in the absence of further training, subjects reliably chose "Yes" when presented with Y1, SAME, and the red square. The full range of tasks used in this part of the experiment (see Figure 5 for some examples) established the following derived sameness relations: Green SAME Y1, Red SAME Y2, Blue SAME Y3, and Yellow SAME Y4.

During the third stage, the Subjects were then exposed to a number of tasks that tested for sequence responses controlled by a variety of relational networks. On each trial, the following words appeared at the top of the computer screen: "Look at the computer screen and then press the four colored keys on the keyboard" (the 1, 4, 7, and 0 keys were covered with Green, Red, Blue, and Yellow squares, respectively). On one trial, the following stimuli were presented (reading from bottom-to-top): Y1 BEFORE Y2 BEFORE Y3 BEFORE Y4. The prior history of relational training and testing in accordance with BEFORE, AFTER, and SAME predicts the following sequence response: Green(Y1)→Red(Y2)→Blue(Y3)→Yellow(Y4). On another trial, the following stimuli were presented: Y1 AFTER Y2 AFTER Y3 AFTER Y4, and the sequence, Yellow(Y4)→Blue(Y3)→Red(Y2)→Green(Y1) was predicted. In fact, all subjects, one as young as 10 years, reliably produced these and other predicted sequence responses across all of the testing tasks. From the perspective of RFT these untrained sequence responses constitute a model of rule-governed behavior because they were produced by the transformation of multiple stimulus functions in accordance with a relational network composed of multiple stimulus relations (in this case, Before, After, and Same).

The generative power of the REP does not stop there, however. In a subsequent stage of the experiment, subjects were presented with the following stimuli on the upper of half of the computer screen:

Y1 SAME Z1/ "Yes"
Y2 SAME Z2/ "Yes"
Y3 SAME Z3 / "Yes"
Y4 SAME Z4 / "Yes"

On the lower half of the screen, the following rule was presented: Z1 BEFORE Z2 BEFORE Z3 BEFORE Z4. As in previous stages, Z1 was presented at the bottom with the other elements successively further up the screen. The stimuli, Z1 to Z4, were nonsense syllables.

Again subjects responded in accordance with the relational network by producing the following sequence: Green(Z1)→Red(Z2)→Blue(Z3)→Yellow(Z4), and they reversed this sequence when presented with: Z1 AFTER Z2 AFTER Z3 AFTER Z4. In fact, we have generated large numbers of novel sequence responses using this general approach with both adults and children. The procedures have proved to be so much more effective than matching-to-sample in generating relatively complex forms of derived relational responding, and have also gone somewhat towards producing an empirical model of rule-governance. This is an important step because it may allow us to analyze systematically some of the more interesting features of rule-governed behavior. Imagine, for example, that a subject produces a sequence response that is in accordance with a trained and tested relational network, but a punisher is delivered for doing so. What will the subject do on the next trial? Repeat the original performance based on the relational network, or emit a new sequence? And what variables would allow us to increase the likelihood of one or other of these outcomes? By conducting this type of research it should be possible to subject rule-governed behavior to a level of functional analysis that has not been possible previously. We are certainly excited by this prospect.

Conclusion

In the current chapter we have described how RFT approaches the study of human language in terms of derived stimulus relations. We have also attempted to show why we favor this approach over the currently available alternatives. Specifically, we argued that relational operants are classes of operant behavior, but their results are abstracted and arbitrarily applicable stimulus relations, not necessarily stimulus classes. We also emphasized that the concept of stimulus class, which has an important place in behavior analysis, needs to be added to, not thrown over. We feel strongly that it is better to make the needed conceptual and methodological modifications than to deal with the distortion that is resulting from an attempt to hold to the concept of stimulus class as the single organizing principle and result in the area of derived stimulus relations. Finally, by embracing the concept of stimulus relation, we have started to develop new procedures for analyzing these relations, and have even moved quite rapidly toward a functional analysis of rule-governance. From the beginning, behavior analysis had as its purpose the analysis of complex human behavior (e.g., Skinner, 1938). To us, RFT is useful only to the degree that it is a vehicle to help us accomplish that goal. Behavior analysis spent seventy years in preparation. It is time to walk into the lion's den that language and cognition presents.

References

Baer, D. M., Peterson, R. F., & Sherman, J. A. (1967). The development of imitation by reinforcing behavioral similarity to a model. *Journal of the Experimental Analysis of Behavior, 10,* 405-416.

Barnes, D. (1994). Stimulus equivalence and relational frame theory. *The Psychological Record, 44,* 91-124.

Barnes, D. (1996). Naming as a technical term: Sacrificing behavior analysis at the altar of popularity. *Journal of the Experimental Analysis of Behavior, 65,* 264-267.

Barnes, D., Browne, M., Smeets, P.M., & Roche, B. (1995). A transfer of functions and a conditional transfer of functions through equivalence relations in three to six year old children. *The Psychological Record, 45,* 405-430.

Barnes, D., & Hampson, P.J. (1993a). Stimulus equivalence and connectionism: Implications for behavior analysis and cognitive science. *The Psychological Record, 43,* 617-638.

Barnes, D., & Hampson, P.J. (1993b). Learning to learn: The contribution of behavior analysis to connectionist models of inferential skill in humans. In G. Orchard (Ed.), *Neural computing research and applications I* (pp. 129-138). London, England: IOP.

Barnes, D., & Hampson, P.J. (1997). Connectionist models of arbitrarily applicable relational responding: A possible role for the hippocampal system. In J. W. Donahoe & V. P. Dorsel (Ed.), *Neural network models of cognition: biobehavioral foundations* (pp. 496-521). Netherlands: Elsevier.

Barnes, D., Hegarty, N., & Smeets, P.M. (1997). Relating equivalence relations to equivalence relations: A relational framing model of complex human functioning. *The Analysis of Verbal Behavior, 14,* 57-83..

Barnes, D., & Holmes, Y. (1991). Radical behaviorism, stimulus equivalence, and human cognition. *The Psychological Record, 41,* 19-31.

Barnes, D., & Keenan, M. (1993). A transfer of functions through derived arbitrary and non-arbitrary stimulus relations. *Journal of the Experimental Analysis of Behavior, 59,* 61-81.

Barnes, D., Lawlor, H., Smeets, & Roche, B. (1995). Stimulus equivalence and academic self-concept among mildly mentally handicapped and nonhandicapped children. *The Psychological Record, 46,* 87-107.

Barnes, D., McCullagh, P. D., & Keenan, M. (1990). Equivalence class formation in non-hearing impaired children and hearing impaired children. *The Analysis of Verbal Behavior, 8,* 19-30.

Barnes, D., & Roche, B. (1996). Stimulus equivalence and relational frame theory are fundamentally different: A reply to Saunders' commentary. *The Psychological Record, 46,* 489-507.

Barnes, D., & Roche, B. (1997). Relational frame theory and the experimental analysis of human sexual arousal: Some interpretive implications In K. Dillenberger, M.F. O'Reilly, & M. Keenan (Eds.), *Advances in behaviouranalysis* (pp. 183-204). Dublin, Ireland: UCD Press.

Barnes, D., Smeets, P.M., & Leader, G. (1996). New procedures for generating emergent matching performances: Implications for stimulus equivalence. In T.R.Zentall and P.M. Smeets (Eds.), *Stimulus class formation in humans and animals* (pp. 153-171). Netherlands: Elsevier.

Biglan, A. (1995). *Changing cultural practices: A contextualist framework for intervention research.* Reno, NV.: Context Press.

Chase, P. N., & Danforth, J. S. (1991). The role of rules in concept learning. In L. J. Hayes & P. N. Chase (Eds.), *Dialogues on verbal behavior* (pp. 205-225). Reno, NV: Context Press.

Cullinan, V., Barnes, D., & Lyddy, F. (in press). Human language and Skinner's Verbal Behavior: Answering the nativist criticisms with Relational Frame Theory. In S. C. Hayes and D. Barnes (Eds.) *Relational frame theory: Creating an alternative behavioral agenda in language and cognition.* Reno, NV.: Context Press

de Rose, J. T., de Souza, D. G., Rossito, A. L., & de Rose, T. M. S. (1992). Stimulus equivalence and generalization in reading after matching-to-sample by exclusion. In S. C. Hayes & L. J. Hayes (Eds.), *Understanding verbal relations* (pp. 69-82). Reno, NV: Context Press.

de Rose, J. C., McIlvane, W. J., Dube, W.V., Galpin, V. C., & Stoddard, L. T. (1988). Emergent simple discrimination established by indirect relation to differential consequences. *Journal of the Experimental Analysis of Behavior, 50,* 1-20.

Devany, J. M., Hayes, S. C., & Nelson, R. O. (1986). Equivalence class formation in language-able and language-disabled children. *Journal of the Experimental Analysis of Behavior, 46,* 243-257.

Dougher, M. J., Auguston, E., Markham, M. R., Greenway, D. E., & Wulfert, E. (1994). The transfer of respondent eliciting and extinction functions through stimulus equivalence classes. *Journal of the Experimental Analysis of Behavior, 62,* 331-352.

Dymond, S., & Barnes, D. (1994). A transfer of self-discrimination response functions through equivalence relations. *Journal of the Experimental Analysis of Behavior, 62,* 251-267.

Dymond, S., & Barnes, D. (1995). A transformation of self-discrimination response functions in accordance with the arbitrarily applicable relations of sameness, more than, and less than. *Journal of the Experimental Analysis of Behavior, 64,* 163-184.

Dymond, S., & Barnes, D. (1996). A transformation of self-discrimination response functions in accordance with the arbitrarily applicable relations of sameness and opposition. *The Psychological Record, 46*, 271-300.

Fields, L., Adams, B. J., & Verhave, T. (1993). The effects of equivalence class structure on test performances. *The Psychological Record, 43*, 697-712.

Gatch, M. B., & Osborne, J. G. (1989). Transfer of contextual stimulus function via equivalence class development. *Journal of the Experimental Analysis of Behavior, 51*, 369-378.

Gewirtz, J. L., & Stengle, K. G. (1968). Learning of generalized imitation as the basis for identification. *Psychological Review, 5*, 374-397.

Green, G., Stromer, R., & Mackay, H. A. (1993). Relational learning in stimulus sequences. *The Psychological Record, 43*, 599-615.

Hayes, S. C. (1991). A relational control theory of stimulus equivalence. In L. J. Hayes & P. N. Chase (Eds.), *Dialogues on verbal behavior* (pp. 19-40). Reno, NV: Context Press.

Hayes, S. C. (1994). Relational frame theory: A functional approach to verbal events. In S. C. Hayes, L. J. Hayes, M. Sato, & K. Ono (Eds.), *Behavior analysis of language and cognition* (pp. 9-30). Reno, NV: Context Press.

Hayes, S.C., (1996). Developing a theory of derived stimulus relations. *Journal of the Experimental Analysis of Behavior, 65*, 309-311.

Hayes, S.C., & Barnes, D. (1997). Analysing derived stimulus relations requires more than the concept of stimulus class. *Journal of the Experimental Analysis of Behavior, 68*, 235-244

Hayes, S. C., Devany, J. M., Kohlenberg, B. S., Brownstein, A. J., & Shelby, J. (1987). Stimulus equivalence and the symbolic control of behavior. *Revista Mexicana de Analisis de la Conducta, 13*, 361-374.

Hayes, S.C., Gifford, E. V., & Ruckstuhl, L. E. (1996). Relational frame theory and executive function: A behavioral approach. In G. R. Lyon & N. A. Krasnegor (Eds.), *Attention, memory, and executive function* (pp. 279 - 306). Baltimore, MD: Paul H. Brookes.

Hayes, S. C., & Hayes, L. J. (1989). The verbal action of the listener as the basis for rule-governance. In S. C. Hayes (Ed.), *Rule-governed behavior: Cognition, contingencies, and instructional control* (pp. 153-190). New York: Plenum Press.

Hayes, S. C., & Hayes, L. J. (1992). Verbal relations and the evolution of behavior analysis. *American Psychologist, 47*, 1383-1395.

Hayes, S. C., Kohlenberg, B. S., & Hayes, L. J. (1991). The transfer of specific and general consequential functions through simple and conditional equivalence relations. *Journal of the Experimental Analysis of Behavior, 56*, 119-137.

Hayes, S. C., Strosahl, K., & Wilson, K. G. (in press). *Acceptance and commitment therapy*. New York: Guilford.

Hayes, S. C., & Wilson, K. G. (1993). Some applied implications of a contemporary behavior-analytic view of verbal events. *The Behavior Analyst, 16*, 283-301.

Hayes, S. C., & Wilson, K. G. (1994). Acceptance and commitment therapy: Altering the verbal support for experiential avoidance. *The Behavior Analyst, 17*, 289-303.

Hayes, S. C., & Wilson, K. (1996). Criticisms of relational frame theory: Implications for derived stimulus relations. *The Psychological Record, 46,* 221-236.

Holcomb, W. L., Stromer, R., Mackay, H. (1996). Transitivity and emergent sequence performances in young children. *Journal of Experimental Child Psychology, 65,* 96-124.

Horne, P.J., & Lowe, C.F. (1996). On the origins of naming and other symbolic behavior. *Journal of the Experimental Analysis of Behavior, 65,* 185-241.

Horne, P.J., & Lowe, C.F. (1997). Toward a theory of verbal behavior. *Journal of the Experimental Analysis of Behavior, 68,* 271-296

Kohlenberg, B. S., Hayes, S. C., & Hayes, L. J. (1991). The transfer of contextual control over equivalence classes through equivalence classes: a possible model of social stereotyping. *Journal of the Experimental Analysis of Behavior, 56,* 505-518.

Lipkens, R. (1992). *A behavior analysis of complex human functioning: Analogical reasoning.* Unpublished doctoral dissertation. University of Nevada, Reno.

Lipkens, R., Hayes, S. C., & Hayes, L. J. (1993). Longitudinal study of derived stimulus relations in an infant. *Journal of Experimental Child Psychology, 56,* 201-239.

Lowe, C.F., & Horne, P.J. (1996). Reflections on naming and other symbolic behavior. *Journal of the Experimental Analysis of Behavior, 65,* 315-340.

McIlvane, W. J., Dube, W. V., Kledaras, J. B., Iennaco, F. M., & Stoddard, L. T. (1990). Teaching relational discrimination to individuals with mental retardation: Some problems and possible solutions. *American Journal on Mental Retardation, 95,* 283-296.

McIlvane, W. J., Dube, W. V., & Callahan, T .D. (1995). Attention: A behavior analytic perspective. In G. R. Lyon, & N. A. Krasnegor (Eds.), *Attention, memory, and executive function* (pp. 97-117). Baltimore, MA.: Paul H. Brookes.

Neuringer, A. (1986). Can people behave randomly?: The role of feedback. *Journal of Experimental Psychology: General, 115,* 62-75.

Owen, J. L. (Ed.) (1997). *Context and communication behavior.* Reno, NV: Context Press

Pinker, S. (1994). *The language instinct.* London: Penguin Books.

Pryor, K. W., Haag, R., & O'Reilly, J. (1969). The creative porpoise: Training for novel behavior. *Journal of the Experimental Analysis of Behavior, 12,* 653-661.

Reese, H. W. (1968). *The perception of stimulus relations: Discrimination learning and transposition.* New York: Academic Press.

Roche, B., & Barnes, D. (1996). Arbitrarily applicable relational responding and sexual categorization: A critical test of the derived difference relation. *The Psychological Record, 46,* 451-475.

Roche, B., & Barnes, D. (1997). A transformation of respondently conditioned stimulus functions in accordance with arbitrarily applicable relations. *Journal of the Experimental Analysis of Behavior, 67,* 275-303.

Roche, B., Barnes, D., & Smeets, P. M. (1997). Incongruous stimulus pairing and conditional discrimination training: Effects on relational responding. *Journal of the Experimental Analysis of Behavior, 68,* 143-160.

Russell, J., McCormack, T., Robinson, J., & Lillis, G. (1996). Logical (versus associative) performance on transitive reasoning tasks by children: Implications for the status of animals' performance. *The Quarterly Journal of Experimental Psychology, 49B,* 231-244.

Sidman, M. (1990). Equivalence relations: Where do they come from? In D. E. Blackman & H. Lejune (Eds.), *Behaviour analysis in theory and in practice: Contributions and controversies* (pp. 93-114). Hove, England: Erlbaum.

Sidman, M. (1992). Equivalence relations: Some basic considerations. In S. C. Hayes and L. J. Hayes (Eds.), *Understanding verbal relations* (pp. 15-27). Reno, NV, Context Press.

Sidman, M. (1994). *Equivalence relations and behavior: A research story.* Boston, MA: Authors Cooperative.

Skinner, B. F. (1938). *Behavior of organisms.* New York: Appleton-Century-Crofts.

Skinner, B. F. (1957). *Verbal behavior.* New York: Appleton-Century-Crofts.

Smeets, P. M., & Barnes, D. (1997). Emergent conditional discriminations in children and adults: Stimulus equivalence derived from simple discriminations. *Journal of Experimental Child Psychology, 66,* 64-84.

Steele, D., & Hayes, S. C. (1991). Stimulus equivalence and arbitrarily applicable relational responding. *Journal of the Experimental Analysis of Behavior, 56,* 519-555.

Watt, A., Keenan, M., Barnes, D., & Cairns, E. (1991). Social categorization and stimulus equivalence. *The Psychological Record, 41,* 33-50.

Wilson, K., & Hayes, S. C. (1996). Resurgence of derived stimulus relations. *Journal of the Experimental Analysis of Behavior, 66,* 267-283.

Wulfert, E., & Hayes, S. C. (1988). Transfer of a conditional ordering response through conditional equivalence classes. *Journal of the Experimental Analysis of Behavior, 50,* 125-144.

Notes

The first author dedicates this chapter to Yvonne, Siobhan and Connor. Address correspondence to Dermot Barnes at Department of Psychology, National University of Ireland, Maynooth, County Kildare, Ireland.

Chapter 9

Applications of Research on Rule-Governed Behavior

M. Carmen Luciano
University of Almería

The focus of this chapter is the practical implications of experimental research on human beings when they behave as speaker and as listener. We learn to do or say something as the result of direct contingencies of reinforcement, because what other people do or say is functional for us to behave or act consequently. Furthermore, verbally competent subjects are able not only to follow instructions but in some conditions to describe the relation between behavior and its consequences. Even when we are able to describe these contingencies, however, sometimes we behave in a different way to that to be expected if our behavior were under control of such descriptions.

Skinner (1969) distinguished between rule-governed and contingency-shaped behavior, in which the first is determined by verbal stimuli or rules and the second is shaped by its consequences. He specified that the difference between the two is motivational, so that rule-governed behavior undermines or mitigates the consequences directly produced by behavior. Empirically, Keller and Schoenfeld (1950) indicated that schedule performance was disrupted by instructions and Ayllon and Azrin (1964) showed the first data regarding the effect of instructions in producing faster and less variable changes in behavior. Research since then has proceeded slowly and perhaps in a disorganized way, and before reviewing research on this topic we will need to consider what is a rule in a functional perspective.

Rule-governed behavior is not a well defined term, because formal and functional definitions of a rule are mixed in the colloquial and technical language. It happens that more interest has been focused on the formal characteristics than the functional, as is often the case in cognitive psychology (Hayes, 1986; Reese, 1989). The focus here, however, is to summarize the situation regarding the functional definition of rules. First there is a brief review of speaking and listening as the basic elements in an understanding of rule-governed behavior, as well as the problem of rule definition and, consequently, the problem of identifying the conditions under which rule-governed behavior may operate. Second, there is a summary of the research in rule-governed behavior. Third, applications derived from the research on rule-governed behavior are considered.

Speaking and listening

Verbal behavior is a phenomenon in which speaker's and listener's functions might occur in different individuals or in the same person. Skinner (1957) included both functions in his approach to verbal behavior, but gave more emphasis to the speaker's behavior as he himself has noted (Skinner, 1989). Even when a listener's behavior was not classified, the speaker's behavior included actions by the listener (Winokur, 1976). The following quotation from Chase and Danforth (1991) summarized this point:

> "Verbal behavior is a relation in which: (1) a response is emitted by an individual, (b) the critical consequence is provided by the behavior of another individual (the listener), (c) the listener's behavior is explicitly conditioned to respond to the stimuli produced by the first individual, (d) and the explicit conditioning of the listener involves conditioning to arbitrary stimulus relations, probably conditioning to relational classes, for example, equivalence classes.... This feature indicates that verbal behavior involves arbitrary, social, or culturally determined relations among events in the world, symbols, pictures, gestures and sounds" (p. 206).

Analyses of the speaker's behavior have in fact also been very scarce, however. Reasons for this have been considered by Sundberg (1991) and are beyond the scope of this chapter. However, experimental studies of mands, tacts, intraverbals, echoics, textuals, transcriptions, and autoclitics have been mostly analyzed in terms of the acquisition of a speaker's functions in work designed to help retarded children and others to speak and improve language as well as to understand and follow rules (see Sundberg, 1991).

Descriptive autoclitic behavior involves the discrimination of one's own behavior. It therefore involves, in one or another way, listener-behavior. Being a listener means to respond to some stimuli as verbal, as happens in all the interactions in which speaker-behavior is being conditioned by the act of the listener. More than ten years ago, Zettle and Hayes (1982) emphasized the role of the listener in complex verbal interactions, and they explicitly defined the listener as verbal while categorizing different types of listener's behavior.

The first issue to confront when analyzing research in this area is how to define "rule", and thus when rule-governed behavior occurs. This is the focus of the following section.

Rules and technical terms

Rule and instructions are terms used in the ordinary way of speaking as well as in the psychological literature (see Reese, 1989). As with many other terms and with different sciences (Deitz, 1986), to increase understanding colloquial terms must be refined to give rise to new terms which do not have the history of the language community. The problem in the case of the term rule is not only with respect to the term itself but also with regard to the causal role given to the rules, which makes a functional analysis more difficult (Hayes, 1986; Hayes & Brownstein, 1986; Skinner, 1957).

Skinner (1969) distinguished between rules in a formal and a functional account when he indicated that the rule is a series of two or more verbally sequential events which govern people's behavior. However, stating a rule as speaker-behavior and following a rule as listener-behavior (labeled as descriptive vs. prescriptive rules, respectively) needs to be distinguished (Andronis, 1991; Reese, 1989). The statement of a rule might be complete, specifying the conditions in which behavior will have a type of consequence, or incomplete with respect to the consequences or the conditions in which the behavior has to be produced. Problems arise at several points, but in this context the most important relates to the term "specifying" and thus the term "rule" and "rule-governed behavior".

Skinner (1957) considered that a rule is a verbal stimulus and that a verbal stimulus is a product of verbal behavior. Parrot (1987) indicated that a rule is different from a verbal stimulus because otherwise rule-governed behavior might not be different from echoic or intraverbal behavior. Hayes (1986) claimed that " a stimulus is verbal only when it is both the product of verbal behavior and is heard by a speaker capable of emitting the same behavior. That is, only when the speaker and listener repertoires combine to control responding should a stimulus be considered verbal" (p. 356). Catania, Matthews, and Shimoff (1990) considered that " unlike non-verbal events, verbal events function both as stimuli and as responses ... Such equivalences characterize verbal behavior" (p. 225).

All these quotations agree with regard to the bidirectional relationships which distinguish verbal stimuli from other stimuli. But as Schlinger (1990, p. 81) emphasized, agreement between behavior analysts is probably about a functional definition of rules, but not about what type of function(s) we reserve for the term "rule".

It is generally accepted that a rule is not simply a discriminative stimulus (a stimulus in which a given response has been reinforced), but is a statement that provides an indirect or derived function to stimuli. Skinner (1969) adopted the term "contingency-specifying stimulus". But the meaning of "specifying" here is not clear, nor how a stimulus comes to have such a function (Hayes & Hayes, 1989; Horne & Lowe, 1996; Vaughan, 1989).

In classifying a rule as "a contingency-specifying stimulus", Skinner indicated something about the content of the rule, namely that it has to alter the listener's behavior concerned with its function. And this function is what characterizes that "verbal statement" or "verbal formula" (L. Hayes, 1991) as a rule that might function as an establishing operation, which in turn alters the function of other stimuli producing different or changed responses (Michael 1982).

Zettle and Hayes (1982) provided a functional classification which focuses on the consequences given when following a particular rule, distinguishing between the ply (producing pliance behavior) and the track (producing tracking behavior). A third functional class is augmental (producing augmenting behavior). As defined in Hayes, Zettle and Rosenfarb (1989), "pliance" is "the fundamental unit of rule following and is rule-governed, under the control of apparent socially mediated consequences for a correspondence between the rule and relevant behavior ... , and involves consequences for rule-following *per se* mediated by the verbal community" (p. 203). Counterpliance is functionally defined in a similar way. "Tracking" behavior is rule-governed behavior "under the control of the apparent correspondence between the rule and the way the world is arranged; ... the speaker does not mediate compliance" (p. 206). "Augmenting" behavior is a very subtle form of rule-governed behavior, "under the control of apparent changes in the capacity of events to function as reinforcers or punishers" (p. 206).

Rules have been classified as general, specific, strategic, paradoxical, opened, closed (Baer, 1997; Hayes, Brownstein, Hass, &Greenway, 1986; Martínez-Sánchez & Ribes-Iñesta, 1996). Rules are also classified according to the temporal relationship between the first accomplishment indicated in the verbal statement and the contact with the relevant consequences, explicit or implicitly specified in the rule. An example would be the direct-acting rules and rules that are not direct acting proposed by Malott (1989) as effective and highly ineffective, respectively. Baum (1995, p. 6) states that "much human behavior starts out as rule-governed behavior and switches to long-term control". Furthermore, "when one speaks of a rule being internalized, it means that control over the behavior has shifted from the proximate contingency to the ultimate contingency" (p. 6). In this light, the first rule-following episode would need to be separated in time from subsequent responses in order to analyze the behavior (Andronis, 1991; Luciano, 1992).

At present, no definitive functional definition of rules has been completely accepted and the situation in the literature is confused not only with regard to the functional definition of a rule, but also with regard to its proper label (Horne & Lowe, 1996). However, a technical terminology might take into account several points in relation to the framework of behavior analysis:

(1) The definition of rules should be only functional, not in the form of the verbal stimulus.

(2) The rule should be an antecedent verbal stimulus or verbal statement or verbal formula with words and, explicit or implicitly, a relation between the elements involved in the verbal statement, that is the autoclitic frames. These words should form part of equivalence classes into appropriate autoclitic frames or relational frames.

(3) Perhaps it would be necessary to differentiate between the verbal statement or verbal formula that for the first time produces or changes a behavior (by altering the function of another stimulus) from that verbal statement which is used or followed after the behavior has been produced and its consequences have followed. By then, the verbal stimulus or nonverbal stimulus (here acting for the first time as a verbal stimulus) has acquired discriminative properties and consequently no rule is involved.

(4) The type of motivational variables in the history of the subject which make a particular verbal statement functional in a particular condition would need to be emphasized in the analysis of rule-governed behavior. Appeals to tracking or plying behavior need to check the course of

the behavior while managing consequences. Otherwise, it will be difficult to classify a "rule" as a track or a ply the first time a rule is given and produces some change in behavior: the first episode is socially mediated and the second may be controlled by the natural conse quences of the particular behavior in the conditions given.

(5) A problem arises when socially mediated consequences might be provided by the subject himself in the context of speaker and listener, especially when it is recognized that public and private social conse quences have differential effects on behavior, as the experimental and clinic literatures show (Hayes, Zettle & Rosenfarb, 1989).

To sum up, the use of technical terms to define the function of particular verbal stimuli will be more useful in developing our understanding in the research arena than retaining confused terms derived from colloquial language.

Rule-governed behavior

Catania (1992) emphasized that "what people do depends on what they are told to do. Such behavior, mainly determined by verbal antecedents, has been called rule-governed behavior" (p. 248). For Hayes (1986) "rule-governed behavior can be thought of as behavior controlled by antecedent verbal stimuli. In this analysis, rule-governed behavior is a type of verbal behavior" (p. 357). Horne and Lowe (1996) have preferred the term "verbally controlled" instead of rule-governed behavior. As indicated by Skinner (1989), listener behavior needs more experimental atten tion. The classification of rule-governed behavior mainly as pliance and tracking filled the gap Skinner left on these topics (Hineline & Wanchisen, 1989). There remains the task of isolating the variables needed to study the characteristics of rule-governed behavior. That is, the issue is the relation of these verbal, contextually determined, behaviors in relation to the appearance of new patterns of behavior without being explicitly trained, or in relation to behavior which remains unchanged or which would have changed if the rules had not been introduced.

How can it be known that behavior is rule-governed?.

Rule-governed behavior is behavior in which a verbal stimulus or formula has participated as one variable of control. For example, the mother says to her son "when you visit your grandmother, ask her about her last trip". After some days, the boy visits her grandmother and asks her for the first time in his life about her travelling activities. But is this a rule-governed behavior? Understanding the mother's rule is a prerequisite to complying with the verbal stimuli. But such understanding, or equivalence, is not sufficient to ensure that a rule will be followed, nor that the behavior which appears is rule-governed.

Understanding. Understanding is evaluated through different procedures, some more suitable than others and not all of them possible in a given circumstance. According to Skinner (1957, pp. 290-297), understanding involves catching the meaning in a rule or in the speaker's behavior. He emphasized that understanding is behaving in the appropriate way, which means to act in a way equivalent to the statement from the speaker's point of view. Speaking with meaning and listening with understanding (Hayes & Hayes, 1989) is the issue here, or in other words, an equivalence, arbitrary or not, between speaker and listener behaviors, which is understanding.

Hayes, Zettle and Rosenfarb (1989) indicated three ways to evaluate understanding, first verbal networks (questions about the rule or substitutions but keeping the functional structure), second transfer of control (evaluations of the psychological functions transferring from one stimulus to a related one), and third the so-called "silent dog" method (see below), which additionally evaluates control by a rule over ongoing behavior.

Understanding is evaluated in the context of equivalence, either words to other words, words to acts or functions, or examples about the relation between the elements through metaphors (Catania, 1992; Skinner, 1957). One more and definitive test is to ask subjects to simulate the action equivalent to the words in the rule. Repeating a "rule" (as echoic behavior) does not entail understanding. For such understanding to take place it is necessary that words and actions form part of the same equivalence class and that the autoclitic frames as relational responding be part of the subject's history. As Hayes and Hayes (1989) noted, when the verbal formula involves only one word it is easier than when verbal events are themselves related verbally. When several words come together in a sentence to form a rule, each word participates in respective equivalence classes together with the relational words (or autoclitic frames in Skinner's words) which are arbitrary conditional relational responding (see Hayes & Hayes, 1989; also Hayes, Gifford & Wilson, 1996). Understanding a rule involves precisely having a history in which these equivalence classes have been formed; otherwise the rule will not be understood and thus cannot be followed.

When is a Rule Involved?

Concern about the procedures used to infer rule use is the focus of discrepancies between different psychological conceptualizations. Shimoff (1986) warned against accepting rule-governance on the basis of the information given by subjects after performance. Matthews, Shimoff and Catania (1987, p. 70) proposed to use "a contingency space-analysis of 'say-do' sequences in which the subject sometimes does not say". Hayes (1986, 1989) proposed "the silent dog" method to infer rule-use based on three criteria that have to be interlocking: (1) demonstrating that the talk-aloud requirement does not influence performance when compared with performance without talking aloud; (2) making verbalization relevant to the task because task irrelevant verbalization may fail to influence behavior, and, (3) introducing variables that violate talk-aloud and lead to changes.

Reese (1989) evaluated several criteria according to their persuasiveness. The least persuasive criteria are to assume that the behavior is regular, or its development is discontinous, or the participant is aware of the rule use. More persuasive is the consistency of observed behavior, but this is not a definitive criterion due to behavioral variability. Most persuasive is when more than one behavior is considered and generalization of the rule use is observed in a new behavior or task.

Research on Rule-Governed Behavior

Research on the experimental analysis of rule-governed behavior began with Ayllon and Azrin (1964), who used instructions to produce a faster and less variable behavior change in clients, and Kaufman, Baron and Knopp (1966), who showed that instructional responding was insensitive to the actual programmed contingencies. At the same time, Lovaas (1961) used the first procedure to adjust verbal-nonverbal correspondence and other researchers showed disruptions of basic schedule performance when humans participated as subjects (see Lowe, 1979). By the 1980's, three lines of research had emerged, research done on the topic of (in)sensitivity to contingencies, on say-do correspondence training, and on equivalence.

(In)sensitivity to Contingencies

Rule-governed and contingency-shaped behaviors have been studied in two ways, in the first of which schedule sensitivity has been monitored with subjects of different ages, and in the second of which schedule sensitivity has been monitored through the direct manipulation of shaped or instructed behavior or indirectly through the manipulation (shaping or instructing) of the verbal behavior describing the goal behavior.

Studies of the first type, using a developmental methodology, were correlational and replicated and extended previous knowledge of different patterns of responding on fixed-interval schedules when the participants were adults. Children with unsophisticated or no verbal behavior showed patterns of behavior similar to those of non-human organisms (with scallop and postreinforcement pause). Children 5-6 years old performed in a mixed way. Older children behaved as adults, either by a constant rate of responding with no scallop or postreinforcement pause, or by making only one or two responses at the end of each interval (Bentall, Lowe & Beasty, 1985; Lowe, Harzem & Bagshaw, 1978). These studies were interpreted as reflecting the influence of an additional variable that probably had a different function from the stimuli controlling schedule performance by direct contingencies. This variable was the verbal behavior of the participants, who might be describing to themselves what was happening in the experimental situation.

The second methodology of studying schedule (in)sensitivity is experimental and involves different procedures and mixed results. Studies by Catania, Matthews and Shimoff showed that when performance is instructed rather than shaped, participants are insensitive to schedule changes (Matthews, Shimoff & Catania, 1977; Shimoff, Catania & Matthews, 1981). Moreover, participants' behavior continued to be insensitive even when it was in contact with contingencies, but at this point contradictory data resulted from the effect of different types of contingencies (see Baron & Galizio, 1983; Galizio, 1979; Gomez-Becerra, 1996). As Skinner (1969) indicated, verbal behavior prevents direct contact with contingencies since verbal behavior responds to contingencies through classes of responding.

Catania, Mathews and Shimoff (1990) considered insensitivity to be a characteristic of rule-governed behavior, but such a view was premature (Cerutti, 1989;

Galizio, 1979; Malott, 1989). Rule-following behavior is a behavior more reinforced than other types of behavior, and so insensitivity may be more a cultural artifact than a characteristic of verbal behavior (Galizio, 1979). Hayes, Brownstein, Zettle, Rosenfarb and Korn (1986) have suggested that instead of talking about insensitivity it would be better to emphasize competing contingencies, with sensitivity in one direction being insensitivity in the other, and vice versa. Thus behavior will depend in each case on the strength of motivational variables according to the particular history of following rules and the present conditions. In this way shaped behavior would be more sensitive to a change in direct contingencies and less sensitive to changes described in the rules, while instructed performance would be less sensitive to changing contingencies and more sensitive to changes described in rules. In each case, behavior would change according to the variables involving while learning classes of responding.

Other studies have focused on shaping verbal statements about behavior, showing greater sensitivity to changes in contingencies than when the required performance was instructed (Catania, Matthews & Shimoff, 1982). However, contradictory data have also been found (see, Hayes, Brownstein, Zettle, Rosenfarb & Korn, 1986). Other studies have been oriented to the analysis of different verbal content as a source of insensitivity. For example, Hayes, Brownstein, Haas and Greenway (1986) differentiated general from specific content in rules, with the former producing more variability of responding and so more sensitivity than instructions with specific content. Additionally, more sensitivity to changing contingencies appeared after shaping a variable pattern of responding (LeFrancois, Chase & Joyce, 1988).

Considering data from different studies and reviews (Baron & Galizio, 1983; Chase and Danforth, 1991), Luciano (1992) concluded that the different variables studied with respect to sensitivity could be related to either of two conditions in which it was difficult to discriminate or there were competing contingencies. The first, discrimination of own behavior, corresponds functionally to similarity or contrast between the content of the rule and the actual performance and contingencies in a particular context. The second reflects competitivity between social consequences for following rules and the direct consequences of actual performances. Thus, (in)sensitivity would result from either of these two conditions, although only when the first (discrimination) is operating is it appropriate to talk about (in)sensitivity to specific contingencies.

Say-Do-Say (Report) Correspondence Research

Several authors have recommended the study of rule-governed behavior in the context of say-do correspondence research (Catania, 1992; Hayes and Hayes, 1989; Reese, 1989; Vaughan, 1989). However, in these studies, verbal functions may have been confused with the discriminative function of a verbal statement. Reviews by Herruzo and Luciano (1994), Lloyd (1994) and Paniagua (1990, 1997) focused on say-do or do-say correspondence, different types of say-do training, and different feedback (as report) and the relation between saying and doing.

Generally speaking, in the say-do research, "saying" by the child is prompted by the experimenter and the content of the verbalization is a choice for the child (for example, between playing with one toy or another). When given the conditions for doing (studies differ in the delay period), the child acts and after a while a report of the relation between what the child said and did is reinforced. Studies differ in the way the saying is produced (most of them instructing statements about what the child should do), and also in the way the report is produced.

Most of the studies are examples of pliance as rule-governed behavior in which social reinforcement occurred on a point to point relation between the content and the performance. However, one of the problems is assuming a verbal control where such may not exist. For example, the child says that she is going to play with the ball, and after a while, is confronted with the stimuli in the context in which her behavior will be evaluated as say-do correspondence or not. At this point, the stimuli present in the situation do not necessarily function merely as a verbal stimulus (in the sense of Hayes & Hayes, 1989) but they may function as a discriminative stimulus which controls the response of having the toy and playing with it because of previous interactions with the toy. In the last case, previous interactions might have given direct function to the ball because of being related to direct and/or social consequences.

To resolve this problem, it is necessary to go back to criteria for specifying participation of a rule in the context of say-do behavior (or a behavior-behavior episode) by appealing to sequences of say-do when sometimes the subject does not say (Matthews, Shimoff & Catania, 1987), by appealing to the content of the verbalization (Stokes, Osnes & Guevremont, 1987), or by using rule following generalization criteria (Luciano & Herruzo, 1991).

In spite of the problems surrounding formal-functional definition of the say-do relation, systematic data showed that a pattern of say-do correspondence as well as do-report is obtained through differential social contingencies for say-do correspondence and noncorrespondence. Moreover, generalized rule-governance is obtained by applying say-do training to different exemplars as it is with any other class of behavior (as indicated by Stokes & Baer, 1977). At the conceptual level, it could be said that in say-do correspondence studies the behavior at the beginning would qualify as pliance but after the subject responds and contacts the direct consequences, successive rule following would qualify as tracking, or even no rule-governed behavior would be operating, as indicated by Baum (1995).

To end, both approaches analyzed, (in)sensitivity and say-do correspondence, focus on the same goal, the study of rule-governance in the context of bringing behavior under verbal control or mitigating verbal control. Following instructions involves understanding and being sensitive to the consequences associated with following instructions because the history of doing this has been successful, either because of social reasons or because of automatic consequences of the behavior. Skinner (1969) indicated that rule-governance occurs because previous behavior in response to similar verbal stimuli has been reinforced. Rule-following is, then, an operant behavior which is independent of the topography (Baron & Galizio, 1983), an operant functional class like imitative behavior (Baer & Sherman, 1964; Baer, Williams, Osnes & Stokes, 1985).

Skinner (1984, p. 610) said that

" the distinction (between rule-governed behavior and contingency-shaped behavior) is an important one, and contingencies of reinforcement are present in both. The contingencies which control the behavior of following a rule are usually not the contingencies specified in the rule, but they exist and must not be ignored".

Previous research has investigated contingency management but says nothing about how understanding is generated and how rules could be followed in new circumstances other than those specifically signaled in the verbal statement. These are points directly treated in equivalence research.

Equivalence and Nonequivalence Research

Research on the experimental analysis of stimulus equivalence as relational responding has developed at an impressive pace in the last decade (see Sidman, 1994 and Zentall & Smeets, 1996 for reviews). This research addresses:

(1) the conditions under which different physical stimuli become equivalent, and the conditions under which equivalence relations (relational equivalence responding between words, actions, objects, sensory stimulation) or nonequivalence responding (as in comparative relations) are formed and produced without direct training (Sidman, 1994; Zentall & Smeets, 1996);

(2) the transfer of functions to other stimuli without a direct interaction, by reason of being part of a particular class of equivalence or nonequivalence in which one of the stimuli has acquired a function (discriminative, conditional, punisher, reinforcer - see, Barnes, Browne, Smeets & Roche, 1995; Barnes & Keenan, 1993; Dougher, Auguston, Markham, Greenway & Wulfert, 1994; Dougher & Markham, 1996; Hayes, Kohlenberg & Hayes, 1991; Roche & Barnes, 1997; Wulfert & Hayes, 1988);

(3) the transfer of functions through stimulus generalization (Fields, Reeve, Adams & Verhave, 1991);

(4) the formation and characteristics of equivalence through many nodes (Fields, Adams, Verhave & Newman, 1990); and

(5) transferring from one type of responding to another (Barnes, Browne, Smeets & Roche, 1995; Chase & Iman, 1987; Ferro, 1993; Hayes, Thompson & Hayes, 1989).

These studies have been accomplished by any of three types of experimental formats, matching to sample (with two or more comparisons), simple discrimination or respondent type conditioning (two stimuli together in the same spatial situation or in temporal sequence), and conditional matching to sample (given a contextual cue, one stimulus is discriminative for another, but given another contextual cue, the same stimulus is discriminative for a different one). Theoretical accounts of equivalence and nonequivalence responding are currently controversial not only with regard to types of terminology but with respect to the role of verbal behavior. The series of studies by Horne and Lowe (1996, and this volume) on the "role of naming", the relational frame theory (Hayes & Hayes, 1989; Hayes, Gifford & Wilson, 1996; Barnes, Healy & Hayes, this volume) and the approach of Sidman to equivalence data have set the stage for more research and rich discussion (see Horne & Lowe, 1996 and Horne & Lowe, 1997, comments and replies; and the review of Zentall & Smeets, 1996). However, it is beyond the scope of this paper to present these controversies. The goal here is an attempt to signal the relevance of research on rule-governed behavior, separating the action of constructing rules from the acts of following them. In doing that, it is easy to agree with Hayes and Barnes (1997) when they recently claimed "rule-governance is even less well understood, both empirically and conceptually, than derived stimulus relations" (p. 239).

The following examples show how to study rule-governed behavior through equivalence classes. The first example describes a derivation of transferring functions through equivalence when the function was directly associated with one of the members. Then the conditions will be considered in which a rule might generate a new behavior or alter a behavior pattern as well as derived rule-following through the transfer of functions.

Example 1: Suppose three dissimilar stimuli (three people, A, B and C) are members of an equivalence class. Suppose one of them (A) is involved in a negative interaction (X), say A-X. Now the function is transferred to the other members of the class without any explicit association or training, simply because the three are part of the same equivalence class (the same "family" or category, A-B-C).

Example 2: But, now suppose that one person is confronted with a verbal statement in which the name of a person "R" ("Ricardo") and a description of an action "Z" ("go away") is related by means of a particular autoclitic frame or relational responding or contextual cue ("When.... then.."), for example when "R", then "Z" ("when Ricardo, then go away"). Suppose that in the particular history of this person, the name "R" is symmetrical or reciprocal (Hineline, 1997) to the physical presence of the person called Ricardo, say R-"R" ("R", Ricardo as a name, and R, Ricardo as physical person), and "Z" is equivalent to the act Z itself. Assuming that the other elements involved in rule-governed behavior are present (e.g., the person is inclined to follow the rule because following the advice given by the person who gave the actual rule to him has been successful and there are no other functions associated with R competing with Z), then when the person R appears, Z is highly possible.

That is, verbal stimuli have controlled a behavior (Z) with a non-verbal stimulus (R) for the first time just because the verbal formula was provided and because symmetrical or reciprocal relations and autoclitic frames were part of the person's history and because of a successful history of following rules. Moreover, the rule would also be effective with different stimuli to R, say H and S, if R, H, and S are part of an equivalence class and no other competing function to Z is associated with H and S.

Example 2 presents the relevance of this research with regard to rule-governed behavior when a new response is derived under the control of a rule via equivalence relations, that is, it involves understanding and rule-governance given the appropriate conditions (Hayes & Hayes, 1989; Hayes, Zettle & Rosenfarb, 1989).

Equivalence research (1) shows new relationships between stimuli, (2) shows "meaning" without direct training, (3) shows how functions are transferred among members of equivalence classes, (4) shows how the same stimuli might be part of different classes (or related in different ways) depending on conditional contextual stimuli, (5) shows how a rule might be followed for the very first time because it affords the conditions for understanding, and (6) shows how a rule might be construed by verbally competent subjects on the basis of the experience given in the experiment. Moreover, (7) it provides data on generalized responding by the application of a relational frame (based on a contextual cue) to new situations ("overarching behavioral classes" is the term selected by Hayes & Wilson, 1993 on the principle of generalization). New relational responding happens when several exemplars or relations have directly been trained and the relation between stimuli may be construed or described through these experiences. Finally, (8) experiments have also shown how particular relations or functions given to several stimuli prevent the formation of equivalence (Eikeseth & Baer, 1997); and have also shown the disruption or breaking of a pattern of equivalence responding in favor of another pattern (Gomez, Barnes & Luciano, 1997).

It should be mentioned that breaking rule-following directly and indirectly through a pattern of generalized responding would permit the formation of new relationships. In one way or another, a pattern of broken equivalence would compete with one of the strongest, and common patterns of relational responding in the subject's history, producing adaptation or otherwise depending on conditional social conditions. As indicated by Hayes and Barnes (1997) and Horne and Lowe (1996, 1997), equivalence classes are common in the way we interact with the world: our history is replete with adaptive equivalence classes because the cultural world involves objects, actions and words going together in spatial and temporal relations. Skinner (1969) spoke about constructing and following rules in the context of problem solving, when the speaker is also his own listener. He analyzed the function of self-mands, the automatic and social consequences when the speaker is his own listener, in problem solving and other contexts (Skinner, 1957). Equivalence experiments as problem-solving tasks are facing this analysis directly.

Applications

Applications of research on rule-governed behavior extend to any point of human activity in which verbal statements or verbal formulae act as rules. As previously indicated, conceptual problems involving rules and, consequently, rule-governance need much discussion in addition to the results of experimental procedures. In spite of these problems, the research done has provided an excess of information that, needless to say, will be more extended and appropriately defined in the future to analyze psychological problems based on Hayes and Follette's (1992) classification of weak, strong, appropriate or inappropriate rule-control. With respect to the utility of the research in an applied arena, three questions emerge with importance to many topics of applied concern. First, how can the probability of following rules as a class and of reporting those rules be sustained and increased? Second, how do rules give rise to new rule-governed behavior and how do they alter the function of other stimuli? Third, how can the behavior-behavior relationship be broken?

Increasing the Probability of Rule-Governance

The conditions under which socialization takes place include situations in which human beings need to learn to behave under instructional control because otherwise the behavior will inevitably produce contact with aversive automatic or social contingencies. The person needs to learn to behave according to the verbal formulae provided by the community for the behavior to become insulated from direct contingencies (creating a history of sensitivity to the social contingencies provided, primarily as plying rule-following). First, from an applied perspective, the formation of the rule-following class will be described as well as the behavior of reporting what has been done by whom. Second, the conditions will be considered in which merely giving a rule generates rule-following.

Rule-following behavior as a class begins very early in development. Parents reinforce many different responses according to particular verbal statements or mands provided by them, with the introduction of prompts (guiding or modeling the behavior) and a minimum temporal relation, at the beginning, between the instruction and the action. These interactions are very frequent in early development and, when properly reinforced, generate the important class of plying rule-following. Based on the research done, what instructors need to know is how to provide "clear" verbal statements or formulae according to the child's history (or the use of prompts that have to be faded out) as well as the necessary social reinforcement describing the relationship between the instructions and the behavior so that one behavior can be attached to the other in the two directions: say-do and do-report.

During development, social contingencies provide many opportunities for the child to respond to many experiences, among them, cause-effect natural relations and "cause-effect" logical relations according to the language and beliefs of adults. The details of the descriptive repertoire will depend on the questions and feedback provided by the adults around, and make a difference with respect to other behavior on how the child learns to know about himself (Skinner, 1957); hence, public interactions are necessary for the adjustment of verbal statements to the cultural pattern of knowing himself. Furthermore, it is during early development that is formed the basis for "self-control behavior", especially when the child is taught to describe the relation between doing something now and having later a relevant consequence.

When many interactions of rule-following behavior and the report of it have been reinforced, it is said that one instructional (conditional) class (or several conditional classes) has been formed. It is then that a verbal formula (with understanding) may be an occasion to act as a rule and produce rule-governance on its first occurrence without any prompt from others. However, verbal formulae and understanding are not sufficient to produce rule-following. A history of generalized conditional rule-following and the absence of competing functions (in the context of rule-following) are also necessary. When the rule has been followed, maintenance of rule-following patterns will depend on the specific natural outcome (social and/ or automatic) as well as the social contingencies maintaining the particular rule-following classes. And generalization of the behavior under the control of a rule occurs to other situations with physical common properties, as any other generalization occurs.

In an applied perspective, it should be emphasized that the components of the verbal formula (in a range from closed to open) influence (less or more) variable responding, respectively. Closed verbal formulae are better for reducing variability in responding, and open verbal formulae are the choice when the goal is to generate variability of responding. Additionally, rules may include explicitly a conditional aspect or conditional frame which determines the (mal)adaptive function of the rule-following behavior. For example, "if my husband/doctor says so, it has to be true, then go ahead!", or "this is a good cookie for me but I have eaten right now, so I must wait two hours" in contrast to a general rule which could be dangerous if followed ("this is a good cookie for me, go ahead" or "it has to be true", respectively). The same reasoning follows the analysis of hypnosis, which has been reconstrued according to conditional relations (the therapist's ceremony) in which some instructions have a particular value or function for particular individual histories (Cangas & Pérez-Alvárez, 1997).

At this point, it is necessary to comment on some characteristics of so-called self-instructional training. From the research done in say-do correspondence, it is not always obvious that self-instruction acts as a rule, and when it does it is necessary to explain how the behavior-behavior relationship is established (Hayes & Brownstein, 1986). The relevant variable identified to form a behavior-behavior relation needs to be considered, and this is the differential social contingencies on the description of what is said and what is done, or what is done and what is said. Furthermore, the collateral effects on "loci" in the person or attributional styles (Guerin & Foster, 1994; Lloyd, 1994; Luciano, 1995; Street, 1994; Whitman, Burgio & Johnston, 1984) would result from the type of feedback provided by others and by the subject him/herself about who obtained the results, who decided to do a particular action, and so on. The type of descriptions used as social feedback develops or changes personal perspectives in which the subject learns to know about him/herself.

Finally, when the description about what is going on enters into an equivalence class the effects are extended in many aspects. One is related to what is called "remembering the experience" and "refeeling it". No matter the reason, when the description appears, it also brings the emotional behavior correlated with the experience. In a given experience, the objects and movements with respect to them in a spatial and temporal relation, the emotional behavior and the verbal behavior with regard to all these elements form an equivalence class. When the subject "remembers" the experience, s/he does so in many senses and under different conditions associated with the experience. That is, the description brings the emotional effects to the present circumstances, and given this, the emotional feelings (negative or positive) may provide the conditions for conditioning new situations, new objects, new people.

Enhancing rule-governed behavior is relevant in many contexts: education, hospital, family, policy, and so on. All these contexts contain frequent use of advice, recommendations towards future action, verbal statements that might make a difference when necessary. However, they do not work, because instructing is not sufficient (see analyses of preventive programs in Takanishi, 1993, and Wulfert & Biglan, 1994). Parents or any other educators as speakers need to know that shaping or instructing verbal formulae makes a difference for the listener to discriminate the conditions under which s/he might behave according to the verbal statement and the motivation for following the verbal formula. Then, to shape or to instruct the verbal formula about what to do and its report will be more appropriate depending on the goal, on the type of rule-following history, and other contextual variables. The probability of following a verbal statement (shaped or instructed) is related to the subject's history according to his success in doing what others tell him or doing what he tells himself. To follow instructions when given by others or shaped (by experience) involves understanding as well as the presence, or not, of competing contingencies, and involves the possibility of reporting the behavior.

Controlled studies concerning these points have been conducted in different contexts. For example, on individual behavior consistencies, on dental hygiene, classroom behavior, hyperactive behavior, psychiatric patients, study-time, children's compliance, adjusting to rules by old people, by professionals (Gil-Roales, 1996; Gómez-Becerra & Luciano, in press; Luciano, Gómez, Plaza & Ybarra, 1997; Paniagua, 1992; Reitman & Gross, 1996; Ribes & Sánchez, 1992; Sowers, Lloyd & Lloyd, 1977; Tracy, Briddell & Wilson, 1974; Wulfert & Biglan, 1994).

Indirect Effects of Rules

When rule-governed behavior has been produced it may generalize to other situations, as may any other behavior. More importantly here is the fact that when a verbal formula is given for the first time it not only may generate rule-following according to the particular or formal characteristics of the rule but also generate rule-following in an arbitrary way according to equivalence and nonequivalence relations. Moreover, a verbal formula alters patterns of responding. Then, we pay attention to rule-following in arbitrary circumstances not specified in the rule as well as rules that alter patterns of behavior, which are directly connected to the experimental literature of equivalence relations.

Rule-following in arbitrary circumstances not specified in the rule and the transfer of functions are possible through the members of the equivalence (or nonequivalence) relational classes; then one rule or one function given to one member would be applied to other members in the equivalence class. The applied implications of these facts are enormous not only to explain emerging behavior during development but to change behavior when that is the objective in the therapeutic context.

Some examples follow: If you read or are told "Cristina is wonderful, so kind, please, offer her your help", and Cristina is in an equivalence class with Alfredo, with no competing functions to that specified in the rule, then rule-following may appear on the first occasion with respect to Alfredo before rule-following occurring with respect to Cristina. In this case, a function given in a rule with respect to one stimulus is transferred to another stimulus in an equivalence relation. The importance of such rule-following may explain the development of (mal)adaptive rule-following. When this behavior happens, it is subject to the contingencies of the interaction with Alfredo and the contingencies of the rule-governed class conditional to the context or person who gave the rule.

Transferring and expanding the function given to one member of a class may alter a pattern of responding. One example of this is when the "self" is specifically involved in the description of a particular experience as happens when a punishment interaction (threatening and abusing a person) is accompanied by saying that "the person is stupid and it is necessary to do this because this is what he deserves". After that, the person may describe himself in a maladaptive way which prevents him from responding to other situations as he did before, even when no direct negative interactions have occurred in these circumstances. This happens because the functions given in the abuse interactions have been transferred to other responding sharing the self in common.

These indirect functions of verbal behavior have been included in the elegant and landmark clinical strategies provided by Hayes (1984), Hayes and Wilson (1994), and Kohlenberg and Tsai (1991).

Breaking the Behavior-Behavior Relationship

As the experimental literature on behavior-behavior relationships increases, more is known about how to form this relationship and about how to break it. Some cases in which breaking relations is a goal would be (1) when unnecessary statements need to be eliminated, (2) when a rule or description about oneself is maladaptive, (3) when rules control inappropriate behavior with negative consequences in the long term, (4) when rules are inappropriate descriptions of what is going on with devastating effects, as it is the case when they are taken as hallucinations (Luciano, 1992). The first two cases will be described here.

In the first case, performance needs to be freed of particular verbal control because otherwise it is maladaptive. These are cases in which several responses need to be chained without verbal statements in between, otherwise responses will not be in contact with direct contingencies (for example, multiplying with statements about how to multiply, or trying not to be lost in a second language conversation while making statements on the grammatical rules of that language). Relevant stimuli should be presented in a more salient and automatic way to prevent the verbal formula and to mitigate or eliminate the possibility of verbal statements. To prevent rule-following when it is not necessary, teachers have to pay attention to the conditions which will prevent verbal formulae, for example by introducing appropriate prompts (pointing or modeling, but not using echoics, tacting, or questions about the relation of stimuli). The analysis to differentiate the behaviors in which it is necessary "to stop and think" (describing the conditions), or "not to stop", is important in a functional analysis. This contrasts with a cognitive analysis in which in many situations children are asked to formulate relations and then this verbal formula acts as a rule preventing the automatic process (Hall, 1980).

The second case indicated is the breaking the behavior-behavior relations while incorporating new relations, which involves the possibility of forming new beliefs or descriptions about oneself and others, for example when thinking is related to another behavior and this relation results in maladaptive functioning. This happens when someone describes himself in a self-damaging way and then responds according to it, this then being consequated by contingencies that "confirm" the "bad thinking" and so, maintain the behavior-behavior relation (Hayes and Wilson, 1993).

One strategy for changing behavior-behavior relationships is to give a different function to the verbal formula, taking into account the natural social contingencies maintaining the relation to be broken and the new relation to be established. In the relation "complaining verbal behavior about oneself / crying / escape responding", for example, the "complaining verbal behavior" might be decontextualized from the other behavior if it is demanded when the person is behaving positively, for example, when s/he is smiling that will serve as an incompatible establishing operation for complaining. One more example is the use of proverbs (Pelechano, 1991). Another example to decontextualize is by repeating and repeating a verbal statement so that it becomes unrelated to the behavior, a technique called "literality" (Hayes, 1987).

Another strategy to break a behavior-behavior relation (say A-B) is through the incorporation of a contextual cue as conditional stimulus to generate a pattern of different behavior-behavior relations. This contextual cue (X) is incorporated with one behavior (say A) of the relation to be broken, and responding in a different and adaptive way (R1) to A in the context of X is formed (X-A-R1). This new interaction gives a new function to particular verbal behavior (A) which could be transferred to other members of the class (B-R1) and so, in the context of X, A and B relation becomes broken because of new ways of responding. Hence, a behavior-behavior relation is changed by introducing a different context which produces a new one in which, as example, the subject confronts aversive thinking without trying to escape from it but accepting it as it is. As is known from experiments on breaking relations, when the contextual cue is used with several examples and the relation is broken, then other relations are broken when the contextual cue is present in some way. This means that it is not necessary to break all the maladaptive relations, but only a few of them. As indicated previously, these operations have to do with the client's reports of his/her behavior in the therapeutic context and other natural contexts and involve taking into account the social consequences provided to maladaptive ways of behaving which maintained the behavior-behavior relation and compete with the new functions of behaving.

A radical conception of verbal behavior has permitted us, as Hayes and Wilson (1994, p. 289) indicated, "to develop during the last 15 years a set of techniques designed to alter the way verbal relations function" (as by the use of paradoxes, metaphors, literality), especially because "the process by which the verbal behavior that occurs within sessions influences the client's behavior outside the session ... is because the verbal stimuli participate in equivalence classes" (Kohlenberg, Tsai & Dougher, 1993, p. 278). The prime contextual therapies (see Hayes, 1987) have developed as Functional Analytic Psychotherapy of Kohlenberg and Tsai (1991) and Acceptance and Commitment Therapy (Hayes & Wilson, 1994; Hayes, Jacobson, Follette & Dougher; 1994; Kohlenberg, Hayes & Tsai, 1993).

Research on these therapies is as yet limited but promising, for example with regard to many other therapies (see a review in Perez-Alvarez, 1996), and empirically with regard to AIDS (Wulfert & Biglan, 1994), depressive and anxiety behavior (Dougher & Hackbert, 1994; Kohlenberg & Tsai, 1994), and other clinical topics (see Hayes & Wilson, 1993).

Many possibilities confront researchers who will have to take into account conceptual and methodological problems which are as yet unresolved. Language and behavior-behavior relations are the focus of much variability in human activity. The experimental and conceptual literature conducted upon the theoretical analysis published by Skinner in 1957 have produced, and still produce, conceptual knowledge about the enormous complexity of explaining behavior.

References

Andronis, P. (1991). Rule-governance: Enough to make a term mean. In L. J. Hayes & P. N. Chase (Eds.), *Dialogues on verbal behavior* (pp. 226-235). Reno, NV: Context Press.

Ayllon, T., & Azrin, N. H. (1964). Reinforcement and instruction with mental patients. *Journal of the Experimental Analysis of Behavior, 7,* 327-331.

Baer, D. M. (1997). Some meanings of antecedent and environmental control. In D. M. Baer & E. M. Pinkston (Eds.), *Environment and behavior* (pp. 15-29). Oxford: Westview Press.

Baer, D. M., & Sherman, J. A. (1964). Reinforcement control of generalized imitation in children. *Journal of the Experimental Analysis of Behavior, 1,* 37-49.

Baer, D. A., Williams, J. A., Osnes, P. G., & Stokes, T. F. (1985). Generalized verbal control and correspondence training. *Behavior Modification, 9,* 477-489.

Barnes, D., Browne, M., Smeets, P., & Roche, B. (1995). A Transfer of functions and a conditional transfer of functions through equivalence relations in three-to six-year-old children. *The Psychological Record, 45,* 405-430.

Barnes, D., & Keenan, M. (1993). A transfer of functions through derived arbitrary and nonarbitrary stimulus relations. *Journal of the Experimental Analysis of Behavior, 59,* 61-82.

Baron, A., & Galizio, M. (1983). Instructional control of human operant behavior. *The Psychological Record, 33,* 495-520.

Baum, W. M. (1995). Rules, culture and fitness. *The Behavior Analyst, 18,* 1-22.

Bentall, R. P., Lowe, C. F., & Beasty, A. (1985). The role of verbal behavior in human learning: II. Developmental differences. *Journal of the Experimental Analysis of Behavior, 43,* 165-181.

Cangas, A. J., & Pérez-Alvarez, M. (1997). Transformación de las instrucciones en sugestiones mediante procedimientos operantes. *Psicothema, 9,* 167-174.

Catania, A. C. (1992). *Learning.* Englewoods Cliffs, NJ: Prentice-Hall.

Catania, A. C., Matthews, B. A., & Shimoff, E. H. (1982). Instructed versus shaped human verbal behavior: interactions with nonverbal responding. *Journal of the Experimental Analysis of Behavior, 38,* 233-248.

Catania, A. C., Matthews, B. A., & Shimoff, E. H. (1990). Properties of rule-governed behavior and their implications. In D. E. Blackman & H. Lejeune (Eds.), *Behaviour analysis in theory and practice* (pp. 215-226). London: Lawrence Erlbaum Associates.

Cerutti, D. T. (1989). Discrimination theory of rule-governed behavior. *Journal of the Experimental Analysis of Behavior, 51,* 259-276.

Chase, P. N., & Danforth, J. S. (1991). The role of rules and concept formation. In L. J. Hayes & P. N. Chase (Eds.), *Dialogues on verbal behavior* (pp. 205-236). Reno, NV: Context Press.

Chase, P. N., & Iman, A. A. (1987). Establishing equivalent intraverbal relations. *Revista Mexicana de Análisis de la Conducta, 13,* 375-388.

Deitz, S. M. (1986). Understanding cognitive language: the mental idioms in children's talk. *The Behavior Analyst, 9,* 161-166.

Dougher, M. J., Auguston, E., Markham, M. R., Greenway, D. E., & Wulfert, E. (1994). The transfer of respondent eliciting and extinction functions through stimulus equivalence classes. *Journal of the Experimental Analysis of Behavior, 62,* 331-351.

Dougher, M. J., & Hackbert, L. (1994). A behavior-analytic account of depression and a case report using acceptance-based procedures. *The Behavior Analyst, 17,* 321-334.

Dougher, M. J., & Markham, M. R. (1996). Stimulus classes and the untrained acquisition of stimulus functions. In T. R. Zentall & P. M. Smeets (Eds.), *Stimulus class formation in humans and animals* (pp. 137-152). North-Holland: Elsevier.

Eikeseth, S., & Baer, D. M. (1997). Use of a preexisting verbal relation to prevent the properties of stimulus equivalence from emerging in new relations. In D. M. Baer & E. M. Pinkston (Eds.), *Environment and behavior* (pp. 138-143). Oxford: Westview Press.

Ferro, R. (1993). *Formación de reglas y formación de equivalencias en un estudio aplicado* (Proyecto Doctorado). Granada: Universidad de Granada.

Fields, L., Adams, B. J., Verhave, T., & Newman, S. (1990). The effects of nodality on the formation of equivalence classes. *Journal of the Experimental Analysis of Behavior, 53*, 345-358.

Fields, L., Reeve, K. F., Adams, B. J., & Verhave, T. (1991). Stimulus generalization and equivalence classes: A model for natural categories. *Journal of the Experimental Analysis of Behavior, 55*, 305-312.

Galizio, M. (1979). Contingency-shaped and Rule-governed behavior: Instructional control of human loss avoidance. *Journal of the Experimental Analysis of Behavior, 31*, 53-70.

Gil Roales-Nieto, J. (1996). *Un procedimiento Sistemático de Intervención en Promoción de la Salud Bucodental* (Research Report). Almería: Universidad de Almería.

Gómez, S., Barnes, D., & Luciano, M. C. (1997, July 10-13). *Breaking equivalence relations and reducing the variability.* Paper presented at the Third European Meeting for the Experimental Analysis of Behaviour, Dublín, Ireland.

Gómez-Becerra, I. (1996). *Investigación sobre el fenómeno de sensibilidad-insensibilidad a las contingencias y el papel de la conducta verbal.* , Almería, Spain.

Gómez-Becerra, I., & Luciano, M. C. (in press). Correspondencia entre "saber" y "hacer". El caso del comportamiento del educador. *Psicothema.*

Guerin, B. And Foster, M. T. (1994). Attitudes, beliefs and behavior: Saying you like, saying you believe, and doing. *The Behavior Analyst, 17* (155-164).

Hall, R. J. (1980). Cognitive behavior modification and information-processing skills of exceptional children. *Exceptional Education Quarterly, 1*, 9-15.

Hayes, L. (1991). Substitution and reference. In L. J. Hayes & P. N. Chase (Eds.), *Dialogues on Verbal Behavior* (pp. 3-18). Reno: Nevada: Context Press.

Hayes, L. J., Thompson, S., & Hayes, S. C. (1989). Stimulus equivalence and rule following. *Journal of the Experimental Analysis of Behavior, 52*, 275-292.

Hayes, S. C. (1984). Making sense of spirituality. *Behaviorism, 12*, 99-110.

Hayes, S. C. (1986). The case of the silent dog-verbal reports and the analysis of rules: A review of Ericsson and Simon's 'Protocol analysis: Verbal reports as data". *Journal of the Experimental Analysis of Behavior, 45*, 351-363.

Hayes, S. C. (1987). A contextual approach to therapeutic change. In N. S. Jacobson (Ed.), *Psychotherapists in clinical practice: Cognitive and behavioral perspectives* (pp. 327-387). New York: Guilford.

Hayes, S. C., & Barnes, D. (1997). Analyzing derived stimulus relations requires more than the concept of stimulus class. *Journal of the Experimental Analysis of Behavior, 68*, 235-243.

Hayes, S. C., & Brownstein, A. J. (1986). Mentalism, behavior-behavior relations, and a behavior-analytic view of the purposes of science. *The Behavior Analyst, 9*, 175-190.

Hayes, S. C., Brownstein, A. J., Haas, J. R., & Greenway, R. E. (1986). Instructions, multiple schedules and extinction: distinguishing rule-governed from schedule-controlled behavior. *Journal of the Experimental Analysis of Behavior, 46*, 137-147.

Hayes, S. C., Brownstein, A. J., Zettle, R. D., Rosenfarb, I., & Korn, Z. (1986). Rule-governed behavior and sensitivity to changing consequences of responding. *Journal of the Experimental Analysis of Behavior, 45*, 237-256.

Hayes, S. C., Gifford, E. V., & Wilson, K. G. (1996). Stimulus classes and stimulus relations: Arbitrary applicable relational responding as an operant. In T. R. Zentall & P. M. Smeets (Eds.), *Stimulus class formation in humans and animals* (pp. 279-299). North-Holland: Elsevier.

Hayes, S. C., & Hayes, L. J. (1989). The verbal action of the listener as a basis for rule-governance. In S. C. Hayes (Ed.), *Rule-governed behavior: cognition, contingencies, and instructional control* (pp. 153-190). New York: Plenum.

Hayes, S. C., Jacobson, N. S., Follette, V. M., & Dougher, M. J. (Eds.). (1994). *Acceptance and change: content and context in psychotherapy.* Reno, NV: Context Press.

Hayes, S. C., Kohlenberg, B. S., & Hayes, L. J. (1991). The transfer of specific and general consequential functions through simple and conditional equivalence relations. *Journal of the Experimental Analysis of Behavior, 56*, 119-137.

Hayes, S. C., & Wilson, K. G. (1993). Some applied implications of a contemporary behavior-analytic account of verbal events. *The Behavior Analyst, 16*, 283-301.

Hayes, S. C., & Wilson, K. G. (1994). Acceptance and commitment therapy: Altering the verbal support for experiential avoidance. *The Behavior Analyst, 17*, 289-304.

Hayes, S. C., Zettle, R. D., & Rosenfarb, I. (1989). Rule-following. In S. C. Hayes (Ed.), *Rule-governed behavior, cognition, contingencies, and instructional control* . New York: Plenum .

Herruzo, J., & Luciano, M. C. (1994). Procedimientos para establecer la "correspondencia decir-hacer". Un análisis de elementos y problemas recientes. *Acta Comportamentalia, 2* , 192-218.

Hineline, P. N. (1997). How, then, shall we characterize this elephant. *Journal of the Experimental Analysis of Behavior, 68* , 297-300.

Hineline, P. N., & Wanchisen, B. A. (1989). Correlated hypothesizing and the distinction between contingency-shaped and rule-governed behavior. In S. C. Hayes (Ed.), *Rule governed behavior: cognition, contingencies and instructional control* (pp. 221-268). New York: Plenum Press.

Horne, P. J., & Lowe, F. (1996). On the origins of naming and others symbolic behavior. *Journal of the Experimental Analysis of Behavior, 65*, 185-241.

Horne, P. J., & Lowe, C. F. (1997). Toward a theory of verbal behavior. *Journal of the Experimental Analysis of Behavior, 68*, 271-296.

Kaufman, A., Baron, A., & Knopp, R. E. (1966). Some effects of instructions on human operant behavior. *Psychonomic Monograph Supplements, 1*, 243-250.

Keller, F. S., & Schoenfeld, W. N. (1950). *Principles of psychology.* New York: Appleton-Century-Crofts.

Kohlenberg, R. J., Hayes, S. C., & Tsai, M. (1993). Radical behavioral psychotherapy: Two contemporary examples. *Clinical Psychology Review, 13*, 579-592.

Kohlenberg, R. J., & Tsai, M. (1991). Functional analytic psychotherapy: *Creating intense and curative therapeutic relationships.* New York: Plenum.

Kohlenberg, R. J., & Tsai, M. (1994). Improving cognitive therapy for depression with functional analytic psychotherapy: Theory and case study. *The Behavior Analyst, 17,* 305-320.

Kohlenberg, R. J., Tsai, M., & Dougher, M. J. (1993). The dimensions of clinical behavior analysis. *The Behavior Analyst, 16,* 271-282.

LeFrancois, J. R., Chase, P. N., & Joyce, J. N. (1988). The effects of a variety of instructions on human fixed-interval performance. *Journal of the Experimental Analysis of Behavior, 49,* 383-393.

Lloyd, K. E. (1994). Do as I say, not as I do. *The Behavior Analyst, 17,* 131-140.

Lovaas, O. I. (1961). Interaction between verbal and nonverbal behavior. *Child Development, 32,* 329-336.

Lowe, C. F. (1979). Determinants of human operant behavior. In M. D. Zeiler & P. Harzem (Eds.), *Advances in the Analysis of Behavior* (Vol. 1, pp. 159-192). Chichester: John Wiley.

Lowe, C. F., Harzem, P., & Bagshaw, M. (1978). Species differences in temporal control of behavior II: Human performance. *Journal of the Experimental Analysis of Behavior, 29,* 351-361.

Luciano, M. C. (1992). Significado aplicado de los tópicos de inestigación básica conocidos como relationes de Equivalencia, Decir-Hacer y Sensibilidad e Insensibilidad a las contingencias. *Análisis y Modificación de Conducta, 18,* 805-859.

Luciano, M. C. (1995). *Análisis y modificación de conducta. infancia y adolescencia.* Almería: Universidad de Almería.

Luciano, M. C., Gómez-Becerra, I., Plaza, M. C., & Ybarra, J. L. (1997, July 10-13). *Shaped verbal behavior in correspondence training with old people.* Paper presented at the Third European Meeting for the Experimental Analysis of Behaviour, Dublin, Ireland.

Luciano, M. C., & Herruzo, J. (1991, April). *Saying and doing: Maintenance and generalization.* Paper presented at the Experimental Analysis of Behavior Group Meeting, London.

Malott, R. W. (1989). The achievement of evasive goals: Control by rules describing contingencies that are not direct acting. In S. C. Hayes (Ed.), *Rule-governed behavior: cognition, contingencies, and instructional control* (pp. 269-324). New York: Plenum Press.

Martínez-Sánchez, H., & Ribes-Iñesta, E. (1996). Interactions of contingencies and instructional history on conditional discrimination. *The Psychological Record, 46,* 301-318.

Matthews, B. A., Shimoff, E., & Catania, A. C. (1977). Uninstructed human responding: Sensitivity to ratio and interval contingencies. *Journal of the Experimental Analysis of Behavior, 27,* 453-467.

Matthews, B. A., Shimoff, E., & Catania, A. C. (1987). Saying and doing: A contingency-space analysis. *Journal of Applied Behavior Analysis, 20,* 69-74.

Michael, J. (1982). Distinguishing between discriminative and motivational functions of stimuli. *Journal of the Experimental Analysis of Behavior, 37*, 144-155.

Paniagua, F. A. (1990). A procedural analysis of correspondence training techniques. *The Behavior Analyst, 13*, 107-119.

Paniagua, F. A. (1992). Verbal-nonverbal correspondence training with ADHD children. *Behavior Modification, 16*, 226-252.

Paniagua, F. A. (1997). Verbal-nonverbal correspondence training as a case of environmental antecedents. In D. M. Baer & E. M. Pinkston (Eds.), *Environment and behavior* (pp. 43-48). Oxford: Westview Press.

Parrot, L. (1987). Rule-governed behavior: An implicit analysis of reference. In S. Modgil & C. Modgil (Eds.), *B.F.Skinner: Consensus and controversy* (pp. 265-276). London: Falmer Press.

Pelechano, V. (1991). La Psicología de los refranes, Psicologemas, 5(37-64).

Pérez-Alvarez, M. (1996). *Tratamientos psicológicos*. Madrid: Editorial Universitas, S. A.

Reese, H. W. (1989). Rules and rule-governance: Cognitive and behavioristic view. In S. C. Hayes (Ed.), *Rule-governed behavior: cognition, contingencies, and instructional control* (pp. 3-84). New York: Plenum.

Reitman, D., & Gross, A. M. (1996). Delayed outcomes and rule-governed behavior among "noncompliant" and "compliant" boys: A replication and extension. *The Analysis of Verbal Behavior, 13*, 65-78.

Ribes, E., & Sánchez, S. (1992). Individual behavior consistencies as interactive styles: their relation to personality. *The Psychological Record, 42*, 369-387.

Roche, B., & Barnes, D. (1997). A transformation of respondently conditioned stimulus functions in accordance with arbitrarily applicable relations. *Journal of the Experimental Analysis of Behavior, 67*, 275-301.

Schlinger, H. D. (1990). A reply to behavior analysts writing about rules and rule-governed behavior. *The Analysis of Verbal Behavior, 8*, 77-82.

Shimoff, E. (1986). Post-session verbal reports and the experimental analysis of behavior. *The Analysis of Verbal Behavior, 4*, 19-22.

Shimoff, E., Catania, C. A., & Matthews, B. (1981). Uninstructed human responding: Sensitivity of low-rate performance to schedule contingencies. *Journal of the Experimental Analysis of Behavior, 36*, 207-228.

Sidman, M. (1994). *Equivalence relations and behavior: A research story*. Boston: Authors Cooperative.

Skinner, B. F. (1957). *Verbal Behavior*. New York: Appleton-Century-Crofts.

Skinner, B. F. (1969). *Contingencies of reinforcement. A theoretical analysis*. Englewood Cliffs, NJ: Prentice Hall.

Skinner, B. F. (1984). An operant analysis of problem solving (Contingencies and rules: author's response). *Behavioral and Brain Sciences, 7*, 583 - 613.

Skinner, B. F. (1989). The behavior of the listener. In S. C. Hayes (Ed.), *Rule-governed behavior: cognition, contingencies, and instructional control* (pp. 85-96). New York: Plenum Press.

Sowers, J. A., Lloyd, K. E., & Lloyd, M. E. (1977). The effects of a class-based point system on planned-actual study time and actual-reported study time correspondence. *Journal of Personalised Instruction, 2*, 43-46.

Stokes, T. F., & Baer, D. M. (1977). An implicit technology of generalization. *Journal of Applied Behavior Analysis, 10*, 349-367.

Stokes, T. F., Osnes, P. G., & Guevremont, D. C. (1987). Saying and doing: A commentary on a contingency-space analysis. *Journal of Applied Behavior Analysis, 20*, 161-164.

Street, W. R. (1994). Attitude-behavior, congruity, mindfulness, and self-focused attention: A behavior-analytic reconstruction. *The Behavior Analyst, 17*, 145-154.

Sundberg, M. L. (1991). 301 Research topics from Skinner's Book Verbal Behavior. *The Analysis of Verbal Behavior, 9*, 81-96.

Takanishi, R. (1993). The opportunities of adolescence: Research, interventions, and policy. *American Psychologist, 48*, 85-87.

Tracy, D. A., Briddell, D. W., & Wilson, G. T. (1974). Generalization of verbal conditioning to verbal and non-verbal behavior: Group therapy with chronic psychiatric patients. *Journal of Applied Behavior Analysis, 7*, 391-402.

Vaughan, M. E. (1989). Rule-governed behavior in behavior analysis: A theoretical and experimental history. In S. C. Hayes (Ed.), *Rule-governed behavior: cognition, contingencies and instructional control* (pp. 97-118). New York: Plenum Press.

Whitman, T., Burgio, L., & Johnston, M. B. (1984). Cognitive behavioral interventions with mentally retarded children. In A. E. Meyers & W. E. Craighead (Eds.), *Cognitive behavior therapy with children* (pp. 193-228). New York: Plenum Press.

Winokur, S. (1976). *A primer of verbal behavior: An operant view.* Englewood Cliffs, NJ: Prentice-Hall.

Wulfert, E., & Biglan, A. (1994). A contextual approach to research on AIDS prevention. The *Behavior Analyst, 17*, 353-364.

Wulfert, E., & Hayes, S. C. (1988). The transfer of conditional sequencing through conditional equivalence classes. *Journal of the Experimental Analysis of Behavior, 50*, 125-144.

Zentall, T. R., & Smeets, P. M. (Eds.). (1996). *Stimulus class formation in humans and animals.* Norh-Holland: Elsevier Science.

Zettle, R. D., & Hayes, S. C. (1982). Rule-governed behavior: A potential theoretical framework for cognitive-behavior therapy. In P. C. Kendall (Ed.), *Advances in cognitive-behavioral research and therapy* (pp. 73-118). New York: Academic Press.

Notes

Parts of this chapter were presented at the Third European Meeting for the Experimental Analysis of Behaviour, Dublin, Ireland, 1997, and the chapter was completed in 1997. Address correspondence to Carmen Luciano, Department of Psychology, University of Almeria, E-04120 Almeria, Spain.

Chapter 10

Building a Bridge Between Research in Experimental and Applied Behavior Analysis

David P. Wacker
The University of Iowa

Building a Bridge Between Research in Experimental and Applied Behavior Analysis

The purpose of this chapter is to discuss the need for bridge studies - analyses of behavior that provide links between more basic and more applied experimental analyses - in behavior analysis, to describe recent examples of applied behavior analysis studies of aberrant behavior that function as bridge studies, and to identify potential difficulties in publishing bridge studies. As discussed by Mace (1994) and Poling, Alling, and Fuqua (1994), there has been a disconnection between basic and applied research in behavior analysis. As an example of this disconnection, Poling et al. (1994) reported the existence of few cross-citations between the Journal of Applied Behavior Analysis (JABA) and the Journal of the Experimental Analysis of Behavior (JEAB). Given that JABA and JEAB are the leading journals for behavior analysts interested in applied and basic research, respectively, and that whatever link remains between applied and basic researchers would be represented in these journals, the disconnection between applied and basic research would appear to be nearly complete.

Fortunately, behavior analysts have often voiced concern over this disconnection (Hake, 1982), and JABA has launched several initiatives to foster greater integration of basic and applied research. These initiatives, begun by Nancy Neef during her term as Editor (1992-1995), have included the routine publication of discussion articles ("Developments in Basic Research and Their Potential Applications") and the publication of a special issue in 1994 dedicated to bridge studies (see Mace & Wacker, 1994). These initiatives have led to a still small but growing applied literature that is directly connected to basic processes.

The Notion of Bridge Studies

Hake (1982) described behavior analysis as existing along a continuum, with basic research residing on one side of the continuum and applied research on the other side. The studies in the middle, then, are bridge studies. Bridge studies, thus, are analyses of behavior that provide a link between basic (fundamental mechanisms that underlie responding) and applied (application of basic mechanisms to socially relevant behavior) research. A bridge study offers an analysis of behavior that would have almost equal appeal to both basic and applied researchers. The study would serve both to increase our understanding of basic mechanisms and to address (or have clear implications for) an applied problem.

As discussed by Wacker (1996), bridge studies also offer an exciting possibility to behavior analysts: reciprocity between basic and applied research. Too often, it seems, this goal of reciprocity is mistakenly considered to be a unidirectional process whereby applied researchers apply, to a greater or lesser extent, basic principles described by basic researchers. In a reciprocal relationship, applied researchers apply basic processes to socially relevant behavior and especially to behaviors that have proven difficult to treat. Difficulties in these applications are used to stimulate further basic research on those underlying mechanisms which, in turn, provide the basis for even more effective treatment. Thus, bridge studies stimulate both applied and basic research, with applied studies focusing on the degree to which a mechanism can be applied and basic researchers studying specific aspects of the mechanism that have applied value.

Kazdin (1978) provided a nice summary of this type of reciprocal relationship in behavior therapy prior to and during the 1960's. The relationship between the clinic and the lab was often reciprocal, leading to a series of rather powerful therapeutic procedures.

The reciprocal aspect of bridge studies is amplified by current applied studies based on the metaphor of behavioral momentum (resistance to extinction) and basic studies of concurrent and chained schedules of reinforcement (see Mace, 1994, for a summary; and see Nevin, 1996, and Fisher & Mazur, 1997, for more recent discussions). Nevin, Tota, Torquato, and Shull (1990) studied numerous variables related to the persistence of behavior when that behavior encounters a challenge such as periods of extinction. The focus of much of this research was to study rate of responding and rate of reinforcement on resistance to extinction. The initial applications of this mechanism by Mace and colleagues (1988) involved increasing the probability that a client would comply with a nonpreferred request. This was accomplished by preceding that request with a series of high-probability requests. Although the applications were initially successful, some failures to replicate emerged, leading both applied and basic researchers to study this phenomenon further (see Nevin, 1996).

Similarly, Neef, Shade, and Miller (1994) sought to apply various dimensions of reinforcement that had been described previously by Herrnstein (1961) and McDowell (1982). In this case, the basic studies had focused on identifying various dimensions of reinforcement that influenced response allocation to two or more choices. The applied studies evaluated whether manipulating similar dimensions of reinforcement might be useful for promoting improved output of academic work. Although these treatments were generally successful, several applied difficulties emerged in these studies, leading to numerous questions regarding various components of these procedures such as changeover delays (see Fisher & Mazur, 1997).

In both sets of bridge studies discussed thus far, applied researchers encountered a difficult-to-treat, socially valid behavior. Initial treatments were close approximations of basic processes developed in research labs with other topographies of behavior. The initial applications showed great promise but also raised numerous applied and basic questions which, in turn, led to additional research.

Applied Implications of Bridge Studies

As shown in the examples of bridge studies discussed in the previous section, one applied implication of conducting these studies is the development of new treatments. The use of high-probability requests and concurrent choices (schedules of reinforcement) are relatively new treatments for use in applied contexts. Other treatments derived from behavioral economics (Kerwin, Ahearn, Eicher, & Burd, 1995), establishing operations (Vollmer & Iwata, 1991), and stimulus equivalency (de Rose, de Souza, & Hanna, 1996) are being developed at a rather rapid pace in JABA. The development of new treatments that are effective with treatment-resistant behavior has obvious applied value. What is critical to note is that all of these new treatments mentioned above were derived from basic processes and were first described as potential treatments in bridge studies. This outcome alone, the development of new treatment, provides sufficient support for the importance of bridge studies to applied behavior analysts.

To applied researchers, there are at least two other equally important implications of bridge studies. First, bridge studies alter the way we study treatment. Rather than comparing Treatment X to Treatment Y, we instead analyze the conditions under which X or Y might be effective. Instead of attempting to hierarchically order treatments in terms of effectiveness, we instead attempt to study when (under what conditions) one treatment is preferred over another. This change in our analysis has led to different research questions, such as asking why behavior change occurred rather than showing only that change occurred. Bridge studies assist us to improve our understanding of how behavior interacts with the existing environment, which is the fundamental question that applied researchers are attempting to answer.

Relatedly, because we are probing why behavior changes, we are better able to assess behavior. Linking target behavior to basic processes provides for new assessment methodologies as well as new treatments. We can probe behavior during predetermined conditions to determine whether behavior reliably changes with changes in these conditions. Perhaps the best example of the impact of bridge studies on applied research has been the evolution of functional analysis methodologies of aberrant behavior.

Functional Analysis

Historically, the treatment of aberrant behavior displayed by persons with developmental disabilities, such as self-injury or aggression, was based on topography, the direction of desired behavior change (i.e., punishment), or whatever "hot" approach was currently in favor. Basing treatment on these criteria led to a rather large but confusing repertoire of treatments that each were successful on at least some occasions with some clients. It also led to a rather large number of comparison-type studies (comparing Treatment X to Treatment Y) that usually failed to explain why one treatment was more successful than another during any particular investigation. One of the most negative side effects of this situation was the "politicizing" of behavioral treatment. As discussed by Carr, Robinson, and Palumbo (1990), the wrong questions were being asked because the conditions under which any given treatment might be effective were unknown.

Linking treatment to basic processes permits us to "match" needed treatment to the target response in specified contexts. By analyzing behavior within specific contexts, we can begin to study the antecedent and consequent variables controlling behavior. A functional approach to assessing and treating aberrant behavior seeks to identify the environmental contingencies maintaining behavior and to implement treatments that disrupt those maintaining contingencies, apply them to more adaptive responses, or both. The issue, then, is not whether one treatment is better than another, but what environmental variables maintain behavior.

Carr (1977) provided operant hypotheses regarding why aberrant behavior occurred (positive, negative, and sensory reinforcement). Based on these hypotheses, Iwata, Dorsey, Slifer, Bauman, and Richman (1982/1994) developed an assessment methodology for directly analyzing each source of reinforcement for each client evaluated. The methodology, termed a functional analysis, consisted of a series of analogue conditions in which both the establishing operations and reinforcers were manipulated for each type of hypothesized reinforcement. Thus, for positive reinforcement in the form of attention, attention was diverted unless aberrant behavior occurred. When aberrant behavior occurred, attention was delivered contingently. For negative reinforcement, a demand was presented unless aberrant behavior occurred. As control conditions, the client was (a) left alone in a room with nothing to do (sensory reinforcement) and (b) provided with free access to stimulating preferred toys and attention. Each of these four conditions is repeated multiple times, and rate of aberrant behavior within and across conditions is evaluated within a multielement design. If a distinct pattern of behavior emerges (e.g., high, steady rate in attention condition only), then the function of aberrant behavior is identified.

The primary applied implication of this approach to assessment is that treatment is matched to function. If behavior is maintained by attention, time-out or extinction might be applied during treatment and might be coupled with reinforcement of a desired response such as appropriate mands (Carr & Durand, 1985). Conversely, treatments are also ruled out. Time-out would not be indicated for behavior maintained by negative reinforcement in the form of task avoidance. The results of a functional analysis, then, provide for a very logical, systematic means by which to select treatments, to combine interventions into a treatment package, and to rule out treatments for a given individual.

On a more conceptual or basic level, this type of analysis permits us to better understand behavior or, more precisely, to study how aberrant behavior interacts with different aspects of the environment. This increased level of understanding permits us to treat behavior more effectively because we are better able to predict how behavior will respond to changes in the environment.

The link between the variables assessed to known dimensions of reinforcement has also led to an advantage few applied researchers had anticipated: robustness (Derby et al., 1992). Various forms of functional analysis procedures have been described in the literature, with some being a brief version of the original methodology (e.g., Northup et al., 1991) and others focusing on different variables, such as antecedents (e.g., Carr & Durand, 1985). Each of these versions has shown remarkable success, probably because each, despite their differences, is based explicitly on basic, underlying mechanisms. Thus, selection of one version of functional analysis procedures over another is largely a matter of preference.

Of equal importance is that, whereas the initial applications focused on aberrant behavior displayed by persons with developmental disorders, replications of these procedures are showing similar successes with other behaviors and populations (Cooper et al., 1992). This type of generalizability is rare in applied research and might very well be due to the strong link established with basic principles in the original bridge study conducted by Iwata et al. (1982/1994).

Categorical Description as an Inherent Difficulty in Bridge Studies

Although bridge studies have some obvious advantages for applied researchers, authors of these studies face some major obstacles for dissemination. The first difficulty an author faces, of course, is that bridge studies are extremely difficult to conduct. Studies that appeal to both basic and applied researchers will be rare and require substantial skill.

This obvious difficulty aside, the community of behavior analysts who serve on editorial boards can also offer a major challenge because research is often viewed categorically. Studies and journals are divided into applied and basic categories and some studies, therefore, can be difficult to disseminate because they are, in fact, bridge studies.

This problem of dissemination was addressed conceptually by Hake (1982). If we view research in behavior analysis as existing along a continuum, then the categorical distinction between applied and basic research becomes more blurred. As proposed by Wacker (1996), only studies on either end of the continuum are categorized, with the middle area begin more relative than categorical. Given that bridge studies are rare, plotting the existing studies in behavior analysis would result in a u-shaped curve as shown in Figure 1. Thus, the frequency of most studies in JEAB would be on the basic end of the continuum and most studies in JABA would be on the applied end. In other words, a skewed distribution would be evident for both journals, with the tails of each distribution constituting bridge studies.

The goal is not to extend the tails of either distribution but to increase the frequency of bridge studies relative to the overall curve. Thus, the goal is to increase

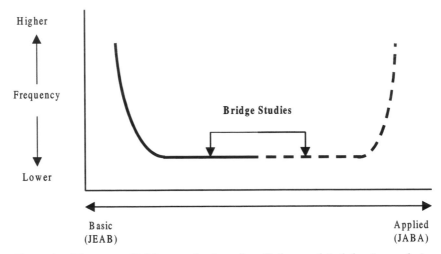

Figure 1.   The current link between basic and applied research in behavior analysis.

the proportion of existing studies rather than to increase the length of the tails in each distribution.

This goal, while obtainable, challenges editorial boards. In JABA, for example, the issue of social validity can be a bit troubling for some reviewers who evaluate a bridge study. Some bridge studies will, of course, have obvious social validity, but many others will be further out on the continuum. There are currently no guidelines for how far away from the applied end of the distribution a study can be and still be publishable in JABA.

As an example of why this can be problematic, consider the original functional analysis study by Iwata et al. (1982/1994). This study does not meet most criteria for social validity. Behavior was assessed in controlled analogue situations, aberrant behavior was reinforced, and no treatment was offered for aberrant behavior other than extinction. The study "simply" showed the responsiveness of aberrant behavior to different types of reinforcement.

What if functional analysis, as a methodology, had never been published because it lacked social validity? Consider now how such a study might be reviewed as a bridge study. It provided a needed link between a socially meaningful response and some of the basic processes that controlled that response. It provided a strong conceptual and methodological basis for later studies which did, in fact, directly establish its social validity. It increased our understanding of a behavior that was quite destructive.

Socially valid treatments may begin with behavior analyses that are linked conceptually but not contextually with meaningful behavior. By disseminating studies that increase our understanding of meaningful behavior, or of treatments often used in society, we build the base needed to develop socially valid treatments. These steps toward developing socially valid treatments, as in the development of all models in science, are often quite small. However, these small steps, as exemplified via functional analysis, can lead to large outcomes.

References

Carr, E. G. (1977). The motivation of self-injurious behavior: A review of some hypotheses. *Psychological Bulletin, 84,* 800-816.

Carr, E. G., & Durand, V. M. (1985). Reducing behavior problems through functional communication training. *Journal of Applied Behavior Analysis, 18,* 111-126.

Carr, E. G., Robinson, S., & Palumbo, L. W. The wrong issue: Aversive vs. nonaversive treatment. The right issue: Functional versus nonfunctional treatment. In A. C. Repp & N. N. Singh (Eds.), *Perspectives on the use of nonaversive and aversive interventions for persons with developmental disabilities* (pp. 361-379). Sycamore, IL: Sycamore Publishing Co.

Cooper, L. J., Wacker, D. P., Thursby, D., Plagmann, I. A., Harding, J., Millard, T., & Derby, M. (1992). Analysis of the effects of task preferences, task demands, and adult attention on child behavior in outpatient and classroom settings. *Journal of Applied Behavior Analysis, 25,* 823-840.

de Rose, J. C., de Souza, D. G., & Hanna, E. S. Teaching reading and spelling: Exclusion and stimulus equivalence. *Journal of Applied Behavior Analysis, 29,* 451-469.

Derby, K. M., Wacker, D. P., Sasso, G., Steege, M., Northup, J., Cigrand, K., & Asmus, J. (1992). Brief functional assessment techniques to evaluate aberrant behavior in an outpatient setting: A summary of 79 cases *Journal of Applied Behavior Analysis, 25,* 713-721.

Fisher, W. W., & Mazur, J. E. (1997). Basic and applied research on choice responding. *Journal of Applied Behavior Analysis, 30,* 387-410.

Hake, D. F. (1982). The basic-applied continuum and the possible evolution of human operant social and verbal research. *The Behavior Analyst, 5,* 21-28.

Herrnstein, R. J. (1961). Relative and absolute strength of response as a function of frequency of reinforcement. *Journal of the Experimental Analysis of Behavior, 4,* 267-272.

Iwata, B. A., Dorsey, M. F., Slifer, K. J., Bauman, K. E., & Richman, G. S. (1994). Toward a functional analysis of self-injury. *Journal of Applied Behavior Analysis, 27,* 197-209. (Reprinted from Analysis and Intervention in Developmental Disabilities [1982], 2, 3-20.)

Kazdin, A. E. (1978). *History of behavior modification.* Baltimore: University Park Press.

Kerwin, M. E., Ahearn, W. J., Eicher, P. S., & Burd, D. M. (1995). The costs of eating: A behavioral economic analysis of food refusal. *Journal of Applied Behavior Analysis, 28,* 245-260.

Mace, F. C. (1994). Basic research needed for stimulating the development of behavioral technologies. *Journal of the Experimental Analysis of Behavior, 61,* 529-550.

Mace, F. C., Hock, M. L., Lalli, J. S., West, B. J., Belfiore, P. Pinter, E., & Brown, D. K. (1988). Behavioral momentum in the treatment of noncompliance. Journal of *Applied Behavior Analysis, 21*, 123-141.

Mace, F. C., & Wacker, D. P. Toward greater integration of basic and applied behavioral research : An introduction. *Journal of Applied Behavior Analysis, 27,* 569-574.

McDowell, J. J. The importance of Herrnstein's mathematical statement of the law of effect for behavior therapy. *American Psychologist, 37,* 771-779.

Neef, N. A., Shade, D., & Miller, M. S. (1994). Assessing influential dimensions of reinforcers on choice in students with serious emotional disturbances. *Journal of Applied Behavior Analysis, 27,* 575-583.

Nevin, J. A. (1996). The momentum of compliance. *Journal of Applied Behavior Analysis, 29,* 535-547.

Nevin, J. A., Tota, M. E., Torquato, R. D., Shull, R. L. (1990). Alternative reinforcement increases resistance to change: Pavlovian or operant contingencies? *Journal of the Experimental Analysis of Behavior, 53,* 359-380.

Northup, J. Wacker, D., Sasso, G., Steege, M., Cigrand, K., Cook, J., & DeRaad, A. (1991). A brief functional analysis of aggressive and alternative behavior in an outclinic setting. *Journal of Applied Behavior Analysis, 24,* 509-522.

Poling, A., Alling, K., & Fuqua, R. W. (1994). Self- and cross-citations in the Journal of Applied Behavior Analysis and the Journal of the Experimental Analysis of Behavior: 1983-1992. *Journal of Applied Behavior Analysis, 27,* 729-731.

Vollmer, T. R., & Iwata B. A. (1991). Establishing operations and reinforcement effects. *Journal of Applied Behavior Analysis, 24,* 279-291.

Wacker, D. P. (1996). Behavior analysis research in JABA: A need for studies that bridge basic and applied research. *Experimental Analysis of Human Behavior Bulletin, 14,* 11-14.

Notes

Portions of this chapter were presented at the Third European Meeting for the Experimental Analysis of Behaviour (July 1997), Dublin, Ireland. Correspondence can be addressed to David P. Wacker, Ph.D., The University of Iowa, 251 University Hospital School, 100 Hawkins Drive, Iowa City, IA 52242 (E-mail: david-wacker@uiowa.edu).

Chapter 11

Functional Analysis of Precurrent Contingencies Between Mands and Destructive Behavior

Wayne W. Fisher, Iser G. DeLeon and David E. Kuhn
*The Kennedy Krieger Institute and Johns Hopkins
University School of Medicine*

Functional Analysis

The assessment and categorization of aberrant behavior has traditionally been based on its structural characteristics and the extent to which certain responses co-occur (e.g., the combination of distractibility, impulsivity, and overactivity has often led to the diagnosis of attention-deficit-hyperactivity disorder [ADHD]). Another approach to assessing and categorizing aberrant behavior is according to its function. Other fields of science, such as microbiology, have long understood the importance of analyzing both the structure and function of dynamic entities. In recent years, behavior analysts interested in the study and treatment of aberrant behavior have similarly begun to assess and categorize these responses not only according to their structural characteristics (e.g., aggression, pica, self-injury), but also in terms of their function. For example, a boy with ADHD might display loud, inappropriate vocalizations at one point in time because it gets him dismissed from a nonpreferred academic activity, math class. He may display this same response at another time because it results in attention from his peers or the teacher. Analyzing and categorizing behavior in terms of its function allows us to determine why the behavior occurs and helps us develop more specific and successful treatments.

From a behavioral perspective, aberrant behaviors are viewed as operant responses that are maintained because they serve some desirable or beneficial function. Skinner (1938) proposed the concept of the operant to help explicate how the consequences a response has produced in the past affect its future probability. That is, responses that have previously produced desirable or beneficial outcomes in a given situation are the ones that are most likely to be repeated in the future under similar circumstances. By contrast, responses that have resulted in undesirable or detrimental consequences are unlikely to be repeated. Thus, over time, the environment selects and the individual displays relatively more of the behaviors that produce desirable or beneficial outcomes and less of other behaviors. Skinner called this process operant selection, and it is somewhat analogous to Darwin's concept of natural selection. Operant selection is not the only variable that influences the probability of aberrant behavior (e.g., biological mechanisms play a critical role as well), but it is certainly an important one.

If one accepts the proposition that the future probability of a response is greatly influenced by the outcomes it has produced in the past (i.e., its reinforcement history), then how do we incorporate this notion into the assessment and treatment of aberrant behavior? Over the past 16 years, a specific approach called the functional analysis model (Neef & Iwata, 1994) has been developed to analyze and categorize aberrant behavior according to its function. Functional analysis attempts to identify the environmental consequences and related antecedents that currently maintain an individual's aberrant behavior. An important and relatively unique characteristic of functional analysis is that the variables of interest (the environmental antecedents and consequences of the aberrant behavior) are systematically manipulated and their effects are directly measured using single-case research methods.

The Development and Impact of Functional Analysis Methods

Functional analysis, as a specific method for analyzing, understanding, and developing treatments for aberrant behavior, began in 1982 with the publication of the seminal paper by Iwata and colleagues (Iwata, Dorsey, Slifer, Bauman, & Richman, 1982/1994). However, there were a number of earlier studies that analyzed relations between a single, specific environmental variable and problem behavior (Berkson & Mason, 1964; Carr, Newsom, & Binkoff, 1980; Lovaas & Simmons, 1969). The method developed by Iwata and colleagues represented a major advance because it provided a procedure that could be used with individual clients to simultaneously analyze the three prevailing operant hypotheses regarding self-injurious behavior (SIB) articulated by Carr (1977). These three hypotheses were that SIB was maintained by (a) negative reinforcement (escape from, or avoidance of nonpreferred activities); (b) positive reinforcement in the form of contingent attention; and (c) automatic reinforcement (e.g., the sensory stimulation automatically produced by the response). The functional analysis method developed by Iwata and colleagues provided a way of determining whether an individual's SIB was maintained by one or more of these sources of reinforcement (e.g., maintained exclusively by attention or a combination of attention and automatic reinforcement).

Iwata et al. (1982/1994) developed a functional analysis method that consisted of a control condition (play) and three test conditions (attention, demand, & alone). Each test condition was developed to analyze one of the hypotheses articulated by Carr (1977). In the attention condition, the client was expected to play quietly with toys while an adult was busy (e.g., reading a newspaper). The adult briefly attended to the client only after each occurrence of SIB. If the rates of SIB were consistently higher in this condition than in the control condition, then it was concluded that the individual's SIB was maintained by attention.

The client was prompted to complete nonpreferred tasks during the demand condition. These tasks were terminated and the relevant materials were removed for 30 seconds following occurrences of SIB, which is a reaction caregivers often have to this behavior (e.g., the caregiver stops the task and gives the person an opportunity to "calm down"). If the rates of SIB were consistently higher in the demand condition than in the control condition, then it was concluded that the individual's SIB was maintained by negative reinforcement in the form of escape from nonpreferred tasks.

SIB maintained by the sensory stimulation it automatically produces is most likely to occur in situations in which there are no competing sources of reinforcement (when the individual has nothing else to do). Therefore, to assess for an automatic reinforcement function, the client was placed in a room alone without toys or materials (i.e., the alone condition). If the rates of SIB were consistently higher in the alone condition than in the control condition, then it was concluded that the individual's SIB was maintained by automatic (or sensory) reinforcement.

In the control condition (play), the client and therapist played together with preferred toys or leisure materials. The therapist provided praise about once every 30 seconds after a 5-second period during which SIB was absent. This condition was designed to simulate an enriched environment, which served as a control for the test conditions.

The client was exposed to each of the test and control conditions multiple times in a randomized order over several days (about 5 to 10 15-minute sessions per condition). The results of the analysis were graphed and visually inspected to identify the function or functions of SIB. Figure 1 shows an example of a functional analysis

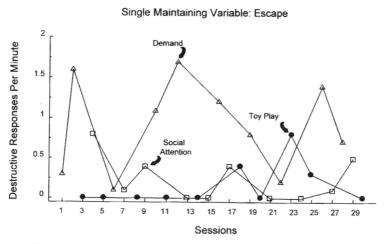

Figure 1. The rates of destructive responses per minute during an analogue functional analysis.

graph for an individual who displayed aberrant behavior maintained by escape from nonpreferred task

The functional analysis method developed by Iwata and colleagues has markedly improved our ability to assess and treat aberrant behaviors. Previous behavioral interventions involved the application of reinforcers not related to behavioral maintenance or punishers designed to "override" the reinforcement contingencies that maintained problem behavior (Mace, 1994). Functional analysis provides a much more rational method of selecting and developing behavioral interventions, ones that are directly relevant to the environmental variables that gave rise to the aberrant behavior.

Fisher, Piazza, Alterson, and Kuhn (in press) described three additional advancements that have resulted from the development of the functional analysis method. First, functional analysis has provided us with a tool with which to better understand the influence of operant mechanisms on severe behavior disorders. That is, epidemiological investigations using the functional analysis method developed by Iwata and colleagues (Iwata, Pace, Dorsey, et al., 1994), or variations of this method (Derby et al., 1992), have largely supported the operant hypotheses described by Carr (1977).

Second, the functional analysis method has resulted in the refinement of specific behavioral procedures like extinction, differential reinforcement, and punishment. For example, Iwata, Pace, Cowdery and Miltenberger (1994) showed that extinction procedures differ dramatically depending on the function of the problem behavior. In fact, it is difficult to envision how one could design a specific extinction procedure without first identifying the reinforcement contingency maintaining the problem behavior, yet such practices were fairly common prior to the development of functional analysis. For example, the technique called planned ignoring has sometimes been referred to as an extinction procedure, but it should function like extinction only for behavior maintained by contingent attention, and it may actually increase responses maintained by negative or automatic reinforcement (e.g., Dura, 1990; Iwata, Pace, Cowdery et al., 1994). Differential reinforcement (DR) procedures may be more effective when the reinforcer that previously maintained problem behavior is identified through a functional analysis and then used to reinforce appropriate behavior. This benefit may occur because DR procedures using the reinforcer that previously maintained problem behavior decrease motivation for the response (e.g., providing attention contingent on appropriate behavior may prevent deprivation of attention, which in turn should reduce motivation to display attention-maintained SIB).

Third, functional analysis research has led to the development of a variety of innovative and effective interventions (e.g., Bowman, Fisher, Thompson, & Piazza, 1997; Carr & Durand, 1985; Chapman, Fisher, Piazza, & Kurtz, 1993; Dunlap, Kern-Dunlap, Clarke, & Robbins, 1991; Horner, Day, Sprague, O'Brien, & Heathfield, 1991; Kennedy & Souza, 1995; Mace & Belfiore, 1990; Pace, Iwata, Cowdery, Andree, & McIntyre, 1993; Touchette, MacDonald, & Langer, 1985; Vollmer, Iwata, Zarcone, Smith, & Mazaleski, 1993). These interventions have often involved one or more of the following: (a) removal of the specific reinforcement contingency responsible for the maintenance of the aberrant behavior (e.g., escape extinction; Iwata et al., 1990); (b) teaching the client to access the reinforcer for aberrant behavior through appropriate behavior (e.g., functional communication training; Carr & Durand, 1985); (c) altering the establishing operation that evokes problem behavior maintained by a given reinforcement contingency (e.g., noncontingent reinforcement; Vollmer et al., 1993); (d) identifying reinforcers that effectively compete with automatically-maintained behavior (e.g., matched stimuli; Piazza et al., in press); and (e) teaching the client to better tolerate the situations that lead to aberrant behavior (e.g., demand fading; Pace et al., 1993). As should be readily apparent, the effectiveness of each of these techniques is dependent on our ability to accurately identify the function(s) of aberrant behavior.

Alterations and Variations of The Functional Analysis Method

Iwata et al. (1982/1994) originally developed their functional analysis method for individuals with mental retardation who exhibited severe SIB. Over the past 15 years, these basic procedures have been adapted and used with a variety of disorders and target behaviors. Functional analysis methods have been applied to tantrums (Repp & Karsh, 1994), elopement (Piazza et al., 1997), breath holding (Kern, Mauk, Marder, & Mace, 1995), various manifestations of aberrant speech (Frea & Hughes, 1997; Mace & Lalli, 1991; Pace, Ivancic, & Jefferson, 1994) and ingestion of a variety of potentially harmful items or substances (Chapman et al., 1993; Mace & Knight, 1986; Piazza, Hanley, & Fisher, 1996). As such, the functional analysis method has proven useful in the assessment and treatment of a diverse variety of behavior problems. Moreover, although functional analysis methods have been used primarily to assess aberrant behavior displayed by persons with mental retardation, these procedures have also proven useful with less severe and more common behavior problems (e.g., Cooper et al., 1992; Northup et al., 1995).

The functional analysis method developed by Iwata et al. (1982/1994) has been modified by various investigators for purposes such as increasing (a) its efficiency (e.g., Northup et al., 1991), (b) its accuracy (Vollmer, Marcus, Ringdahl, & Roane, 1995), (c) its generality to natural environments (e.g., Mace & Lalli, 1991) or different populations (e.g., Northup et al., 1995), and (d) its applicability to idiosyncratic or complex antecedent, behavior, consequence relations (e.g., Horner, Day, & Day, 1997).

One general type of alteration to the functional analysis method developed by Iwata et al. (1982/1994) has been primarily methodological in nature, and the aim has been to produce clearer results and, therefore, more useful information regarding the functions of aberrant behavior. Some of these changes have involved modifications of the experimental design. For example, Vollmer et al. (1995) examined the utility of extended alone sessions in clearing up the results of inconclusive functional analyses. Their rationale was that inconclusive results sometimes stem from multiple treatment interference given the rapidly alternating conditions of the original functional analysis design. By contrast, a series of alone sessions should eliminate the effects of multiple treatment interference. For example, attention-maintained behavior may be evoked during the alone condition because the individual is deprived of attention, and because attention is delivered either contingently or noncontingently in other conditions (i.e., carry-over effects). Such carry-over effects should extinguish more readily during a consecutive series of alone sessions because no attention is delivered throughout the series. Alternatively, if behavior is automatically reinforced, responding should persist in the absence of any social consequences during the series of alone sessions.

Another design change developed to control for the potential interaction effects stemming from rapidly alternating conditions is the pairwise-comparison method described by Iwata, Duncan, Zarcone, Lerman, and Shore (1994). These authors examined behavior under a series of phases in which a single test condition (e.g., demand) was compared to the control condition (play) in each phase. The pairwise-comparison thus decreases the effects of multiple treatment interference because only two conditions are alternated per phase, yet provides a continuous control condition throughout the assessment that would be lacking if a strict reversal design was used (i.e., testing only one condition per phase). For two participants, this design succeeded in producing clear functional analysis outcomes whereas the results of a multielement analysis produced somewhat undifferentiated results.

A different sort of methodological alteration has involved the manner in which the results of a functional analysis are interpreted. As described above, functional analysis results are inspected visually to determine if rates of behavior under any of the test conditions are substantially different from the control condition. Hagopian et al. (1997) developed structured criteria for visually inspecting functional analysis results and showed that the use of these criteria can increase the reliability and validity of the interpretation.

A second general type of alteration has been to combine or replace experimental functional analyses with indirect and direct descriptive assessments (e.g., rating scales, interviews, scatterplots; direct observations in the natural environment) with analogue functional analyses (Belfiore, Browden, & Lin, 1993; Lerman & Iwata, 1993; Mace & Lalli, 1991; Sasso et al., 1992; Touchette et al., 1985). Combining descriptive assessments with experimental functional analyses is sometimes done to help ascertain how much confidence one should have regarding whether or not the function of problem behavior has been accurately identified (Lalli & Goh, 1993). The experimental analysis examines whether various contingencies function as reinforcement for problem behavior, and the descriptive assessments help determine the extent to which those contingencies actually occur in the natural environment. Mace and Lalli (1991) suggested that one should feel most confident when both the descriptive assessment and experimental analysis identify the same operant function(s). Other reasons for combining these two types of assessments are (a) to develop more specific and/or streamlined experimental analyses (Iwata, 1994; Lalli & Goh, 1993); or (b) to identify idiosyncratic operant mechanisms, such as specific establishing operations related to the function for aberrant behavior (e.g., Carr,

Yarbrough, & Langdon, 1997; Fisher, Adelinis, Thompson, Worsdell, & Zarcone, in press; Horner et al., 1997; O'Reilly, 1997).

Some authors have suggested that indirect and direct descriptive assessments may be used as inexpensive and efficient alternatives to experimental functional analyses (Durand & Crimmins, 1988). However, rating scales designed to identify behavioral function tend to be unreliable (Sigafoos, Kerr, Roberts, & Couzens, 1993; Sturmey, 1994; Zarcone, Rodgers, Iwata, Rourke, & Dorsey, 1991). Scatterplot analyses can be somewhat more reliable but are often difficult to interpret (Kahng et al., in press). Descriptive assessments that employ direct observation methods tend to be much more reliable, but the extent to which they produce results equivalent to an experimental analysis remains in question (Lerman & Iwata, 1993; Mace & Lalli, 1991; Sasso et al., 1992).

A third type of modification of the functional analysis method has involved manipulation of the components of individual assessment conditions. For example, Fisher, Piazza, and Chiang (1996) found that variations in the duration of reinforcement across functional analysis conditions sometimes substantially alters the results, because the target response is less likely to occur while reinforcement is available. If reinforcement is delivered for different amounts of times across conditions (as prescribed in the original procedure), those conditions with shorter reinforcement durations may produce considerably higher rates of responding. Similarly, several investigations have found that other reinforcement parameters (e.g., quality of reinforcement) or antecedent events (e.g., rate of demand presentation) can influence functional analysis results (Fischer, Iwata, & Worsdell, 1997; Fisher, Ninness, Piazza, Owen-DeSchryver, 1996; Smith, Iwata, Goh, & Shore, 1995).

Functional Analysis and Interresponse Relations

Again, the key contribution of functional analysis methods to the treatment of aberrant behavior is to permit clinicians to identify the conditions that give rise to and maintain aberrant behavior. One class of conditions that has begun to receive increasing attention involves various relations between separate responses or operant classes. Given that behaviors often occur in close temporal proximity, it seems reasonable to hypothesize that they can influence each other in various ways. There has been a great deal of basic research examining relations between responses and, through functional analyses, clinicians have begun to see parallel relations in the development, maintenance, and treatment of aberrant behavior. In what follows, we briefly describe some examples of these interresponse relations and how they have been implicated in cases of aberrant behavior. Subsequently, we will focus more acutely on interresponse relations in which one response alters the probability of reinforcement for another response.

Operant class membership. Two or more responses may be related in that they belong to the same operant class. An operant class is a set of response topographies that produce the same environmental outcome (Johnston & Pennypacker, 1993). Members of such a class can all be evoked by the same antecedent conditions, and unless they are physically incompatible, may occur simultaneously or in close temporal proximity given those conditions. For example, in an uncomfortably cold room, an individual may both put on a sweater and close an open window. Similarly, aberrant behaviors may tend to co-occur because they are occasioned by the same antecedent conditions and function to produce the same environmental outcomes. Studies employing functional analyses have revealed that highly distinct forms of aberrant behavior are sometimes functionally related in this manner (Derby, Fisher, & Piazza, 1996; Lalli, Mace, Wohn, & Livezy, 1995). Furthermore, some approaches to treatment rely on establishing new responses as members of the same functional class as aberrant behavior. Once the appropriate behavior has been incorporated into the response class, the probability of its occurrence can be raised above that of the inappropriate behavior through a variety of mechanisms including extinction (e.g., Lalli, Casey, & Kates, 1995; Shirley, Iwata, Kahng, Mazaleski, & Lerman, 1997) or punishment (Fisher, Piazza, Cataldo, et al., 1993; Wacker et al., 1990) of the aberrant response or by selecting appropriate responses that are relatively less effortful than the challenging behavior (e.g., Horner & Day, 1992; Horner, Sprague, O'Brien, & Heathfield, 1990).

Responses as reinforcers. Two responses may also be correlated because they are both involved in a contingent relation. That is, the first response is reinforced by the second. Hypotheses regarding behavior as reinforcement have evolved considerably over the years (Premack, 1959, 1965; Sheffield, Roby, & Campbell, 1954; Timberlake and Allison, 1974). These hypotheses share the central notion that contingent access to a behavior that is restricted below its free-operant level will function as reinforcement for other behavior. This sort of relation, in which access to one response functions as reinforcement for another one, sometimes develops between different classes of aberrant behavior. For example, Smith, Lerman, and Iwata (1996) recently described a case in which such a relation developed between SIB and self-restraint. Specifically, their analysis revealed that SIB, a relatively low probability response, was being maintained by contingent access to self-restraint, a response that was much more probable.

Motivational interresponse relations. Behaviors can also be related such that the first response functions as an establishing operation for the second. Establishing operations alter the momentary value of reinforcers and evoke behavior that have, in the history of the organism, produced those reinforcers (Michael, 1982; 1993). For example, water deprivation momentarily increases the value of water as a reinforcer and temporarily increases the frequency of behaviors that have resulted in access to water. Establishing operations may also decrease the frequency of behavior by decreasing the value of the events that maintain the behavior. In a similar way some responses can, as a sort of side effect, alter motivation for aberrant behavior. For example, physical exercise has been shown to decrease aberrant behaviors, such as aggression, SIB, and stereotypies even though the contingencies for these behaviors remained unchanged (e.g., Allison, Basile, & MacDonald, 1991; Baumeister & MacLean, 1984). One explanation of the effects of antecedent exercise is that this activity (i.e., response) acts as an establishing operation and lowers the efficacy of the reinforcers that maintain aberrant behavior (Smith & Iwata, 1997). Although it has not been reported, it is also possible that exercise could potentially increase the effectiveness of the reinforcers that maintain aberrant behavior. For example, activities that produce fatigue could potentially increase the effectiveness of escape as reinforcement.

Functional Analysis of Mands and Destructive Behavior

Precurrent Contingencies, or Facilitative Interresponse Relations

Discriminative stimulus control is said to occur when a change in responding is reliably produced by a stimulus that is correlated with the availability of reinforcement, and one response may function as a S^D for another response (Skinner, 1957). However, in precurrent contingencies the function of the first response is not only discriminative. Precurrent responses actually increase the probability of reinforcement. Skinner (1953) used the term precurrent behavior to describe one relation of this sort, in which one response (the precurrent response) created the opportunity for reinforcement for a subsequent response (the current response).

Parsons, Taylor, and Joyce (1981) described three ways in which a precurrent response can affect a current response. First, the precurrent response "can alter the probability that the organism makes functional contact with the discriminative events controlling the current operant (p. 253)." The responses often termed "attending" and "observing" appear to serve this function. For example, Kelleher (1958) exposed two chimpanzees to conditions in which left key pressing was either reinforced with food on a fixed-interval 30 s (FI 30") schedule or placed on extinction during randomly alternating periods. Each condition was correlated with a different color on the food key, but in the absence of responding on a different key (the stimulus key), the food key lamp remained dark. Presses on the stimulus key illuminated the food key, providing discriminative cues regarding the contingencies currently in operation for the food key. As such, stimulus key presses functioned as precurrent responses that put the participants in contact with discriminative events regarding food key presses, the current response. The results showed that stimulus key presses maintained at rates much higher than that required to keep the food key illuminated and that both participants developed clear discriminations such that responding was much higher during the periods associated with the FI 30" schedule.

A precurrent response can also increase the probability that the current response meets the functional parameters of the response class. Behavior that is sometimes termed "mediating" may fit this pattern. For example, Laties, Weiss, and Weiss (1969) placed rats on differential reinforcement of low rate schedules such that lever presses were reinforced with sweetened condensed milk, but only for responses that followed the preceding response by 18 s. All five rats eventually developed collateral responses (e.g., tail nibbling, licking bars on the grid floor) between lever presses and the development of collateral behavior was associated with increases in the percentage of reinforced lever presses. Furthermore, blocking collateral behavior resulted in a corresponding decrease in the percentage of reinforced lever presses. When lever pressing was placed on extinction for two subjects, lever pressing decreased as expected, but the collateral response displayed by both rats ceased before the lever pressing. It appears, then, that the collateral behaviors were maintained by the increased probability that lever pressing would be sufficiently spaced, thereby increasing the probability of reinforcement for lever presses.

Finally, a precurrent response can alter the probability that the current response is reinforced by directly changing the schedule for the latter response. A recent example of the formation of this sort of relation was reported by Polson and Parsons (1994). Four college students earned points exchangeable for money by pressing the right button on a computer mouse. During baseline periods, each response was reinforced with .02 probability. During experimental phases, presses on the left key increased the probability of right-key reinforcement from .02 to .08 for 15 s. Three of the four participants readily learned to press the left key, in the absence of any instruction, during the experimental phases. By contrast, when there was no precurrent contingency, changeovers to the left key responses declined. Rate of right-key pressing remained constant regardless of the condition, but a higher proportion of right-key response were made within 15 s of a left key response during the experimental periods. A similar pattern emerged for the fourth participant, but only after exposure to a condition in which right-key responses in the normal state were reinforced with zero probability, but with a .08 probability following a left-key response.

Further examples of this sort of relation stem from the use the verbal units that Skinner (1957) termed autoclitics. Autoclitics are verbal responses that are based on or depend on other verbal responses and often function to alter a listener's reaction to other verbal responses. For example, the autoclitic "I think" that precedes the subsequent verbal unit "her name is Sally" functions to convey the weakness of the relationship between "her name is Sally" and the variables that control it. The listener is then able behave in accordance with the weakness of that relation (e.g., by not simply assuming that her name is Sally upon introducing himself).

With regard to the present topic, some forms of autoclitics increase the probability that other verbal responses meet with reinforcement, as is sometimes observed with autoclitics that accompany mands. Skinner (1957) defined a mand as a verbal operant under the control of a relevant motivational state and that typically specifies its reinforcer (e.g., "Give me a drink"). Skinner further states that such verbal operants are more effective when prefaced with an autoclitic such as "I demand." As such, the autoclitic, as a precurrent response, functions to increase the likelihood that the mand, the current response, will contact reinforcement. Problem behavior may also function as a precurrent response that increases the probability that a mand will be reinforced. But before discussing this specific type of precurrent contingency, it may be useful to discuss Skinner's analysis of the mand and its controlling stimuli more fully.

Skinner (1957) proposed a model of interaction between a speaker and a listener relative to the stimuli that evoke (i.e., deprivation and aversive stimulation) and reinforce mands. A mand will specify positive reinforcement when an individual experiences deprivation (e.g., "Give me a drink") and negative reinforcement in the presence of aversive stimulation (e.g., "Please turn off the alarm"). For example, with this paradigm, the listener functions as a discriminative stimulus (S^D) that occasions a mand (e.g., "Give me a drink") when the speaker experiences deprivation or aversive stimulation. Next, the mand functions as a S^D and occasions a response (e.g., giving water to the speaker) from the listener. Delivery of the requested item functions both as reinforcement for the mand and as a S^D that occasions an additional response from the speaker (e.g., saying "thank you"). However, a mand does not always guarantee that the requested reinforcer will actually be delivered. For example, children frequently request that parents buy them toys when at the store, and parents often deny such requests (e.g., saying "No, you have enough toys at home").

Skinner (1957) also suggested that a speaker (e.g., the child) can increase the probability that a listener (e.g., the parent) will reinforce a mand through either positive reinforcement (e.g., thanking the parent when the requested toy is delivered) or negative reinforcement (e.g., throwing a tantrum when the parent denies the request). Although Skinner's paradigm focused on mands and their relevant antecedents and consequences, his paradigm may be just as relevant to the analysis of these secondary responses (e.g., saying "thank you", throwing a tantrum) that alter the future probability of reinforcement for mands.

Precurrent Relations Between Mands and Aberrant Behavior

We have begun to study how aberrant behaviors like aggression, self-injury, and property destruction may function as precurrent responses. That is, we hypothesize that some individuals display aberrant behavior (e.g., aggression) not because this response produces reinforcement directly, but because it increases the probability that another response, the mand, will produce reinforcement. We further hypothesize that precurrent contingencies may develop between destructive behavior and the probability of reinforcement for mands because the two types of responses together produce a wider array of preferred reinforcers more effectively and efficiently than either response alone. Before discussing this hypothesis more fully it may be helpful to present a case from a study by Bowman et al. (1997).

The children in the Bowman et al. (1997) study had well-developed verbal repertoires and frequently "bossed" their parents around (e.g., often manding for particular foods or toys that were not readily available, or the initiation or discontinuation of specific activities). We noticed that these children manded for a wide array of idiosyncratic objects and activities that frequently changed from one day to the next. In addition, they frequently made seemingly unreasonable requests (e.g., having two family members sit in each chair during meals, one person on the others lap), and surprisingly, the parents and family members generally complied with these unusual requests. Destructive behavior generally occurred when the child's mands were not reinforced (e.g., when the parent said "No").

Figure 2 shows a sequential model of how we hypothesize the precurrent contingency occurs between destructive behavior and the probability of reinforcement for mands. The sequence begins with a child request or mand, which is evoked by an establishing operation (usually deprivation or aversive stimulation). The adult may then either comply with or deny the child's request. Compliance with the request functions as reinforcement for the child's mand and, at least momentarily, removes its establishing operation. By contrast, the establishing operation remains in effect if the parent does not comply with child's request. In addition, responding (i.e., the child's mand) without reinforcement (i.e., delivery of the requested object or activity) may serve as an establishing operation for other responses typically evoked by reinforcement deprivation during extinction, such as tantrums, aggression, or SIB. These aberrant responses are often aversive to the parent, and thus they function as negative reinforcement and increase the probability that the parent will comply with child mands in the future. That is, the parent may learn to avoid destructive behavior by complying with the child's mands whenever possible.

In this model, there are three relevant behaviors, two emitted by the child (mands and destructive behavior) and one by the parent (compliance). The reinforcement for the mand is the delivery of the requested object or activity.

Mands and Behavioral Function

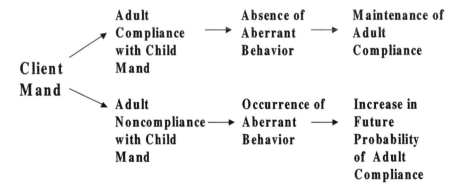

Figure 2. A model of the hypothesized precurrent relation between mands and destructive behavior.

Destructive behavior functions as a precurrent response that increases the probability that the requested object or activity will actually be delivered. The function of adult compliance is to avoid destructive behavior.

Bowman et al. (1997) developed a specific functional analysis method designed to evaluate whether a precurrent contingency between the probability of reinforcement for mands and destructive behavior would maintain the latter response. Figure 3 shows the results of two functional analyses conducted with a participant from the Bowman et al. study. Jerry was a 12-year-old boy with a seizure disorder, PDD, mild to moderate mental retardation, and attention deficit-hyperactivity disorder. The top panel of the figure shows the results of an assessment of destructive behavior using the functional analysis method developed by Iwata et al. (1982/1994). As can be seen, the rates of destructive behavior were highly variable both within and between conditions, and thus no clear function for the behavior was identified. The bottom panel shows the findings from a second functional analysis (called the mand analysis), which was based on the hypothesis that destructive behavior was a precurrent response that increased the probability of reinforcement for mands.

In the control condition of the mand analysis, the therapist complied with all child requests or mands and destructive behavior produced no social consequences (i.e., extinction). At the start of each test condition, the therapist discontinued reinforcement of mands, but then resumed compliance with mands for 30 seconds contingent on destructive behavior. The results in the bottom panel clearly show that destructive behavior occurred exclusively in the condition where its function was to increase reinforcement for mands.

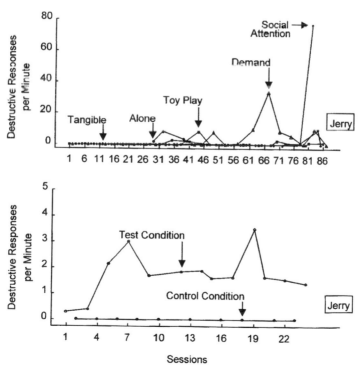

Figure 3. The rates of destructive responses per minute during the analogue functional analysis (top panel), and the mands analysis (bottom panel) for Jerry. (From Bowman, L. G., Fisher, W. W., Thompson, R. H., & Piazza, C. C. (1997). On the relation of mands and the function of destructive behavior. Journal of Applied Behavior Analysis, 30, 257; reprinted by permission of the Society for The Experimental Analysis of Behavior).

Bowman et al (1997) also showed how information about this sort of precurrent contingency could be used to develop and effective intervention for destructive behavior. Figure 4 shows the results of the treatment evaluation conducted with Jerry. The baseline in this analysis was identical to the test condition of the mand analysis (i.e., destructive behavior functioned to increase reinforcement for mands). During functional communication training with extinction (FCT + EXT), Jerry was taught a more appropriate precurrent response (the statement, "Please play by my rules"), which resulted in reinforcement of mands for 30 seconds. During treatment, destructive behavior was placed on extinction (i.e., it produced no social conse-quence). This treatment reduced destructive behavior considerably, but did not eliminate it. We then added another treatment component, a response cost in which the therapist immediately discontinued reinforcement of mands contingent on destructive behavior. The combination of differential reinforcement of an alterna-tive precurrent response (i.e., communication) and a response cost reduced destruc-tive behavior to near-zero levels. The next step in the treatment process (data not shown) was to gradually teach Jerry the difference between appropriate mands (which continued to produce reinforcement) and those that were inappropriate (which were placed on extinction). In addition, Jerry was also taught that even appropriate mands would not produce reinforcement at all times (e.g., during work activities).

We argue that a precurrent relation between mands and destructive behavior may develop in some individuals because the combination of these two responses are more efficient and effective at producing reinforcement than either response

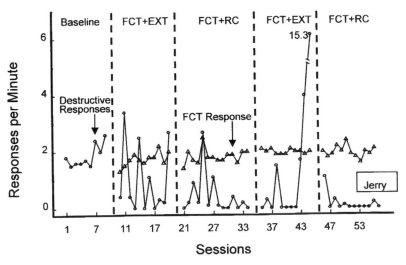

Figure 4. The rates of destructive behavior and communication responses per minute during the treatment evaluation for Jerry. (From Bowman, L. G., Fisher, W. W., Thompson, R. H., & Piazza, C. C. (1997). On the relation of mands and the function of destructive behavior. Journal of Applied Behavior Analysis, 30, 259; reprinted by permission of the Society for The Experimental Analysis of Behavior).

alone. Most people seek a variety of reinforcers, and their relative preferences for these objects and activities may change from one moment to the next. Because of this, mands provide a highly efficient way for a speaker (e.g., the child) to specifying the reinforcer that is most preferred at a given point in time. However, mands do not insure that the listener (e.g., the parent) will deliver the requested reinforcer. By contrast, destructive behavior provides little or no information to the listener regarding the reinforcer that is most preferred by a speaker at a given point in time. Nevertheless, destructive behavior displayed by a child is often aversive to a parent (or other caregiver), and as such, it should act as an effective establishing operation for escape or avoidance contingencies. Thus, the two responses together have complementary functions. Mands specify a variety of preferred reinforcers at various points in time and destructive behavior increases the probability that the specified objects or activities will actually be delivered.

The Bowman et al. (1997) investigation focused on the functions of the two child behaviors (mands and destructive behavior) in our model, but not on the hypothesized function of the critical parental response (i.e., parental compliance maintained by avoidance of child destructive behavior). Although this remains an untested hypothesis within the model, the findings of other studies suggest that it is a reasonable hypothesis (e.g., Carr, Taylor, & Robinson, 1991; Wahler & Dumas, 1986). In one such study, Carr et al. found that, over time, adults reduced the number and type of instructional demands they presented to children who exhibited problem behavior during work situations. This change in adult behavior did not occur when they worked with children who did not display problem behavior. Consistent with our model, Carr et al. hypothesized that the adults in their study found the children's aberrant behavior aversive, and so they stopped presenting those demands that evoked the aberrant behavior (i.e., a punishment effect). Our model and the one proposed by Carr et al. are based on the premise that our understanding of and ability to treat problem behavior may be enhanced by viewing aberrant behavior as a component of an interaction between a child and an adult.

We have conducted mand analyses with multiple participants and thus far it appears that this analysis may be most appropriate with two groups of clients. All of the participants whose destructive behavior served as a precurrent response that increased the probability of reinforcement of mands had been diagnosed with either (a) oppositional defiant disorder or (b) pervasive developmental disorder (PDD). Interestingly, the type of mands emitted by these two groups differed qualitatively in ways that were consistent with their respective diagnoses.

The individuals with oppositional defiant disorder emitted a much wider and more complex array of mands (e.g., making up an increasingly complex set of rules for an ongoing card game, requiring the adult to perform silly or embarrassing responses). Anecdotally, it appeared to us that dictating the adult's activity (i.e., being in charge or the boss) was often more reinforcing than the actual stimuli that were delivered following a given mand. For example, these children would often emit multiple mands, each one followed by adult compliance, without consuming any of the requested items (e.g., "Get me a ball", "Now turn on the TV", "Now get me some water" without ever playing with the ball, watching the TV, or drinking the water). Among the children diagnosed with a pervasive developmental disorder, we rarely (if ever) saw this pattern of responding. Thus, having interpersonal control (being able to dictate the actions of another person) appeared to be highly reinforcing for the children diagnosed with oppositional defiant disorder, and sometimes more reinforcing than the specific items or objects that were delivered following the mands.

The children with pervasive developmental disorder often displayed mands that permitted them, either alone or in conjunction with the adult, to emit stereotypic or ritualistic behavior. For example, one individual with autism would sometimes mand to be left alone, and then would engage in stereotypic behavior. Another individual would mand for family members to participate in a given ritual (e.g., when getting into the family van, each member was required to enter the van in a specific order and to sit in a specific seat in order to avoid an outburst of destructive behavior). Thus, in part, the precurrent contingency that developed between destructive behavior the probability of reinforcement for mands allowed these individuals with PDD increased access to preferred stereotypies and rituals, and helped them to better "maintain sameness in their environments".

Concluding Comments

The functional analysis method developed by Iwata et al. (1982/1994) was originally designed specifically for the assessment of SIB. Its use has been extended to a variety of other problems and populations. Although this method appears to have fairly wide applicability, there may be specific situations in which these methods should be altered in order to better meet the needs of a given problem or population. The analysis of interresponse relations among aberrant behavior (e.g., property destruction and stereotypies) or between aberrant and appropriate behavior (e.g., mands and destructive behavior) may represent examples of this type of situation. The analyses used in the clinical investigations described above to evaluate interresponse relations borrow important features from the functional analysis method developed by Iwata et al. Perhaps the most important of these features are that the hypothesized establishing operation and consequence for problem behavior are present in the test condition and one or preferably both of these variables are absent from the control condition. Future researchers may wish to keep these important features in mind as they attempt to further refine the functional analysis method for use with unique behavior disorders.

References

Allison, D. B., Basile, V. C., & MacDonald, R. B. (1991). Brief report: Comparative effects of antecedent exercise and lorazepam on the aggressive behavior of an autistic man. *Journal of Autism and Developmental Disorders, 21,* 89-94.

Baumeister, A., & MacLean, W. (1984). Deceleration of self-injurious and stereo-typic responding by exercise. *Applied Research in Mental Retardation, 5,* 385-393.

Belfiore, P. J., Browder, D. M., & Lin, C. (1993). Using descriptive and experimental analyses in the treatment of self-injurious behavior. *Education and Training in Mental Retardation, 28,* 57-65.

Berkson, G., & Mason, W. A. (1964). Stereotyped movements of mental defectives: IV. The effects of toys and the character of the acts. *American Journal of Mental Deficiency, 68,* 511-524.

Bowman, L. G., Fisher, W. W., Thompson, R. H., & Piazza, C. C. (1997). On the relation of mands and the function of destructive behavior. *Journal of Applied Behavior Analysis, 30,* 251-265.

Carr, E. G. (1977). The motivation of self-injurious behavior: A review of some hypotheses. *Psychological Bulletin, 84,* 800-816.

Carr, E. G., & Durand, V. M. (1985). Reducing behavior problems through functional communication training. *Journal of Applied Behavior Analysis, 18,* 111-126.

Carr, E. G., Newsom, C. D., & Binkoff, J. A. (1980). Escape as a factor in the aggressive behavior of two retarded children. *Journal of Applied Behavior Analysis, 13,* 101-117.

Carr, E. G., Taylor, J. C., & Robinson, S. (1991). The effects of severe behavior problems in children on the teaching behavior of adults. *Journal of Applied Behavior Analysis, 24,* 523-535.

Carr, E. G., Yarbrough, S. C., & Langdon, N. A. (1997). Effects of idiosyncratic stimulus variables on functional analysis outcomes. *Journal of Applied Behavior Analysis, 30,* 673-686.

Chapman, S., Fisher, W., Piazza, C. C., & Kurtz, P. F. (1993). Functional assessment and treatment of life-threatening drug ingestion in a dually diagnosed youth. *Journal of Applied Behavior Analysis, 26,* 255-256.

Cooper, L. J., Wacker, D. P., Thursby, D., Plagmann, L. A., Harding, J., Millard, T., & Derby, M. (1992). Analysis of the effects of task preferences, task demands, and adult attention on child behavior in outpatient and classroom settings. *Journal of Applied Behavior Analysis, 25,* 823-840.

Derby, K. M., Fisher, W. W., & Piazza, C. C. (1996). The effects of contingent and noncontingent attention on self-injury and self-restraint. *Journal of Applied Behavior Analysis, 29,* 101-110.

Derby, K. M., Wacker, D. P., Sasso, G. M., Steege, M., Northup, J., Cigrand, K., & Asmus, J. (1992). Brief functional assessment techniques to evaluate aberrant behavior in an outpatient setting: A summary of 79 cases. *Journal of Applied Behavior Analysis, 25,* 713-722.

Dunlap, G., Kern-Dunlap, L., Clarke, S., & Robbins, F. R. (1991). Functional assessment, curricular revision, and severe behavior problems. *Journal of Applied Behavior Analysis, 24,* 387-397.

Dura, J. R. (1990). Facial screening fails in the treatment of stereotypy. *Psychological Reports, 67,* 1171-1174.

Durand, V. M., & Crimmins, D. B. (1988). Identifying the variables maintaining self-injurious behavior. *Journal of Autism and Developmental Disorders, 18,* 99-117.

Fischer, S. M., Iwata, B. A., & Worsdell, A. S. (1997). Attention as an establishing operation and as reinforcement during functional analyses. *Journal of Applied Behavior Analysis, 30,* 335-338.

Fisher, W. W., Adelinis, J. D., Thompson, R. H., Worsdell, A. S., & Zarcone, J. R. (in press). Functional analysis and treatment of destructive behavior maintained by termination of "Don't" (and symmetrical "Do") requests. *Journal of Applied Behavior Analysis.*

Fisher, W. W., Ninness, H. A.C., Piazza, C. C., & Owen-DeSchryver, J. S. (1996). On the reinforcing effects of the content of verbal attention. *Journal of Applied Behavior Analysis, 29,* 235-238.

Fisher, W. W., Piazza, C. C., Alterson, C. J., & Kuhn, D. E. (in press). Interresponse relations among aberrant behaviors displayed by persons with autism and developmental disabilities.

Fisher, W., Piazza, C., Cataldo, M., Harrell, R., Jefferson, G., & Conner, R. (1993). Functional communication training with and without extinction and punishment. *Journal of Applied Behavior Analysis, 26,* 23-36.

Fisher, W. W., Piazza, C. C., & Chiang, C. L. (1996). Effects of equal and unequal reinforcer duration during functional analysis. *Journal of Applied Behavior Analysis, 29,* 117-120.

Frea, W. D., & Hughes, C. (1997). Functional analysis and treatment of social-communicative behavior of adolescents with developmental disabilities. *Journal of Applied Behavior Analysis, 30,* 701-704.

Hagopian, L. P., Fisher, W. W., Thompson, R. H., Owen-DeSchryver, J., Iwata, B. A., & Wacker, D. P. (1997). Toward the development of structured criteria for interpretation of functional analysis data. *Journal of Applied Behavior Analysis, 30,* 313-325.

Horner, R. H., & Day, H. M. (1991). The effects of response efficiency on functionally equivalent, competing behaviors. *Journal of Applied Behavior Analysis, 24,* 719-732.

Horner, R. H., Day, H. M., & Day, J. R. (1997). Using neutralizing routines to reduce problem behaviors. *Journal of Applied Behavior Analysis, 30,* 601-614.

Horner, R. H., Sprague, J. R., O'Brien, M. M., & Heathfield, L. T. (1990). The role of response efficiency in the reduction of problem behaviors through functional equivalence training: A case study. *Journal of the Association for Persons with Severe Handicaps, 15,* 91-97.

Horner, R. H., Day, H. M., Sprague, J. R., O'Brien, M., & Heathfield, L. T. (1991). Interspersed requests: A nonaversive procedure for reducing aggression and self-injury during instruction. *Journal of Applied Behavior Analysis, 24,* 265-278.

Iwata, B. A. (1994). Functional analysis methodology: Some closing comments. *Journal of Applied Behavior Analysis, 27,* 413-418.

Iwata, B. A., Pace, G. M., Kalsher, M. J., Cowdery, G. E., & Cataldo, M. F. (1990). Experimental analysis and extinction of self-injurious escape behavior. *Journal of Applied Behavior Analysis, 23,* 11-27.

Iwata, B. A., Dorsey, M. F., Slifer, K. J., Bauman, K. E., & Richman, G. S. (1994). Toward a functional analysis of self-injury. *Journal of Applied Behavior Analysis, 27*, 197-209. (Reprinted from Analysis and Intervention in Developmental Disabilities, 2, 3-20, 1982.)

Iwata, B. A., Duncan, B. A., Zarcone, J. R., Lerman, D. C., & Shore, B. A. (1994). A sequential, test-control methodology for conducting functional analyses of self-injurious behavior. *Behavior Modification, 18*, 289-306.

Iwata, B. A., Pace, G. M., Cowdery, G. E., & Miltenberger, R. G. (1994). What makes extinction work: An analysis of procedural form and function. *Journal of Applied Behavior Analysis, 27*, 131-144.

Iwata, B. A., Pace, G. M., Dorsey, M. F., Zarcone, J. R., Vollmer, T. R., Smith, R. G., Rodgers, T. A., Lerman, D. C., Shore, B. A., Mazaleski, J. L., Goh, H., Cowdery, G. E., Kalsher, M. J., McCosh, K. C., & Willis, K. D. (1994). The functions of self-injurious behavior: An experimental-epidemiological analysis. *Journal of Applied Behavior Analysis, 27*, 215- 240.

Johnston, J. M., & Pennypacker, H. S. (1993). *Strategies and tactics of behavioral research* (2nd edition). Hillsdale, NJ: Lawrence Erlbaum Associates, Inc.

Kahng, S., Iwata, B. A., Fischer, S. M., Page, T. J., Treadwell, K. R. H., Williams, D. E., & Smith, R. G. (in press). Temporal distributions of problem behavior based on scatter plot analysis. *Journal of Applied Behavior Analysis.*

Kelleher, R. T. (1958). Stimulus-producing responses in chimpanzees. *Journal of the Experimental Analysis of Behavior, 1*, 87-102.

Kennedy, C. H., & Souza, G. (1995). Functional analysis and treatment of eye-poking. *Journal of Applied Behavior Analysis, 28*, 27-37.

Kern, L., Mauk, J. E., Marder, T. J., & Mace, F. C. (1995). Functional analysis and intervention for breath holding. *Journal of Applied Behavior Analysis, 28*, 339-340.

Lalli, J. S., & Goh, H. (1993). Naturalistic observations in community settings. In J. Reichle, & D. P. Wacker (Eds.), *Communicative alternatives to challenging behavior: integrating functional assessment and intervention strategies* (Vol. 3, pp. 11-39). Baltimore MD: Paul H. Brookes Publishing Co.

Lalli, J. S., Casey, S., & Kates, K. (1995). Reducing escape behavior and increasing task completion with functional communication training, extinction, and response chaining. *Journal of Applied Behavior Analysis, 28*, 261-268.

Lalli, J. S., Mace, F. C., Wohn, T., & Livezey, K. (1995). Identification and modification of a response-class hierarchy. *Journal of Applied Behavioral Analysis, 28*, 551-559.

Lerman, D. C., & Iwata, B. A. (1993). Descriptive and experimental analysis of variables maintaining self-injurious behavior. *Journal of Applied Behavior Analysis, 26*, 293-319.

Lovaas, O. I., & Simmons, J. Q. (1969). Manipulation of self-destruction in three retarded children. *Journal of Applied Behavioral Analysis, 2*, 143-157.

Mace, F. C. (1994). The significance and future of functional analysis methodologies. *Journal of Applied Behavior Analysis, 27*, 385-392.

Mace, F. C., & Belfiore, P. (1990). Behavioral momentum in the treatment of escape-motivated stereotypy. *Journal of Applied Behavioral Analysis, 23,* 507-514.

Mace, F. C., & Knight, D. (1986). Functional analysis and treatment of severe pica. *Journal of Applied Behavior Analysis, 19,* 411-416.

Mace, F. C., & Lalli, J. S. (1991). Linking descriptive and experimental analysis in the treatment of bizarre speech. *Journal of Applied Behavior Analysis, 24,* 553-562.

Michael, J. (1982). Distinguishing between discriminative and motivational functions of stimuli. *Journal of the Experimental Analysis of Behavior, 37,* 149-155.

Michael, J. (1993). Establishing operations. *The Behavior Analyst, 16,* 191-206.

Neef, N. A., & Iwata, B. A. (1994). Current research of functional analysis methodologies: An introduction. *Journal of Applied Behavior Analysis, 27,* 211-214.

Northup, J., Broussard, C., Jones, K., George, T., Vollmer, T. R., Herring, M. (1995). The differential effects of teacher and peer attention on the disruptive classroom behavior of three children with a diagnosis of attention deficit hyperactivity disorder. *Journal of Applied Behavior Analysis, 28,* 227-228.

Northup, J., Wacker, D., Sasso, G., Steege, M., Cigrand, K., Cook, J., & DeRaad, A. (1991). A brief functional analysis of aggressive and alternative behavior in an outpatient setting. *Journal of Applied Behavior Analysis, 24,* 509-522.

O'Reilly, M. F. (1997). Functional analysis of episodic self-injury correlated with recurrent otitis media. *Journal of Applied Behavior Analysis, 30,* 165-168.

Pace, G. M., Ivancic, M. T., & Jefferson, G. (1994). Stimulus fading as treatment for obscenity in a brain-injured adult. *Journal of Applied Behavior Analysis, 27,* 301-305.

Pace, G. M., Iwata, B. A., Cowdery, G. E., Andree, P. J., & McIntyre, T. (1993). Stimulus (instructional) fading during extinction of self-injurious escape behavior. *Journal of Applied Behavior Analysis, 26,* 205-212.

Piazza, C. C., Fisher, W. W., Hanley, G. P., LeBlanc, L., Worsdell, A. S., Lindauer, S. E., & Keeney, K. M. (in press). Assessment and treatment of the social and automatic functions of pica. *Journal of Applied Behavior Analysis.*

Piazza, C. C., Hanley, G. P., Bowman, L. G., Ruyter, J. M., Lindauer, S. E., & Saiontz, D. M. (1997). Functional analysis and treatment of elopement. *Journal of Applied Behavior Analysis, 30,* 653-672.

Piazza, C. C., Hanley, G. P., & Fisher, W. W. (1996). Functional analysis and treatment of cigarette pica. *Journal of Applied Behavior Analysis, 29,* 437-450.

Premack, D. (1959). Toward empirical behavior laws I. Positive Reinforcement. *Psychological Review, 66,* 219-233.

Premack, D. (1965). Reinforcement theory. In D. Levine (Ed.), *Nebraska Symposium on Motivation* (Vol. 13, pp. 123-180). Lincoln: University of Nebraska Press.

Repp, A. C., & Karsh, K. G. (1994). Hypothesis-based interventions for tantrum behaviors of persons with developmental disabilities in school settings. *Journal of Applied Behavior Analysis, 27,* 21-31

Sasso, G. M., Reimers, T. M., Cooper, L. J., Wacker, D., Berg, W., Steege, M., Kelly, L., & Allaire, A. (1992). Use of descriptive and experimental analysis to identify the functional properties of aberrant behavior in school settings. *Journal of Applied Behavior Analysis, 25*, 809-821.

Sheffield, F. D., Roby, T. B., & Campbell, B. A. (1954). Drive reduction versus consummatory behavior as determinants of reinforcement. *Journal of Comparative and Physiological Psychology, 47*, 349-354.

Shirley, M. J., Iwata, B. A., Kahng, S., Mazaleski, J. L., & Lerman, D. C. (1997). Does functional communication training compete with ongoing contingencies of reinforcement? An analysis during response acquisition and maintenance. *Journal of Applied Behavior Analysis, 30*, 93-104.

Sigafoos, J., Kerr, M., Roberts, D., & Couzens, D. (1993). Reliability of structured interviews for the assessment of challenging behavior. *Behaviour Change, 10*, 47-50.

Skinner, B. F. (1938). *The Behavior of Organisms*. Cambridge, MA: Copley Publishing Group.

Skinner, B. F. (1957). Verbal behavior. Cambridge, MA: Prentice-Hall.

Smith, R. G., & Iwata, B. A. (1997). Antecedent influences on behavior disorders. *Journal of Applied Behavior Analysis, 30*, 343-375.

Smith, R. G., Iwata, B. A., Goh, H., & Shore, B. A. (1995). Analysis of establishing operations for self-injury maintained by escape. *Journal of Applied Behavior Analysis, 28*, 515-535.

Smith, R. G., Lerman, D. C., & Iwata, B. A. (1996). Self-restraint as positive reinforcement for self-injurious behavior. *Journal of Applied Behavior Analysis, 29*, 99-102.

Sturmey, P. (1994). Assessing the functions of aberrant behavior: A review of psychometric instruments. *Journal of Autism and Developmental Disorders, 24*, 293-304.

Timberlake, W., & Allison, J. (1974). Response deprivation: An empirical approach to instrumental performance. *Psychological Review, 81*, 146-164.

Touchette, P. E., MacDonald, R. F., & Langer, S. N. (1985). A scatter plot for identifying stimulus control of problem behavior. *Journal of Applied Behavior Analysis, 18*, 343-351.

Vollmer, T. R., Iwata, B. A., Zarcone, J. R., Smith, R. G., & Mazaleski, J. L. (1993). The role of attention in the treatment of attention-maintained self-injurious behavior: Noncontingent reinforcement and differential reinforcement of other behavior. *Journal of Applied Behavior Analysis, 26*, 9-21.

Vollmer, T. R., Marcus, B. A., Ringdahl, J. E., & Roane, H. S. (1995). Progressing from brief assessments to extended experimental analyses in the evaluation of aberrant behavior. *Journal of Applied Behavior Analysis, 28*, 561-576.

Wacker, D. P., Steege, M. W., Northup, J., Sasso, G., Berg, W., Reimers, T., Cooper, L., Cigrand, K., & Donn, L. (1990). A component analysis of functional communication training across three topographies of severe behavior problems. *Journal of Applied Behavior Analysis, 23*, 417-429.

Wahler, R. G., & Dumas, J. E. (1986). Maintenance factors in coercive mother-child interactions: The compliance and predictability hypothesis. *Journal of Applied Behavior Analysis, 19,* 13-22.

Zarcone, J. R., Rodgers, T. A., Iwata, B. A., Rourke, D. A., & Dorsey, M. F. (1991). Reliability analysis of the Motivation Assessment Scale: A failure to replicate. Research in *Developmental Disabilities, 12,* 349-360.

Notes

Address correspondence to: Wayne W. Fisher, Ph.D., Neurobehavioral Unit, Kennedy Krieger Institute, 707 N. Broadway, Baltimore, MD 21205.
E-mail: Fisher@KennedyKrieger.org

This manuscript was supported in part by Grant MCJ249149-02 from the Maternal and Child Health Service of the U.S. Department of Health and Human Services.

Chapter 12

Behavioral History: Implications for Applied Behavior Analysis

Ian Taylor, Mark F. O'Reilly and Giulio Lancioni
*University of Ulster at Jordanstown, University College,
Dublin, and University of Leiden*

> When we reinforce an organism on Monday and see the effect on Tuesday,
> it is reassuring to suppose that Monday's reinforcement produced knowl-
> edge which survived until Tuesday or a memory which could be recalled on
> Tuesday. (Skinner, 1969, p. 277)

One of the goals of the experimental analysis of behavior has been to demonstrate that behavior is a lawful and orderly function of an organism's environment (Skinner, 1953). The environment, however, is not limited to current conditions: Behaviour is a function of present contingencies only through past experience (Branch, 1987). That is, current responding reflects an interaction between control by current contingencies and past ones. The field of behavior analysis has tended to focus on current contingencies that minimize the extent and duration of past experiences (i.e., an emphasis on temporally proximal contingencies that may conceal the effects of temporally distal ones). It is assumed that if current variables fully account for behavior, there is no need to specify past experiences (Freeman & Lattal, 1992). Such a proposition, however, may not be justified. Variability in responding, for example, may sometimes result in part from historical variables (Carr, 1994). History effects may therefore be a useful construct to describe sources of control over present behavior that have not been eliminated by current contingencies. Historical variables may sometimes confound the obtained functional relations between responding and current contingencies. Without a known history of current responding, the effects of important environmental variables may remain unspecified.

Access to Historical Variables

In seeking information on past events the behavior analyst can ask an individual to verbally report the events. When distal events are remote, complex, and inaccessible, proximal events such as verbal self-reports are all the more useful. The tact is a useful conceptualization of verbal self-reports of historical events which an individual has elusive or special contact with (Skinner, 1957). A person's verbal community provides differential reinforcement for correspondence between events and the reporting of them. The process of reinforcing accurate tacts of past events continues throughout a person's life with the verbal community relying on intermittent corroboration by chance witnesses and consistencies in the telling and retelling of an event. Unfortunately, historical behavioral events may be invented or misconstrued when there are immediate reinforcers for doing so. They may be constructed, or confabulated depending on the contingencies in operation. Given these inherent difficulties, an alternative to having individuals verbally report past history is for the experimenter to provide an experimental history relevant to the experimental task under consideration. In line with this rationale, Sidman (1960) suggested that historical variables can be studied systematically by arranging certain experiences and then evaluating the effects of those experiences on subsequent performance. A database is beginning to emerge in both the basic and applied literature making use of such a research strategy.

Experimental Histories: Basic Animal Research

Behavioral history has been examined in animal research by establishing patterns of responding for two groups under different schedules and subsequently examining the effects of initial conditioning on responding to a common third schedule of reinforcement (e.g., Freeman & Lattal, 1992; Poppen, 1982b; Weiner, 1969). For example, Urbain, Poling, Millam, and Thompson (1978) initially exposed groups of rats to either fixed-ratio (FR) or differential-reinforcement-of-low-rates (DRL) schedules. Subsequent exposure to fixed-interval (FI) schedules resulted in behavioral patterns similar to the high or low response rates that developed under the previous conditions. Wanchisen, Tatham, and Mooney (1989) replicated the findings of Urbain et al. (1978) and showed that FI performance of rats differed as a result of the presence or absence of a history of responding on variable-ratio (VR) schedules.

More recently, Freeman and Lattal (1992) examined the effects of behavioral history in pigeons. They conducted a series of experiments in which the pigeons were exposed to a variety of schedule combinations. Initially the pigeons were exposed to a FR schedule in one session and a DRL schedule in another session each under different stimulus conditions. The FR schedule established a history of responding significantly higher than the DRL schedule. The pigeons were then exposed to the same FI schedule under the respective stimulus conditions. Rates of response remained higher under the conditions previously associated with the FR schedule. This differential rate of responding was maintained for approximately 15-40 sessions. Similar findings occurred in a second experiment examining the effects of FR and DRL schedules on subsequent VI response patterns. A third experiment replicated the findings of the first two experiments using a multiple schedule to generate high and low rates of responding within individual baseline sessions.

In an extension of the above research, LeFrancois and Metzger (1993) examined the effects of immediate and remote history. Two groups of rats were initially conditioned on a DRL schedule. One group was subsequently exposed to an intervening FR schedule while the other group was not. Responding by the group exposed to the FR schedule was influenced by the intervening schedule. LeFrancois and Metzger concluded that current responding is more likely to be influenced by immediate history than by remote history.[1] This experiment and the set of experiments conducted by Freeman and Lattal (1992) suggest that if behavior has been established under stimulus control in the past, then past schedule performance affects current responding in the presence of these stimuli. These data also suggest that the effects of such histories of reinforcement can be relatively persistent.

Experimental Histories: Basic Human Research

Harold Weiner demonstrated in his early research that human behavior is susceptible to the influence of history effects. Weiner (1965) found that given initial exposure to a FR schedule, subsequent human performance on a FI schedule was of the high rate type. In contrast, following a history of DRL performance, a low-rate FI pattern of responding predominated. Weiner found these effects to be remarkably permanent, showing little sign of diminishing over several experimental sessions. Similar findings highlighting the effects of reinforcement histories were obtained by Weiner (1969). Participants were given either a FR 40 or DRL 20-s history before the introduction of FI schedules of different values. The participants were adult hospital workers who were reinforced by points for pressing a button on a console. Each participant had at least 10 one-hour sessions on a given schedule. Following a FR history, participants responded at a high and constant rate on the fixed-interval schedule, which changed little as schedule values were increased. Unlike the FR history participants, the DRL history participants produced low-rate performances on all values of the FI schedule.

In a similar analysis, Poppen (1982b) trained young adults to press a lever for points exchangeable for money. They were programmed on concurrent schedules in which one component was a FI and the other component either a FR (Experiment 1) or a DRL (Experiment 2). Two general patterns of FI responding—post-reinforcement pause or constant rate—occurred in both experiments as a function of the parameter values of each component. Also, patterns of interaction between the component schedules developed in which responding or point delivery on one component appeared to be discriminative for responding on the other component. Once a pattern of responding was established, it tended to persist even when the parameter values of the schedule were changed. On many schedules, participants with an experimental history responded differently than did naive participants, although certain schedule values were resistant to the history effect.

Strong effects of reinforcement history have been demonstrated on schedules other than the FR and FI schedules (e.g., variable-interval [Weiner, 1965]; avoidance schedules [Weiner, 1969] and extinction [Weiner, 1982]) even when the persistence of a given form of responding resulted in the loss of a considerable proportion of available reinforcement. Weiner (1969) suggests that such effects (he later referred to these effects as "behavioral inertia"; Weiner 1970) could not be due to simple response induction from one schedule to another. He supports this proposition by arguing that research has shown, for example, that response rates which previously occurred on a DRL schedule may be substantially altered when a FI schedule is introduced (depending on the value of the FI); a DRL responding history is sufficient, however, to change all subsequent performance on the FI schedules to low-rate patterns of responding.

Verbal Behaviour and History

Behaviour analysts have begun to explore possible mechanisms responsible for the effects of behavioral history on current responding in humans. Recent experimental research has focused on the role of verbal behavior. Poppen (1982a,b) has argued that there is a link between verbal histories and reinforcement histories and has gone as far to suggest that the history effects observed in laboratory studies of human operant behavior (e.g., Duvinsky & Poppen , 1982; Poppen, 1972, 1982a,b; Weiner, 1964, 1969, 1970) are simply instances of self-rule governance. Similarly, Lowe (1979) has argued that history effects are mediated by a person's verbal statements of the contingencies. More recently, Lattal and Neef (1996) suggested that a person's verbal repertoire is often considered to be a history variable. This proposition suggests not just the importance of learning history in accounting for behavior, but implies the importance of verbal behavior in conjunction with history. Recent experimental research lends support to this hypothesis (see Mace, Neef, Shade, & Mauro, 1994).

Catania, Shimoff, and Matthews (1989) conducted a series of experiments examining the relationship between rules and contingencies of reinforcement. Previously, Matthews, Catania, and Shimoff (1985) had found individual differences in the effects of shaped contingency descriptions on button pressing rates. Based on these results Catania and his colleagues hypothesized that some of the variability could be attributed to differences in participants' pre-experimental verbal repertoires. The subsequent study described below (i.e., Catania et al., 1989) was designed to examine this hypothesis more closely.

In Experiment 1, to determine whether button pressing rates depended on a participant's verbal formulation of how to respond under given contingencies, they sampled "performance hypotheses" at the beginning and end of each experimental session. Participants read descriptions of three schedules (i.e., random-ratio, random-interval and differential-reinforcement-of-low-rate) and were then asked to write down how to earn the most points. During sessions, accurate contingency descriptions were shaped by reinforcing successive approximations with money. Results showed that some participants did not include different rates of responding in their hypotheses about random ratio and random interval performances, and differences in the random-ratio and random-interval rates did not occur during shaping trials. In contrast, the remaining participants generated performance hypotheses in which random-ratio rates were higher than random-interval rates. Subsequent shaping of appropriate descriptions of these contingencies was accompanied by corresponding random-ratio and random-interval differences. Catania and his colleagues concluded from these data that the variable effects of identifying contingencies depend on variations in the correlated repertoires with which participants enter an experimental setting (i.e., the participants' ability to describe the contingencies appropriately). Also, shaping contingency descriptions can control responding only if the participant can report that different rates of responding are appropriate for different schedules.

In Experiment 2, Catania et al. (1989) hypothesized that it should be possible to create reliable schedule-appropriate performance by providing participants with accurate hypotheses about how to respond on random-ratio and random-interval schedules (i.e., provide participants with an appropriate verbal repertoire). Participants were given pre-session lessons describing the random-ratio and random-interval schedules and specifying rates of responding appropriate for each. Data indicated that when accurate performances were established by pre-session lessons, shaped contingency descriptions were associated with differences in pressing rates appropriate to each schedule. Rates of pressing were subsequently found to be controlled by participants' contingency descriptions in four cases, sensitive to contingencies and independent of contingency descriptions in two cases, and apparently under competing verbal and contingency control in one case. For participants with an extensive history of correctly identifying contingencies, contingency descriptions were controlled by the contingencies, and pressing rates were appropriate to those contingencies.

Recent research by Hackenberg and Joker (1994) has tested the hypothesis that verbal histories and reinforcement histories are related. They assessed response allocation of adult human participants when correspondence between instructions and contingencies was progressively less congruent. Instructional control was established quickly where instructions accurately reflected the schedules in operation. As the instructions became progressively more inaccurate, however, response allocation became more variable and produced more reinforcement, resulting in a shift from instructional to schedule control. The extent to which response allocations were controlled by the schedule contingencies varied according to the point at which instructional control first broke down, suggesting that the history of consequences for following inaccurate instructions can have enduring effects on behavior.

Verbal Behaviour, History, and Experimental Control

An analysis of verbal behavior is problematic in that it is unrecorded, it is a product of an unknown history, and it is controlled by unspecified contingencies. Such verbal behavior may depend on prior non verbal responding, may be similar to earlier verbal behavior upon which non verbal responding depended, or it may be related to prior non verbal responding in other undetermined ways (Harzem, Lowe, & Bagshaw, 1978). Most research examining verbal behavior involves verbal stimuli whose controlling properties have been established prior to the start of an experiment. Little is known about the circumstances under which these properties have developed. This is not to say that accounts of instructional control as a form of discriminative stimulus control cannot be constructed on the basis of interpretations of naturally occurring behaviors. A common observation is that socialization of children includes reinforcement of instructed responding by parents and other adults, and a plausible assumption is that instruction-following by adults in the laboratory taps this complex history. But unlike conclusions reached from laboratory studies of discriminative control, such accounts of instructional control are speculative, and a full analysis of instructional effects as a form of discriminative control must await direct study.

To give a complete specification of the environmental determinants of the verbal behavior recorded during any experiment would require an account of specific environmental interactions in each participants childhood that led to the development of the current verbal behavior and then the additional experiences with similar cues and equivalent verbal stimuli leading to the eventual rule formulation in the course of the experiment (Horne & Lowe, 1993). It is not experimentally possible or feasible to trace individuals verbal behavior back to early environmental histories within a verbal community (Skinner, 1945, 1957).

Given these inherent difficulties, a number of studies have been reported in the experimental literature which have attempted to control for the emergence of verbal behavior within the experimental context. For example, Catania, Matthews, and Shimoff (1982) showed that a participant's verbal behavior relevant to an experimental task could be shaped in the experimental setting. They arranged that college students' button presses produced points exchangeable for money according to multiple random-ratio random-interval schedules, with separate buttons for each schedule (i.e., a left and a right button respectively). After exposure to each schedule, students completed left button and right button sentences (guesses). Every 3 min, students completed written sentences describing "the way to turn the green lights on" (i.e., to earn points) on each of the two buttons. Correct response-rate guesses were established by reinforcing successive approximations with money (i.e., "press fast" or "press quickly" for the random-ratio button and "press slow" or "press slowly" for the random-interval button). Similarly, in Matthews et al. (1985) and Shimoff, Matthews, and Catania (1986), college students earned money by pressing on multiple random-interval random-ratio schedules and, after every exposure to the pair of schedules, by writing statements about either contingencies or the appropriate way to press the buttons. As with the Catania et al. (1982) study, correct verbal statements were shaped by reinforcing successive approximations with money. Besides the empirical findings that this series of studies have generated, they are important because they demonstrate that self-rules can be studied as operant behavior, directly and objectively measured under well specified conditions, recorded on a more or less continuous basis, and most importantly, brought under some degree of experimental control.

Behavioral History and Applied Behaviour Analysis

The experimental research reviewed above suggests that applied behavior analysts need to consider the role of behavioral history in their analyses. Lattal and Neef (1996) have argued that applied behavior analysts acknowledge the importance of behavioral history, but have generally tended to ignore it. They suggest a number of reasons why this may be so. First, it is impossible to know the reinforcement history which lead to the development of a particular behavior and as a result there is little that can be done about it. Many applied behavior analysts have therefore adopted the position that history effects should be ignored and treated as an inevitable source of variability over which there is little control (Baer, 1977). A second reason why applied behavior analysts have tended to ignore the effects of historical variables is the assumption that current responding may be affected by different conditions than those under which it originally developed. It is therefore assumed that an arrangement of current conditions should override the effects of prior conditioning.

In terms of a complete behavior analysis, it may be a limiting position for applied behavior analysts to argue that the relevance of history depends on whether or not applied behavior analysts have arranged it. For example, consider attempts to establish a history that will render behavior insensitive to immediate contingencies by providing participants with inaccurate instructions about schedule contingencies. If experimenter provided verbal behavior results in behavior persisting in the presence of competing contingencies during an experimental session, then behavior analysts must appreciate that a participants pre-experimental history may also affect current operant responding.

Despite the inherent difficulties associated with the incorporation of history effects into any analysis, history effects are beginning to be addressed in the applied behavioral literature. For example, Mace et al. (1994) conducted a study of concurrent schedule reinforcement of academic behavior. Three adolescent students with special educational needs were given a choice between completing one of two available sets of math problems. Time allocated to the two sets of math problems was primarily a function of the reinforcement rate obtained from each set. Changes in the schedules were not followed by changes in allocation patterns until adjunct procedures (e.g., changeover delays, limited holds, timers, and demonstrations) were introduced. All three participants appeared to be sensitive to the scheduled contingencies in the first phase of concurrent variable-interval variable-interval reinforcement. Familiarity with concurrent schedules, however, appeared to produce insensitivity to participants responding to changing consequences with particular response patterns tending to persist.

Recent research by Taylor and O'Reilly (1997) has attempted to provide a known history of covert self-rules within an experimental context.[2] Four participants with intellectual disabilities were successfully taught (using modelling and role play techniques) to perform the steps of a supermarket shopping task analysis in classroom and supermarket training settings. Additionally, they were taught to use appropriate verbal self-instructions to prompt each step of the task analysis in training and non training settings. Taylor and O'Reilly argued that the self-instruction training protocol provided a methodology to control for the emergence of self-rules within an experimental context (i.e., the self-instructional training provided a means whereby a set of self-rules was shaped over a number of training sessions). The emergence of self-instruction was documented under well-specified conditions, recorded on a more or less continuous basis, observed over a period of time, and brought under some degree of experimental control.

To date, there are few examples of historical effects reported in the applied literature (but see recent research on behavioral momentum and prior social context variables below). Given that the effects of history are fairly well established in the basic research, it is unclear why such effects have not been reported more often in the applied literature. One possibility for their omission is that the methodology typically used by applied behavior analysts does not lend itself to the reporting of history effects. The traditional methodologies used by applied behavior analysts are multiple baseline and reversal designs. With these designs it is necessary to demonstrate an immediate experimental effect. Research in which behavior tends to persist despite the implementation of an appropriate intervention may, therefore, not be submitted for publication. Arguably the effects of history are more prevalent than the reported literature suggests (see Lattal & Neef, 1996 for a number of other reasons why history effects have not been widely reported in the applied literature).

Implications for Intervention Development

An implicit assumption of many interventions adopted by applied behavior analysts is that operant behavior is controlled by current reinforcement contingencies. Basic research with both animal and human participants has, however, systematically demonstrated that previous experiences also influence schedule-controlled behavior (Baron & Leinenweber, 1995; Freeman & Lattal, 1992; Wanchisen et al., 1989; Weiner, 1969). This growing body of literature also demonstrates the diminution of this control as experience under other schedules increases. Indeed, "the assumption that history effects are not indefinite as behavior adapts to the present environment is the raison d'être for applied behavior analysis" (Lattal & Neef, 1996, p. 216). For the applied behavior analyst, the significant consideration is not that the effects usually diminish over time but that they persist as long as they do (Freeman & Lattal, 1992). This analysis raises important issues for applied behavior analysts. Specifically, they must ask themselves how historical variables can be incorporated into their analyses and related to applied problems. A consideration of behavioral history should assist applied behavior analysts to design interventions that remove or take advantage of historical influences on current responding.

One area of applied research where a recognition of the role of behavioral histories may lead to more effective interventions is when behavior is resistant to change. Some reinforced behavior can persist for a time even when the response-reinforcer relation maintaining the behavior is no longer in operation. In such cases, for interventions to be effective, they must compete effectively with the target behavior's resistance to change. Applied behavior analysts have only recently begun to consider the role of behavioral resistance when developing interventions (Mace & Wacker, 1994). Such research, however, has focused exclusively on temporally proximal variables (Mace, 1994). For example, one recent application involves presenting a sequence of instructions likely to be complied with by an individual (i.e., high-probability or high-p instructions) immediately before an instruction to perform a low-probability (low-p) response (Davis, Brady, Hamilton, McEvoy, & Williams, 1994; Ducharme & Worling, 1994; Houlihan, Jacobson, & Brandon, 1994; Mace, Hock, Lalli, West, Belfiore, Pinter, & Brown, 1988; Mace, Lalli, Shea, Lalli, West, Roberts, & Nevin, 1990; Mace, Mauro, Boyajian, & Eckert, 1997; Taylor, O'Reilly, & Lancioni, 1996; Zarcone, Iwata, Mazaleski, & Smith, 1994). Essentially, these interventions arranged a conditioning history providing a high rate of reinforcement for a high rate of responding that, in turn, increased compliance to the low-p instruction.

Mace (1994) suggests that in addition to temporally proximal variables, temporally distant factors may facilitate behavioral persistence during extinction. One temporally distant variable identified by Mace is abandoned extinction schedules. For example, the father who gives in before his son's aggressive behavior has been completely extinguished. A second temporally distant variable identified by Mace is the history of a behavior with various schedules of reinforcement. For example, parents may allow a child to be aggressive in the house but restrict aggression outside the home. In the home, parental reactions may follow a variety of variable-ratio and variable-interval schedules. Outside the family home, rapid consequences for aggressive behavior may follow fixed-ratio and fixed-interval schedules. Such schedule changes may prevent easy discrimination of the operating contingencies promoting behavioural resistance when the behavior analyst is called to deal with the child's aggressive outbursts.

Behavioural History: A Case of an Establishing Operation

The need for applied behavior analysts to incorporate history effects into their analyses is consistent with the calls from time to time to expand the basic unit of analysis to examine contextual influences on the three term contingency relation (of which prior conditioning history will undoubtedly play a major role). These contextual influences have typically been described as an establishing operation or a setting event (Kantor, 1959; Michael, 1982).

Michael (1993) defines an establishing operation as:

an environmental event, operation or stimulus condition that affects an organism by momentarily altering (a) the reinforcing effectiveness of other events and (b) the frequency of occurrence of that part of the organism's repertoire relevant to those events as consequences. (p. 191)

Alternatively, the term setting event, which was originally adopted from the writings of Kantor, has been used in a similar manner to describe the effect of events, operations and stimulus conditions that inhibit or facilitate the occurrence of existing stimulus and response functions (Kantor, 1959; Kennedy & Itkonen, 1993).[3] One of the dominant themes in recent applied behavioural research has been the development of strategies, such as analogue analysis assessments, which provide a detailed analysis of the operant function of aberrant behavior (see Iwata, Dorsey, Slifer, Bauman, & Richman, 1982/1994). The focus of such assessments has been on temporally proximate conditions (immediate antecedents and consequences) that evoke and maintain aberrant responding. The need to research other variables that impact the probability of temporally immediate behavior-environment relations during these analogue assessments has been stressed (Kennedy & Itkonen, 1993; Kennedy & Meyer, 1996; O'Reilly, 1995; 1996; 1997). For example, O'Reilly and Carey (1996) systematically manipulated prior classroom conditions to explore their effects on performance under analogue assessments for a 7-year-old girl with severe intellectual disabilities who exhibited aggressive behavior. Results demonstrated consistently higher levels of aggression during analogue assessment conditions when the teacher attended to the girl's aggression immediately prior to the analogue assessment. It was argued that the density of reinforcement for aggression (i.e., reinforcement for aggression was delivered on a FR1 schedule in the classroom by the teacher) produced persistence of responding during the analogue assessment.

In an extension of this research, O'Reilly, Lancioni, and Emerson (in press) examined the influence of prior social conditions on levels of aberrant behavior under analogue assessments with two individuals with severe developmental disabilities. Social conditions that occurred regularly for these individuals were systematically controlled prior to analogue analyses. Data indicated that exposure to prior social contexts influenced levels of aberrant behavior in analogue conditions in idiosyncratic ways for both participants. For one participant, teacher attention for aggression (delivered on a FR1 schedule) prior to analogue assessment conditions produced high levels of aggression in the classroom and in the subsequent analogue analysis assessment. Levels of aggression within the analogue analysis were significantly less if the teacher did not attend to the aggression prior to the analysis. Analogue analysis results for the second participant produced clear patterns of escape-maintained self-injury within the analogue analysis. Escape-maintained self-injury was higher under the analogue analysis conditions if such escape behaviors were reinforced (on a FR1 schedule) immediately prior to the analogue analysis.

O'Reilly et al. (in press) identified a number of reasons why the analysis of prior social context may be important in a functional analysis. First, if prior social interactions (these were referred to as contextual variables) can influence performance under analogue conditions, then the results of such analyses might want to be interpreted with greater caution. Second, the systematic analysis of contextual variables such as behavioural history may begin to allow researchers to understand how such variables enter into functional relationships with immediate maintaining contingencies. Finally, it is important to keep in mind the defining characteristics of a functional analysis (Oliver, 1995). Behaviour should be examined in terms of its antecedents and consequences, these variables should be empirically determined, and all necessary and sufficient conditions should be considered. If these conditions are not satisfied we are in danger of attributing functions that are not operative or omitting functions that are (see Oliver & Head, 1993).

Unfortunately, to date, the calls to incorporate setting events or establishing operations such as prior history into their analyses have not been taken up with great enthusiasm by applied behavioural researchers until relatively recently. There are two obvious reasons why this may be the case. First, behavior analysts have traditionally understood setting events as extraneous variables which need to be controlled in order to achieve and demonstrate conditioning effects (Schlinger, 1993). Setting events have therefore not been traditionally conceptualized as independent variables in their own right. Second, Wahler and Fox (1981) predicted that a number of legitimate methodological concerns with incorporating setting events in to the analysis of behavior. While they propose that applied behavioural research has resulted in an undue emphasis on temporally proximate conditions (i.e., immediate antecedents and consequences) they note that expanding the analysis to temporally distant behavior-environment interactions may change the focus of our research from causal to descriptive or correlative analyses. This is because setting events are often only amenable to molar rather than micro units of analysis, are sometimes temporally distant and are often not susceptible to systematic manipulations. The very nature of many of historical variables (i.e., temporally distant and not amenable to a micro analysis) makes it difficult to adapt causal methodologies (i.e., functional analysis techniques) to such a task.

Conclusion

The applied and experimental research discussed above indicates that operant behavior is not determined exclusively by contemporary requirements for reinforcement. It illustrates how immediate schedule circumstances interact with historical variables to control behavior. As such, this research offers a broader context for discussing behavior and raises important issues for applied behavior analysts concerning how behavior is conceptualized and studied.

To date, behavior analysts (both experimental and applied researchers) have only begun to scratch the surface of the "problem of history" (Poppen, 1989). Early experimental work avoided the problems of history by employing naive, non human organisms and research designs that eliminated the effects of earlier experience on later behavior by focusing on "steady state" performance. Weiner's pioneering research with human participants (some of which was reviewed above–see Weiner, 1982 and 1983, for a comprehensive review of the various aspects of reinforcement history in humans that have been examined), recent experimentation with non humans (see Freeman & Lattal, 1992, for a review), and the recent applied research by Mace, O'Reilly and colleagues has opened the door to the study of history as an important variable in applied behavior analysis. Such research has demonstrated lawful relationships between performance on current schedules of reinforcement as a function of experience on prior schedules of reinforcement and that, in the case of human participants, this could be accomplished despite the diverse learning histories of each participant. We return to our original contention, namely, that behavior is a function of present contingencies only through past experience (Branch, 1987). If applied behavior analysts are to fully acknowledge this article of faith in word and deed, they must begin to address the issue of behavioural history in a systematic and coherent way. The analysis presented in this chapter provides a conceptual basis upon which to move forward and can be seen as an initial step to that end.

References

Baer, D. M. (1977). Perhaps it would be better not to know everything. *Journal of Applied Behavior Analysis, 10,* 167-172.

Baron, A., & Leinenweber, A. (1995). Effects of a variable-ratio conditioning history on sensitivity to fixed-interval contingencies in rats. *Journal of the Experimental Analysis of Behavior, 63,* 97-110.

Bentall, R. P., & Lowe, C. F. (1987). The role of verbal behavior in human learning III: Instructional effects in children. *Journal of the Experimental Analysis of Behavior, 47,* 177-190.

Bentall, R. P., Lowe, C. F., & Beasty, A. (1985). The role of verbal behavior in human learning II: Developmental differences. *Journal of the Experimental Analysis of Behavior, 43,* 165-181.

Branch, M. N. (1987). Behavior analysis: A conceptual and empirical base for behavior therapy. *The Behavior Therapist, 4,* 79-84.

Carr, E.G., (1994). Emerging themes in the functional analysis of problem behavior. *Journal of Applied Behavior Analysis, 27,* 393-399.

Catania, A. C., Matthews, B. A., & Shimoff, E. (1982). Instructed versus shaped human verbal behavior: Interactions with nonverbal responding. *Journal of the Experimental Analysis of Behavior, 38,* 233-248.

Catania, A. C., Shimoff, E., & Matthews, B. A. (1989). The experimental analysis of rule-governed behavior. In S. C. Hayes, (Ed.), *Rule-governed behavior: Cognition, contingencies, and instructional control* (pp. 119-152). New York: Plenum Press.

Davis, C. A., Brady, M., Hamilton, R., McEvoy, M., & Williams, R. (1994). Effects of high-probability requests on social interaction of young children with severe disabilities. *Journal of Applied Behavior Analysis, 27,* 619-637.

Ducharme, J. M., & Worling, D. E. (1994). Behavioral momentum and stimulus fading in the acquisition and maintenance of child compliance in the home. *Journal of Applied Behavior Analysis, 27,* 639-647.

Duvinsky, J. D., & Poppen, R. (1982). Human performance on conjunctive fixed-interval schedules. *Journal of the Experimental Analysis of Behavior, 37,* 243-250.

Freeman, T. J., & Lattal K. A. (1992). Stimulus control of behavioral history. *Journal of the Experimental Analysis of Behavior, 57,* 5-15.

Hackenberg, T. D., & Joker, V. R. (1994). Instructional versus schedule control of humans' choices in situations of diminishing returns. *Journal of the Experimental Analysis of Behavior, 62,* 367-383.

Harzem, P., Lowe, C. F., & Bagshaw, M. (1978). Verbal control in human operant behavior. *The Psychological Record, 28,* 405-423.

Horne, P. J., & Lowe, C. F. (1993). Determinants of human performance on concurrent schedules. *Journal of the Experimental Analysis of Behavior, 59,* 29-60.

Houlihan, D., Jacobson, L., & Brandon, P. K. (1994). Replication of high-probability request sequence with varied interprompt times in a preschool setting. *Journal of Applied Behavior Analysis, 27,* 737-738.

Iwata, B.A., Dorsey, M., Slifer, K., Bauman, K., & Richman, G. (1994). Toward a functional analysis of self-injury. *Journal of Applied Behavior Analysis, 27,* 197-209. (Reprinted from Analysis and Intervention in Developmental Disabilities, 2, 3-20, 1982).

Kantor, J. R. (1959). *Interbehavioral psychology.* Granville, Ohio: Principia Press.

Kennedy, C. H., & Itkonen, T. (1993). Effects of setting events on the problem behavior of students with severe disabilities. *Journal of Applied Behavior Analysis, 26,* 321-327.

Kennedy, C. H., & Meyer, K. A. (1996). Sleep deprivation, allergy symptoms, and negatively reinforced problem behavior. *Journal of Applied Behavior Analysis, 29,* 133-135.

Lattal, K. A., & Neef, N. A. (1996). Recent reinforcement-schedule research and applied behavior analysis. *Journal of Applied Behavior Analysis, 29,* 213-230.

LeFrancois, J. R., & Metzger, B. (1993). Low-response-rate conditioning history and fixed-interval responding in rats, *Journal of the Experimental Analysis of Behavior, 59,* 543-549.

Lowe, C. F. (1979). Determinants of human operant behaviour. In M. D. Zeiler, and P. Harzem, (Eds.), *Advances in analysis of behaviour,* Vol 1: Reinforcement and the organisation of behaviour (pp. 159-192). Chichester: Wiley.

Lowe, C. F., Beasty, A., & Bentall, R. P. (1983). The role of verbal behavior in human learning: Infant performance on fixed-interval schedules. *Journal of the Experimental Analysis of Behavior, 39,* 157-164.

Mace, F. C. (1994). Basic research needed for stimulating the development of behavioral technologies. *Journal of the Experimental Analysis of Behavior, 61,* 529-550.

Mace, F. C., Hock, M. L., Lalli, J. S., West, B. J., Belfiore, P., Pinter, E., & Brown, D. K. (1988). Behavioral momentum in the treatment of noncompliance. *Journal of Applied Behavior Analysis, 21,* 123-141.

Mace, F. C., Lalli, J. S., Shea, M. C., Lalli, E. P., West, B. J., Roberts, M., & Nevin, J. A. (1990). The momentum of human behavior in a natural setting. *Journal of the Experimental Analysis of Behavior, 54,* 163-172.

Mace, F. C., Mauro, B. C., Boyajian, A. E., & Eckert, T. L. (1997). Effects of reinforcer quality on behavioral momentum: Coordinated applied and basic research. *Journal of Applied Behavior Analysis, 30,* 1-20.

Mace, F. C., Neef, N. A., Shade, D., & Mauro, B. C. (1994). Limited matching on concurrent-schedule reinforcement of academic behavior. *Journal of Applied Behavior Analysis, 27,* 585-596.

Mace, F. C., & Wacker, D. P. (1994). Toward greater integration of basic and applied behavioral research: An introduction. *Journal of Applied Behavior Analysis, 27,* 569-574.

Matthews, B. A., Catania, A. C., & Shimoff, E. (1985). Effects of uninstructed verbal behavior on nonverbal responding: Contingency descriptions versus performance descriptions. *Journal of the Experimental Analysis of Behavior, 43,* 155-164.

Michael, J. L. (1982). Distinguishing between discriminative and motivational functions of stimuli. *Journal of the Experimental Analysis of Behavior, 37,* 149-155.

Michael, J. L. (1993). Establishing operations. *The Behavior Analyst, 16,* 191-206.

Oliver, C. (1995). Self-injurious behaviour in children with learning disabilities: Recent advances in assessment and intervention. *Journal of Child Psychology and Psychiatry, 30,* 909-927.

Oliver, C., & Head, D. (1993). Self-injurious behaviour: Functional analysis and interventions. In R. S. P. Jones & C. B. Eayrs (Eds.), *Challenging Behaviour and Intellectual Disability: A Psychological perspective* (pp. 12-33). Avon England: BILD Publications.

O'Reilly, M. F. (1995). Functional analysis and treatment of escape-maintained aggression correlated with sleep deprivation. *Journal of Applied Behavior Analysis, 28,* 225-226.

O'Reilly, M. F. (1996). Assessment and treatment of episodic self-injury. *Research in Developmental Disabilities, 17,* 349-361.

O'Reilly, M. F., & Carey, Y. (1996). A preliminary analysis of the effects of prior classroom conditions on performance under analogue analysis conditions. *Journal of Applied Behavior Analysis, 29,* 581-584.

O'Reilly, M. F. (1997). Functional analysis of episodic self-injury correlated with recurrent otitis media. *Journal of Applied Behavior Analysis, 30,* 165-167.

O'Reilly, M. F., Lancioni, G., & Emerson, E. (in press). A systematic analysis of the influence of prior social context on aggression and self-injury within analogue analysis assessments. *Behavior Modification.*

Poppen, R. (1972). Effects of concurrent schedules on human fixed-interval performance. *Journal of the Experimental Analysis of Behavior, 18,* 119-127.

Poppen, R. (1982a). The fixed-interval scallop in human affairs. *The Behavior Analyst, 5,* 127-136.

Poppen, R. (1982b). Human fixed-interval performance with concurrently programmed schedules: A parametric analysis. *Journal of the Experimental Analysis of Behavior, 37,* 251-266.

Poppen, R. (1989). Some clinical implications of rule-governed behavior. In S. C. Hayes (Ed.), *Rule-governed behavior, cognition, contingencies and instructional control* (pp. 325-357). New York: Plenum Press.

Schlinger, H. D. (1993). Establishing operations: Another step toward a functional taxonomy of environmental events. *The Behavior Analyst, 16,* 207-209.

Shimoff, E., Matthews, B. A., & Catania, A. C. (1986). Human operant performance: Sensitivity and pseudosensitivity to contingencies. *Journal of the Experimental Analysis of Behavior, 46,* 149-157.

Sidman, M. (1960). *Tactics of scientific research.* New York: Basic Books.

Skinner, B. F. (1945). The operational analysis of psychological terms. *Psychological Review, 52,* 270-277.

Skinner, B. F. (1953). *Science and human behavior.* New York: Macmillan.

Skinner, B. F. (1957). *Verbal behavior.* New York: Appleton-Century-Crofts.

Skinner, B. F. (1969). *Contingencies of reinforcement: A theoretical analysis.* New York: Appleton-Century-Crofts.

Taylor, I., & O'Reilly, M. F. (1997). Toward a functional analysis of private verbal self-regulation. *Journal of Applied Behavior Analysis, 30,* 43-58.

Taylor, I., O'Reilly, M. F., & Lancoini, G. (1996). An evaluation of an ongoing consultation model to train teachers to treat challenging behaviour. *International Journal of Disability, Development and Education, 43,* 203-218.

Urbain, C., Poling, A., Millam, J., & Thompson, T. (1978). D-amphetamine and fixed-interval performance: Effects of operant history. *Journal of the Experimental Analysis of Behavior, 29,* 385-392.

Wahler, R. G., & Fox, J. J. (1981). Setting events in applied behavior analysis: Towards a conceptual and methodological expansion. *Journal of Applied Behavior Analysis, 14,* 327-338.

Wanchisen, B. A., Tatham, T. A., & Mooney, S. E. (1989). Variable-ratio conditioning history produces high-and-low-rate fixed-interval performance in rats. *Journal of the Experimental Analysis of Behavior, 52,* 167-179.

Weiner, H. (1964). Conditioning history and human fixed-interval performance. *Journal of the Experimental Analysis of Behavior, 7,* 383-385.

Weiner, H. (1965). Conditioning history and maladaptive human operant behavior. *Psychological Reports, 17,* 935-942.

Weiner, H. (1969). Conditioning history and the control of human avoidance and escape responding. *Journal of the Experimental Analysis of Behavior, 12,* 1039-1043.

Weiner, H. (1970). Human behavioral persistence. *The Psychological Record, 20,* 445-456.

Weiner, H. (1982). Histories of response omission and human operant behavior under a fixed-ratio schedule of reinforcement. *The Psychological Record, 32,* 409-434.

Weiner, H. (1983). Some thoughts on discrepant human-animal performances under schedules of reinforcement. *The Psychological Record, 33,* 521-532.

Zarcone, J. R., Iwata, B. A., Mazaleski, J. L., & Smith, R. G. (1994). Momentum and extinction effects on self-injurious escape behavior and noncompliance. *Journal of Applied Behavior Analysis, 27,* 649-658.

Notes

[1] Lattal and Neef (1996) suggest that this finding may have important implications for functional analysis techniques. Functional analyses are concerned primarily with identifying the contingencies maintaining current responding. Such analyses, however, involve putting in place more immediate contingencies and schedules of reinforcement. The possibility exists that the observed behaviors may come to be controlled more by the immediate contingencies established by the functional analysis than by the contingencies the functional analysis is designed to assess. This may be particularly true if the functional analysis is protracted.

[2] Some researchers have pointed out that adult humans come to the experimental setting with an extensive repertoire of formulating rules and responding to them (e.g., Poppen, 1982a). Given that such a repertoire reflects the individual's own unique history, any general laws emerging from such research may be questionable. As a result, a number of researchers have begun to study the origins of rule-governed behaviour. Developmental research conducted by Lowe and his colleagues is some of the most important conducted in this area (Lowe, Beasty, & Bentall, 1983; Bentall, Lowe, & Beasty, 1985; Bentall & Lowe, 1987).

[3] Historical variables are consistent with the conceptualizations of establishing operations and setting events postulated by Michael and Kantor. Prior conditioning history can affect an organism by altering the reinforcing effectiveness of other events (i.e., can inhibit or facilitate the occurrence of existing stimulus and response functions). The impetus for the inclusion of prior conditioning history into applied behaviour analyses may well come from the acceptance that setting events must be incorporated into applied research efforts in general.

Chapter 13

Telling Tales About Behavior Analysis: Textbooks, Scholarship and Rumor

Sandy Hobbs, David Cornwell and Mecca Chiesa
University of Paisley, Paisley, Scotland and University of Strathclyde, Glasgow, Scotland

B.F. Skinner has described reactions to accounts of the raising of his second daughter Deborah in the baby-tender or "Air-Crib". Particularly striking are what he called "horror stories":

> A prominent psychiatrist, author of several popular books, told an acquaintance of ours that our daughter had become psychotic. I wrote to say that I was trying to trace the story and wondered where he had heard it. He did not tell me, though he apologized profusely. A well-known British critic, visiting the United States one summer, said to our friend Harry Levin [the Harvard Shakespearean scholar], "Isn't it too bad about the Skinners' daughter, the one they raised in the box, killing herself!" "Well, when did she do that?" said Professor Levin, "I was swimming with her only yesterday." (Skinner, 1979, p. 40).

What would clearly have been rather unpleasant experiences for the Skinner family take on a different significance for students of folklore who have studied in some detail what are called variously "contemporary legends" or "urban legends" (Bennett & Smith, 1993; Brunvand, 1993). These stories often circulate very widely, being told as true, but efforts to confirm their veracity generally end in failure. Even when an occasional source for a story is found, the narrated versions often differ significantly (Fine, 1992). Since these stories are not true, it is reasonable to ask what causes them to be told so frequently. Although this seems a "psychological" question there are few psychologists amongst those studying them (Cornwell & Hobbs, 1992). Many features of these stories have been delineated, including recurring motifs and characteristic modes of telling (Bennett & Smith, 1996; De Vos, 1996). From a behavioral perspective, one may ask what reinforcers shape and maintain the story telling (Hobbs & Cornwell, 1991).

The stories about Deborah Skinner have some characteristics which suggest their legendary character. Death is a common feature in contemporary legends. One collection of 194 stories has 51 dealing with dying or corpses, 67 if we include the death of animals (Fleming & Boyd, 1994). "Going mad" is an outcome for those who have had a particularly harrowing experience (Jansen, 1973). Skinner's failure to find a source is also telling.

That some critics of Skinner's child rearing methods have made false claims to bolster their views may tell us something about the standing of behaviorism in our society. It may seem somewhat remote, however, from the issue of how behavior analysis is presented in academic works. A large gap divides textbooks from gossip, it might be thought. Unfortunately, there is reason to believe that the gap is not as wide as it should be.

Representation and Misrepresentation

There is a fairly substantial literature on the representation of behavior analysis in psychology texts and other sources (for example, Cooke, 1984; DeBell & Harless, 1992; Jensen & Burgess, 1997; Todd, 1987; Todd & Morris, 1983, 1992). A special interest group within the Association for Behavior Analysis, ABA-International and its newsletter, *Balance*, is devoted to the accurate representation of behavior analysis in academic and popular sources, the need for which clearly presupposes the existence of faulty representations. Our agenda here is to contribute to this body of knowledge by providing additional data, looking at potential ways of quantifying the accuracy of presentations of behavior analysis, and offering further research questions.

In the first place, we would encourage the adoption of a behavior analytic approach. If behavior analysts claim that they are misrepresented in the scholarly or popular media, and if they hope to do anything to change that state of affairs, it is reasonable to argue that the scientific and conceptual rigour applied to effecting change in other areas would enhance efforts to monitor and ensure accuracy. Todd (1994) in his study of textbook treatments of Watson, has introduced a welcome degree of system and quantification into his analysis. However, with the exception of a study of "fraud, fakery and fudging" (Blakely, Poling, & Cross, 1986), we are not aware of any behavior analysis of concepts such as "misrepresentation" or "error" which seem helpful in considering, for example, the way in which behavior analysis is presented in psychology textbooks. In the texts cited above, a number of terms are employed without detailed conceptual analysis, "myth" and "folklore" being among them. Furthermore, the term "misrepresentation" implies the possibility of something presumably called "representation". The challenge facing scholars in this field is how to deal with these concepts in a behavior-analytic way. Decisions need to be taken about what the main categories of analysis should be.

Trying Out a Checklist

One strategy which attempts to systematize evaluations of the presentation of behavior analysis in textbooks is to propose a checklist of statements that describe the behavior analytic position on a series of issues. A text can then be compared with the checklist to ascertain the extent to which it includes or ignores specific issues, or to what extent it "gets it wrong".

Roger F. Bass put up such a checklist for discussion in an issue of *Balance* published in 1996 or 1997. (Unfortunately, *Balance* does not have an ISBN number or a date of issue, so we are unable to reference this source precisely.) Bass suggests sixteen items in the form of assertions:

1. Genetic influences are acknowledged. Behavior analysis is not exclusively environmental.
2. Behavior analysis acknowledges and provides an analysis of important inner processes and behaviors including thoughts, feelings, and emotions. It is not 'empty organism" or "black box" psychology.
3. Human individuality and uniqueness are concepts compatible with behavior analysis.
4. Human experience includes "knowing" and "conscious awareness" in the behavior analytic view.
5. Behavior analysts provide analysis of concepts such as "meaning", "purpose", and "intention".
6. Terms such as "ethics", "morals", and "value judgment" are consistent with the behavior analytic perspective.
7. Behavior analysis is not anti-theoretical and, in fact, is itself undergirded by a comprehensive theory.
8. Behavior analysis advocates positive methods of control over punishment.
9. Behavior analysis is consistent with democracy.
10. The enormous differences (as well as similarities) between humans and lower animals are evident to behavior analysts.
11. There exists a broad and growing research literature on behavioral applications in clinics, schools, and homes, etc.
12. Behavior analysts would not replace teachers with machines.
13. Complex human behavior such as language and relationships are dealt with by behavior analysts at the theoretical, experimental, and applied levels.
14. The richness of human experience is valued and is a focus for behavior analysts.
15. Behavior analysts are interested in other perspectives. They are not isolated, closed to criticism, and ignorant of other perspectives.
16. Behavior analysis is alive and vital rather than out of the mainstream, dying, or dead.

A further three items concern presentations of history and theoretical perspectives, the experimental science of behavior analysis, and applications of behavior analysis, with an additional category of "Unusual inaccuracies, not fitting into any of the above categories". Bass suggests that these items could be rated as Accurately Represented, Misrepresented, or No Mention.

The checklist concludes with six items of erroneous statements that have appeared in textbooks:

- all behaviors are equally conditionable;
- Skinner and Watson shared the same viewpoints on all key issues;
- air-cribs are "Skinner boxes";
- behavior analysts ignore the individual's physiology;
- valid explanation must derive from a hypothetico-deductive model;
- definitions of reinforcement and punishment include references to emotions and feelings.

In the spirit in which it was intended, i.e., in the spirit of discussion, we attempted to use the checklist to evaluate the presentation of Skinner's work by looking at references to Skinner in one British text, Taylor, Sluckin, Davies, Reason, Thomson, and Colman (1982).

The book's index indicates that Skinner is mentioned at nine points in the text. Figure 1 summarizes what we found at each entry. In two cases, B and D, there were descriptions without comment. The descriptions themselves were not of a sort to cause us to question their accuracy. In six cases, Skinner's position is questioned, as seen by the presence of words such as "however" (C, F, H, I), "controversial" (A), "challenged" (E). Finally, we have in case G the phrase "if we choose to disagree" with a position introduced as a quotation from Skinner which has not been expounded in the text. In the text we examined, the presence of Skinner's name seems to be predominantly a prelude to presenting an alternative (and presumably supposedly more correct) position. This finding may point the way to a useful unit of analysis: how often is Skinner "set up" in this manner? On how many occasions do authors follow reference to Skinner with terms such as "however", "challenged" and so on?

Attempting to apply the Bass checklist told us little. All sixteen positive (and presumed accurate) assertions simply fell into the "no mention" category. One assertion, "the enormous differences (as well as similarities) between humans and lower animals are evident to behavior analysts" could arguably rate as misrepresented under item E, Figure 1, in that Skinner's name is linked to the equipotentiality premise. Another assertion "complex human behavior such as language and relationships are dealt with by behavior analysts at the theoretical, experimental, and applied levels" could arguably be rated as both "no mention" and "misrepresented" since the context in which Verbal Behavior (Skinner, 1957) and language theory are related allows for this. We also found that the three items concerning presentations of history and theoretical perspectives, experimental science of behavior analysis, and applications of behavior analysis could not be applied to the text we examined, while only one of the five erroneous statements proposed was found in the text, again relating to the equipotentiality premise that "all behaviors are equally conditionable". Thus, out of a checklist of 26 items, we were able to find one clear problem relating to the equipotentiality premise. The remaining issues either did not occur or were not applicable to this text.

Some of the checklist assertions are not as straightforward as they might initially seem. For example, one of the categories of correct representation is as follows: "Behavior analysis is alive and vital rather than out of the mainstream, dying or dead". If Skinner's point of view is regularly denied, then his position may be implied

A. pp 36-37 (In Chapter 2, Comparative and Ecological perspectives)
Description of Skinner Box. Work shows certain general principles apply across species [NO REF]
"*controversial*".

B. pp 340-341 (In Chapter 13, Learning)
Account of operant conditioning [REFS: Skinner, 1938, (not in ref. list) Ferster and Skinner, 1957, and three others]

C. p 343 (In Chapter 13, Learning)
"Followers of Skinner" treat academic study, language, social behaviour as types of operant conditioning.
"*However...*"

D. p 352 (In Chapter 13, Learning)
Incidental reference to Skinner Box.

E. pp 358-359 (In Chapter 13, Learning)
Constraints on learning: superstitious behaviour [REF: Skinner, 1953 (not in ref. list)] Equipotentiality premise "derives from the writings of Pavlov, Skinner and others [NO SKINNER REF.]
"*Challenged*" [REFS INCLUDE Breland and Breland, 1961]

F. p 361 (In Chapter 13, Learning)
Skinner opposed to intermediary concepts [REF Skinner, 1950 (not in ref. list)]
"*However...*"

G. p 384 (In Chapter 1, Voluntary behaviour)
"scientific analysis of behavior dispossesses autonomous man..." [Skinner, 1971 (not in ref list)] *If we choose to disagree* with [this] assertion...basic question: how are voluntary movements formed?

H. pp 443-444 (In Chapter 17, Language)
Learning theory approaches. S-R and S-O-R models. Skinner on shaping of child's pronunciation as example. [REF Skinner, 1957]
"*However...*"

I. p 567 (In Chapter 21, Models of personality)
Behaviouristic approaches , Skinner listed [NO REFS]
"*...however...*" "More flexible versions of behaviourism are most popular..."

Figure 1. Mentions of Skinner in Taylor et al. (1982)

to be "dying" (although that is rather a large leap of inference). We would note too how difficult a concept "mainstream" is in this context. The statement implies that to say behavior analysis is not mainstream would be somehow incorrect. However, it is equally arguable that the state of contemporary psychology could quite accurately be said to involve the marginalizing of behavior analysis, however regrettable that might be.

A similar point can be made concerning "Behavior analysts are interested in other perspectives. They are not isolated, closed to criticism, and ignorant of other perspectives". The first part of the statement does not allow for specification of what it is about other perspectives that interests behavior analysts (they may be interested simply for the purpose of criticism), while in relation to the second part of the statement it can again be argued that behavior analysts are in fact isolated, for example, through being unable to publish empirical findings in journals whose editorial stance rejects their inductive and single-subject methodology. Indeed, Coleman and Mehlman (1992) explore the notion of isolation by looking at citation patterns within and between behavioral and other journals. They argue that the trends previously found by Krantz (1971, 1972) persist; instances of self-citation within their sample of behavioral journals remains high, while instances of cross-citation between behavioral and other journals remains low. However, the isolation these trends apparently indicate is not necessarily pathological. They note that "very high self-citing rates are found in journals of some apparently healthy hard-science specialities" (p. 48) and caution that "journal-level self-citation is a complexly determined, molar-level feature of scientific information usage, the proper interpretation of which has not been agreed upon" (p. 48). Some features of "isolation" may in fact be desirable in terms of "intradisciplinary self-sufficiency, consensus, focus, etc." (Coleman & Mehlman, 1992, p. 49).

Although the checklist refers to Behavior Analysis, the example we have looked at deals with Skinner only. This raises an important question: what counts as behavior analysis? Should a list be compiled of individuals willing to call themselves behavior analysts? Can the field be organized by the numerous books that describe its conceptual and empirical approach? Or do behavior analytic journals better frame the field? If behavior analysts disagree, how would we reasonably expect a textbook to handle that fact? Are there any criticisms of behavior analysis which could be regarded as fair?

Although we were unable to evaluate an introductory text using Bass's checklist, it stimulated us to consider some of the questions that need to be refined. For example, Item E in Figure 1 initially seems a straightforward example to fit the checklist assertion of an erroneous characterization of behavior analytic views: All behaviors are equally conditionable. However, the notion of equipotentiality in the text being examined is not attributed directly to Skinner, but is said to "derive from" his writing. It is striking that whilst equipotentiality is vaguely associated with Skinner without a reference, the Breland and Breland (1961) paper on "The Misbehavior of Organisms" is explicitly cited as evidence against equipotentiality. Our first and general impression was that the passages considered include some which are clearly under-referenced.

References as Units of Analysis

One advantage of considering referencing is that it allows for some precision and quantification in textual analysis. There is a well developed area of research covering citation analysis, which charts lines of intellectual influence in an empirical way (see, for example, Cronin, Snyder, and Atkins's [1997] comparison of the major writers cited in sociology books and journals). There is also a growing body of research which demonstrates how inaccurate citations in academic works often are (see, for example, White's [1987] review of trends over four decades).

Both approaches are appropriate for present purposes: the former allows us to try to gauge the strength of the influence of behavior analysis in psychology textbooks, while the latter approach (accuracy of references) may provide indicators of the treatment of behavior analysis.

Although style manuals provide guidelines for the straightforward matter of documenting assertions, the practices involved in compiling a reference list are a subject of debate (e.g., Bazerman, 1981; Gilbert, 1977; Langham, 1995). In relation to behavior analysis, Chiesa (1994) has pointed out how references can function as subtle implications. For example, she notes that where Mahoney (1989) asserts that "respected scientists [have] challenged or revised radical behaviorist accounts of learning" (p. 1374) he substantiates the assertion with reference to several papers, including Rescorla's (1988) "Pavlovian conditioning: It's not what you think it is", While it will not come as a surprise to behavior analysts that "even the most superficial reading of Skinner's work illustrates that his system differs in important scientific and philosophical ways from Pavlov's" (Chiesa, 1994, p. 12), for the uninformed reader, "Mahoney's assertion and subsequent reference imply the opposite" (Chiesa, 1994, p. 12). Further, our example given above wherein Skinner's writing is mentioned but not directly referenced suggests that an absence of references may say as much about representations as their presence. With these issues in mind, and in the context of a European contribution to the literature on representation, we set out to compare samples of British and American textbooks.

Finding a Measure of "Neglect"

Our sample consisted of six British texts published since 1980 and six U.S. texts published in the same period. In addition, we decided to consider a general introductory text which is unusual in that it was written from an explicitly behavior analytic standpoint (Poling, Schlinger, Starin, & Blakely, 1990). Since we do not yet have objective ways to specify "correct" treatment of behavior analysis, we used this book as a kind of "target behavior" against which to compare these other texts. It provides an indication of the extent to which behavior analysts might expect coverage of their field in textbooks.

One hypothesis we hoped to test is that behavior analysis would receive less coverage in British texts than in their American counterparts. It occurred to us that neglect of behavior analysis might be more readily quantified than distortion. Looking for ways of collecting data that would be as precise as possible, we decided to try two "measures" that could be defined relatively clearly: (1) the frequency of citations to three journals reporting conceptual and empirical research in the behavior analytic tradition, *Journal of the Experimental Analysis of Behavior* (JEAB), *Journal of Applied Behavior Analysis* (JABA), *The Behavior Analyst*; and (2) how often works by Skinner were cited.

Table 1: Articles Cited

| | Source | |
	All Periodicals	Behavior Analysis*
UK TEXTS		
Dobson et al, 1981	215	0 (0.00%)
Taylor et al., 1982	790	2 (0.25%)
Lloyd et al., 1986	432	1 (0.23%)
Gross, 1992	696	1 (0.14%)
Malim et al., 199	279	0 (0.00%)
Radford & Govier, 1991	489	3 (0.61%)
Total	2701	7 (0.26%)
USA TEXTS		
Baron et al., 1980	829	4 (0.48%)
Lefton, 1982	834	6 (0.71%)
Hothersall, 1985	430	4 (0.91%)
Coon, 1992	1152	4 (0.35%)
Zimbardo, 1992	1401	9 (0.64%)
Fernald, 1997	899	12 (1.33%)
Total	5445	39 (0.70%)
BA TEXT		
Poling et al., 1990**	206	40 (19.4%)

* Percentages are of all periodical articles cited in that book.
** Includes 1 citation of Behavior Analysis and Social Action.

As Table 1 shows, neither British nor American texts cite many articles from behavior analytic journals, but the American texts cite more (39) than the British (7). (21 citations were to JABA articles, 23 to JEAB, 2 to *The Behavior Analyst*.) The somewhat higher level of citation in the American texts holds when figures are converted to percentages of the total number of articles in a given book. On average, American texts cite two and a half times as many behavior analytic articles as British texts do. Both British and American texts cite proportionally many fewer behavior analytic articles than does the book written by behaviorists, the forty behavior analytic articles cited there being one more than the total for all six of the other American textbooks.

We next checked for citations of Skinner in our sample. Somewhat to our surprise, given the higher number of references in American texts, there was little

Table 2: Skinner Works Cited

	All References	Skinner Books + Articles+Total
UK TEXTS		
Dobson et al, 1981	487	2+1=3 (0.62%)
Taylor et al., 1982	1612	5+1=6 (0.37%)
Lloyd et al., 1986	839	3+0=3 (0.36%)
Gross, 1992	1520	5+1=6 (0.39%)
Malim et al., 1992	223	4+0=4 (1.79%)
Radford & Govier, 1991	948	2+0=2 (0.21%)
Total	5629	24 (0.43%)
USA TEXTS		
Daron et al., 1980	1311	5+1=6 (0.44%)
Lefton, 1982	1299	1+3=4 (0.31%)
Hothersall, 1985	839	4+0=4 (0.48%)
Coon, 1992	2037	2+2=4 (0.20%)
Zimbardo, 1992	2854	4+4=8 (0.28%)
Fernald, 1997	1264	4+3=7 (0.55%)
Total	9604	33 (0.34%)
BA TEXT		
Poling et al., 1990	470	10 (2.13%)

difference between the two country samples in the number of Skinner works referenced, the typical number being around four or five (see Table 2). The British references are to earlier works, only 21 per cent being to works after 1957, in comparison to 38 per cent in the American textbooks and 56 per cent in the behavior analysis textbook. The British textbooks refer proportionally more to Skinner's books than articles (88% books amongst British references as opposed to 61% amongst the American). There is a general tendency for American textbook writers to cite proportionally more articles than books (mean percentage journal articles cited are 59% and 48% in American and British texts respectively) which might explain this finding. However, there is the possibility that it relates to issues discussed in the following paragraphs.

How can we interpret the different tendency suggested by our findings? We have employed two criteria of "neglect" of behavior analysis: citations of behavior analytic journal articles and citations of works by Skinner. On the first criterion, journal citations, British textbooks do pay less attention to behavior analysis than their American counterparts. When we ask about reasons for this comparative neglect, answers might be found in data relating to the geographic origins of behavior analysis journals (the United States) and the geographic locations of their subscribers. According to figures supplied by the journal managements, JABA, JEAB and *The Behavior Analyst* have respectively 1327, 778 and 112 institutional subscribers in the United States, while the equivalent figures for Britain are 54, 25 and 8. We can safely suggest that the relative neglect of behavior analysis in British textbooks reflects the paucity of behavior analytic practitioners in Britain. Quite simply, there appear to be few British psychologists practicing, teaching, and disseminating behavior analysis.

By this same measure (journal citations), both British and American texts appear negligent when compared with the behaviorally orientated textbook. However, on the second criterion (references to Skinner), British and American textbooks are roughly equal. Furthermore, comparison to the behavioral textbook suggests much less clear evidence of neglect.

Why should there be a difference here? One possibility is the way in which citations are used. A journal article in this context is likely to be cited in a positive way, as a source for an empirical assertion, for example. In contrast, a book may well be cited negatively, for the purpose of criticism, as well as positively. It may be significant that the most cited book by Skinner is *Verbal Behavior* (1957) which has eight appearances. This is not because the authors of the textbooks are endorsing Skinner's analysis of verbal behavior. Generally, it seems to be mentioned to provide a contrast to Chomsky's approach (see the analysis of Taylor et al. [1982] above). If this distinction is correct, introductory textbooks, particularly British ones, may be said to neglect research findings published in behavior analytic journals. They are not so negligent of Skinner as an individual. Whether his work is given full and fair treatment, however, is another matter.

Are Citations Clear and Accurate?

Let us turn now from the question of the neglect of behavior analysis to the relation between accuracy and clarity of citations. In a short section, "Evaluation of the Behaviourist Approach", one of the British texts (Malim, Birch, & Wadeley, 1992, pp. 32-33) lists some criticisms. These include:

"tend to overlook the realm of consciousness and subjective experience."

"does not address a possible role of biological factors in human behaviour."

"cannot account for the production of spontaneous, novel or creative behaviour."

While it would be easy to argue that these statements libel behavior analysis, a caveat is necessary: no individual writers are cited as the object of these criticisms. The reader would have to make an inference to assume that they are directed at Skinner. Secondly, it is unclear from the text whether the authors are simply reporting these criticisms or whether they are endorsing them. Our overall impression is that the intention is to leave the reader with an unfavorable picture of behaviorism. But should we as behavior analysts be dealing in vague, overall impressions? There may well be methods of text analysis worth exploring that would allow such impressions to be tested in a manner that would go some way to satisfying behavior analysts' emphasis on quantification and rigor.

It is also possible to find broadly fair and positive accounts of behavior analysis. An example is a passage in another British textbook (Radford & Govier, 1991, p. 804). Having propounded the view that "any account of behaviour must deal with three levels...physiological, individual, and social", the text goes on to indicate that few psychologists have actually done this. Freud is cited as one who failed to do so, H. J. Eysenck as one who has tried, while "Skinner similarly seeks to take account of genetics, an individual's learning history, and the functional importance of social environments."

Compared with the previously cited criticisms of behaviorism this is fair indeed. But consider the position of the reader who wishes to follow up this positive account of Skinner. No references to Skinner are cited at this point in the text and the consolidated references at the end of the book will lead the reader only to *Verbal Behavior* (Skinner, 1957). The references also include *Schedules of Reinforcement* (Ferster & Skinner, 1957) but that is to be found at F for Ferster. Even if the naive reader did find both works, can we say that these two volumes offer the best introductions to Skinner's work? Behavior analysts may wish to consider which of Skinner's numerous publications they would recommend as appropriate for text-book readers at the introductory level, and whether there are more appropriate texts by authors other than Skinner.

These referencing issues are worth pursuing a little further. First let us, with apologies, offer another rather non-behavioral impression; namely that textbook writers are rather careless in their referencing when dealing with behaviorism. We do have some hard evidence on this which suggests that the issue is worth pursuing as a research question. Gross (1992) deals in some detail with Skinner and operant conditioning on pages 173 to 185. In the text, 33 different works are referenced in the standard way, i.e. author's surname and date of publication; for example, "Skinner (1938)" and "Skinner (1948)". However, readers who wish to follow up these works by finding the full details in the consolidated reference list will discover that they do not appear there. Neither do "Azrin and Holz (1966)" or "Seligman (1974)". (The omission of the publication details of these works makes it impossible to identify them without resorting to inference. These works cannot appear in our list of references.) Indeed of 33 citations, 17, slightly more than half, do not appear in the reference list. Although such carelessness might be characteristic of the treatment of behaviorism, it is also possible that the author is generally careless with citations. As a check on this, we reviewed another section of the book (pp. 269-285), this time dealing with perception. A total of 40 works were cited, only 3 of which were not in the list of references. With accuracy on operant conditioning, 48%, and accuracy on perceptual adaptation, 93%, there are reasonable grounds for complaint. Furthermore, it is worth finding out if this violation of referencing conventions in the case of behavior analysis is an isolated occurrence, or if it is one instance of a more general pattern.

Some Suggestions

The evidence we have cited supports the proposition that behavior analysis is neglected in British introductory textbooks relative to their American counterparts, and suggests that their authors are out of touch with the conceptual and empirical advances made in the field since Skinner's early efforts. This raises two big questions: Why is this the case? And what can be done about it?.

On the "why" question, we can reasonably suppose that the phenomenon has multiple causes, and two factors stand out. The first we have already alluded to; the relative scarcity of behavior analytic practitioners in the British psychological community. It may simply be the case that British behavior analysts have not yet disseminated theoretical and applied findings sufficiently widely for textbook authors to take notice. It may also be the case that as a consequence, British psychologists take Skinner to be the only noteworthy representative of the field.

Friman, Allen, Kerwin, and Larzelere (1993), using citation analysis, described the existence of three thriving schools of psychology, cognitive, psychoanalytic and behavioral (although it should be noted that they define behavioral psychology more widely than behavior analysis alone). Insofar as these approaches do not interact, then it is understandable that textbook writers who belong in the main to the largest stream in modern psychology, the cognitive, will tend to be ignorant of the behaviorist stream.

The second factor is the character of the introductory textbook not just as an aspect of psychology but as a feature of society generally. Paul (1988) has discussed the rise of the typical contemporary introductory psychology textbook, particularly in relation to the almost doubling of undergraduate college enrolment in the United States in the 1960's. She notes that the most rapid expansion occurred in the two-year community college sector, a sector that more closely resembles high schools than traditional colleges in that faculty consisted of fewer Ph.D.s and were expected to focus on teaching and "to do lots of it": "many instructors were ill-prepared to teach a wide range of courses at the college level. Few had Ph.D.s, and a majority taught part-time. Because their students were often not well-prepared academically, community college instructors demanded simpler texts" (Paul, 1988, p. 32).

According to Paul, these books shifted their emphasis from content to style so that they are now enticingly multicolored but only superficially comprehensive. Above all, they compete in a market where hundreds of thousands of students are studying psychology at an introductory level. These factors may not all hold true of British textbooks: however, the basic fact is that British textbooks, like their American counterparts, are products offered in the market place. As Paul notes, "texts are adopted by professors, not students" (1988, p. 33), so that psychology teachers have a key role in determining the success of a textbook by setting it as required or recommended reading. Thus a successful textbook will be one which fits the assumptions and biases of the mainstream teachers.

We should remember that introductory texts have other flaws aside from their treatment of behavior analysis and that these also need explaining. For example, data in textbooks dealing with a number of prominent topics have been shown to be seriously distorted. These include the heritability of intelligence (see, for example, Kamin, 1977, Chapter 6, and Paul, 1985), while other distortions noted in secondary sources include the use of "phantom citations" (McKnight, 1979) and a preference in textbooks for idealized over actual data (Shepard, 1983).

Turning to the second question, what is to be done? Some suggestions are fairly obvious. Write detailed critiques and send them to authors and publishers. Teach students to be sceptical about introductory texts. Do not use introductory texts at all. Write our own introductory texts. If our finding that important referencing conventions are seriously violated in the case of behavior analysis can be replicated, then this provides a clear criticism that can be passed on to publishers and textbook authors. While we would not wish to discourage anyone from adopting any of these strategies, as yet we have no guarantee of their success. Before attempting to change the behavior of authors and editors, we would be wise to apply standard behavior analytic practices to textbook evaluation. That is, a fruitful approach might lie in the analysis of the development and function of modern textbooks along with an analysis of textbook writers' behavior.

Behavior analysis has made substantial contributions to the clinical and educational fields, but its success is based on long and painstaking data collection and analysis. Introductory psychology textbooks are the products of human behavior. Whatever is wrong with these textbooks can only be understood and corrected if we have an adequate way of analyzing the behavior involved. The behavior is complex, but that is simply a given which we have to accept. In looking at other areas of human behavior, behavior analysts do not assume that any of it is beyond analysis. The same holds true of textbook writing.

Telling Tales: The Social Transmission of Knowledge

In his introduction to *The Structure of Scientific Revolutions*, Kuhn (1970, p. 1) draws attention to the way in which textbooks function to organize the knowledge of a given discipline so that the systematization of the knowledge (the textbook) in a sense becomes the knowledge. For behavior analysts, the field of social forces that create knowledge is almost virgin territory, although others, such as scholars of rumor, contemporary legend, and the sociology of science have tackled knowledge transmission in their own way and in their own terminology. It may be worth considering some of the ways in which these seemingly discrete fields of inquiry can be drawn upon to guide research questions and suggest appropriate methods that would further a behavior analysis of the textbook and the influences on its production.

A rumor scholar has suggested that:

Popular beliefs and scholarly knowledge develop in separate communication channels but in quite similar ways; they differ mostly in the extent to which use of critical ability is institutionalized... The development of human knowledge is a social process. Both popular outlook and scholarly knowledge are shaped through the successive testing of hypotheses and the retention of the successful ones. (Shibutani, 1966, pp. 160-161).

The language is not behavioral, but the issue is worth taking seriously by behaviorists. How does scholarly knowledge develop? What, in practice, distinguishes scholarly knowledge from popular belief? Where does the textbook stand between scholarship and rumor transmission in terms of critical standards?

In the field of contemporary legend, scholars have concluded that these stories circulate in print and other media as well as by word of mouth (Hobbs, 1978; Mullen, 1972; Smith & Hobbs, 1990) and there is a parallel with research in the psychology of rumor, where rumor in the mass media is seen as significant as oral transmission (Rosnow, 1991). There are, of course, differences between newspapers and psychology textbooks. However, the fact that textbook writers may claim to employ higher standards of scholarship and evidence does not automatically mean that the standards are actually higher. Their behavior may be under the control of variables similar to those which control the behavior of journalists.

A justification for exploring this possibility is that a number of the most famous studies in psychology have been shown to be seriously misrepresented in secondary texts. In a famous attempt to establish a laboratory equivalent to the transmission of rumor, Allport and Postman (1947) employed a procedure in which a subject describe a picture to another subject, who then described it to a third, and so on. They found many distortions in the chain of "serial reproduction". For example, a picture of a subway train with a white man holding an open razor often ended up with a description in which it was a black man who had the razor. Treadway and McCloskey (1987) report that this finding is frequently misreported. In particular, the distortion is sometimes described as occurring in the recall of the first subject rather than in the chain of secondary account. Similar mistakes appear in accounts of Asch's (1956) experiments on conformity and independence of judgement (see Friend, Rafferty, & Bramel, 1990). Following the discovery that Cyril Burt's claims were based on fraudulent data, Paul (1988) examined subsequent claims concerning the heritability of intelligence in textbooks:

> The scandal's primary effect was on the reference sections of the texts. These were invariably updated. As a result, many books cited as references articles that characterized as worthless the data reported authoritatively in the discussion. (p. 31)

And in relation to the numerous misreporting of Watson and Rayner's (1921) "Little Albert" experiment, Paul notes that "once a story is established, it is almost impossible to dislodge" (1988, p. 32).

We stress that these examples represent only a small sample of those published. This being so, we must consider to what extent distortions of behavior analysis are unique and to what extent they are examples of a wider problem.

We believe that the communication obstacles between behavior analysis, rumor studies, and contemporary legend scholarship can be overcome to allow a fruitful cross-fertilization. Hobbs and Cornwell (1991) have suggested a behavior analysis model for the study of contemporary legend (see Figure 2) where story telling is conceptualized as an example of social interaction. The behavior of the teller is influenced by that person's reactional biography, by the setting and by the behavior of the listener. The same set of variables influence the behavior of the listener. What relevance can a model developed to deal with story telling, gossiping or cracking jokes have to understanding the behavior of psychologists? The simplest and most direct answer to the question is this: psychologists tell stories. We are referring here not to the private lives of psychologists but to their professional activities. One work by writers in the behavior analysis tradition provides us with an example. In *Principles of Behavior Analysis* (Grant & Evans, 1994), the authors have attempted to construct the text on behavior analytic principles. In explaining how they set about this, they may incidentally produce some clues to a behavior analytic method of analyzing

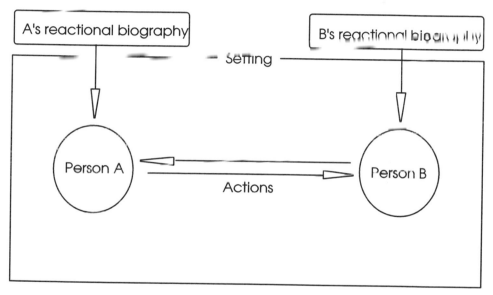

Figure 2 Behavior Analysis Model of Contemporary Legend

textbooks. However, we find it particularly telling that these authors, describing their own behavior in writing the text, include the following passage:

> Although this text consists mainly of true stories, in some cases we have altered aspects of the stories... We have given the subjects names to make the material more readable... We have made omissions and minor alterations in aspects of the studies for illustrative purposes. (p. x)

Here we have textbook writers, by their own accounts, changing actual events in order to make "a good story", just as people do when they pass on rumors or contemporary legends (Hobbs, 1987). Lest it be thought that this is meant as a condemnation of these authors, let us say, first, that we believe they are simply being open about aspects of textbook composition which others keep to themselves, and secondly, Grant and Evans draw attention to the dangers when they write,

In a few cases in which we have made substantial alterations of experiments, we have suggested that interested readers compare (cf.) our rendition to the original source.

The effort required to follow this suggestion may make such a comparison unlikely, and the "more readable" stories may circulate. Consider the following example. Coon (1992) suggests that students may demonstrate for themselves the power of social reinforcers by shaping the behavior of their teacher. They should smile and show interest when the teacher moves in one direction, but yawn and look bored when the move is in the opposite direction:

This trick has been a favorite of psychology graduate students for decades. For a time one of my professors delivered all his lectures from the right hand side of the room while toying with the cords from the venetian blinds. (We added the cords in the second week!) (p. 201)

Chrisler (1988) refers to such anecdotes as "legion". Writers on contemporary folklore have treated the story as an example of modern legend (Brunvand, 1989, 1991; Hobbs, 1991, 1992). What is particularly relevant here is that the story is told in a textbook of psychology. We suggest that the author may have found the story evoked favorable responses in conversation or in class and as a consequence repeats the telling in this different context. Skinner (1980) suggested a similar explanation for the survival of classic tales for children:

Perhaps "Jack the Giant Killer"... is reassuring to the small child in a world of towering grown-ups - but perhaps it is simply a story adults have found effective in holding the attention of children because they fear giants... In the latter case, it is the story teller who perpetuates the story, whose "need" is satisfied. The gripping concern which keeps the child motionless and reinforces story telling may be injurious rather than remedial. (p. 310)

A similar situation may prevail in textbook writing, when writers seek to enliven their texts. Of course, this can only be speculation because we do not have the necessary information about the writer's reactional biography. We are not yet at the stage where we can hope to experiment on the process of textbook composition.

References

Allport, G. W., & Postman, L. (1947). *The psychology of rumor*. New York: Holt.

Asch, S. E. (1956). Studies of independence and conformity. *Psychological Monographs, 70*, Whole No. 416.

Baron, R. A., Byrne, D. E., & Kantowitz, B. H. (1980). *Psychology: Understanding behavior*. (2nd edition) New York: Holt, Rinehart and Winston.

Bazerman, C. (1981). What written knowledge does: Three examples of academic discourse. *Philosophy and the Social Sciences, 11*, 361-387.

Bennett, G., & Smith, P. (1993). *Contemporary legend: A folklore bibliography*. New York: Garland.

Bennett, G., & Smith, P. (Eds.) (1996). *Contemporary legend: A reader*. New York: Garland.

Blakely, E., Poling, A., & Cross, J. (1986). Fraud, fakery, and fudging: Behavior analysis and bad science. In A. D. Poling & R. W. Fuqua (Eds.), *Research methods in applied behavior analysis* (pp. 313-330). New York: Plenum Press.

Breland, K., & Breland, M. (1961). The misbehavior of organisms. *American Psychologist, 16*, 681-684.

Brunvand, J. H. (1989). *Curses! Broiled again! The hottest urban legends going*. New York: Norton.

Brunvand, J. H. (1991). More on the trained professor. *Foaftale News, 24*, 5-6.

Brunvand, J. H. (1993). *The baby train and other lusty urban legends*. New York: Norton.

Chiesa, M. (1994). *Radical behaviorism: The philosophy and the science*. Boston: Writers' Cooperative.

Chrisler, J. C. (1988). Conditioning the instructor's behavior: A class project in psychology of learning. *Teaching of Psychology, 15*, 135-137.

Coleman, S. R., & Mehlman, S. E. (1992). An empirical update (1969-1989) of D. L. Krantz's thesis that the experimental analysis of behavior is isolated. *The Behavior Analyst, 15*, 43-49.

Cooke, N. L. (1984). Misrepresentations of the behavioral model in preservice teacher education textbooks. In W. L. Heward, T. E. Heron, D. S. Hill & J. Trap-Porter (Eds.) *Focus on behavior analysis in education* (pp. 197-217). Columbus OH: Charles E. Merrill.

Coon, D. (1992). *Introduction to psychology: Explorations and application*. (6th ed.) St. Paul MN: West.

Cronin, B., Snyder, H., & Atkins, H. (1997). Comparative citation rankings of authors in monographic and journal literature: a study of sociology. *Journal of Documentation, 53*, 263-273.

Cornwell, D., & Hobbs, S. (1992). Rumour and legend: Irregular interactions between social psychology and folkloristics. *Canadian Psychology, 33*, 609-613.

DeBell, C. S., & Harless, D. K. (1992). B.F. Skinner: Myth and misperception. *Teaching of Psychology, 19*, 68-73.

De Vos, G. (1996). *Tales, rumors, and gossip: Exploring contemporary folk literature in grades 7-12*. Englewood CO: Libraries Unlimited.

Dobson, C. B., Hardy, M., Heyes, S., Humphrey, A., & Humphreys, P. (1981). *Understanding psychology*. London: Weidenfeld and Nicholson.

Fernald, L. D. (1997). *Psychology*. Upper Saddle River NJ: Prentice-Hall.

Ferster, C. B., & Skinner, B. F. (1957). *Schedules of reinforcement*. New York: Appleton-Century-Crofts.

Fine, G. A. (1992). *Manufacturing tales: Sex and money in contemporary legends*. Knoxville TN: University of Tennessee Press.

Fleming, R. L., & Boyd, R. F. (1994). *The big book of urban legends*. New York: Paradox Press.

Friend, R., Rafferty, Y., & Bramel, D. (1990). A puzzling misrepresentation of the Asch "conformity" study. *European Journal of Social Psychology, 20,* 29-44.

Friman, P. C., Allen, K. D., Kerwin, M. L. E., & Larzelere, R. (1993). Changes in modern psychology: A citation analysis of the Kuhnian displacement thesis. *American Psychologist, 48,* 656-664.

Gilbert, G. N. (1977). Referencing as persuasion. *Social Studies of Science, 7,* 97-113.

Grant, L., & Evans, L. (1994). *Principles of behavior analysis.* New York: Harper Collins.

Gross, R. D. (1992). *Psychology: The science of mind and behaviour.* (2nd ed.) London: Hodder and Stoughton.

Hobbs, S. (1978). The folk tale as news. *Oral History, 6,* 74-86.

Hobbs, S. (1987). The social psychology of a "good" story. In G. Bennett & P. Smith (eds.) *Perspectives on contemporary legend II* (pp. 133-148). Sheffield: Sheffield Academic Press.

Hobbs, S. (1991). The trained professor. *Foaftale News, 21,* 3-4.

Hobbs, S. (1992). Shaping the lecturer's behavior. *Newsletter of the British Psychological Society Scottish Branch, 15,* 9-14.

Hobbs, S., & Cornwell, D. (1991). A behavior analysis model of contemporary legend. *Contemporary Legend, 1,* 93-106.

Hothersall, D. (1985). *Psychology.* Columbus OH: Merrill.

Jansen, W. H. (1973). The surpriser surprised: A modern legend. *Folklore Forum, 6,* 1-24.

Jensen, R., & Burgess, H. (1997). Mythmaking: How introductory psychology texts present B. F. Skinner's analysis of cognition. *The Psychological Record, 47,* 221-232.

Kamin, L. J. (1977). *The science and politics of IQ.* Harmondsworth: Penguin.

Krantz, D. L. (1971). The separate worlds of operant and non-operant psychology. *Journal of Applied Behavior Analysis, 4,* 61-70.

Krantz, D. L. (1972). Schools and systems: The mutual isolation of operant and non-operant psychology as a case study. *Journal of the History of the Behavioral Sciences, 7,* 86-102.

Kuhn, T. S. (1970). *The structure of scientific revolutions.* (2nd edition) Chicago: University of Chicago Press.

Langham, T. (1995). Consistency in referencing. *Journal of Documentation, 51,* 360-369.

Lefton, L. A. (1982). *Psychology.* (2nd ed.) Boston MA: Allyn and Bacon.

Lloyd, P., Mayes, A., Manstead, A. S. R., Meudell, P. R., & Wagner, H. L. (1986). *Introduction to psychology: An integrated approach.* London: Fontana.

Mahoney, M. J. (1989). Scientific psychology and radical behaviorism. *American Psychologist, 44,* 1372-1377.

McKnight, C. (1979). Phantom citation: A case of insulin shock.. *Bulletin of the British Psychological Society, 32,* 353-354.

Malim, T., Birch, A., & Wadeley, A. (1992). *Perspectives in psychology.* Basingstoke: Macmillan Press.

Mullen, P. B. (1972). Modern legend and rumor theory. *Journal of the Folklore Institute,* *9,* 95-108.

Paul, D. B. (1985). Textbook treatments of the genetics of intelligence. *Quarterly Review of Biology, 60,* 317-325.

Paul, D. B. (1988, Winter). *The market as censor. PS Political Science and Politics,* pp. 31-35.

Poling, A., Schlinger, H., Starin, S., & Blakely, E. (1990). *Psychology: A behavioral overview.* New York: Plenum.

Radford, J., & Govier, E. (Eds.) (1991). *A textbook of psychology.* (2nd edition) London: Routledge.

Rescorla, R. A. (1988). Pavlovian conditioning: It's not what you think it is. *American Psychologist, 43,* 151-160.

Rosnow, R. L. (1991). Inside rumor: A personal journey. *American Psychologist, 46,* 484-495.

Shepard, R. N. (1983). "Idealized" figures in textbooks versus psychology as an empirical science. *American Psychologist, 38,* 855.

Shibutani, T. (1966). *Improvised news: A sociological study of rumor.* New York: Bobbs-Merrill.

Skinner, B. F. (1957). *Verbal behavior.* New York: Appleton-Century-Crofts.

Skinner, B. F. (1979, March). My experience with the baby-tender. *Psychology Today,* pp. 28-31, 34, 37-38, 40.

Skinner, B. F. (1980). *Notebooks.* Englewood Cliffs NJ: Prentice-Hall.

Smith, P., & Hobbs, S. (1990). Films using contemporary legend themes/motifs. In G. Bennett & P. Smith (Eds.) *Contemporary legend: The first five years* (pp. 138-148) Sheffield: Sheffield Academic Press.

Taylor, A, Sluckin, W., Davies, D. R., Reason, J. T., Thomson, R., & Colman, A. M. (1982). *Introducing psychology.* (2nd edition) Harmondsworth: Penguin.

Todd, J. T. (1987). The great power of steady misrepresentation: Behaviorism's presumed denial of instinct. *The Behavior Analyst, 19,* 117-118.

Todd, J. T. (1994). What psychology has to say about John B. Watson: Classical behaviorism in psychology textbooks, 1920-1989. In J. T. Todd & E. K. Morris (Eds.) *Modern perspectives on John B. Watson and classical behaviorism* (pp. 75-107). Westport CT: Greenwood Press.

Todd, J. T., & Morris, E. K. (1983). Misconception and miseducation: Presentations of radical behaviorism in psychology textbooks. *The Behavior Analyst, 6,* 153-160.

Todd, J. T., & Morris, E. K. (1992). Case histories in the great power of steady misrepresentation. *American Psychologist, 47,* 1441-1453.

Treadway, M., & McCloskey, M. (1987). Cite unseen: Distortions of the Allport and Postman rumor study in eyewitness testimony literature. *Law and Human Behavior, 11,* 19-25.

Watson, J. B., & Rayner, R. (1920). Conditioned emotional reactions. *Journal of Experimental Psychology, 3,* 1-14.

White, A. (1987). Reference list inaccuracies: A four-decade comparison. *Journal of Counseling and Development, 66,* 195-196.

Zimbardo, P. (1992). *Psychology and life.* (13th edition). New York: Harper Collins.

Chapter 14

Infant Emotions Under the Positive-Reinforcer Control of Caregiver Attention and Touch

Jacob L. Gewirtz and Martha Peláez-Nogueras
Florida International University

In this chapter we summarize several research themes on infant emotional phenomena that we have approached in the operant-learning paradigm. These infant emotional phenomena include: *attachment, fear of the dark, fear of strangers, jealousy* and *depression*. We illustrate how these phenomena can be based on operant-learning processes that, as process explanations, constitute remarkable discrepancies from other nominal conceptions of "process" in the developmental and clinical literatures.

For the most part, infant emotional phenomena have been explored heretofore by nonexperimental means, often under the aegis of nominal process theories that resort to explanatory fictions (e.g., an "insecurely attached" infant, a "depressed" infant). Mainstream developmentalists tend to minimize or exclude entirely the contributions of environmental factors, most specifically of contingent stimuli provided via caregiver behavior and of learning, to the infant (problem) behaviors at issue. Thus, many infant emotional responses are conceptualized in the developmental literature as biologically based, or even worse as resulting from the nonprocess pseudo-causal hollow variable of chronological age (Gewirtz & Peláez-Nogueras, 1996). The developmental literature emphasizes that there are several unique universal emotions present at birth that are prewired to emerge as maturational processes (e.g., Izard, 1992). Also, cognitively-oriented functionalists (e.g., Barrett & Campos, 1987; Campos & Barrett, 1984; Lazarus, 1991) have emphasized prewired innate and universal emotions.

The experiments we describe here do not rule out definitively such unlearned or hereditary explanations of the key outcome behaviors "explained" in the literatures. However, their results do make it likely that much, if not most or all, of the variance in the infant behaviors studied could be accounted for by their relations with the parent-provided proximal antecedent and consequent stimuli.

In our operant-learning studies, when infant attachment, fear of the dark, fear of strangers, jealousy, and depression phenomena were studied under laboratory conditions, with maternal behaviors under experimenter control, these phenomena were shown to result from dramatically-different processes than those identified in the literature. The infant adaptive problem behaviors actually appear to be operants under the control of occasioning stimuli and consequences inadvertently provided, in the contexts in which they appear, by the responding of well-intentioned, loving parents. Even so, the results of our experiments do not rule out definitively the literature's predominant notions that the behaviors denoting attachment, fear, jealousy and depression are innately determined and that, in time, children "grow out" of the problem behaviors involved. The results of our experiments, however, make plausible the idea that those attachment, fear- and jealousy-denoting behaviors may result alternatively from an operant-learning process involving positive rein-forcement. Whenever possible in reports of the experiments that follow, we list the number or proportion of the subjects who conform to the patterns denoting success under the operant-learning paradigm. If binomial tests were used to evaluate the result patterns in terms of probability models, one-tail remote probabilities (p <.0001) in favor of the operant hypothesis would be found in every instance. Such a pattern of successful results should not be surprising, for in our work the sampling of the behavior of every infant subject in every phase of each design continues until the behavior criterion for that phase is attained. In addition, no subject is ever discarded on behavior-score grounds.

Attachment or Separation Anxiety: The Learned Basis of Infant Protests

In the child clinical literature, there has been a systematic failure to take into account whether or not there exists a systematic pattern of parental responding contingent on the infant target behaviors (Gewirtz & Peláez-Nogueras, 1991; Gewirtz & Peláez-Nogueras, 1992). This omission has led infant researchers to treat infant target behavior classes, such as protests occasioned by maternal departures or separations, as symptoms or indices of putative underlying "causes," for instance "attachment" (Bowlby, 1960; Schaffer & Emerson, 1964), "security of attachment" typologies (Ainsworth, Blehar, Waters, & Wall, 1978), or "separation anxiety" (Kagan, 1980; Kagan, Kearsley, & Zelazo, 1978; Weinraub & Lewis, 1977).

From our behavior-analytic perspective, the proximal explanation of the occurrence of these cued responses is far simpler: those infant response patterns appear in the setting in which they occur due to a history of conditioning there, wherein protests were occasioned by antecedent discriminative stimuli, and fol-lowed routinely or intermittently by contingent maternal responses functioning as reinforcing stimuli for those protest responses. The *protest* of the infant may be comprised of cries, screams, fusses, whines, or whimpers; in somewhat older children the protests may involve, in addition, such responses as grabbing the parent's body or clothing, pleading, or imploring. These responses denoting protests seem to be functional equivalents for delaying maternal departures and for cutting short separations from the mother. On this basis, these infant response can function as a class of operants in conditioning contexts, conditionable by their effectiveness in delaying and/or precluding maternal departures, or shortening separations.

Our thesis has been that cued separation protests result typically from an operant-learning-of-protests process in the departure or separation setting in which the protests appear, produced by a prior pattern of well-intentioned, idiosyncratic, maternal reactions contingent on those cued protests. Thus, the process variables manipulated in our experiments involved some of the typical contingent stimuli provided by the mother during her departures, by such of her discrete reactions as stopping, retracing her steps, hesitating, vacillating, turning to, speaking to, reasoning with or- once separated- returning to pick up her protesting child; and during actual separations when she calls or returns to her infant contingent on protests. We have shown that, when contingent, these events can function as reinforcing stimuli to raise the relative incidence of a child's protests (denoting the occurrence of operant conditioning) to discriminative stimuli provided by a mother's preparations to leave, by her actual departures, and by separations, with her being out of sight and earshot.

Our first two studies were designed to ascertain if, and how, infant protests can come under the control of cues and contingencies generated by maternal behaviors during her brief departures or separations from her child. The demonstration that such infant protests can be shaped, maintained, or increased by patterns of contingent maternal responding (provided on the basis of continuous reinforcement: CRF), and decreased or eliminated by maternal responding contingent on alternative-to-protests behaviors (thus providing differential reinforcement of other behavior: DRO), have provided evidence for the conditioned basis of the protests that have been treated as an unlearned, species-specific, index of "attachment" for some other theorists.

The Conditioning of Infant Departure and Separation Protests

In this first experiment (Gewirtz & Peláez-Nogueras, 1991), 23 six- to 11-mo.-old infants received treatments from their mothers, in 8 to 12 successive weekday 6- to 8- trial sessions conducted in our laboratory. Each trial consisted of a departure, a separation and a reunion segment. The departure segment involved the mother, under instructional earphone control, cuing her departure three times via vocal-plus-visual stimuli in a *standard* manner (i.e., standing up, kissing the child while saying "Bye, bye; I'll be right back" and then slowly walking toward the exit door, then stopping and turning to see her child and repeating her verbalizations twice more before closing the door). Each departure segment of a trial lasted approximately 28 secs. The separation segment of the trial (lasting up to 3 min.) began as soon as the mother exited the room and closed the door. The reunion segment lasted 15 sec. The intertrial interval was 60 sec. Under the conditioning (CRF) treatment, the mother's three responses during a departure and a separation were contingent on the infant's protests. In the reversal treatments, the same three maternal responses were contingent (DRO) on other behaviors than infant protest behaviors. The overall percentage interobserver agreement on infant cued protest responses between two independent observers for all subjects was 94.

In this experiment, the same treatment was implemented serially for the departure and separation segments of each trial. That is, contingent maternal responding to infant protests during a departure on the same trial always preceded her contingent responding to infant protests during the brief separation that followed. After a joint criterion was attained in *both* trial segments in that 80% or more of the trials include a protest (usually this occurred between the third and the sixth session), the DRO reversal treatment was introduced (simultaneously) for both departure and separation trial segments. A criterion for terminating the DRO treatment was that, on the last session, the proportion of trials involving protests be 20 % or less. An additional criterion for terminating the DRO treatment during separation segments was the time-duration without protests which was shaped proportionally across sessions up to 3 min. Across trials, the escalating DRO schedule employed during separations with mother outside the room involved her contingent responses shaping nonprotest durations of ever-increasing length. That is, maternal responding was provided contingent on the absence of protests for durations that increased up to three min. Nine infants served in an ABA (DRO-CRF-DRO) reversal design while 13 infants served in a BA (CRF-DRO) design.

The outcome measure used was the proportion of trials-per-daily-session on which the infant made a cued protest. As seen in Figure 1, every one of the nine infant subjects manifested the same inverted-"V", ABA pattern, confirming the effective-

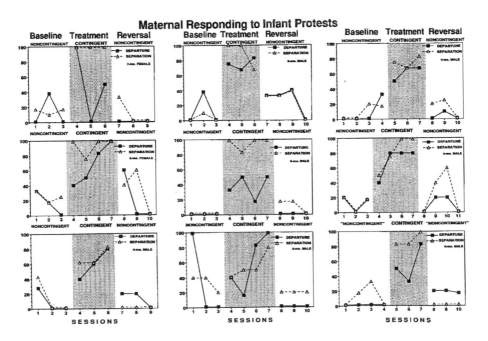

Figure 1. Under the ABA design, departure and separation protest chart of 9 infant subjects.

ness of the treatment separately under departures and separations. On a binomial basis, if each predicted inverted-"V", ABA pattern during departures, and separately during separations, is considered a "head", and every other pattern is considered a "tail", a one-tail test is in order. The one-tail probability of finding this 9-for-9 pattern in each of the two contexts is p < .001.

Based on the individual departure and separation curves of the same nine infants, composite protest curves (see Figure 2) were developed from the *median* percentage of protest trials per session, across the first, next-to-last, and last session scores in each of the three successive treatment phases. These two median curves smooth the two result patterns for the reader. Another result was that mothers of every one of the nine infants remained outside the room during separations, before infant protests were emitted, for much longer durations under the DRO than under the CRF treatment (one-tail binomial probability, p < .001, in every case).

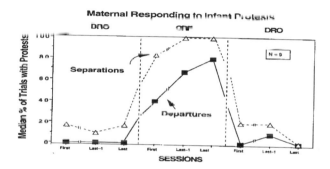

Figure 2. A composite protest chart (N = 9) representing Median Percentage-Protest trials per session, across the first, next-to-last (Last–1) and last session score under each of the three experimental phases of the ABA design.

Under the BA design, both the departure and the separation protests of *every one* of the 13 individual infants decreased from the maternal contingent-reinforcement (CRF) treatment phase to the (DRO) reversal phase of maternal responding differentially contingent on nonprotest behaviors. The one-tail probability of finding 13-for-13 is p < .001 in each of the two contexts, departure and separation. For the ABA and BA design groups, the frequency and content of maternal stimuli provided were implemented to be equivalent under both CRF and DRO treatments. The outcome measure was the proportion of session trials on which the infant made a cued protest.

Conditional Discrimination Between Departures and Separations: The Role of Context

We conducted a follow up study with 18 infants in an attempt to train a discrimination, indexed by protests, between maternal departure and separation contexts (Peláez-Nogueras & Gewirtz, 1990). In addition, we wanted to control for the potential sequence effect in our first experiment where the conditioning for protests was cued first by maternal departures and then by maternal separations. The conditions were implemented in each trial segment sequentially and not independently. That is, a conditioning or reversal procedure (either CRF or DRO) was implemented for infant protests in both the departure segment and the ensuing separation segment of a trial.

Thus, the purpose of this second experiment on the theme of attachment was to condition *opposite* patterns of infant protests serially in the two trial segments (Peláez-Nogueras & Gewirtz, 1990). For one order of conditions, the protests in the departure segment of a trial were followed by a CRF schedule of maternal responding, which was opposite to the DRO schedule being implemented in the separation segment of that trial. For the second order of conditions, the CRF and the DRO sequence was reversed in context; protests in the departure segment were under a DRO schedule while protests during separation were under a CRF schedule. Specifically, infant protests should come under the control of different discriminative contextual stimuli and contingencies generated in successive segments of the same trials by differential maternal behavior. In this frame, under both orders the infant responses generated in the departure and separation contexts were conceptually and operationally distinguished from one another.

As in the first experiment, there were two treatment conditions. A series of S^Ds (discriminative stimuli, which included the mother saying "Bye, bye" while picking up her purse and walking toward the door) set the occasion for infant protests to occur and to be reinforced three times by contingent maternal responses (for example, saying "What is the matter? I'll be right back. Don't worry.") during the departure segment of a trial while, under the ensuing separation segment of the same trial, another series of S^Ds (closing the door and disappearing out of infant's sight and earshot) set the occasion for any other infant response but the protest to be reinforced by the contingent return of the mother to the infant. Thus, discrimination training was implemented, with infant protests coming under the differential control of S^Ds from maternal departures and the ensuing brief separations.

Subjects were 18 infants, ranging in age from 6 to 10 mo, who participated in 8 to 12 daily training sessions in our laboratory. Each session consisted of 6 to 8 trials. Each of two groups received the treatments in one of two orders. For one group of 9 infants in a modified BA reversal design, during every trial the mother's responses (under instructional control) were provided contingent on each infant protest under a CRF schedule during her departures, and under a DRO schedule under the ensuing separation segment of the very same trial, contingent on infant nonprotest behaviors (such as vocalizations, smiles, or play). If in a DRO trial a protest was emitted, 10 sec had to elapse before a nonprotest would be followed by contingent maternal responding. When the response criterion was attained under both segments of the trial, the CRF schedule of maternal responding was reversed by a shift to a DRO schedule. In the second group, 9 infants received a counterbalanced, inverse treatment order: maternal DRO responding followed departure protests and maternal CRF responding followed the ensuing separation protests.

Using the index proportion-of-trials-with-protests in a session, contrasts were made, first, between the concurrent CRF and DRO treatment scores of the final session of the first condition, and, second, between the sequential CRF treatment scores of the final session of the first condition and the DRO treatment scores of the final session of the second condition(s). *Every* infant in each of the two condition orders emitted a behavior pattern in which (a) within treatments, the CRF behavior pattern was higher systematically than the concurrent DRO behavior pattern (for *each* treatment order, 9 of 9, one-tail binomial test $p < .001$), and (b) sequentially, the CRF behavior pattern was systematically higher than the DRO behavior pattern (for *each* treatment order, 9 of 9, one-tail binomial test $p < .001$). Thus, the behavior of all 18 infant subjects conformed to the operant hypothesis: every one could be trained successfully to discriminate between maternal departure and ensuing separation trial segments. This was denoted by their emitting opposite patterns of responding in those two segments of the same trials. To simplify and complete the picture, these results are summarized in Figures 3a and 3b, showing median proportions of infant responses per trial block in each condition.

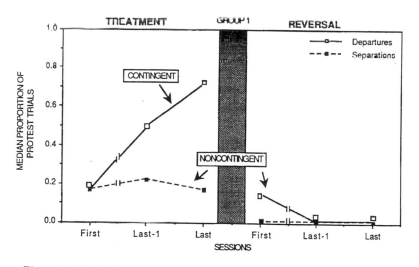

Figure 3a. Under the BA design, the chart shows median proportions of protest trials for maternal contingencies (CRF) following infant protests during departures and contingencies on other behaviors (DRO) following separation protests, in the same session, with subsequent reversal conditions (Group 1, N= 9).

The results of these two experiments supported the assumption that infant protests cued by maternal departures, and during brief separations, that have served

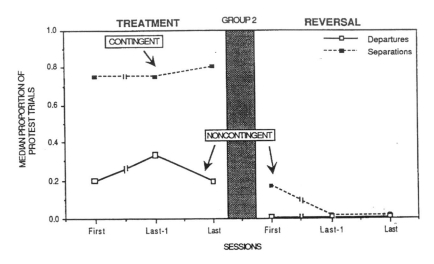

Figure 3b. Under the BA design, the chart shows median proportions of protest trials under maternal contingencies (CRF) following infant protests during separations and contingencies on other behaviors (DRO) following departure protests, in the same session, with subsequent reversal conditions (Group 2, N = 9).

as an "attachment" or "separation anxiety" index in the infancy literature, can be conditioned in the usual departure/separation settings in which they appear, trained under the differential reinforcement contingencies provided by maternal behaviors. These results support the possibility that the protest pattern is very likely to be trained inadvertently in the life settings in which it occurs by the maternal reactions that operate under the conception of positive, responsive, "loving" mothering.

Our two experiments support the conclusion that the contingent maternal responding (under experimenter control) conditioned cued infant operant protests in the laboratory (thus demonstrating internal validity), and it is very likely that conditions like those of our two experiments operate similarly in other life settings for mother-infant dyads (thus providing external validity). By ignoring environmental antecedents, and in particular the patterns of maternal behaviors routinely contingent on separation-cued infant protests that very-likely had been occurring prior to and during standardized assessments in laboratory settings, cited studies such as those by Ainsworth and associates, Schaffer and Emerson, Weinraub and Lewis, and Kagan and associates were led conceptually to consider infant separation protests to be symptoms or indices of putative underlying "causes". Those causes – which we believe to be fictional- are "attachment" for Bowlby and for Schaffer and Emerson, "security or insecurity of attachment" in the case of Ainsworth, "separation distress" for Weinraub and Lewis, and "separation anxiety" for Kagan and his associates. We believe that the proximal explanation based on a functional analysis that focuses on the reinforcement contingencies for infant protests is more parsimonious than the concepts those researchers have proposed.

In the same way that emotional behavior denoting "attachment" were approached, the emotional conceptions of "fear of the dark," "fear of strangers," and "jealousy" were examined experimentally. These phenomena are also conventionally conceived of as resulting from unlearned panhuman emotions. They can all involve protests, and were thus also addressed in human-infant subjects in terms of operant learning under positive reinforcement in three experiments.

Children's "Fear of the Dark" and "Fear of Strangers"

We employed methods similar to those reported earlier to study three additional developmental themes that have been approached in the literature by nonexperimental means. Such approaches completely ignore the contributions to the child behavior problem class of learning processes such as result from caregiver behaviors provided contingent on infant protests. We refer to protests that have been taken to be indicators of the *"fear of the dark"* and the *"fear of strangers"* in infants and children. Such protests have been reported to be emitted by infants when there is change from illumination to darkness. Similarly, protests or locomotor-avoidance responses at the approach of a "stranger" have been taken to denote the fear of strangers. Under the nominal theories employed in the literature, these fearful protests and avoidance behaviors have been conceived of as universal and unlearned (Izard, 1992). Yet, these operants may not always be valid indicators of fear, as they are under positive reinforcer control. The protest and approach and avoidance responses toward strangers often may result from operant conditioning to the onset of darkness or the approach of a stranger (as discriminative stimuli) by contingent attention, functioning as positive reinforcement, provided by well-intentioned, concerned parents.

Fear of the dark. In this experiment (Sanchez, Gewirtz, & Peláez-Nogueras, 1998) on the "fear of the dark", 10 normal 6- to 8-mo.-old infants sat strapped in a highchair for 25 min per day, from 10 to 20 weekdays, with their mothers seated immediately behind them (operating under instructional control), in a single-subject alternating-treatments and reversal design in the presence and in the absence of light in a room. For five infants, the effects of contingent maternal attention (CRF) on protest behaviors, and on nonprotest behaviors through differential reinforcement (DRO), were compared across four experimental phases: (a) baseline, (b) CRF for protests in light and DRO in darkness, (c) CRF for protests in darkness and DRO in light, and (d) Reversal or elimination of protest both in darkness and light contexts. The order of contexts and treatments were counterbalanced for the other 5 infants. Facial expressions of the infants confronting darkness were recorded by infrared camera and their vocal behavior (other than protests) scored.

When protest frequencies were compared in subjects within concurrent, and separately within sequential, CRF and DRO treatments, every one of the 10 infants showed increasing and dramatically greater protest frequencies in the CRF than in the DRO treatment, separately in the light and in the dark conditions (see Figures 4a and 4b). In addition, no difference in facial expressions for any one of the 10 infants was found between the light and the dark condition. Thus, it was demonstrated that what some take to be fear-denoting protests are as readily conditioned in illumination as in darkness by contingent maternal attention.

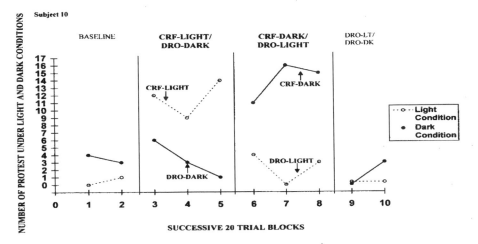

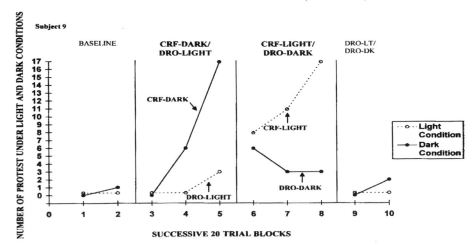

Figures 4a and 4b. Number of protests per trial block involving concurrent and sequential contrasts between CRF and DRO contingency conditions, in illuminated and dark contexts, for two representative infants in two treatment orders.

Fear of strangers. Empirical studies have shown that not all children show a fear-of-strangers response, nor do all researchers conceive that the 'fear of strangers' is related to age or developmental level. The presumed ubiquitous 'fear of strangers' was explored from a conditioning perspective (Lum Lock, Gewirtz, Peláez-Nogueras, & Markham, 1997). Six 8- to 10-mo-old infants participated in a four-phase single-subject design: (A_1) baseline; (B_1) parent attention contingent on infant approaches to female strangers; (A_2) parent attention contingent on the infant avoidance of/ withdrawal from the strangers; and (B_2) parent attention contingent on infant approaches to the strangers. The baseline assessed the infant's initial approach rate to the female stranger in the absence of maternal-provided cues or contingencies. Under the two conditioning phases (B_1, B_2), infant locomotor approach responses to the stranger were shaped and maintained by the mother's contingent attention (on a CRF schedule); for the A_2 reversal phase, attention was provided (on a DRI schedule) contingent on the infant's avoidance of the stranger (this was a DRI, differential reinforcement of incompatible behavior, schedule, because reinforcement was contingent on behavior incompatible with approach).

Each trial began with the infant on the right side of a playpen, beyond a red line that divided the playpen in two, with mother seated two feet away adjacent to the side where she could (under experimenter instructional control) shape and control by providing discriminative and contingent (reinforcing) stimuli for her infant's approach and avoidance behavior to the approaches of a series of female "strangers." From a distance of 3 m, a stranger female approached the infant on repeated trials, on each occasion initiating contact by smiling and talking. When the infant locomoted in the stranger's direction across the red dividing line, an approach was scored. When the infant locomoted away from the stranger, across the red dividing line, or remained beyond the red line away from the stranger, an avoidance response was scored. In every session, three to six different strangers participated with each infant, rotating after five trials.

In Figure 5, the homogeneous behavior patterns of every one of four infant subjects, rising from baseline level in the first contingency phase, declining in the reversal phase, and again increasing in the final contingency phase, illustrates how each infant learned to approach or avoid the female stranger depending on the discriminative and reinforcing stimuli provided by the mother. For two infants, the behavior pattern was identical, except for an unsatisfactory rising or declining baseline, accepted in error by the experimenter. Thus, as indicated by the work on infant "fear of the dark," the results of this experiment suggest that behaviors denoting the "fear of strangers" in life settings may be influenced via an operant-conditioning process by maternal behavior.

Jealousy. Various infant behaviors that have previously been taken to denote infant "jealously/rivalry" can, through operant learning, come readily under the control of discriminative cues and contingencies provided by the behavior of the mother. Jealousy in siblings and from an infant to a sibling can occasion that infant's jealous protests, with the mother's attentive reorienting (under the experimenter's

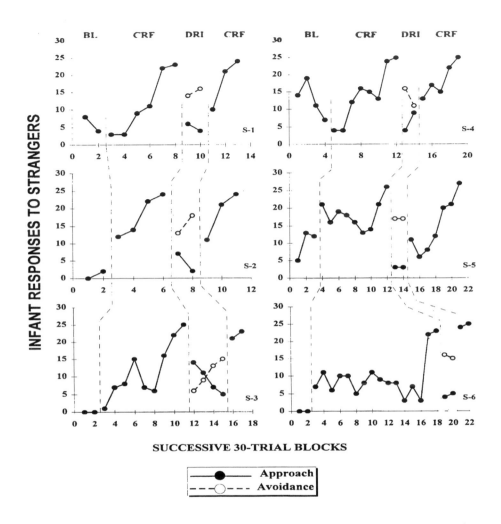

Figure 5. Under the control of maternal contingencies, the chart shows infant approach and avoidance responses to encounters with female strangers (N = 6). BL-No Parent Attention, CRF-Attention Contingent on Approach, DRI-Attention Contingent on Avoidance

instructional control) to the protesting child serving to reinforce those jealous protests. An experiment (Roth, Gewirtz, & Markham, in press) was conducted to investigate the role of maternal attention in occasioning and maintaining jealous behavior as an operant. Four 11- to 14-month-old–twin pairs participated concurrently in a "dual" single-subject design. One infant from each pair completed a CRF-DRO-DRO (BAA) design with shaping while the other twin completed a yoked DRO-CRF-DRO (ABA) design, also with shaping. During the DRO phases, maternal attention was made contingent upon behavior other than jealous protests

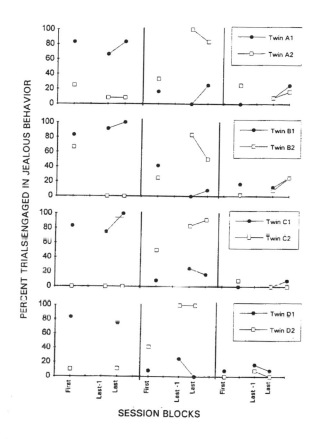

Figure 6. Percentage of trials on which jealous protests were emitted by four twin infant pairs: Twins 1 are under a CRF/DRO/DRO design and Twins 2, concurrently, are under a DRO/CRF/DRO design.

and, during the CRF phases, maternal attention was contingent on behavior denoting jealousy (see Figure 6).

Just as in our previous experiments on departure and separation protests, and on "fear of the dark" and "fear of strangers", it was found that the infants' jealous protests decreased during DRO phases and increased during CRF phases of maternal responding. Results showed that maternal attention to one twin infant can function as a discriminative stimulus for jealous protests of the second twin infant, and that the restoration of maternal attention to protests of the second twin can function as a positive reinforcer to shape and increase those jealous protests. These results represent a behavioral demonstration of how environmental events can operate to establish and maintain protests that denote jealous behavior in siblings.

The studies summarized thus far are all based on demonstrations involving simple reversal designs (sometimes joined with alternating treatments designs) initially with continuous reinforcement of operant classes. In the first two separation-protest experiments, the plan was to use relatively-large numbers of subjects in group designs. This was because at the time we were not confident that mothers would be willing and able to bring their infants to the lab repeatedly, for 10 or more visits. We discovered subsequently that many mothers could come often enough, making single-subject designs feasible.

The Reinforcing Effects of Touch on Behavior of Infants of Depressed Mothers

In developmental psychology, research has focused, for the most part, on investigating the effects of maternal facial, orienting, and vocal stimuli on infant social development and learning. However, the systematic investigation of the role of the caregiver's tactile stimulation as an active social component and potential reinforcer for infant behavior has been neglected. Very few studies have been designed to explore the socio-communicative functions of maternal touch during face-to-face interactions, and there has been no attempt to separate the effects of various components or modalities of social stimuli during interactions to determine their relative discriminative and reinforcing values. The paucity of studies leaves a gap in our understanding of early social learning.

The effects of maternal depression. Having a "depressed" mother increases by three times a child's risk of developing the abnormalities characteristic of depressed mothers (Weissman, Prusoff, Gamon, Merikangas, Leckman, & Kidd, 1984). Researchers have identified depressed mothers as unresponsive, insensitive to the infant's behavior cues, ineffective, noncontingent, emotionally flat, negative, disengaged, intrusive, avoidant of confrontation, and generally, less competent and uninvolved in interactions with their infants (Cohn & Tronick, 1983; Cohn, Matias, Tronick, Connell, & Lyons–Ruth, 1986; Field, 1984; 1992; Peláez-Nogueras, Field, Cigales, Gonzalez, & Clasky, 1994; Peláez-Nogueras, Field, Hossain, & Pickens, 1996).

Experiencing early interaction disturbances places infants of depressed mothers at risk for later affective and socioemotional disorders. Infants of depressed mothers (the "depressed infants") appear to develop a "depressed mood style," as early as at 3 months. These infants typically exhibit less attentiveness, fewer smiles, more frequent fussiness, more frequent gazing away, and lower activity levels when interacting with their depressed mothers compared to infants of nondepressed mothers (Cohn, Campbell, Matias, & Hopkins, 1990; Gelfand & Teti, 1990; Goodman, 1992). At one year, infants show growth and developmental delays if their mothers remain depressed. Thus, depressed mothers and their infants appear to *share* their behavior "states," spending more time in negative attentive and affective behavior states than nondepressed mothers-infant dyads (Field, Healy, Goldstein, & Guthertz, 1989).

Touch as intervention. The series of studies we have been conducting was designed to investigate the effects of various laboratory manipulations of maternal behavior on infant learning of social and attentive responses during interaction. These studies were directed to examining how caregiver *touch* stimuli provided contingent on infant behavior can function to condition those behaviors denoting "mood states". We wanted to determine also if there would be an increased effectiveness of touch when part of a compound stimulus (auditory and visual) presentation as a reinforcer for infant behaviors denoting positive and negative moods (Peláez-Nogueras, Field, Cigales, Gewirtz, Gonzalez, Clasky, & Sanchez, 1997; Peláez-Nogueras, Gewirtz, Field, Cigales, Malphurs, Clasky, & Sanchez, 1996).

A *synchronized-reinforcement* procedure was developed in which the onset and offset of adult stimulation is controlled by the onset and offset of the infant eye-contact response with the caregiver/experimenter. In addition to determining the efficacy of touch stimulation as a reinforcing event, this procedure permitted evaluation of whether or not infants would show a preference for social compound stimuli that included touch over compound stimuli that did not include touch, in a face-to-face situation with an adult experimenter. Also, the synchronized-reinforcement procedure permitted the comparison of the effects of different types of touch stimulation, for example stroking vs. tickling on infant behavior (Peláez-Nogueras et al., 1997). Infants' responses indicated a preference for stroking over tickling.

Subjects were 10 normal full-term infants, 6 males and 4 females, who ranged in age from 1.6 to 3.5 mos at the start of our first touch-conditioning study. In the high-risk clinic where the study was conducted, these infants were labeled "depressed infants," given that they were born of depressed adolescent mothers and their rate of positive emotional responses (smiling, cooing) was low. A mother was considered to be "depressed" based on cutoff scores on the Beck Depression Inventory (BDI) (Beck, Ward, Mendelson, Mach, & Erbaugh, 1961). The 21 BDI items are scored on a 4-point scale indicating absence/presence and severity of depressed feelings, behaviors and symptoms. The scale is a commonly-employed instruments in research on non-clinically depressed samples. The mothers of these infants had BDI scores of 13 or greater and were considered depressed.

At the beginning of the experiment, the infants were seated in an infant seat, located on a table top, with face 20 inches from the experimenter's. A single-subject alternating-treatments (ABA, BAB) design was implemented. Each daily session consisted of three periods. The Touch (A) and No-touch (B) treatments were alternated across periods.

During the *Touch treatment*, each time the infant began eye contact, the experimenter responded contingently by smiling, vocalizing and rubbing/massaging rhythmically both of the infant's legs and feet using the five fingers of both of her hands, for the duration of the infant's eye-contact responding. Deep but gentle pressure was used in slow circular motions at a rate of approximately one circular rub

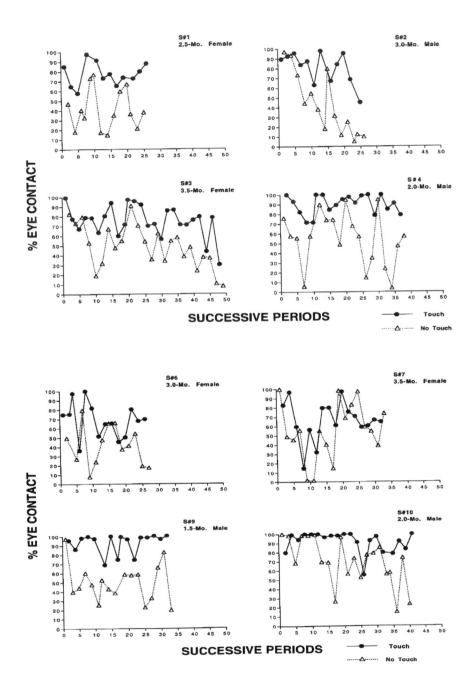

Figure 7a and 7b. Percentage of time each of 8 infants made eye contact across periods as a function of Touch vs. No–Touch treatment.

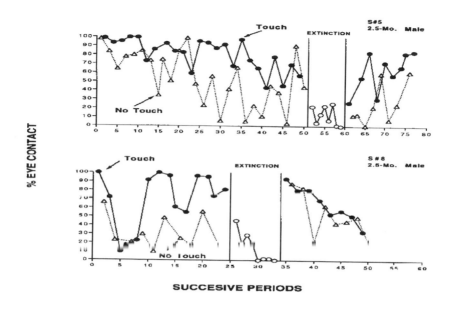

Figure 7c. Percentage of time two infants, who received an extinction phase, made eye contact across periods as a function of Touch vs. No–Touch treatment.

The *No–Touch treatment* was identical, except that no touch was provided. That is, each time the infant began eye contact with the experimenter, the latter responded contingently by smiling and cooing to the infant (but no touch was provided). Under both conditions, as soon as the infant looked away from the experimenter's eyes, the experimenter stopped smiling at, vocalizing to (and touching in the Touch condition) the infant. The experimenter continued facing and looking at the infant with a neutral face, until the infant again emitted an eye–contact response.

In both treatment conditions, during the 30–sec interval between periods the infant was turned away from the experimenter, and rocked and entertained with a toy by a second experimenter. The total duration of a session was 7 min. The total number of sessions for each subject ranged from 11 to 30 ($M = 14$), and the total number of treatment periods across sessions ranged from 26 to 75 ($M = 40$).

To test the reversibility of the eye–contact response, a subsample of two subjects received a reversal (extinction) phase. The comparison between the Touch and the No-Touch treatment showed that the Touch treatment was associated with a higher percentage (i.e., *longer* periods) both of infant eye contact and of responses denoting positive affect (smiles and vocalizations), and lower percentage of responses denoting negative affect (cries and protests).

The individual data show a higher percentage of eye contact (the target response) across successive conditioning periods for all subjects. The two infant subjects who received the reversal (extinction) probes showed reversibility of their eye–contact response (see Figure 7c). However, when the stimulation treatments were reintroduced in the last phase, eye–contact and positive affect increased only in one subject. In general, all infants spent more time making eye contact with the adult experimenter during the Touch treatment than in the No–touch treatment (see Figures 7a and 7b).

The results indicated that, under the synchronized conjugate-reinforcement schedule, a stimulus compound comprised of touch together with auditory and visual stimuli was a more effective reinforcer for infant eye-contact responding than a compound that did not include touch. The results supported our assumption that familiar caregivers who are nondepressed can provide effective contingencies as part of preventive intervention programs to occasion and maintain more positive and fewer negative behaviors in the infants than do depressed mothers typically.

In the case of infants of depressed mothers, it is suggested that the operant contingencies provided, not by mothers but by others, can produce positive social behavior (eye-contact) and mood enhancing responses (infant smiles and vocalizations) that reverse depression-like behaviors in the infants. In general, it appears caregiver's touch has strong influences on human behavior and may be used successfully in intervention programs with at-risk populations including the depressed and the aged.

Conclusion

The developmental themes enumerated in this chapter were addressed experimentally in terms of operant-learning conceptions, with parent behavior providing antecedent discriminative, and consequent reinforcing, stimulus events for units of infant behavior. The outcomes under scrutiny were found to result from dramatically-different processes than those proposed in the developmental and clinical literatures. Infant's problem or adaptive behaviors were found to be comprised of discriminated operants apparently under the close control of discriminative stimuli and consequences provided via the responding of well-intentioned loving parents (caregivers), acting possibly under the influence of popular theories in the field. While the results we have described do not rule out definitively the explanations of the denotative behaviors found in the literatures surveyed, they make it likely that some, if not much or all, of the variance in the behaviors at issue could be accounted for by relations with the proximal antecedent and consequent environmental factors that we have been studying.

The experiments on infant protests we have reported illustrate potential pathways to development in the child of problem-behavior patterns (that is, fussing, whimpering, instrumental crying, and rage) that can result from these early mother-infant chains of interaction that interfere with behaviors denoting social competence. We believe that results like those reported can provide bases for designing preventive interventions that parents and other caregivers might use to preclude, eliminate or at least minimize maladaptive behaviors while potentially increasing more developmentally-appropriate behavioral patterns. The processes highlighted by application of the operant-learning paradigm are *un*expected under the routine conceptions of process that have been applied in the literature, yet reflect a level of analysis that, from moment to moment, reflects the parental/environmental influence on developmentally-important infant behaviors. Indeed, in the behavior arenas surveyed the well-intentioned, loving, caregiver creates problem-behavior patterns that, subsequently, require much effort to set right.

References

Ainsworth, M. S., Blehar, M. C., Waters, E., & Wall, S. (1978). *Patterns of attachment.* Hillsdale, NJ: Erlbaum.

Barrett, K. C., & Campos, J. J. (1987). Perspectives on emotional development II: A functionalist approach to emotional development. In J. D. Osofsky (Ed.), *Handbook of infant development* (3rd edition), (pp. 55-578). New York: John Wiley & Sons.

Beck, A. T., Ward, C. H., Mendelson, M., Mach, J. E., & Erbaugh, J. (1961). An inventory for measuring depression. *Archives of General Psychiatry, 4,* 561–571.

Bowlby, J. (1960). Separation anxiety. *International Journal of Psychoanalysis, 41,* 89-113.

Campos, J. J., & Barrett, K. C. (1984). Toward a new understanding of emotions and their development. In C. E. Izard, J. Kagan, & R. B. Zajonc (Eds.), *Emotions, cognition, and behavior* (pp. 17-37). New York: Cambridge University Press.

Cohn, J. F., Matias, R., Tronick, E. Z., Connell, D., & Lyons–Ruth, K. (1986). Face-to–face interactions of depressed mothers and their infants. In E. Z. Tronick & T. Field (Eds.) *Maternal Depression and Infant Disturbance*, New Directions for Child Development, no. *34*. San Francisco: Jossey–Bass.

Cohn, J. F., Campbell, S. B., Matias, R., & Hopkins, J. (1990). Face–to–face interactions of postpartum and nondepressed mother–infant pairs at two months. *Developmental Psychology, 26,* 185–193.

Cohn, J. F., & Tronick, E. Z. (1983). Three–month–old infants' reaction to simulated maternal depression. *Child Development, 54,* 185–193.

Field, T. (1984). Early interactions between infants and their postpartum depressed mothers. *Infant Behavior and Development, 7,* 527–532.

Field, T. (1992). Infants of depressed mothers. *Developmental and Psychopathology, 4,* 49–66.

Field, T., Healy, B., Goldstein, S., & Guthertz, M. (1990). Behavior state matching in mother–infant interactions of nondepressed versus depressed mother–infant dyads. *Developmental Psychology, 26,* 7–14.

Gelfand, D. M., & Teti, D. M. (1990). The effects of maternal depression on children. *Clinical Psychology Review, 10,* 329-353.

Gewirtz, J. L., & Peláez-Nogueras, M. (1991). The attachment metaphor and the conditioning of infant separation protests. In J.L. Gewirtz & W. M. Kurtines (Eds.), *Intersections with attachment* (pp. 123-144). Hillsdale, NJ: Erlbaum.

Gewirtz, J. L., & Peláez-Nogueras, M. (1992). Infants' separation difficulties and distress due to misplaced maternal contingencies. In T. Field, P. McCabe, & N. Schneiderman (Eds.), *Stress and coping in infancy and childhood* (pp. 19-46). Hillsdale, NJ: Erlbaum.

Gewirtz, J. L., & Peláez-Nogueras, M. (1996). In the context of gross environmental and organismic changes, learning provides the main basis for behavioral development. In S. Bijou & E. Ribes (Eds.), *New directions in behavioral development*, (pp. 15-34). Reno NV: Context Press.

Goodman, S. (1992). Understanding the effects of depressed mothers on their children. In E. F. Walker, B. Cornblatt, R. Dworkin (Eds.). *Progress in experimental personality and psychopathology research* (Vol 15, pp. 47-109). New York: Springer.

Izard, C. E. (1992). Basic emotions: Relations among emotions, and emotion-cognition relations. *Psychological Review, 99*, 561-565.

Kagan, J., Kearsley, R.B., & Zelazo, P.R. (1978). *Infancy: Its place in human development.* Cambridge, MA: Harvard University Press.

Lazarus, R. S. (1991). *Emotion and adaptation.* New York: Oxford University Press.

Lum Lock, K., Gewirtz, J. L., Peláez-Nogueras, M. & Markham, M. (1997, May). Infants' "fear of strangers" may be a learned phenomenon. In P. Miller (Chair), *Environmental influences on fearful behavior in young children,* symposium conducted at the annual meeting of the Association for Behavior Analysis, Chicago, IL.

Peláez-Nogueras, M., & Field, T., Cigales, M., Gonzalez, A., Clasky, S. (1994). Infants of depressed mothers show less "depressed " behavior with their nursery teachers. *Infant Mental Health Journal, 15*, 358-367.

Peláez-Nogueras, M., Field, T., Cigales, M., Gewirtz, J. Gonzalez, A., Clasky, S., & Sanchez, A. (1997). The effects of systematic stroking versus tickling and poking on infant attention and affect. *Journal of Applied Developmental Psychology, 18*, 169-177.

Peláez-Nogueras, M., Field, T., Hossain, Z., & Pickens, J. (1996). Depressed mothers' touching increases infant positive affect and attention in still-face interactions. *Child Development, 67*, 1780-1792.

Peláez-Nogueras, M. & Gewirtz, J. L. (1990, May). Discrimination training of infant protests. Paper presented at the Annual Convention of The Association for Behavior Analysis: International (ABA), Nashville, TN.

Peláez-Nogueras, M. & Gewirtz, J. (1997). The context of stimulus control in behavior analysis. In D. M. Baer & E. M. Pinkston (Eds.), *Environment and behavior*, (pp. 30-42). Boulder CO: Westview Press.

Peláez-Nogueras, M, Gewirtz, J. L., Field, T., Cigales, M., Malphurs, J., Clasky, S., & Sanchez, A. (1996). Infants' preference for touch stimulation in face-to-face interactions. *Journal of Applied Developmental Psychology, 17*, 199-213.

Sanchez, A., Gewirtz, J. L., & Peláez-Nogueras, M. (1988, May). Toward a discrimination between children's respondent and operant responses denoting fear. In

S. Petrovich, Chair, *Development of operant responses in infants.* Symposium conducted at the annual meeting of the Association for Behavior Analysis, Orlando, FL.

Schaffer, H. R., & Emerson, P. E. (1964). The development of social attachments in infancy. *Monographs of the Society for Research in Child Development, 29* (3, Serial No. 94).

Roth, W. E., Gewirtz, J. L., & Markham, M. R. (in press). Maternal attention evokes and reinforces jealousy behavior in twin infants. *The Psychological Record.*

Weinraub, M., & Lewis, M. (1977). The determinants of children's responses to separation. *Monographs of the Society for Research in Child Development, 42,* (4, Serial No. 172).

Weissman, M. M., Prusoff, B. A., Gammon, G. D., Merikangas, K. R., Leckman, J. F., & Kidd, K. K. (1984). Psychopathy in children (ages 6-18) of depressed and normal parents. *Journal of the American Academy of Child Psychiatry, 23,* 78-84.

Chapter 15

Consumer Situation: An Operant Interpretation[1]

Gordon R. Foxall
Cardiff Business School, University of Wales

The Meaning of Behavior

Radical behaviorist interpretation is a matter of locating behavior, that is, of reconstructing the contingencies that produced it, without the direct aid of experimental method. This might be misunderstood by some as imposing external order on observed actions of sentient beings and, indeed, operant accounts of contingency-shaped behavior are often criticized for omitting the actor's "subjective" experience of situations. Behaviorists have tackled the question of individual reaction by accounting for a person's behavior within the situation; the account includes consideration of the individual's verbal behavior, the rule-governance of his or her earlier activities, and the continuity of behavior over time. This is achieved by reference to the individual's environmental history (Skinner, 1974), for the meaning of an operant response is to be found in what has preceded it. According to Skinner, the meaning of an act is not found in the current setting: neither in the discriminative stimuli that compose the setting, nor in the responses that take place there, nor in their outcomes. Rather, it is located solely in the history of exposure to similar contingencies which have brought behavior under the control of the current situation (p. 91).

Meaning is thus defined in terms of the function of a response, not, as the structuralists would have it, in its topography. Topographies of behavior may resemble one another closely, but the meanings of the behaviors, as found in past contingencies, may differ markedly. Two customers may buy neckties from the same assistant, but the meaning of doing so can be quite different if the first tie is bought as a present (and therefore controlled by a history of gift giving) while the second is bought for personal use (and controlled by a history of wearing ties to the office). The meanings do not depend on the reinforcer (the type of tie) but on these histories of buying, giving, wearing, and their outcomes.

The Behavioral Perspective Model

The Behavioral Perspective Model (BPM) is a neo-Skinnerian model of situational influence on consumer behavior in which the responses of consumers are held to be determined by the contingencies of reinforcement under which they are emitted (Foxall, 1990). Consumers' approach and avoidance/escape behaviors, as well as emotional responses (or, at least, the verbal behavior by which they are described), are posited to be functions of situational influence. The scope of the consumer behavior setting is defined by the behaviorally-contingent reinforcement signaled by the setting elements as they are mobilized by the consumer's learning history. The meaning of the behavior which is emitted in those circumstances is uniquely a product of the interaction between the discriminative stimuli that comprise the behavior setting and the individual's history of reinforcement and punishment in similar settings (Foxall, 1996). Consumer behavior can, therefore, be contextualized in a manner absent from cognitive consumer research in which the mainsprings of overt behavior are sought in intrapersonal information processing. In the BPM, the consumer's behavior is located at the intersection of his or her learning history and the current behavior setting. These coordinates define the *consumer situation*, a device which explains consumer behavior by locating it in space and time (Foxall, 1996).

The BPM proposes that consumer behavior is situated at the intersection of the behavior setting in which it occurs (the spatial perspective) and the learning history of the consumer (the temporal perspective) (Foxall, 1990). The resulting construct of the *consumer situation* has been used to interpret observed patterns of consumer behavior including purchase and consumption, saving and domestic asset management, the adoption and diffusion of innovations and "green" consumption (Foxall, 1994; 1996). The interpretation proceeds essentially in terms of the three-term contingency, albeit critically appraised and re-presented in line with the provisions outlined above. Each of the elements of this summation facilitates the interpretation of consumer behavior as a situationally-influenced activity. The resulting model, which complements the social cognitive interpretations of consumption which currently dominate consumer research (Foxall, 1997a; Kardes, 1994), introduces to consumer research a three-stage operant interpretation of consumer choice.

The following discussion develops the model through three stages of interpretive detail which successively elaborate the basic model and locate consumer response with increasing specificity. The first is the *operant classification* of consumer behavior which explores the role of different sources of reinforcement in establishing the equifinality class to which an operant consumption response belongs. The second is the allocation of a consumer response to a particular *contingency category*; this means extending the idea that consumer behavior is located at the intersection of a learning history and a behavior setting by showing (a) how these combine to determine the *scope* of the setting, and (b) how consumer behavior setting scope and operant classification are used to locate consumer choice in terms of the overall pattern of environmental contingencies maintaining it. The third, the exploration of the *consumer situation*, further elaborates this intersection and shows how the process of consumer decision making is a function of the spatial/regulatory and historical components of consumer behavior setting scope.

Operant Classification

The Consequences of Behavior

Lee (1988, pp. 135-7) proposes as the first question of operant interpretation, "What is this person doing?". This is an inquiry into the consequences being produced. Equivalent forms of this question are: "What is this act?" and "What is the meaning of this act?". The traditional answer, as we have seen, would be couched exclusively in terms of the individual's learning history.[2] Unfortunately, unlike the learning history of the rat or pigeon whose entire lifetime has been altruistically given over to advancing the experimental analysis of behavior, that of the middle-aged consumer in Harrods is not empirically available. We might be able to surmise a certain amount, and the consumer might be able to tell us an uncertain amount, but we shall be left wondering whether we have elucidated the current act in terms of a reconstructed environmental history with any validity.

Yet we cannot simply observe the current behavior and its outcomes in order to uncover its meaning. We have already seen that topographically similar responses may produce disparate consequences; so may topographically dissimilar responses belong to the same functional class. Operant interpretation requires that, in addition to whatever evidence is obtainable for reconstructing the individual's learning history, elements of the current behavior setting and the kinds of reinforcement or punishment that follow them be taken into consideration. The BPM indicates the form which an answer to Lee's question would take in the context of consumer behavior. Isolating the operant classes relevant to consumer behavior is not just a case of saying which responses produced "similar ends". It can be more sophisticated than that, identifying the sources of reinforcement appropriate to a set of responses which binds them together as an operant.

The Dual Consequences of Consumer Behavior

Economists have usually ignored or been unable to deal professionally with the social psychological causation of consumer behavior (Earl, 1990; Mason, 1981). The BPM is founded upon two variables which capture the social psychological influences on consumer behavior. Each of these variables is based on a conception of social psychological influence relative to a significant counter-influence. First, the concept of the consumer's behavior setting scope contrasts social with individual influences on responding. Consumer behavior setting scope indicates how far persons other than the consumer control the settings in which consumption occurs. This continuum thus provides a measure of personal versus social locus of control. Secondly, the ratio of instrumental to informational reinforcement allows social psychological influences (informational reinforcers) to be contrasted with economic influences (utilitarian reinforcement). The ratio of utilitarian to informational reinforcement indicates how far the consequences of a consumer's actions are supplied by others (in the form of social approval or socially-learned feelings of self-esteem) rather than by the requirements of the consumer's biological and innate individual constitution.

Bifurcation of Reinforcement

The consumer behavior setting – a store, a library, an opera house, or a crack dealership – consists of four kinds of element or discriminative stimuli: physical, social, temporal and regulatory. These antecedent stimuli signal the possibility of three kinds of consequence (Figure 1). The first is utilitarian reinforcement which we define as consisting in the functional properties (economic and technical) of the

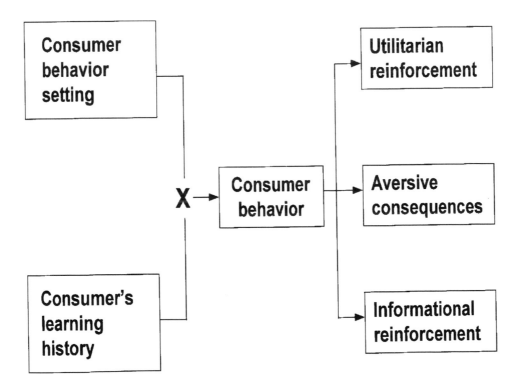

Figure 1. Antecedent stimuli signaling three possible conseqences

reinforcer, often reported verbally in terms of the satisfaction which consuming them brings.

Utilitarian reinforcement consists in the practical outcomes of purchase and consumption – the functional benefit, value-in-use, economic/pragmatic/material satisfactions received by consumers as a result of acquiring, owning and/or using an economic product or service. It is purely instrumental, consisting in itself and for itself; it is concrete and likely to be constant across social systems. Incentives are usually of this kind. Hence, utilitarian reinforcement arises from the characteristics of the product or service obtained in purchase or used in consumption; this corresponds to the use of utility in economics to refer to "the direct satisfaction that goods and services yield to their possessors" (Gould & Kolb, 1964). Utility theory in economics derives essentially from the psychology of hedonism (Menger, 1956; Griffin & Parfitt, 1987; Viner, 1925). Hence, while utilitarian reinforcement is akin to value-in-use, it derives not only from the functional performance of a product or service but from the feelings associated with owning and consuming it. In addition to the functions performed by a product or service, utilitarian consequences of consumption include the positive affect generated in the process. Utilitarian reinforcement refers, therefore, to all of the benefits derived directly from possession and application of a product or service: it is reinforcement mediated by the product or service.

Informational reinforcement, by contrast, is symbolic, usually mediated by the responsive actions of others, and closely akin to exchange value. It consists not in information per se but in feedback on an individual's performance. Informational reinforcement attests to the level of correctness or appropriateness of a person's performance as a consumer. Whereas utilitarian reinforcement stems from economic and functional payoffs of buying and using goods, informational reinforcement results from the level of social status, prestige and acceptance achieved by a consumer by his or her efforts. It is usually publicly determined, judged by others according to their rules, and thus of primarily social significance. In as much as it is mediated by other people, it is verbal (Skinner, 1957), consisting of speech, gestures and in private thoughts (Skinner, 1974). From the viewpoint of the consumer, informational reinforcement rests on a comparative judgement of how well he or she is using time and energy relative to other uses to which they would be put: "How well am I exchanging my time and effort for the acquisition of groceries?" If the consumer is being relatively inefficient, he or she may either speed up the shopping trip or postpone purchasing further items. If efficient, they can use the time and energy left over to accomplish something else. From the social viewpoint, the public consumption of a prestigious product or service is exchanged for the goodwill, praise, positive responses and so on of others, i.e., for esteem and social status. Public or private, informational reinforcement is symbolic, representative, referential, cultural; the behaviors it reinforces are likely to differ sharply from social system to social system.[2]

In short, *utilitarian* reinforcement refers to the acceptance of positive benefits of purchasing, owning or consuming economic products and services (goods); these benefits are functional, conferring material satisfactions, the utility of orthodox microeconomic theory. Utilitarian reinforcers are frequently referred to as incentives both in general discourse and in applied behavior analysis. *Informational* reinforcement is performance feedback, an indication of how well the consumer is doing. It may confer social status and/or self-satisfaction, or it may simply constitute a reference point denoting progress to date. Informational reinforcement is associated with verbal behavior because the meaning of the behavior is always mediated by a person, usually someone other than the actor but perhaps by him/herself. There is empirical evidence that utilitarian and informational reinforcement have separate influences on behavior in both human operant experiments conducted under laboratory conditions (Wearden, 1988), in token economy studies (Foxall, 1995), and in the field experiments of applied behavior analysis directed towards the reduction of environmentally-deleterious consumption (Foxall, 1996). The distinction between utilitarian and informational sources of reinforcement is empirically supported. This account is necessarily brief. Further conceptual and empirical justification is offered in Foxall (1990, 1996, 1998).

Contingency- and Rule-Derived Reinforcement

The usual functional distinction made of reinforcers is between primary and secondary. *Primary reinforcers* such as sexual satisfaction, water and food are effective from birth and for almost all species. Their effectiveness is not dependent upon their relationship with other reinforcers; the apparent biological determination of these inherent reinforcers has led to their being known as *natural*. *Secondary reinforcers* acquire their capacity to influence the rate of behavior in the course of the individual's experience; their power to do so depends upon their being repeatedly paired with primary reinforcers. An example is money, with which many primary reinforcers can be obtained. Some authors also speak of *social reinforcers*, including praise, affection and attention, which are a combination of primary and secondary reinforcers.

A more useful functional distinction in the present context is between *contingency-derived reinforcers* and *rule-derived reinforcers*. Contingency-derived reinforcers are both primary and secondary. Their effect is apparent in the contingency-shaping of behavior; it derives from the impact which behavior has directly upon its environment. These reinforcers are generally associated with pleasurable effects for the individual who is in a state of reinforcer deprivation (though behavior analysts usually avoid the notion that something is reinforcing because it is pleasant). But evolution has required that most acts whose rate is influenced by primary reinforcers have pleasant outcomes: eating sugar and avoiding pain, for instance. Secondary reinforcers such as foods, furniture, housing, and music usually also have a utilitarian effect. Contingency-derived reinforcers are, therefore, *utilitarian* reinforcers.

Rule-derived reinforcers have their effect only by virtue of being specified in rules – e.g., money is a measure of individual prestige as well as a medium of exchange, the meanings of other tokens such as university degrees. None of these derives its reinforcing power from "nature"; none is a reinforcer from the organism's birth. They are only useful/reinforcing in so far as they are symbols, i.e., as they point to something else – a level of performance, success, access to a job, etc. Rule-derived reinforcers are social and verbal; their effect is on behavior that is mediated by others (where "the other" may be the individual him/herself). Such instructed behavior, the verbal behavior of the listener, is reinforced by the individual's level of achievement of socially- (or personally-) prescribed goals; the behavior consists of pliance or tracking. In the case of pliance, the informational reinforcement derives from the praise, recognition, acknowledgment extended by the mediating individual(s) to the rule-follower. (Informational punishment may be the result of noncompliance or counter-compliance). In the case of tracking, the informational reinforcement derives from consonance between the physical environment as it is experienced and as it was described by the mediating individual (who may the behaver). (Informational punishment would result from a lack of such consonance.) These reinforcers are always secondary. They derive power from the social status and/or self-esteem conferred as a result of the behaviors they maintain. Rule-derived reinforcers are, therefore, *informational* reinforcers.

It may be worth emphasizing here that one-to-one mapping of primary/ secondary reinforcement on to utilitarian/ informational reinforcement is not implied by this reasoning. Primary reinforcement emphasizes utilitarian but may, in humans at least, have an informational component. Human awareness and competitiveness can, for instance, make success in survival a matter of status. Secondary reinforcement involves both utilitarian and informational reinforcers: by demonstration, consumer operants comprise elements of each. Social/verbal reinforcement emphasizes informational but entails the emergent utilitarian consequences included in social status and self-esteem.

Hence, the most that we can deduce with respect to the distinction between contingency-shaped and rule-governed behavior is this: the former is shaped and maintained *predominantly* by utilitarian reinforcement; the latter, *predominantly*, by informational reinforcement. The impression should not be given that we are speaking here of utilitarian and informational reinforcers as inalienably distinct entities as though there were some things or events that always and invariably reinforce via utility while others always and invariably reinforcer informationally. We are speaking of the functions of reinforcers. Function is always determined by the situation. Most things or events which are consequences of behavior have both utilitarian and informational functions: jewelry is mainly informational but also performs a utilitarian function; air conditioners are principally utilitarian but may add to one's social status (especially in a West European country where they are relatively scarce as compared with the US).

Primary and secondary reinforces are often differentiated on the basis of the speed with which they cease to reinforce. Primary reinforcers may be permanent and universal in their effectiveness; but there is no logical reason why secondary reinforcers should be either. Informational reinforcers are more contingent still upon social usages: fashions, forms of address, fad products, etc. quickly cease to reinforce and may punish when they no longer confer membership of a group. Powdered wigs may, alas, be gone forever.

Moreover, the effects of utilitarian and informational reinforcers may be mutually-strengthening. Since informational reinforcement is contrived and symbolic, its power stems ultimately from its association with contingency-derived or utilitarian reinforcement. It reinforces only in so far as it is linked with the reinforcers provided by the contingencies themselves, only in so far as the rules it reflects are consonant with those environmental contingencies. Hence the behaviors that confer informational reinforcement lead ultimately to pleasure just as surely as do the utilitarian reinforcers with which they are associated. Where those utilitarian reinforcers are secondary, they are effective only in so far as they are related to primary reinforcers. This is only to say that the ultimate reinforces are always primary – natural, non-contingent, biological. The BPM classification of consumer operants reflects this: all four operant classes of consumer behavior are reinforced by a combination of utilitarian and informational reinforcement rather than by one or other of these.

Since this is a functional classification of reinforcers, any particular item such as money might have both utilitarian and informational effects. Money has generally been regarded as a secondary reinforcer which derives its power from the primary reinforcers which can be acquired with it. But it can also play the role of an informational reinforcer: social status and self-esteem both stem from the performance feedback provided by a high salary or bank balance. Operationally, therefore, the interpretation of the meaning of money will depend upon the situation under investigation. Furthermore, operational measures of utilitarian and informational reinforcement (whether these are being used in a quantitative analysis or qualitative interpretation of consumer behavior) must reflect the pleasurable/utilitarian and social/personal functions of reinforcers respectively. That is, we should look for expressions (verbal and nonverbal) of pleasure or usefulness in order to identify utilitarian reinforcers; and for considerations of status/self-esteem in order to identify informational reinforcers.

Operant Classes of Consumer Behavior

We can now elaborate our understanding of the nature of an operant class as applied to consumer choice. An *operant class* of consumer behavior consists of a set of responses which, irrespective of their topographical (dis)similarities, correspond in terms of the pattern of reinforcement which maintains them, i.e. the configuration of relatively high/relatively low utilitarian reinforcement and relatively high/relatively low informational reinforcement associated with their continuance.

The actual procedure by which these four classes of behavior were initially derived is as follows (see Foxall, 1990). On the basis of the BPM reinforcer variables, four theoretical classes were known to be possible: high, high; high, low; low, high; and low, low. Broad kinds of consumer behavior were allocated to each of these on an the basis of the definitions of utilitarian and informational reinforcement and the responses maintained by "incentives" and "feedback" in the applied behavior analysis of environmental conservation. Only when this had been done satisfactorily were labels attached to the operant classes.

The first operant class suggests behaviors which supply high levels of incentive and high levels of status/esteem. Activities leading to personal accomplishment seem to belong here: cultural achievements which bring more than the pleasure of listening to a performance or reading a classic novel for the joy of the story.

Consumer behaviors maintained by a high level of utilitarian reinforcement but, relatively speaking, a low level of informational reinforcement suggest entertainments, pleasures, the amelioration of one's own suffering; in short the hedonistic activities involved in increasing one's pleasure and/or decreasing one's pain.

Table 1.

Operant Classes of Consumer Behavior	**High Utilitarian Reinforcement**	**Low Utilitarian Reinforcement**
High Informational Reinforcement	Accomplishment	Accumulation
Low Informational Reinforcement	Hedonism	Maintenance

Where informational reinforcement is high but utilitarian relatively low, the characteristic behaviors indicate saving and collecting. Incremental acquisition is not without its satisfactions from day to day or week to week and ultimately such behavior depends upon the utilitarian benefits of having the products in question. But the behaviors of gradually saving and collecting are maintained by feedback on performance: how much interest has my saving attracted? How many more points do I need for the bonus gift? How soon do these magazines transform themselves into an encyclopedia?

Finally, there are behaviors maintained by relatively low levels of both utilitarian and informational reinforcement. These ought to include activities which are routine or mandatory, the minimal consumer responses one needs to effect to stay alive or duties one must perform to continue to exist as a citizen.

These four operant classes of consumer behavior can be described, respectively, as Accomplishment, Hedonism, Accumulation and Maintenance (Table 1). (In order to avoid tedium, the qualifier "relative" is henceforth omitted, though utilitarian/informational reinforcements are always relative, as are open and closed consumer behavior settings).

Contingency Category Analysis

Consumer Behavior Setting Scope

The *consumer behavior setting* consists of the current discriminative stimuli that signal reinforcement and punishment contingent upon the emission of a purchase or consumption response. The discriminative stimuli that compose the setting may be physical (e.g. point-of-sale advertising, the product array, a store logo), social (principally the physical presence of co-shoppers, other diners in a restaurant, the waiter, the salesperson), temporal (the hours of opening of a store, the duration of a special offer, Christmas) or regulatory (self- and other-rules that specify contingencies). Rule-governed behavior is actually a social phenomenon but deserves separate treatment (Foxall, 1997a). In addition to the suggestion of several behavior analysts that operant principles are most clearly visible in the control of behavior in settings such as a factory, an army or a school, there is abundant evidence for this distinction in the operant literature on consumer behavior. Token economies are relatively closed settings in which consumer behavior conforms very strictly to the ordinal utility theory of microeconomics (which is operant), to the extent of being capable of delineation by demand curves. Consumer behavior investigated in field experiments of applied behavior analysis is clearly under environmental control but not to the same degree. The extent to which consumer behavior can be attributed unambiguously to control by environmental contingencies varies with the *scope* of the setting in which it takes place. The animal laboratory, from which principles of operant behaviorism were derived, presents a particularly closed setting, one in which the elements of the three-term contingency can be objectively identified and behavior therefore traced unambiguously to its environmental effects. The further behavior settings stray from this degree of closedness, the harder it is for the operant psychologist to ascribe activities within them unreservedly to operant conditioning. Even in the animal laboratory, there exists scope for alternative interpretations: in terms, for instance, of classical conditioning or cognitive decision making. The human operant laboratory, for example, presents a less closed context, one from which escape is relatively easy; while nonhumans face no option but being in the setting, human participants on occasion remove themselves from the experimental situation.

The settings in which human consumer behavior takes place are more open still: though a continuum of such settings is evident, from the relatively closed confines of a large group awareness training session to the relatively open variety store. Closed and open settings may also be distinguished in terms of the verbal behavior that characterizes each. In closed settings, the other-instructions and contingencies are precise: in order to get a passport, a consumer must obey the rules to the letter. In open settings, the consumer has more control over his or her behavior through self-instructions, and specific other rules are less likely to be determinative. There may be several other-rule configurations to "choose" among; further, there is the possibility of behavior being directly controlled by the contingencies: as one spots new products, devises new ways of finding presents, and so on. Even if the view is taken that most consumer behavior is rule-governed, open settings allow self-rules to a far greater extent than closed. Moreover, human behavior that is entirely contingency-shaped is rare. Self-rules, devised and followed by the same individual, are particularly effective instructions, which may be more isolated from the contingencies than other-rules (Catania, Matthews, & Shimoff, 1990). Thus *behavior setting scope* is the extent to which the current consumer behavior setting compels a particular pattern of behavior (as a national opera house induces people to wear evening dress, remain seated and silent during arias, and applaud wildly at the end; compare a rock concert where one is free to walk about, shout, sing, smoke, eat and drink and do many other things during the performance). The scope of the former is said to be (relatively) closed; that of the latter, (relatively) open.

The Role of Learning History

The importance of learning history is amply demonstrated by the repeated finding that prior behavior is an important determinant of current responding. It is not sufficient to attribute the influence of prior behavior simply to "habit", which is to redescribe it rather than explain it. The continuance of behavior is to be accounted for by the consequences it produces and whether or not a stream of behavior is continued into the near future depends on the stimulus control which influences it and the maintenance of the pattern of reinforcement that is its distal cause.

The potency of a learning history is manifested within a particular behavior setting: prior learning establishes what will act as a discriminative stimulus in that setting by embodying the consequences, reinforcing and punishing, of earlier behavior in the presence of the relevant setting elements. The BPM links past behavior, behavior setting elements, and outcomes by arguing that learning history primes elements of the setting to act as discriminative stimuli for utilitarian and informational reinforcement/punishment contingent upon the performance of specific responses. The BPM provides an alternative, noncognitive synthesis of empirical results gained in both attitude research and operant investigations of instructed behavior (Foxall, 1997a).

The BPM Contingency Matrix

The second stage, then, in locating consumer behavior is to summarize the probable effect of behavior setting stimuli on the probability of an approach or avoidance response currently taking place. The BPM proposes eight general contingency categories defined by the operant class to which the situated behavior in question belongs and the scope of the behavior setting in which it occurs (Figure 2). Allocating consumer behavior to one or other of these on a functional basis (i.e., in terms of the consequences produced and the stimuli that signal them) occur at a second level of analysis. Employing dichotomous variables to represent the causative elements of the model, actual consumer situations can be categorized among eight contingency configurations, depending on whether the consumer behavior setting is relatively closed or relatively open, whether utilitarian reinforcement is relatively high or low, and whether informational reinforcement is relatively high or low.

A *contingency category* summarizes the contingencies of reinforcement pertaining to a set of consumer situations. It thus presents in outline the pattern of reinforcement which typically maintains the response in question, and the scope of the consumer behavior setting in which it occurs. Since pattern of reinforcement is defined by the relative levels of two sources of reinforcer, utilitarian and informational, there are eight contingency categories (shown in the BPM contingency

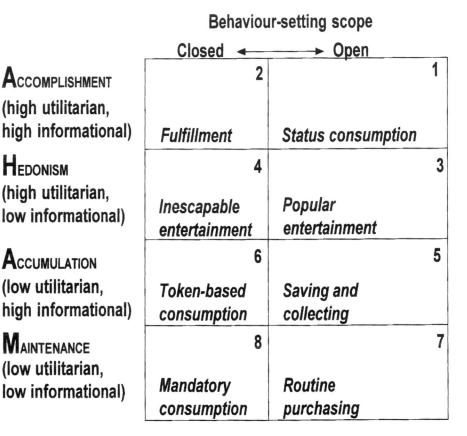

Figure 2. The BPM Contingency Matrix

matrix, Figure 2). The BPM contingency matrix suggests a *functional* typology of consumer situations: the placing of any particular consumer behavior within this scheme depends on the pattern of utilitarian and informational reinforcement which maintains it. Saving up belongs in CC5 because it is primarily maintained by informational reinforcement, secondarily by utilitarian. The behavior is best regarded as Accumulation. But collecting antiques would be CC1 or 2 because it is Accomplishment: behavior maintained by high levels of both utilitarian and informational reinforcement.

The consumer situations and behaviors assigned to each of these eight contingency categories are defined functionally rather than morphologically and topographically identical behaviors may be assigned at different times to different operant classes and contingency categories depending on the interpretation of the combination of contingencies maintaining them. The labels employed in Figure 2 are, therefore, ultimately arbitrary, though they have proved useful in the interpretation of consumer behavior (Foxall, 1994). Some topographically similar behaviors can be allocated to more than one contingency category depending on the particular environmental determinants which are to be emphasized. Status consumption involves both aspects of informational reinforcement: status and/or self-esteem. Collecting, for instance, may not be a public affair: personal (private) reinforcement may be to the fore as the joy of acquisition and ownership etc.

The BPM was initially conceived primarily as an interpretive device. In this section we explore how it might be applied to the description of consumer behavior as it relates to the environmentally-located contingencies which apparently maintain it. In other words, despite the qualification made above that the BPM operant classification and the contingency matrix are based upon functional possibilities rather than final taxonomies of consumer behaviors, is it possible to allocate broad examples of consumer choice to each of the contingency categories at least on a provisional basis? Single responses such as browsing, inspecting, signing, paying, transporting, preparation and using are to be found within any of the categories, but do more molar patterns of consumer behavior *reasonably* belong to specific classes and categories given the logic on which the classification and the matrix were constructed? There is no harm in making the attempt so long as our surmising is at some stage open to empirical examination. Therefore, arbitrary or useful as they must ultimately be, the following generalized descriptions of consumer behaviors and situations which appear to belong to each of the contingency categories provide a summary of consumer choice in relation to the contingencies that maintain it.

Accomplishment. Accomplishment in an open setting consists in general in the *purchase and consumption of status goods*. A familiar instance is pre-purchase consumer behavior for luxuries and radical innovations such as TV satellite dishes, video recorders, exotic vacations, and home computers. These behaviors, including window-shopping and browsing, involve searching for and the comparative evaluation of information about many products and services. Most of the items in question are possessed and used for the pleasure or ease of living they confer, the wellbeing they make possible for the individual: they thereby provide extensive hedonic rewards. But they are often status symbols and their conspicuous consumption also strengthens the behavior in question. They attest directly, and often publicly and unambiguously, to the consumer's attainments, especially economic. Goods in this category are usually highly differentiated – by novel function in the case of innovations, by branding in the case of luxuries. In a closed setting, accomplishment can be generally described as *fulfillment*. In such a context, it comprises personal attainments gained through leisure, often with a strong element of recreation or excitement as well as achievement. This category refers to the material contribution to *fulfillment* and could include both the completion of a personal development seminar or gambling in a casino. Gambling in so closed a setting is an activity maintained by both hedonic and informational consequences. In addition, few consumer behaviors are maintained so thoroughly by social rules. All these elements of the setting unambiguously signal both the positive consequences of approved approach behaviors and the potentially punishing implications of escape or avoidance responses which flout established rules and gaming conventions. Although several games may be available in the casino, there is one principal reinforcer: winning. Pleasure and social approval stem mainly from success, though a certain amount of enjoyment and prestige may be derived from being part of a somewhat exclusive social group and conforming to its code of behavior. Closely defined acts must be performed in order to participate, including obtaining membership, dressing appropriately, entering the game at the right time and in an acceptable manner.

Hedonism. In an open setting, this behavior generally consists of *popular entertainment.* Obvious examples are watching television game shows which provide near-constant hedonic reward, and the reading of mass fiction which contains a sensation on almost every page. Personal cassette players and VCRs have made such reinforcement more immediate to the point of its being ubiquitous. Mass culture presents frequent and predictable, relatively strong and continuous hedonic rewards which are not contingent on long periods of concentrated effort. Indeed, the arrangement of reinforcers is such that viewing, listening or reading for even a short interval is likely to be rewarded. Informational feedback is more obvious on some occasions than others, as when game shows allow the audience to pit their own performances against that of the competing participants, but it is not the main source of reward. Hedonism in closed settings consists as a generalization of inescapable entertainment and amelioration. The behaviors in question are potentially pleasurable but in this context may be irksome because they are unavoidable. As a result, consumption of these products and services may be passive rather than active. An example is the situation in which long distance airline passengers must purchase meals and movies along with their travel. The meals are usually consumed, like the in-flight movies which follow them, without alternative. The setting, which cannot be other than highly restrictive if one is to arrive safely, is further closed by the pulling of blinds, the disappearance of cabin staff, the impossibility of moving around the plane, and the attention of one's fellow passengers to the movie. To try to read or engage in other activities may invite censure.

Accumulation. In an open setting, Accumulation is generally described as *saving and collecting.* For example, purchases for which payments are made prior to consumption – installments for a holiday which can only be taken once the full amount has been paid. Another example is payments into a Christmas club. Discretionary saving with the intention of making a large purchase once a certain amount has accumulated, would fall into this category, too. Promotional deals requiring the accumulation of coupons or other tokens before a product or service can be obtained also belong here. The important reward, in every case, is informational, feedback on how much one has accumulated, how close one is to the ultimate reinforcer. Accumulation occurring in a closed setting may be described, in general terms, as *token-based buying.* This also involves collecting – through schemes in which payment for one item provides tokens which will pay for another. Although some examples of this are quite recent, the practice is simply an extension of the familiar prize schemes open to collectors of cigarette cards or trading stamps. For example, the frequent flyer points earned by frequent flyers on domestic and international airlines constitute informational reinforcers. Some hotels also offer gifts to customers who accumulate points by staying there frequently. The collection of these tokens is reinforced by gaining additional free air travel or hospitality, or by access to different types of reinforcer such as prizes. Purchase and consumption of the basic product, the air travel or accommodation originally demanded are maintained by both the intrinsic hedonic rewards they embody and the feedback on progress that is being made towards the ultimate incentive. The setting is said to be relatively closed because the first item would probably be purchased anyway in some form or other and the consumer's income constraint makes it likely that the second or backup reinforcer would be obtained only in this way.

Maintenance. In an open setting, Maintenance may be generally described as *routine purchasing and consumption.* This includes the regular buying of goods necessary for survival. For example, the habitual purchasing of grocery items at a supermarket. Consumer behavior in these circumstances is indeed routine: it occurs as if reinforcement were available only at fixed intervals. Further, contrary to the usual depiction, the frequent consumer of say, baked beans is highly rational, having tried and evaluated many brands in the relevant product class. But his or her behavior is not static: again in contrast to the received wisdom of the marketing texts, comparatively few such consumers are brand loyal in the sense of always choosing the identical brand in a long sequence of shopping trips. There is so much choice that the consumer enjoys considerable discretion among versions of the product (Ehrenberg, 1972). Maintenance is generally characterized in closed settings as *mandatory purchase and consumption.* It includes all forms of consumer behavior necessary to remain a citizen: the payment of taxes for public and collective goods, for instance. Less extremely, it includes payments into pension schemes linked to employment, payments of endowment insurance premiums linked to mortgages. To this extent, Maintenance is the consumer behavior inherent in pursuing the normal business of citizenship. In the workplace, it may include the enforced use of areas under smoking bans which, for smokers, represent a severe limitation on behavior (though for nonsmokers, particularly the allergic, they constitute an opening of the setting, a measure that permits a wider range of behaviors).

At this second level of analysis it is important to take account of the punishing utilitarian and informational consequences of consumer behavior. Although these do not enter into the operant classification of consumer behavior, in so far as they are signaled by discriminative stimuli, they are important determinants of the scope of consumer behavior settings.

The Consumer Situation

The third level of interpretive analysis is that of the consumer situation. The significance of this construct requires its distinction from that of consumer behavior setting scope. *A consumer behavior setting* comprises the discriminative stimuli which signal the likely consequences of emitting a particular response, i.e. the probable levels of utilitarian and informational reinforcement, and that of aversive outcome.

In other words, it provides a summary of the reinforcement and punishment contingent upon the performance of the requisite response. This is an abstract definition, general and theoretical, because it is dependent on other variables (the consumer's learning and evolutionary histories, for instance) in order to have a concrete influence on behavior.

Consumer behavior setting scope is the extent to which the consumer's current behavior is narrowly determined by elements of the behavior setting in which it is located. It is determined not only by the elements of the behavior setting (social and physical surroundings, temporal frame, regulatory frame) but by the consumer's history of behaving in similar settings and the consequences of having done so. Consumer behavior settings of varying scope may be arrayed on a continuum of closed-open consumer behavior settings, the most closed setting controlling the nature of the consumer's responses entirely and predictably; the most open, having minimal external control over behavior which is accordingly much more difficult to predict.

This is a somewhat more operational idea of the immediate determinant of consumer response: consumer behavior setting *scope* comprehends both the setting and the consumer's learning history which "activates" the setting elements, converting some of them from neutral stimuli into discriminative stimuli which bring behavior under stimulus control. However, this is still a rather abstract depiction of environment-behavior relationships. To that extent and, since these concepts are not unobservables posited at some other realm than observed behavior, both consumer behavior setting and consumer behavior setting scope may be considered examples of the kinds of descriptive theoretical entity which can organize collections of facts, for which Skinner called. Note that the contingency analysis involved in deciding upon the scope of a consumer behavior setting is of a macro-level: strictly speaking, from it we can predict the operant class to which the consumer's response belongs.

However, a *consumer situation* is a particular (concrete, real world) consumer behavior setting and a learning history. It is delineated by the synomorphic presence of a given individual (who embodies a behavioral learning history and an evolutionary history) and a specific consumer behavior setting, e.g., John Smith at the barber's. This is a more empirically amenable entity, not in the sense that it comprises data while the preceding notions of consumer behavior setting and consumer behavior setting scope were hypothetical constructs, but in as much as it is amenable to direct observation in and of itself rather than a précis of empirical relationships at a disaggregated level. It is a description of a situation which has potential for influencing/ determining behavior or making it more predictable.

Consumer behavior is located at the meeting place of the consumer's learning history and the current consumer behavior setting. This intersection is the consumer situation. Both of its components are necessary to the operant reconstruction of the meaning of a particular response or behavior pattern to the consumer. The consumer's learning history determines what can act as a discriminative stimulus of current behavior; that learning history thereby also determines what is a potential reinforcer or punisher. But that learning history, which shapes the individuality, the unique response potential, of the consumer, is activated by the consumer behavior setting. It has no meaning in itself and can confer no significance on the current behavior of the consumer unless an opportunity to act presents itself: that opportunity is afforded by the current setting which primes the learning history's capacity to shape current consumer choice. When this has occurred, whatever consumer behavior takes place is a function of the interaction of historical and current environments: it can be located in time and space.

In practice, this third and most detailed level of analysis relates particular consumer responses – browsing, evaluating, buying, using – to the elements of the consumer situation in which they arise. In accounting for the approach, avoidance and escape responses of consumers, this micro-level interpretation involves identifying the discriminative stimuli that compose the setting, the consequences to which they point, and, as far as is feasible, the learning history of the individual. Ultimately, the purpose is to understand the meaning of the observed pattern of behavior for the individual consumer.

Since direct empirical access to the consumer's learning history is denied the observer, an operant interpretation often necessarily concentrates on those environmental factors that can be observed or inferred, notably elements of the behavior setting. The assumption is – and all interpretive systems rest upon an act of faith that the reinforcing consequences these setting elements offer are broadly those which have shaped and maintained similar behavior in the past; such (setting) elements and (behavioral) consequences can thus be used as a guide to the predisposing/ inhibiting nature of the consumer's learning history. But there is no reason why the resulting account cannot be checked, corroborated, and amended by the individual's own recollection of that history; no reason why the consumer's verbal account cannot provide the interpretation; no reason why the operant interpretation cannot be "thick" rather than "thin". The sole criterion is our resulting understanding of "how the action of interest makes a difference to the person's life. That is, what does the action produce or present that would not be produced or presented otherwise?" (Lee, 1988, p. 137). The framework could easily accommodate a fourth interpretive level to embrace the detailed, self-described and analyzed experience of an individual consumer related to the organizing environment. Moreover, the analysis invites the integration of consumer research not only with operant psychology but with a wider paradigm, selection by consequences. Goldsmith's (1992) statement of the dual causality found in biological evolution has echoes in Kimble's (1996) proposal for a scientific psychology. Kimble argues that "behavior is the joint product of relatively enduring *potentials* for, and relatively more temporary *instigation* to, action". In representing behavior as a function of potential and instigation, the BPM portrays consumer choice as an evolutionary process. In natural selection, potential resides in the genotype, instigation in the environment, behavior in the phenotype. In the BPM, potential (ultimate causation) resides predominantly in learning history (though natural selection has also played its part); the instigating environment (proximate causation) is represented by the consumer behavior setting; and behavior is the outcome of their intersection. The environment is that of the behavior, not the individual (as, in strict behaviorist terms, it is *behavior* which has a learning history rather than a person), and so it includes bodily states such as deprivation as well as economic and social state variables such as financial means, physical surroundings and interpersonal influence. Potential is determined largely by the role of the utilitarian and informational consequences of prior behavior; instigation is a matter of the extent to which that learning history transforms the antecedent stimuli of the current behavior setting into *discriminative* stimuli; behavior consists in economic responses which can be allocated to operant classes based on the pattern of reinforcement which maintains them. As has been noted, the potential for behavior derives from the individual's history of approach and avoidance responses and their consequences.

Nevertheless, while operant consumer research provides ontological diversity, it does not solve the epistemological problems of cognitive explanation. It relies ultimately on the very inference that it seeks to avoid, differing by assuming that proximate causes of another's behavior lie in those behavioral events that are private to him or her rather than that the causes of behavior inhere in an unobservable mental realm. The encouragement of ontological diversity nonetheless represents an advance for the consumer research subdiscipline which has sought so little to emancipate itself from the strictures of social cognition.

Conclusion

Radical behaviorism has traditionally avoided premature theorization. Accusations of the "botanization of responses" arise easily in reaction to classificatory schemes, two-by-two matrices, and intuitive leaps into new areas of application such as those discussed here. Yet theoretical analysis has never been far beneath the surface of operant interpretation (Reese, 1986) and the detailed understanding of complex human interaction in operant terms requires inputs from disciplines other than psychology (in the present context, notably from economics and consumer science) which will inevitably stretch behavior analysis. Operant interpretation cannot be a "top down" exercise, in which behavior analysts arbitrarily impose a view of the world which is merely a fitting of selected observations into the confines of the three-term contingency. Such an exercise would be simplistic to say the least, and regretfully I would claim that much extrapolation of behavior principles gained in the laboratory is indeed unsophisticated due to its lack of detailed comprehension of the behaviors to which it is applied. "Bottom up" operant interpretation begins with the subject matter, incorporates an interdisciplinary perspective where appropriate, and remains flexible in the face of the need to understand its subject matter in terms of environmental contingencies. Such analysis is tentative, leading to hypotheses rather than experimental facts (Lee, 1988) and requires careful conceptual justification and, wherever it can be arranged, empirical examination. Happily, in the case of the interpretation of consumer choice developed in this chapter, both aspects of such work are well under way (Foxall, 1997b, 1997c).

References

Alhadeff, D. A. (1982). *Microeconomics and human behavior: Toward a new synthesis of economics and psychology.* Berkeley, CA: University of California Press.

Catania, A. C., Matthews, B. A., & Shimoff, E. H. (1990). Properties of rule-governed behaviour and their implications. In D. Blackman & H. Lejeune, (Eds.) *Behaviour analysis in theory and practice: Contributions and controversies* (pp. 215–230). London: Erlbaum.

Cone, J. D., & Hayes, S. C. (1980). *Environmental problems/behavioral solutions.* Monterey, CA: Brooks/Cole.

Earl, P. E. (1990). Economics and psychology. A survey. *Economic Journal,* 100, 718–755.

Ehrenberg, A. S. C. (1972). *Repeat buying.* Amsterdam: North Holland. [Second edition, 1988. London: Griffin].

Foxall, G. R. (1990). *Consumer psychology in behavioural perspective.* London: Routledge.

Foxall, G. R. (1994). Behaviour analysis and consumer psychology. *Journal of Economic Psychology,* 15, 5–91.

Foxall, G. R. (1995). Science and interpretation in consumer research: a radical behaviourist perspective. *European Journal of Marketing,* 29, 3-99.

Foxall, G. R. (1996). *Consumers in context: The BPM research program.* London and New York: Routledge/ITP.

Foxall, G. R. (1997a). The explanation of consumer behaviour: From social cognition to environmental control. In C. L. Cooper & I. Robertson (Eds.), *International review of industrial and organizational psychology.* Chichester: Wiley.

Foxall, G. R. (1997b). The emotional texture of consumer environments: A systematic approach to atmospherics. *Journal of Economic Psychology,* 18.

Foxall, G. R. (1997c). *Marketing psychology: The paradigm in the wings.* London: Macmillan.

Foxall, G. R. (1998). Putting consumer behavior in its place: An operant interpretation of purchase and consumption. *The Behavior Analyst,* in press.

Goldsmith, T. H. (1992). *The biological roots of human nature.* New York: Oxford University Press.

Gould, J., & Kolb, W. L. (Eds.) (1964). *A dictionary of the social sciences.* London: Tavistock.

Griffin, J., & Parfitt, D. (1987). Hedonism. In J. Eatwell, M. Milgate, & P. Newman (Eds.), *The new Palgrave: A dictionary of economics.* London: Macmillan.

Guerin, B. (1994). *Analyzing social behavior: Behavior analysis and the social sciences.* Context Press, Reno, NV.

Kardes, F. R. (1994). Consumer judgment and decision processes. In R. S. Wyer, & T. K. Srull (Eds.), *Handbook of social cognition. Volume 2: Application.* Second edition., Hillsdale, NJ: Erlbaum.

Kimble, G. A. (1994). A new formula for behaviorism. *Psychological Review, 101,* 254–8.

Kimble, G. A. (1996). *Psychology: The hope of a science.* Cambridge, MA: The MIT Press.

Lee, V. L. (1988). *Beyond behaviorism.* London: Erlbaum.

Mason, R. (1981). *Conspicuous consumption.* Farnborough: Gower Press.

Menger, C. (1956). *Gruendste der Volkwirtschaftslehre, trans.* J. Dingwall & B. F. Hoselitz. Glencoe, IL: Free Press.

Reese, H. W. (1986). On the theory and practice of behavior analysis. In H. W. Reese, & L. J. Parrott (Eds.), *Behavior science: Philosophical, methodological, and empirical advances.* Hillsdale, IL: Erlbaum.

Skinner, B. F. (1957). *Verbal behavior.* Century: New York.

Skinner, B. F. (1974). *About behaviorism.* Knopf: New York.

Viner, J. (1925). The utility concept in value theory and its critics. *Journal of Political Economy, 33,* 369–87.

Wearden, J. (1988). Some neglected problems in the analysis of human operant behaviour. In G. C. L. Davey & C. Cullen (Eds.), *Human operant conditioning and behaviour modification.* Wiley, Chichester.

Notes

[1] This chapter is derived from a chapter in *Marketing Psychology: The Paradigm in the Wings* by Gordon Foxall, published by Macmillan Press, London, 1997, by kind permission of the publisher.

[2] A defining characteristic of economic behavior, since it includes a reciprocal transfer of rights, lies in its being simultaneously reinforced and punished (Alhadeff 1982). It incurs reinforcement and punishment as direct and specific consequences of its being performed. Economic behavior is determined by the interaction of two response strengths: approach and avoidance, each of which is dependent upon the consumer's learning history, the quality and quantity of reinforcement, reinforcement schedules, and so on (Alhadeff, 1982).

Chapter 16

Walden Two At Fifty

Marc Richelle

Professor Emeritus, University of Liège, Belgium

Fifty years after it was written, *Walden Two,* first published in 1948, is still worth reading, in spite of the disrepute in which behavorists' contributions to psychological sciences have been brought. Looked at from a distance, Skinner's utopian novel appears to have anticipated most of the major problems which contemporary societies are confronted with. In many respects, he certainly was ahead of his time in his criticisms of features characterising modern Western society, which are even more a source of concern today. Although the solutions proposed in the fictional context of a Utopia are not directly transferable to the real world, the kind of social management imagined by Skinner could profitably be used by political managers today as possible source of inspiration in their search for new concepts with respect to employment, preservation of resources, political responsibility, education, etc.

Selecting from the many themes discussed by Skinner through the characters in *Walden Two,* the present chapter points to their relevance to current social and political issues, especially related to the crisis of democracy. It is argued that Skinner's venture into social philosophy, under the cover of a literary genre not usual among scientists, far from reflecting unfounded pretension at extrapolating from animal laboratory to human affairs, was, and still is, a call to psychologists to commit themselves to social responsibility. As such, *Walden Two* remains a seminal introduction to all applications of the experimental analysis of behavior.

Walden Two: An Anecdote?

Walden Two was first published in 1948. It seems appropriate to celebrate the half centenary of Skinner's utopian novel in the context of the present book, which emphasizes the applications of the experimental analysis of behavior. In spite of its success a few years after it was printed, the book has not become a classic of political fiction, and it has little impact, if at all, outside the restricted circles of Skinner's devotees. Those who acknowledge some aspects of Skinner's scientific contributions, while they do not share his theoretical views, and even less his socio-political ideas, usually ignore *Walden Two* as an accident in Skinner's production.

In its issue of December 1996, the *Harvard College Gazette* reported with pride that six members of the Harvard faculty had been ranked among the 100 most influential scientists, past and present, in a selection "compiled with the aid of prominent scientists and historians of science", titled *The Scientific 100.* "Following such luminaries as Isaac Newton, Albert Einstein and Charles Darwin, are physicist

Sheldon Glashow, biologist James Watson, Ernst Mayr, George Gaylord Simpson, Edward O. Wilson, and psychologist B. F. Skinner". Skinner's scientific merits are shortly described, as are those of his distinguished Harvard colleagues; then comes the following statement: "Skinner's ideas about utopian communities governed by principles of behavioral engineering, teaching pigeons to guide missiles, and environmentally controlled cribs, or boxes, for raising children survive only as anecdotes. But his work has had long-term influence in education, particularly special education, and in the treatment of phobias and other behavioral problems." Leaving aside the misinformation contained in the last sentence (the treatment of phobias is a widely recognized success of behavior therapies, but it is not essentially based on Skinner's ideas or experiments), this quotation makes a strange mixture of the major work of Skinner in the field of social philosophy with admittedly somewhat anecdotal, although not insignificant, contributions. The author of the article, William J. Cromie, seems to feel it better to discard *Walden Two* as possibly soiling Skinner's reputation as confirmed by *The Scientific 100*.

There is nothing surprising about this, if we remember how violently Skinner's views on society have been attacked, and distorted from opposite sides of the ideological continuum, from Noam Chomsky to Spiro Agnew. However, had Cromie read *Walden Two*, he might have understood how lucidly Skinner had foreshadowed crucial problems of modern Western civilization, which are still with us today, more acute than ever. And perhaps, instead of rejecting the book among anecdotal and not very commendable productions, he would have encouraged Harvard undergraduates to read it and to reflect about the solutions proposed by Skinner, especially to those issues which seem desperately resistant to novel approaches.

Since Cromie has not done it, let me try to do it. Admittedly, my potential audience is very different from Harvard undergraduates, probably both more receptive and more critical.

A word of warning is necessary before moving ahead. Utopian literature has never been expected to provide models for life or society immediately transferable to real life. People who read Plato's *Republic*, Thomas More's *Utopia*, or St. Augustine's *City of God* do not evaluate these pieces of work with respect to the feasibility of the social system they propose. They do not read them as blueprints of a building designed by an architect, aimed at practical realization. They read them as sources of reflections on human affairs, often encapsulating lucid criticisms of the present state of affairs, and suggesting directions for changes; criticisms and suggestions for changes can be expressed in highly symbolic style, or in sorts of caricatures, amplifying those features which the author wanted to emphasize. Skinner's Utopia should be read with the same spirit. Arguments that it would not work if literally put into practice are beside the point. So are the arguments that it did not work when it was in fact put in practice. The few attempts which were made to build communities after the principles of *Walden Two*, with whatever degree of failure or success, are irrelevant to a profitable reading of *Walden Two*. This is not to blame the founders and members of such communities, nor to deny the significance of their enterprise with respect to Skinner's social philosophy, but the latter can be discussed, taken as a source of inspiration in the search of alternative solutions to our social problems, without any reference to those few real life experiments.

Seven Issues of Current Interest

Let me turn now to those issues of which we are all aware, especially in European societies today, and which are currently considered as symptoms of a crisis of democracy and as the decline of the welfare state. We shall review briefly what Skinner had to say about them fifty years ago.

I shall focus on seven issues (the magical number again!):

1. the fracture between the political class and what has come to be named the civil society - ordinary citizens rather than politicians;
2. the contradiction between the pressure to increased consumption and the awareness of the limited amount of resources available on our small planet;
3. the problem of unemployment;
4. the place of leisure and of culture;
5. the role of the media;
6. the place of women, and more generally social equality;
7. education.

Democratic Society and its Discontent

Recent events in European countries, at the national or European Union levels, have shown more acutely than ever before a number of dysfunctionings in democratic regimes, in spite of the general agreement that democracy , if it is not intrinsically good, is after all less bad than other regimes. In very different contexts, the political debates and votes on the Maestricht Treaty and the dramatic discoveries of criminal child abuse in Belgium in 1996 threw light on the same evil. Politicians are blamed for having lost their relationship with the people they are supposed to represent, for making laws and running society with little concern for being understood by citizens at large, or worse for acting against the people under the cover of technical discourses not accessible to common understanding. The sources of this state of affairs are evidently numerous and complex. Some of them, however, are blatant and can be denounced without sophisticated inquiry.

The failure to maintain clear communication between the political class and civil society is, to a large extent, the result of practices which are by no means intrinsic to democracy: political offices have been increasingly reserved to individuals engaging in life-long political careers, often holding several charges, developing between themselves an allegedly technical style which in turn legitimates their claim to the difficulties of their task, and therefore their status of professional politicians. The very fact that information does not flow from them to the people appears as a demonstration that politics can no longer be left in the hands of ordinary citizens, that it requires hyper-specialized persons. Procedures for elections have favored this view, as well as rules defining access to political charges and offices.

Dissatisfaction among citizens proceeds from increasing discrepancies between words and actions, between electoral propaganda, essentially based on verbal fantasies, and real life contingencies, between the claim to change life and the crude fact that things are maintained as they are. It also proceeds from the number of subgroups, composing the minority in the democratic sense, which never reach their share in power, so that they perceive the democratic government as a despotic ruler. Most of the symptoms we observe today had been identified by Frazier in Walden Two, and alternative practices were thoroughly discussed. The traps and illusions of democracy were so central in Walden Two that Frazier suggested Burris to title his book *The Critics of Democracy*. Frazier by no means preferred despotism to democracy: he objected to democracy, as implemented at that time in the US, which is not very different from what it is today in Europe, for disguising a despotism of the majority instead of being the government for all; for providing politicians with an easy escape from responsibility for their bad actions by turning the blame onto the citizens responsible for voting for them; for favoring emotional and irrational aspects of elections, with little regard to the effective actions of candidates. Walden Two had solved some of these problems by having the right people in the right places - that is, really skilled individuals for given tasks - rather than ambitious individuals obsessed by the prospect of a career. In case they might be tempted to pursue individual profit, their time in office was limited anyhow. As long as other equally skilled persons were available, none of the planners or managers, as the two levels of "government" were called, was impossible to replace. They were not elected, but chosen for their competence. Control by the people was exerted through other channels, any aspect of the rules in operation being permanently open to debate and eventually changed. We could go on either describing Walden Two's practices or paraphrasing Frazier's discourses related to the crisis of democracy. Let me quote a brief passage to summarize an otherwise long story - since, as already said, the whole novel can be taken as an essay on democracy:

> "The government of Walden Two has the virtues of democracy but none
> of its defects. It is much closer to the theory or intent of democracy than
> the actual practice in America today."

None of us would venture to abandon democracy in the present world context. But we are all acutely aware that, as it works now, democracy may run into serious trouble. The challenge we are facing today is to work out new practices closer to the "intent of democracy". Some of these have been envisioned by Skinner and are described in *Walden Two*. Not all of them require revolutionary changes.

Contradictions in Economics

Economics has always been to me a source of perplexity. It is said, and probably rightly (at least to some extent) that economy is the moving engine of any society, and therefore should be the major concern of any government. We also know that approaches to economics are as varied as there are eminent economists and schools of thought, which indeed are many and of the most diverse kinds, including opposite kinds. There is obviously no more consensus among economists on the nature of economical processes and on the way to control them than among psychologists as to the nature of psychological mechanisms and the way to influence them towards some ideal view of human behavior. Notwithstanding this, economists are much more respected, and much more involved in government, than psychologists.

For lack of time and of competence, I shall not indulge in a discussion of current economical issues in the light of solutions given to some of them in *Walden Two*. I shall limit myself to one of the most blatant contradictions to which contemporary citizens are exposed. On one hand, there is a sort of consensus that the market economy is the key to all our problems; the collapse of the communist regimes is given as unquestionable evidence that it is the best way to rule human societies, perhaps the unique modality that fits human nature in the long run, or the one that eventually will perpetuate itself after all others will have been eliminated by some process of natural selection. In what has been called the end of ideology, adhesion to the market economy seems to be the shared common denominator of political parties hitherto opposed precisely on their view of economical mechanisms and their regulation; hence, the solution to the current economic crisis is to stimulate consumption.

On the other hand, there is another apparent consensus that the world economy is now global, and that the limitation of resources should induce humans to sparing rather than wasting behavior - the basic message of ecological movements now reiterated by most official political groups.

The logical contradiction is obvious. But I know of no political program at the moment that clearly solves it. It was solved in *Walden Two*: consuming was maintained at a reasonable level by limiting individually owned goods to what is necessary, taking into account that the community would offer its members the use of all enjoyable items as needed for sport, art, music, etc., as well as basic items such as food, shelter, a bed, and the like. Preservation of natural resources was a major concern of the community, a principle that foreshadowed the ecological stands popularized since then although they are still so far from being perfectly implemented in daily life.

Unemployment

No one would deny that unemployment is the major problem of our society. It is a byproduct of both the global market economy and of the deep changes in instruments of production characterizing the third industrial revolution. In spite of repeated and insistent declarations in favor of creating new jobs, from all parts of the political class, the situation seems to be desperately out of control. There is a general feeling that work should be redistributed (as it has been several times in modern history), but established situations, habits or privileges raise many obstacles to such change. A large part of the active population is overworked, exposed to stress and lives under permanent pressure, including the threat of losing employment, while an increasingly high number of unemployed people experience frustration, anxiety, and a loss of human dignity.

Walden Two had its solutions, not so much to the problem of unemployment (which was not crucial in the years after the war), but to the problem of technological progress which would inevitably sooner or later generate unemployment. Although it was a rural community, Walden Two did not return to old methods of farming that would keep all its members busy performing hard physical work in an idyllic landscape. Walden Two was a center of advanced technology, adding its own creative genius to equipment available from the outside world. The consequent reduction in global workload was faced by "getting rid of the work, not of the worker". This was achieved by the ingenious "credit system", based on the idea that not all jobs are equally attractive, but that a community cannot dispense with them. In the Walden Two credit system, each job is assigned a credit value, and each member is expected to perform a certain amount of "work credits" per year. If one prefers attractive and pleasant jobs, one will have to work more hours, while one who wants to keep as much free time as possible for leisure activities will choose to work fewer hours on less attractive jobs. All in all, citizens of Walden Two work an average of 24 hours per week on duty. This low average is due also to a number of convergent factors, including absence of early retirement, absence of a privileged class, absence of delinquency, good health, and, most important, flexible time schedules - not only for work proper but for other daily activities such as meals, social gatherings, artistic performances, etc., which in turn results in flexibility of working schedules.

A number of words in this description sound familiar: indeed they are part of the current vocabulary when people talk about possible solutions to the problem of unemployment. We are still far from practical implementation of what appear as innovative concepts, although some trends are already visible. We know, for instance, that early retirement, which is frequently proposed to provide jobs for younger people, is a pseudo-solution which imposes a heavier load on a reduced active population. We know that delinquency, drugs, bad health have an enormous social cost and show a complex and viciously circular relation with unemployment. We understand that schedule flexibility and location flexibility would help in saving time, if only by reducing rush hour traffic in big cities. The philosophy of work organization in Walden Two had focussed on all these issues. Hopefully, within a few decades, Walden Two practices with respect to work organization might appear as an anticipation of reality rather than as naive, unrealistic fantasies appropriate only for a small community with no existence but on the pages of a novel.

Leisure and Culture

One of the results and indeed one of the main goals of work organization at Walden Two was to provide time for leisure, to turn energies "toward art, science, play, the exercise of skills, the satisfaction of curiosities, the conquest of nature, the conquest of man - the conquest of man himself, but never of other men...leisure without slavery" (p. 76).

Skinner had foreseen one of the trends of artistic culture which was to develop to an extreme point in contemporary society. Progress in technology and the management of cultural products in business, the star system, and the easy diffusion of pieces of art in records, movies, TV production, etc., while propagating culture to an unpreceded extent, is encouraging the passive consumption of cultural products. People are listening or watching to what they are offered, and which more often than not is of a very poor quality, instead of being induced to engage in active and creative artistic behavior. A logical consequence is that the set of artists from which stars can be recruited will eventually become smaller and smaller with time, and that their level of quality will inevitably decrease, the system leading to its own destruction. The same is true of sport, of course.

The answer to that is a radical shift in perspective: create conditions, some would say contingencies, favorable to the practice of arts by the many, providing them first with time and relaxation, but also with appropriate and accessible facilities - in the case of music, instruments on which to perform, good masters who enjoy transmitting their skills, scores, records, and, most important, audiences. All this in a context of emulation without rivalry - the opposite of the competitive contests so popular today.

Such conditions are not only the key to the enjoyment of art by the largest number of people. They are also the key to individual creativity, an aspect which was repeatedly emphasized by Skinner, substantially in line with his psychological theory of behavior - contrary to the widespread misrepresentation of it as a mechanistic stimulus-response psychology.

Many persons responsible for, or simply concerned with, art or sport education are perfectly aware of these problems, and would agree that Walden Two was close to what should be achieved. The question for the future is: will they succeed in overcoming all those powerful factors which push in the opposite direction?

Although it raises difficult problems for all of us in science, let me touch upon another practice in Walden Two. Scientific research, at least its so-called basic facet, is part of leisure activities, like music or painting or theater. Only applied research strictly oriented to improving productivity, or quality and the like, is part of "jobs", mainly reserved to highly qualified members with special status in the work credit system. But fundamental research has the status of a self-reinforcing activity, which people are willing to "pay for" - which at Walden Two simply means earn work credits in such a way as to obtain more free time. Probably most people engaged in basic research would object that scientific research is now a highly specialized and highly sophisticated field, that they themselves work far more than the average 40 hours per week of most other professions, and that good research is not compatible with the sort of amateurism inherent in leisure activities. I am not sure these objections are fully founded, and anyhow, there might be place for a mixed system. In favour of the Walden Two solution, one might argue that research is indeed a creative activity, comparable with sport and art, which people might like to carry out to compensate for dull jobs; that a wider array of self-rewarding leisure activities will increasingly be needed as the global labor load of a population is reduced as a result of new technologies and of increased life expectancy; that basic research is expensive, in terms of equipment and salaries; and that a condition to have it develop without restraints in the future is to shift at least part of it from the area of paid jobs to the domain of leisure.

The Role of the Media

Planners and managers at Walden Two were too enthusiastic about new technologies to have rejected the tremendous possibilities of TV, personal computers, and Internet, had they "lived" fifty years later. But one can infer how they would have judged the use made of them from the way they used external radio broadcasts. They listened to them, for information, music and entertainments, but they filtered out commercials. This was dictated both by the general distrust of any propaganda, be it to sell goods or political illusions, and by respect for the content of the programs.

This practice would make an enormous difference today as compared with fifty years ago. It sounds even more "utopian" in the present context of management of media in 1998 rather than in 1948. However, media exert a very frightening form of control over a wide range of behavior of all citizens of the world, from consuming habits to decisions in favor of a candidate for election to highest political office, from the shaping of esthetic taste to the building of beliefs and attitudes. The whole system is dependent upon financial power and represents one of the most subtle covert controls ever put to work in human societies. In my view, it is one of the major challenges for those who, like behavior analysts, are willing to develop appropriate counter-controls to those forces which fraudulently assert their commitment to the defence of freedom and dignity.

The Place of Women, and More Generally Social Equality

In spite of abundant declarations and proclaimed intentions, modern societies are far from the alleged ideal of equality. Discrimination towards various groups is still with us, and in many cases it is more present than before. Except in a few countries, women have not yet gained equal status with men; racial discrimination has not been eradicated - on the contrary it is still sometimes dramatically stirred up; minorities are not given the protection they are supposed to receive according to constitutions and laws.

The issue was a central one in *Walden Two*. As I have argued elsewhere (Richelle, 1993), Skinner's Utopia was in one sense an answer to the problem of discrimination against women, which had been a concern for Skinner in his own family life. He designed a community the organization of which was largely aimed at freeing women from the routine of domestic work, by having it organized on a collective basis and fully shared between genders. Dependency upon the male was eliminated by the way housing and child care were arranged.

As indicated above, government by the majority was eliminated to be replaced by a style of management really concerned with the rights of all. More generally, and perhaps unexpectedly, Walden Two was designed to preserve individual idiosyncrasy and interindividual diversity. Social rules were to the service of individual achievement, but individual achievement was never at the expenses of other individuals. The respect of minorities is, ultimately, the respect of individuals.

Education

A large part of *Walden Two* is devoted to the description of child care and education. It was a prelude to the later writings of Skinner on education. It already contained his main criticisms of the educational system as it was in the USA fifty years ago, and his proposals for alternative solutions. All in all, no serious remediation has been given to the defects of educational agencies, and most European countries have recognized for some years a crisis in education. Schools are expensive yet inefficient; preparation for adult life is poor; for many pupils and students school is aversive; violence has entered the school buildings, some of which are protected as severely as airports; teachers are more frustrated than ever and the profession becomes less appreciated; conflicts between pupils, parents and institutional agents are the rule; selection, including on financial criteria, remains the main way to an institution's success. In spite of all these, education remains fertile in good intentions and verbal projects. When one reads or listen to discourses on education, one can only conclude that they sound far more utopian than descriptions of Walden Two. A more pragmatic approach to building adequate contingencies, after the model in force at Walden Two, would lead to more improvement than most reforms we have been experiencing in the past fifty years.

We all know that education is only one part of the global system of social organization, that it reflects economical and political features more than it shapes them. Contrary to what was tried in Walden Two, we cannot start from scratch and build a fully fresh generation. We are rooted in history for better and worse. What we can do is concentrate our efforts at the professional as well as the political level to shift the emphasis from the compulsive concern for economy to a lucid approach to educational issues. Perhaps, if we have any hope to influence the course of human history, it will be by giving priority to education.

Limits of space do not permit to go into more details concerning the possible applications of *Walden Two* to contemporary issues. The admittedly superficial survey I have attempted here suffices to show that many practices in Walden Two, many of the ideas developed by the protagonists in the novel are relevant (which, again, does not mean immediately transferable) to our society today, be it only as stimulation in the search of solutions. Perhaps it is not very important to decide whether these practices and ideas are scientifically founded, as Skinner himself claimed. After all, there they are, and their value can be evaluated by comparison with the failure of current practices. At any rate, if they derive from a scientific analysis of behavior, one can expect that they will improve in the future, as science progresses, for science is not a static body of knowledge, fixed once for ever. The question remains: is a scientifically based control of man over himself, and of human society over itself, possible at all? Are we not reaching the limits of scientifically based control when we turn to human affairs, by some sort of limitation analogical to the consequences of Gödel's theorem, which makes it ultimately impossible for any system to account for itself? A look at the world might prompt, I admit, a pessimistic answer to that question. For all practical purposes, however, we may dispense with the solution of such metaphysical enquiry, and reflect on *Walden Two* with a fresh spirit, as an exercise in imaginative solutions to some of our social difficulties.

References

Cromie, W. J (1996). Harvard scientists ranked among most influential. *Harvard College Gazette*, 1 & 8.

Skinner, B.F. (1948). *Walden Two*. New York: Macmillan.

Richelle, M.N. (1993). *B. F. Skinner: A reappraisal*. Hove: Lawrence Erlbaum Associates.